LOUIS XIV

PHILIPPE ERLANGER

translated from the French by

STEPHEN COX

PRAEGER PUBLISHERS

New York · Washington

BOOKS THAT MATTER

Published in the United States of America in 1970 by Praeger
Publishers, Inc., 111 Fourth Avenue, New York, N.Y. 10003

First published in French by Librairie Arthème Fayard
French Edition ©1965 by Librairie Arthème Fayard
English translation © 1970 by George Weidenfeld & Nicolson Ltd.

Library of Congress Catalog Card Number: 79-109471

Printed in Great Britain

To Her Majesty
Queen Marie-José

Contents

Contents

Contents

A *

Illustrations

Illustrations

Between pages 276 and 277

Louis XIV by Rigaud (Giraudon, Paris)

Louis XIV signing the Revocation of the Edict of Nantes (Radio Times Hulton Picture Library)

Louis XIV in the trenches before Mons (Mansell Collection)

Between pages 308 and 309

The Grand Dauphin (Radio Times Hulton Picture Library)

Louis XIV (Mansell Collection)

Duc de Saint-Simon (Mary Evans Picture Library)

Voltaire (Mansell Collection)

Part One

The Tragic Dawn
[1637-61]

[1]

The Open Mystery

FRANCE's belated entry into the Thirty Years War redoubled the efforts of those conspirators who had continually opposed Louis XIII's First Minister, Cardinal Richelieu, and his policies. In late July 1637 Richelieu informed the King of a plot uncovered by his industrious agents. During her retreats to the Convent of Val-de-Grâce, in Paris, the Queen, Anne of Austria, had been conducting a treasonable correspondence with a secretary at the British embassy, through the medium of her valet, La Porte. The secretary had seen to it that this correspondence did not remain a secret.

On 12 August La Porte was arrested and his papers seized. Chancellor Séguier, accompanied by the Archbishop of Paris, carried out a search at Val-de-Grâce. The Queen began by denying the whole thing, even to the point of perjury, but then realized that the more sensible course was to make various minor admissions in order to conceal the more damaging facts – always providing that La Porte's evidence could be made to tally with his mistress's.

Marie de Hautefort, a maid of honour loved by the King although she was devoted to Anne of Austria, disguised herself as a man and managed to penetrate the Bastille, where she made contact with a mortal enemy of Richelieu, Chevalier de Jars. She passed him a letter containing precise instructions to enable the valet to align his story with the Queen's. De Jars' cell was several storeys above La Porte's, and the vital message was delivered by dint of piercing through the intervening floors and ceilings, without attracting the guards' attention. La Porte was a man of great bravery and loyalty. Even the prospect of torture did not crack him. In her long contest with Richelieu, this round went to Anne of Austria.

The conspirators' secrets were safe, but Richelieu still held proof that the Queen of France had made false statements under oath and had been in contact with a hostile power in time of war. Given Louis' feelings towards her, this would be more than enough to make the position of the sister of the King of Spain permanently untenable. Childless and loveless, a royal consort counted for very little, and the shame of a public trial would probably topple her from the throne and relegate her to a nun's cell for the rest of her life. The

King had never spared those who were nearest to his heart: why should he show lenience to a woman who had been the object of his growing hatred for fifteen years?

Richelieu took his time in mulling over the situation, and came to the reluctant conclusion that the reconciliation between the King and Queen which his enemies desired was equally essential to his own projects. Admittedly, the cabal hoped to bring Louis over to the side of Spain, but this was sheer fantasy and quite beyond Anne's powers. On the other hand a divorce would put paid to any remaining hope of producing a Dauphin who would preserve Richelieu's achievements and make the future secure. By an odd paradox, Richelieu's avowed enemy, the woman who had worked ceaselessly to destroy him, was also his one means of bringing about a final victory.

Richelieu paid the helpless Queen a visit. He confronted her with her lies and had the satisfaction of seeing his haughty adversary stripped of all her dignity before being restored to her regal status by his own hand. The King yielded to the Cardinal's persuasion and consented to a pardon, sanctioned by a solemn declaration, after which their Majesties spent a fortnight together at Fontainebleau. The news of a series of victories in Italy and Holland, La Capelle and Leucate, arrived like harbingers of harmony regained.

All this was only a façade. Louis was not the kind of man to forget a grudge, and his heart was set, not on his wife, but on Marie de Hautefort, whose continuing devotion to the Queen inflamed him still further against her. He longed to banish what he hated most – Spanish intrigues and arrogance, finery and cant.

As for Anne, her nerves were being stretched to breaking-point by the threat of repudiation. She loved life and had always hoped that her later years might bring her the enjoyment she had been denied in her youth. Her strained relations with Louis dated from 1622, when their brief conjugal idyll had ended. The King's sense of duty, and the Pope's urging, had at first induced him to make the appropriate gestures towards perpetuating his line. Anne had unfortunately failed to understand her mission, and after an initial miscarriage had provoked another by indulging in a race with Mme de Chevreuse in the Galerie du Louvre. Louis had tired of his wife, and the Queen's apartments had witnessed the visitation of scandal, in the person of George Villiers, First Duke of Buckingham, and conspiracy, in that of the Duchesse de Chevreuse, who was later to play a leading part in the plots against royal power during Louis xiv's minority. There was no doubt in the King's mind that at least once, during the Chalais affair,* Anne had had hopes of becoming a widow, in order to share the throne with his brother, Gaston of Orléans (known as Monsieur).

---

* Chalais had been a favourite of Louis XIII, but was beheaded for plotting against Richelieu in 1626. – Tr.

The King continued his hunting forays and brooded on the wreck of his emotional life. He had tried to respect the sacrament of marriage and had not even obtained the blessing of offspring from this unbearable union. Marie de Hautefort, who might have brought him comfort, had merely laughed at him. Then there had been the interlude with Louise de La Fayette, his *'beau lis'*. He had told her: 'I shall bring you to Versailles, I want you to be completely mine. . . .' The frightened virgin had crossed herself, and to expiate his brief aberration Louis had made the supreme sacrifice of allowing the young girl to be immured in a convent, God alone being worthy of receiving such perfection. Since that time his one consolation had been his long talks with the novice at the Convent of La Visitation Sainte-Marie, in the Rue Saint-Antoine in Paris. But here too his conscience was under assault, since Mlle de La Fayette felt impelled to arrange the downfall of Richelieu, the end of the war and the reconciliation of their Majesties.

In the winter of 1637, while Anne pined in the Palais du Louvre, the royal residence in Paris, Louis XIII turned to his beloved Versailles for respite from the physical ailments which his doctors treated so learnedly and to so little effect, and from the doubts which tormented him. On 5 December he abruptly decided to call on Mlle de La Fayette and spend the night with the Condés* at Saint-Maur, where the royal bed, furniture, crockery and attendants were dispatched as usual.

Louis was received in the gloomy waiting room in the Rue Saint-Antoine, while the gentlemen of his entourage kept a respectful distance behind the bars which could not shut out a son of Saint Louis. The nun whose task it was to accompany the novice sat motionless in a corner, beads in hand, like some wrinkled statue. The King revealed to Louise his inmost feelings and related his innumerable pathetic, almost childish troubles. Hours went by, and when the King wished to leave it was very late. Rain was flooding down and the gale kept blowing out the lanterns. It so happened that Guitaut, the captain of the guard, was a man who loved his Queen and hated Richelieu. He ventured to say that it would be madness to risk the perils of the countryside and suggested that Louis should sleep at the Louvre.

'Let us wait,' said Louis, 'it will blow over.' But the storm worsened and Guitaut returned to the offensive. Louis now lost his temper. His apartment had been installed at Saint-Maur since morning, and could not now be brought to Paris. In the midst of all the extravagances of his court, the King's needs had remained so simple that when he arrived unexpectedly at any of his residences he was greeted by empty rooms, and took what he needed with him. Guitaut remarked innocently that the Queen would be only too happy to offer bed and board to her august husband. Louis sighed his surrender, and the triumphant Guitaut hurried to the palace.

* The Condé family was a collateral branch of the House of Bourbon. – Tr.

Louis arrived to find that everything possible had been done to please him. The sovereigns dined together in an atmosphere of suppressed excitement on the part of all those present. After a superb meal the royal pillow was placed on the Queen's bed, there being no other available. All the religious communities of Paris had been alerted, probably from the Rue Saint-Antoine, and prayers were rising from all the houses of the pious. His Majesty remained at the Louvre until daybreak.

On 20 January 1638 Renaudot's *Gazette* published the incredible tidings: the Queen was with child! It was a sensational development, which brought princes and noblemen hot-foot to Saint-Germain to present the customary compliments to their Majesties. The obligatory show of joy could not hide their stupefaction, and Gaston of Orléans, faced with the loss of the crown he had so eagerly sought and expected, had to put a good face on his chagrin. On 10 February the King renewed his vow to the Holy Virgin. A procession was to be instituted every 15 August in perpetuity, a medallion was struck and a statue of the Virgin erected on the main altar of Notre-Dame, where the kneeling monarch offered his crown and sceptre at her feet.

Yet still not a single affectionate word or tender gesture passed between the royal couple. This was not to the liking of Marie de Hautefort: Anne of Austria must be shielded against any kind of adverse influence during the months of her pregnancy. Marie was aware of her power and ready for any sacrifice on behalf of her mistress. Louise may have become the image of divine love for the King, but it was said of the petulant Gascon girl (even though 'Louis the Chaste' had never touched her):

> Hautefort la merveille
> Réveille
> Tous les sens de Louis
> Quand sa bouche vermeille
> Lui fait voir un souris.*

Out of affection for the Queen, Marie bestowed many smiles on her strange suitor, and their withered idyll bloomed again. Louis XIII began to enjoy life, suffered less from gout, headaches and internal pains, and – being anxious to keep the maid – stayed close by her mistress. But Marie was too full of scorn and impatience to put up with his hunting stories for long, and in any case a touch of uncertainty would be a useful spur to the King's affections. After barely three months he was once again enduring tiffs, flirtations, scenes, explanations. A spate of letters to Richelieu enumerated every detail, and the Cardinal was forced to take his mind off the Thirty Years War to arbitrate the conflict.

* 'The wonderful Hautefort/rouses/all Louis' senses/when her ruby lips bestow a smile upon him.'

On 22 April the child stirred in the womb, news which certainly caused more rejoicing among the people than did that of the conquest of Guadeloupe, which came soon after. The next day a fête was given at the Arsenal to celebrate the good omen. The Cardinal trailed his ermine and red train through the resplendent crowd and admired the rockets, fireworks and flares as if he were watching some portent written in the skies.

In July the King appointed the Marquise de Lansac Governess of the Children of France, much to the annoyance of Hautefort, who had intended the post for her aunt, Mme de La Flotte. From that time onward Louis could say farewell to any hope of peace and quiet. Goaded beyond endurance by Marie, and infuriated by the Queen's new status, he took refuge among his soldiers.

On 19 August the doctors summoned him back – prematurely. 'I wish I had not arrived so early and was still in Picardy,' the unhappy King wrote to Richelieu. 'Tomorrow I am going to Versailles for two or three days. I have found the female sex as senseless and impertinent as ever. It really is annoying that the Queen has not been brought to bed so that I might go back to Picardy, whether or not you deem it advisable; just so long as I can be away from all these women.' He was exasperated by the alliance of Anne and Marie, and the girl must have realized the danger, for she agreed to a reconciliation which 'could not have gone better,' according to a letter from Minister Chavigny to the Cardinal on 25 July: 'The King, who had been unusually upset and looking very bad-tempered, has come back quite cheerful, and his stomach has eased without the use of the remedies he usually employs.' Three days later public prayers were begun throughout the kingdom. Louis grew impatient, as did the royal family and the entire court, which thronged the château, ready to rush in at the slightest sound, for no child of France must enter life without a host of witnesses.

On 5 September 1638, just nine months after the unexpected encounter at the Louvre, the King was informed that his wife was in labour. The princes of the blood, the Comtesse de Soissons, the Duchesse de Vendôme, Constable de Montmorency, Mme de Sénecé and various others pressed round. Gaston of Orléans craned his neck as if to make sure that there was no trickery afoot. The Queen had a difficult labour, and for a time her life seemed to be in danger. Marie de Hautefort wept, and reproached Louis for not showing more concern. 'The child must be saved,' he replied. 'You will have every consolation for losing the mother.' A quarter of an hour before midday the midwife triumphantly held up the baby who was to become the Sun King. Mme de Sénecé raised the cry: 'It is a Dauphin!'

Cannon roared, bells rang, fifty couriers put spurs to their horses and the King knelt to give thanks to Heaven. It was with some difficulty, however, that he was persuaded to go to his wife and kiss her. He next went to the chapel of

Château-Vieux and heard the Te Deum. Monseigneur the Dauphin, baptized by the Bishop of Meaux and then suckled by Mlle de La Giraudière, was taken to his apartment, Mme de Lansac bearing the precious burden. On either side of the gallery, red musketeers in their white plumes raised gleaming swords as Louis-Dieudonné held his first review.

At Saint-Germain, four silver dolphins spewed out an endless flow of wine. Forty pieces of artillery and three hundred firework displays announced the good news in Paris. There followed two days of continuous dancing, concerts, fireworks, triumphal cars and bonfires. The violins were drowned in the din of fireworks and artillery, and the Palais Cardinal blazed with light. Pealing bells spread the signal for celebrations from town to town as far as Switzerland. France was in ecstasy.

The general rejoicing drowned any malicious murmurs about the special grace which had come so conveniently to the aid of Anne of Austria after twenty-three years of marriage and fifteen of estrangement. It was not until much later that they were heard again, and swelled to create the widespread rumour which took its origin from enemies of the monarchy, free-thinkers and scandalmongers. Although the usually mysterious circumstances of conception may in this case be determined with exactitude, no amount of improbability has ever since discouraged the supporters of the theory of the 'bastard' king. Some even implicated Buckingham – ten years in the grave – and Henry iv's legitimized son the Comte de Moret, who had also died many years before the event. Others claimed that Mazarin was the father. The Queen's guards and her household were all scrutinized for the dashing gentleman – Rochefort, Guitaut, Comminges, Rantzau? – who had been chosen to perpetuate the Bourbon line. The nineteenth-century historian Michelet plumped for Comminges. Even Richelieu himself was entered in the lists.

But there is really no cause for debate. The only peculiar circumstance is that the unforeseen meeting of 5 December could not have happened had it not been for Louis' chaste love for a future Carmelite, a thunderstorm and the opportunism of a captain of the guard devoted to his Queen. Surrounded by spies, and prevented by etiquette from ever being alone, Anne of Austria would have faced insuperable difficulties in committing an act of adultery. As for the alleged impotence of Louis xiii, so often taken as beyond dispute, it is flatly disproved by the journal of Hérouard, the King's doctor, and the Queen's early pregnancies show that his misogynistic inclinations in no way incapacitated him for fathering children.

There was, then, no mystery – or rather, there was something more tangible. Those who had believed that by reconciling Louis xiii with his wife they could create a breach with his Minister had their hopes dashed. The triumph of the Cardinal's implacable enemies (Anne, La Fayette, Hautefort), of the disaffected nobility and the pro-Spanish party, far from saving Spain, ensured her defeat at the hands of Richelieu and guaranteed the success of the royal revolution in France. Gaston of Orléans lost his high rank as heir to the throne and the future ceased to depend on the life of a chronically ailing monarch.

In 1637 Louis XIII and Richelieu, neither of whom had long to live, were striving against all odds to construct a great edifice which could not conceivably survive them. By 1638 they had every right to think that Christendom would no longer be dominated by the House of Austria, that the unity of the realm was assured and that the threat of civil war had lessened. All this because France now had a Dauphin.

[2]

The Child of Discord

LOUIS-DIEUDONNE's parents were as dissimilar as they were disunited, and represented two conflicting dynasties. Far from bringing them together, his existence created a new barrier between them. Against his will, but obedient to tradition, the King left the Dauphin in his mother's care, relying on Mme de Lansac, formerly lady-in-waiting to Henry IV's consort, Queen Margot, to prevent the boy from going over to the enemy. She was made governess because she had never served a foreign queen. For their own part, Louis' enemies regarded Anne's maternal status and its accompanying political power as one of their trump cards.

Foreign observers were even finding portents in the baby's appetite. Grotius, the Swedish ambassador, wrote: 'The Dauphin has already changed wet-nurses three times [he was to have eight altogether]. The ladies chosen for that office say that they cannot fulfil it because this sturdy, temperamental child bites and tears their breasts. *Let France's neighbours beware of such precocious greed!*' It was astonishing that the tubercular Bourbon, worn out before his fortieth year, and the daughter of the degenerate Habsburgs should have produced such a lusty heir.

Louis XIII was already in decline. As illness and medicines sapped his strength, so the darker, more restless side of his nature came to the fore, and the image of this great and stoical martyr to *raison d'Etat* came strangely close to the caricatures which were later to be made of it. Eaten up with pain, scruples and resentment, the King knew himself to be tragically isolated and withdrew behind a wall of suspicion. He soon grew jealous and distrustful of the longed-for son who was now surrounded and admired as the emblem of the future – as if Louis XIII would soon be making way for him. The face he showed to his son in the cradle was severe, morose and rigid: Anne of Austria's shone with eager solicitude, for the hopes and fears of Spain resided in this fat baby with its long robe and flat bonnet, already girded with the Cordon Bleu.

The year 1639 witnessed the downfall of Marie de Hautefort and the phenomenal rise of the little Marquis de Cinq-Mars, whom the King introduced to his wife 'with words that gave strong evidence of his passion'. Anne had the sense to behave very graciously towards the new favourite, and it occurred to Cinq-Mars that a reconciliation between the royal couple might bring greater freedom for himself. At the Château de Saint-Germain, on Christmas Eve, the King gave the order to lay the royal pillow on Anne's bed, and on 28 January 1640 Renaudot's *Gazette* made it known that her Majesty was again with child.

In her final month of pregnancy her peace was shattered by a violent upheaval. Louis XIII came home from the war and went to see the Dauphin, whom he found 'in very good health', but when Cinq-Mars went to caress the child the future Sun King began to scream. His father's intervention only made matters worse. That same evening the infuriated Louis wrote to Richelieu and recounted the incident, concluding: 'My son is much improved in looks, but very stubborn. [Henry IV had said the same about Louis XIII.] I am absolutely determined not to put up with his tantrums.' On 9 September 1640 the King declared to his Minister: 'I am most displeased with my son. *As soon as he sets eyes on me, he yells as if he were looking at the devil and always cries for his mother.* He must be cured of these tantrums and taken away from the Queen's side as soon as possible.'

The subsequent letters of 13 and 14 September are worth quoting at length. On the 13th:

> I am writing these few lines to tell you that thanks to the good offices of Mme de Lansac my son has begged my forgiveness on his knees and played with me for an hour and more. I have given him toys to play with and we are the best of friends. Pray God that this may continue.

On the 14th:

> Thank you for your good advice about the *aversion* that my son was showing signs of developing towards me . . . by the grace of God, I hope that you will already be aware, by means of the letter I wrote to you yesterday morning, how the reconciliation came about. Since that time *he cannot bear to leave me, he tries to follow me everywhere.* I fondle him as much as I can. *I think that a little speech I made in front of some people who were sure to pass it on, and the offices of Mme de Lansac may have contributed to this change.* The speech was to the effect that there were women about my son who were trying to make him afraid of men, and that if these tantrums continued I would replace all his attendants except Mme de Lansac and two women, and that I wanted him to see nothing but men from now on . . . I said this *to make it known that I really might take him away from here.*

Plainly the King was aware that the Dauphin's 'good humour' had its roots in the threat to take him away from the Queen and was by no means certain that this lull would persist. He had put the Dauphin through a strange performance – a two-year-old being compelled to play-act so as not to be parted from his mother. By Louis XIII's own account, it took two days to persuade his son and to rehearse him; the change was brought about partly by

11

Mme de Lansac, but above all by Anne herself, whose fate depended on the outcome. Only a short time before, the future had offered the prospect of widowhood without honour: now, the mother of a child who might become king while still in the cradle could look forward to wielding the absolute power of a Catherine or a Marie de Médicis. Since the health of both King and Cardinal was declining at a frightening rate, she knew that she was at the decisive turning-point of her life. Whatever else happened, she must have the Dauphin by her side when the issue came to a head, and must be in a position to lay claim to the Regency. It is no slander on the Queen to affirm that her terror of losing custody of her son played a part in this calculation – a terror that the child sensed and shared so vividly that he would show affection towards the pallid bogyman with the pointed moustache.

The consequences were to prove quite disproportionate to the event. Louis XIII was never mentioned at his son's court. The Sun King never followed any of his precepts and never remembered him. The second of the Bourbons vanished from the memory of the French people and Louis XIV grew to behave as if he were the sole originator of his dynasty. Hence the deplorable elevation of his bastards, the will which entrusted the substance of power to the eldest of them and the necessity for the Regent to win his legitimate rights after the death of Louis XIV by means of a coup d'état for which the Parlement* exacted the price of regaining certain political prerogatives, and was thus able to oppose any basic reforms during two reigns, and to make the Revolution inevitable.

The Oedipus complex could scarcely be more dangerous than when its effects act to distort the functioning of an absolute monarchy.

About a week after this alarum the Queen gave birth to her second son, Philippe, who received the title of Duc d'Anjou. This event did not improve relations between the parents, and the Queen fell back on her brother-in-law, the many disaffected individuals and the conspiracies which she herself had set in train fifteen years previously. In 1641 she secretly supported the revolt of the King's cousin, the Comte de Soissons, and she also encouraged the Marquis de Cinq-Mars' rash conspiracy against Richelieu, which united against the Cardinal the combined forces of Spain, Monsieur, the Duc de Bouillon and many others.

Before setting off on the conquest of Roussillon, Louis XIII forbade Mme de Lansac to admit Monsieur into the presence of the little Princes if he was accompanied by more than three people. He gave orders that the Princes were to be surrounded by officers whenever Monsieur paid a visit to the Queen.

---

* Under the Ancien Régime, each region of France had its own supreme court of justice, called the *Parlement*. Although its functions were primarily judicial, the Paris Parlement in particular tended to play an increasing political role – Tr.

Richelieu, for his part, posted two observers, practically jailers, close to Anne, with the titles of grand master and maid of honour – the Baron de Brassac and his wife.

Presumably satisfied by these precautions, the King was almost affectionate in his leave-taking. That was in February 1642: in April, for no apparent reason, the Queen received an order from Louis XIII not to leave Fontaine-bleau. Once again there was talk of the Princes being taken from her. Anne wrote to Richelieu in a panic: 'The prospect of being parted from my children at such an early age has caused me pain beyond bearing.' She received no reply. For weeks on end the Brassacs kept her in suspense and led her to believe that her sons might be snatched from her at a moment's notice. On top of this, Cinq-Mars' conspiracy was grinding to a halt. Anne, full of life and vitality, was confronting two sick men whose legacy was in her charge. Realizing that she must safeguard her position and gain a breathing space at all costs, she conveyed to Richelieu a copy of the treaty concluded between the King of Spain, Monsieur and Cinq-Mars. Although we have no formal proof of it, there is no doubt that such a transaction took place.

Cinq-Mars was arrested on 13 June, and on the 15th Louis XIII sent his wife an extremely kind letter bidding her to remain with her children. Yet his greeting was very bad-tempered when they met at Fontainebleau on 25 July, for he could not forgive the woman whom he suspected of precipitating his favourite's downfall. Faced with this new scare, the Queen grovelled to the point of offering to entrust the upbringing of the Princes to Richelieu, even though he had his own eye on the regency – true, the Cardinal was given no more than three months to live at the time. Anne had the satisfaction of being informed of his death on 4 December 1642.

The dead man's three principal colleagues, Chavigny, de Noyers and Cardinal Mazarin, now formed a kind of collegiate government. It would have been in Chavigny's hands had the King been able to forget his leading part in the Cinq-Mars episode. On the other hand, he had great respect for de Noyers and had long been showing signs of genuine friendship for Mazarin. The Italian cardinal destroyed his rival's standing by falsely accusing him of working to establish the Queen as Regent. He then persuaded the ingenuous de Noyers that the intelligent course would be to tender his resignation: the King would refuse it and would confirm him in his authority. De Noyers rose to the bait, his resignation was accepted, and without commotion, almost apologetically, Mazarin took the place of Richelieu.

It was a striking contrast. The new Minister's behaviour was gentle, kindly and accommodating. The clergyman and politician Paul de Gondi, who as Cardinal de Retz wrote some of the most famous memoirs of the time, comments that he seemed to be 'in despair that his dignity as a cardinal did not permit him to humble himself before the world as much as he would have wished.' He took great pains to please and be of service, and showed great devotion towards the Queen. The Dauphin grew used to the frequent appearances of this soft-spoken, suave man who was 'well made, a little above average height, with a fine, lively complexion, fiery eyes, and brown, slightly wavy hair.' Although he had been one of Richelieu's creatures, Anne had been well disposed towards him ever since the day when the Cardinal had presented the young captain of the papal army to their Majesties with the insolent afterthought: 'You will like him, Madame, he looks like Buckingham.' Their two portraits do indeed show some similarity of features between the Italian and the handsome Englishman who had played havoc with the Queen-Infanta's heart.

The Cardinal won favour with Anne by urging the King to pave the way for his own salvation by pardoning the rebels. Richelieu had wanted to strip Gaston of Orléans of his rights and had made arrangements for his downfall. That course was now abandoned, and Monsieur returned to court as gay as ever. It was the first of a long series of reparations thanks to which Louis meant to insure his conscience against any risk of injustice. Richelieu's former enemies – notably the Ducs de Vendôme, Mercoeur and Beaufort, the natural sons and grandsons of Henry IV – left the Bastille or came home from exile. Only four people were not covered by the amnesty: Chateauneuf, formerly Guardian of the Seals and the conspirators' permanent candidate for the office of First Minister, the Duchesse de Chevreuse, too close and too formidable a friend of the Queen, Marie de Hautefort and La Porte.

From 21 February onward, Louis suffered the final onslaughts of the tubercular disease of the lungs and stomach that had been his familiar enemy for twenty years. On 16 March, after a night of torment, he gave up the struggle and an overwhelming sadness increased his pain. On the 27th he asked his doctor, Bouvard, point-blank what his chances were, and when that gloomy worthy did not dare to reply, Louis sighed: 'Your silence tells me that I must die.' He added: 'God is my witness that I have never liked life and that I shall be overjoyed to go to Him.'

Overjoyed as a Christian, perhaps, but as King of France he was assailed by a multitude of troubles, which he confided to Mazarin. He had been unable to end the war and was leaving the nation exposed both to the vengeance of the higher nobility and to enemy attacks. The new sovereign would be four and a half years old, and his natural guardians, his mother and uncle, whom the laws of the realm appointed to govern in his name, had been involved in a case of high treason only a year before. As for the third most important power in the land, Louis II de Bourbon de Condé (Monsieur le Prince), he was an insatiable predator whose ambition was equalled only by his greed and coarseness. Would the dark days of the previous regency recur, and must the achievement of each successive Bourbon be destroyed by his widow? Louis xiii was determined not to have sacrificed his life to the public interest only for a foreign woman to nullify his efforts. Even if it meant disgracing her, he would thwart his wife and deprive her of the means of doing further harm.

Mazarin pointed out the uselessness and danger of drastic measures and proposed the clever middle path of instituting a Regency Council whose decisions would be reached by a majority vote. Thus it would not matter much if the Queen should preside, even if she should take the title of Regent, or if Monsieur should become Lieutenant Général – provided that they were in the right company. Louis gave his consent. In addition to Anne of Austria, Gaston of Orléans and Condé, the members of the Council were to be Chancellor Séguier, Chavigny, Bouthillier and, of course, Mazarin himself. The majority would thus consist of Richelieu's spiritual heirs.

The main problem was the reaction of Anne of Austria. Would she accept such humiliating treatment without protest? Might not the faction which had been regrouping expectantly around her devise some scheme to defend her rights? Mazarin murmured into Anne's credulous ear that it would be folly to protest, and that he had only made these arrangements out of zeal for her welfare. The principal aim was to ensure that the mother of the future King should not be excluded from the Regency. Once in possession of that crucial title, it would be as simple a matter for her to be the real power behind the throne as it had been for Marie de Médicis. The Queen believed him.

The Cardinal, after all, had made it known that he had no personal aspirations and thought of himself simply as a stop-gap. An ambassadorship in some distant country was the height of his ambition. The court was deceived, but not the dying King. If he still had illusions about the value of his will, he had none at all about the man to whom he had decided to entrust his son. He made up his mind to bind them together, and announced that the son of Sicilian fishermen was to become godfather of the heir of Saint Louis (the Dauphin had been only privately baptized).

On 19 April the King suffered 'a hepatitic flux with a species of slow fever.' The following day the door of his bedchamber was opened to admit the Queen and her children, the princes, the *ducs et pairs* and the high officers of the Crown. An official read aloud 'the declaration of his Majesty on the government of his States.' The preamble recalled the main events of the reign and the special blessings which Heaven had dispensed to the King on every critical occasion from his minority to the birth of his two sons 'at a time when we least expected it.' It voiced one of the constant laws of history: 'France has made it truly apparent that, united, she is invincible and that her greatness depends upon her unity as does her ruin on her division.' The declaration proper prescribed the organization of the coming regency. One article specified that Chateauneuf was to remain in the Bastille and Mme de Chevreuse in exile.

At the end of the reading, the King asked if anybody had any objection to make. No one broke the silence. He signed the document, which was then handed over to the First President of the Parlement and the high legal dignitaries for registration. Those present dispersed, except for the Queen and Monsieur, whom Louis enjoined to love and help one another.

The baptism took place on 21 April. Charlotte de Montmorency, Princess de Condé, for whom Henry IV had all but set Europe ablaze, was the godmother, and Mazarin the godfather. The ceremony made a deep impression on the Dauphin, who seems to have confused it with the coronation. When the boy came to see him, still dressed in his robe of silver thread, the King asked him: 'What is your name now?' – 'Louis XIV, papa!' – 'Not yet!'

People remarked on the King's having a 'rosy face' in spite of his incessant racking cough. On 22 April he received the viaticum. The following day he fell into a faint. 'Ah!' he sighed, regaining consciousness in the midst of an over-eager throng, 'these people are coming to see how soon I shall die.' Hearing a burst of laughter from the dressing-room, he murmured: 'That must be the Queen and Monsieur.' This was unfair to his wife, who had been beside herself with grief. His confessor entreated the dying man to abjure this pernicious idea, but he only replied: 'In my present condition, I am obliged to forgive her, but I am not obliged to believe her.'

Louis XIV could truly be called the child of discord.

[3]

The Queen and *Frère Coupechou*

THAT day in April when the little Dauphin believed that he was already Louis
XIV marked an important stage in the career of the man who held him over
the font. Only a short while before, his patron Richelieu had dubbed him,
with a blend of cruelty, affection and contempt, *'illustrissime colmardo'*, or *'frère
coupechou'*, the brother who carried out the most menial tasks in a monastery.

The Revolution was to enable an unknown Corsican lieutenant to become
emperor of the French, and the sons of inn-keepers and lawyers to put on
crowns. The convulsions of the twentieth century brought into prominence
men such as Hitler, Mussolini and Stalin, and made the fate of the world
dependent on them. Even so, it is perhaps even more extraordinary that in an
age when the classes were separated by impassable barriers, everything
depended on 'birth' and social upheaval was unthinkable, the grandson of an
unknown commoner, probably a Sicilian fisherman, and son of a Roman
steward should have become a cardinal, first minister of France and godfather
of a future king of France, at the age of forty.

Pietro Mazzarini, steward of Don Filippo Colonna, Constable of Naples,
nursed high ambitions for his son and wanted him to become a Jesuit.
However, when Giulio left college his sole thought was to enjoy worldly
pleasures. In addition, he had already acquired the thoroughgoing scepticism
which later enabled him to change his tack so easily. At that time he was a
charming sharp-witted young man, ready for anything. Thanks to the
Colonnas, he was able to move in a brilliant society. In order to live up to its
ostentation and lavishness, he took to gambling with such feverish dedication
that his father became apprehensive, and decided to send him away: he
obtained an appointment for Giulio as *cameriere* to the Constable's second
son, Don Girolamo, who took him to Spain, where he was also to complete
his studies.

In the course of the journey to Spain Mazarin, then aged twenty, set out to
charm his younger master. His success was absolute. We have testimony that
the young Colonna 'bore him a more than ordinary affection.' In Madrid
Mazarin did not study law, as had been intended, but his discovery of the
capital of the most powerful Christian empire aroused in him the first sparks

of ambition, which did not prevent him from flinging himself into pleasure and gambling just as he had in Italy. 'How stupid is a man without money!' he would exclaim when he lost.

Eventually, after a run of bad luck, he borrowed money from a notary named Nodardo, making a false statement that he was expecting funds. This gave him the opportunity to make the acquaintance of Nodardo's daughter, with whom he fell in love, but the young Colonna, learning that his friend intended to marry, sent him back to Rome with a letter for the Constable, who read it, reprimanded him severely and refused to let him go back to his Spanish beauty. Mazarin saw that he was at the mercy of circumstance, as he always would be, and found little difficulty in making the best of things.

This episode is of interest because it throws light on the kind of 'trivial' accidents which may determine a great career. If the young Colonna had set less store by the celibacy of his *cameriere,* the fate of the future cardinal would have been quite different. There was to be no further trace of a woman in the career of this sensual figure until the Queen of France entered his life twenty years later.

There followed another and no less fascinating episode. The young man turned his back on a legal career and managed to have himself appointed a captain in the papal army, stationed at Ancona. Upon learning that his mother had fallen sick, he hastened to her side without asking for leave and only paid heed to the consequences of his rashness after she was cured. Far from ruining him, however, this escapade gave him the chance to throw himself at the feet of Urban VIII. Once again his charm worked. The Holy Father, moved by his 'spontaneity', showed the first signs of what turned out to be an enduring and profitable affection.

Sachetti, the apostolic commissioner of the army, also took a liking to Mazarin and made the young man his secretary when he was appointed nuncio extraordinary to Milan in 1628. At the age of twenty-seven Mazarin now found his true vocation – diplomacy. He himself wrote: 'I made myself more important in practice than was warranted by the post I had been given.'

The tangled question of the Mantuan succession was now at its height, with the Spain of Olivarez confronting the France of Richelieu and the two powers already fighting each other through intermediaries. Although the Pope wanted to prevent war at all costs, his emissaries were getting quite out of their depth, and the humble secretary was able to propose a bold initiative which they were only too happy to sanction. He travelled untiringly from one town to another, converting Spanish generals and Italian princes by his intelligence and persuasiveness, until they concluded that he alone was capable of halting and defeating Cardinal Richelieu, the terror of Europe, who was about to cross the Alps at the head of his army. The frivolous and ineffectual Cardinal Antonio Barberini went to Lyons to try to mediate between the two rivals, taking with him Mazarin, the papal captain – and the real ambassador.

The fateful interview took place on 29 January 1630. Mazarin asked for a truce in the course of a three-hour speech whose excessive humility gained not the Holy See's cause, but his own. 'You could talk for twenty years and I would not give way,' said Richelieu, who was nonetheless enchanted by Mazarin's brilliance and invited him to dinner – a considerable distinction. On that day, the Italian discovered both the deep motivations of French policy and the hypnotic power of genius. Later, he wrote: 'I took to him by instinct, even before discovering his great qualities by experience.'

In the spring the French seized the key town of Pignerol in Piedmont and prepared to lay siege to Casale. Once again, the legate Barberini and the indispensable Mazarin attempted to stem the flood. On 10 May, in Grenoble, they were presented by Richelieu to the King himself. Here too, Mazarin failed in his mission but won a victory on a different level. He impressed Louis XIII so much that his Majesty offered him money (standard practice with the diplomats of those times) which the artful Italian took care not to accept.

Guile need not preclude courage. In October the two armies, preparing to fall upon each other outside Casale, were thrown into consternation by the spectacle of Captain Mazarin spurring his horse between them with a cry of 'Peace! Peace!' Moments later the generals were gathered about him and an agreement was reached. For a season, Mazarin was the most popular man in Europe.

It was now generally recognized that the young man had other qualities just as precious as the art of pleasing: 'a surprising power of persuasion, an unparalleled tenacity, once committed to action, and a marvellously flexible character and intelligence which allow him to adjust with ease to any interlocutor, of whatever origin.' Richelieu was quick to suggest that Mazarin should be appointed papal nuncio in Paris, but Urban VIII took offence and refused. Mazarin still did not stint his efforts on behalf of France, and negotiated a treaty with Savoy. In 1632 he went to Saint-Germain where the court gave him a glittering welcome. Girolamo Colonna, now cardinal and legate at Bologna, continued to write affectionate letters to the man whom he addressed as '*Signor Giulio mio*'. After two missions in Mazarin's company, Cardinal Antonio Barberini had not remained immune to his charm. He invited him to take up residence at the Palazzo Barberini, centre of the political, intellectual and social life of the day. Mazarin rewarded him by acting as a go-between with Leonora, his beautiful mistress.

In 1633 everything bore fruit. The valiant captain of Casale became Monsignor, and could wear ecclesiastical costume without having been ordained. He received two canonries, sinecures whose revenues were to be paid by France. The following year he was able to return to France as nuncio extraordinary, once again with orders from Urban VIII to prevent a war between two Catholic kingdoms.

It was now that the statesman and the adventurer fused. At one and the same time Mazarin paid court to Richelieu, even exerting himself to amuse him, and worked tirelessly for the peace in Christendom which he was to establish twenty-five years later. Richelieu, on the other hand, wanted something entirely different: the humiliation of the House of Austria and a French hegemony in Europe. When war did break out (in 1635) the papal envoy fell ill with disappointment and at once began to work for a peace conference, but early in 1636 Spain took offence at his pro-French attitudes and had him recalled. Mazarin went to earth at Avignon, where on his own admission he converted one room of the palace into a gambling den.

He did not stay long, for his friend Cardinal Antonio recalled him to Rome. There he committed himself to his future course. From then on, he was to serve Richelieu – a thankless task, at a papal court whose allegiance was almost totally Spanish. Mazarin wanted to escape from this 'hell' which nevertheless offered so many pleasures, and begged Richelieu to bring him back to France. If the Cardinal did not want him to meddle in policy, let him employ him 'to fix statues and look after the château!' But His Eminence preferred to employ his invaluable agent in Rome.

The death of Father Joseph, Richelieu's *éminence grise*, put a new complexion on things. While it may be doubted whether the Cardinal intended Mazarin to be his eventual successor, it is certain that he meant him to be his chief collaborator. He even went as far as to ask on Mazarin's behalf for the red hat which had been destined for the dead man. It is not true that Mazarin received 'letters of naturalization' which made him a French subject.* He was to govern France without being a Frenchman, just as he was to become a cardinal without being a priest.

Such a prospect must have seemed far-fetched on 14 December 1639, the day he left Rome for good in response to Richelieu's summons. An inveterate gambler, he was staking everything on the sick Cardinal's friendship. In France he was to display on all occasions his wide-ranging talents and versatility. He was already using the method which he himself described so well: 'I dissimulate, I evade, I temper, I arrange everything as amicably as possible.' His reward came on 16 December 1641. Yielding to Richelieu's insistence, the Pope at last appointed his former captain to the office of cardinal. Louis XIII gave Mazarin the biretta, at Valence in February 1642.

From the day after Richelieu's death, the King sought out the advice of the man about whom he was to say that he had 'rendered us such loyal and outstanding services that we are no less assured of him than if he had been

---

*The error was originated by the nineteenth-century historian Chéruel, and has been perpetuated by numerous others.

born our subject.' Many historians have been convinced that in so doing Louis was obeying the express wish of the dying Richelieu in the course of *tête à tête* interviews with the monarch. In fact, in his final recommendations, the Cardinal advised the King only to *make use* of Mazarin. If the latter immediately received a share of the governing power and later the whole of it, he owed it to the friendship and far-sightedness of Louis xiii.

It was natural that, as the King's health declined, the contacts between the future Regent and the First Minister should grow more frequent. Mazarin had about three weeks in which to determine the 'course of history' and of his own destiny, and to work a sex-change on the mentality of a notoriously indolent and frivolous woman. Adopting a widely accepted interpretation, a recent biographer of Louis xiv has written: 'Something flowed between Mazarin and Anne of Austria, a reciprocal and profound love which was to withstand every test, even that of time.'[1] This sudden passion between two people *who had known each other for eleven years* seems hardly credible at a time when both were preoccupied with quite dissimilar problems.

At forty-two years of age, Anne of Austria was no longer the siren who had disturbed even Richelieu at close quarters and captivated Buckingham. She was now a very pale, fair, full-blown matron with green eyes and handsome arms and hands. Only the large nose, too broad at the tip, and the famous lower lip betrayed the Spanish royal blood in this bold woman who loved hunting, food, *honourable* gallantry and the dangerous games of Mme de Chevreuse. In spite of her misfortunes, Philip iii's grand-daughter had a confidence, ease and taste which her ardent piety did little to subdue. With the exception of Marie-Antoinette, no Queen of France ever displayed a more feminine, more flirtatious temperament, but her *gloire** and her fear of God held in check the violence which sometimes dwelt in her.

How would such a woman react if Richelieu's former protégé dared to pay court to her, and in a situation in which his motives would be highly suspect? Here we must examine the whole question of the relationship between Anne of Austria and the *illustrissime colmardo*. Charlotte Elizabeth of Bavaria, second wife of Louis xiv's brother and chronicler of much of his reign through his letters, stated as a fact that 'the widow of Louis xiii did much worse than love Cardinal Mazarin – she married him.' True, the truculent Princess was writing seventy-four years later (in 1717), and if we were to believe this same informant we would have to consider Mme de Maintenon a poisoner and an incendiary.

* The 'classical sense' of this word is defined by the *Grand Larousse* as 'consideration, honour, reputation, proceeding from the merit of a person and with no connotation of signal celebrity.' His *gloire* was the medium in which a monarch must necessarily move: no English word will do. – Tr.

The Duchesse de Chevreuse, Anne's greatest friend and the first victim of Mazarin's new powers, was much less assertive. She told Cardinal de Retz:

... that she had seen in certain of [the Queen's] airs something of those she had adopted with Buckingham; that in others, she had noticed circumstances which led her to believe that there was nothing between them but a liaison of the mind; that one of the most remarkable of those circumstances was the off-hand, even rude way in which the Cardinal behaved with her ... which the duchess, whose inclination was nevertheless malicious, finally interpreted as having two *conflicting meanings, from what I know of the Queen's temperament, so that I do not know what to make of it.*

There are also a number of letters, sometimes clumsily enciphered, which are perplexing for two reasons: on the one hand because of their intimate tone and expressions, on the other because those which seem to offer clinching evidence date from a time when both parties were in their fifties – practically old age at that time. In 1653, when the fifty-one-year-old sovereign wrote: 'Farewell, I am worn out, Mazarin (in code) knows why,' she could still have been referring to a sexual relationship. But by 1660 Mazarin was old, seriously ill and extremely bad-tempered. He had brushed Anne unceremoniously aside from affairs of state and often showed his lack of consideration for her. She was then fifty-nine years old, the equivalent of seventy today, and yet she could write: 'To the last breath, Anne is yours, whatever you may believe.' When the Cardinal died eight months later, the Queen's *femme de chambre*, Mme de Motteville, tells us in her memoirs that Anne 'was moved to tears.' Then she made the strange remark that she had always known him better than anyone else and that she had not thought any the worse of those who advised her to send him away from court. After that, politics became her sole preoccupation.

None of this is conclusive, but there are three things which dispose of any possibility of a physical union between the mother and godfather of Louis XIV. The Queen lived her life in the public eye, and her women slept at the foot of her bed. There were no circumstances in which she might be *alone* – that is, with all of her entourage out of earshot. The doors were always kept open, and any conjugal intimacy between herself and the 'knave of Sicily' would have touched off stronger repercussions than mere gossip and pamphleteering. Anne was a supreme product of Habsburg pride, which was unsurpassed by any other dynasty, and piety, which left no room for compromise. Its attendant mortifications curtailed her life. Such a woman could not have committed 'habitual mortal sin' with a cardinal. A woman proud enough, in years to come, to risk unleashing civil war rather than let Louis XIV marry Marie Mancini could not have married Marie's uncle.

The third factor is that according to the Parisian doctor, Gui Patin, whose letters provide a chronicle of the time, Mazarin 'died in the hope of becoming Pope.' This is confirmed by other evidence and by the general trend of the policy which culminated in the Treaty of the Pyrenees. Mazarin did not expect to die before the age of sixty, and he was familiar with the character of Louis XIV. He had only one way of saving himself from the eventual fate, if not of a Concini, then at least of a Sully,* and that was to inherit the papal crown. But destiny, which had given him so much, refused him that culminating glory.

In the final analysis, the historian's conclusion on Mazarin's relations with Anne of Austria must accord with the Queen's own statement to Mme de Brienne: 'I grant you that I like him, and I may even say tenderly, but the affection I bear him does not go so far as love, or if it does so without my knowledge it is not my senses which are involved but only my mind, which is charmed by the beauty of his.'

That remark throws light on the motivation behind the coup de théâtre which was enacted between 21 April and 18 May 1643. Dazzled and captivated by Mazarin's intelligence, and conquered by his personality, Anne suddenly realized what she ought to have known as soon as her son was born. If she conducted her Regency like Marie de Médicis, tied to Spain and in the power of her immediate coterie, her reign would be without honour and might well come to the same bad end. The downtrodden wife of Louis XIII must forget the past and become the glorious mother of Louis XIV. The former had been the emblem of a party committed to a foreign land: the latter must identify herself with France.

On 14 May 1643 a throng of courtiers invaded the King's bedchamber, which was already pervaded by the smell of death. The King was stifling, but it would never have occurred to him to deprive any of those present of the spectacle of his demise. The idol of the tribe must breathe his last in the same way as he had been born, had consummated his marriage and spent every hour of his existence – in public. Before his people and the world, he would observe the last rites. Yet at the last minute the man succeeded in eluding the persona.

He called for his confessor, Father Dinet, took a little crucifix from around his neck and secretly charged the priest to convey this token to Sister Louise-Angélique, whose name had once been Mlle de La Fayette. Then he tried to accompany the prayers for the dying and soon became out of breath, although he was still heard to whisper 'Jesus!' A short while later he made a gesture of secrecy to Father Dinet and died with a suggestion of a smile, putting a finger to his lips.

Anne of Austria displayed as much grief as propriety required. Then she turned to her elder son and greeted him 'as her king and her son together.'

---

* Concini, an Italian adventurer who held power under the regency of Marie de Médicis, was overthrown and assassinated when Louis XIII came to power (1617). The Duc de Sully, Henry IV's minister, was ousted after the latter's death by Marie de Médicis' party (1611). – Tr.

Suddenly she trembled for him. In circumstances such as these, the French court was still a jungle.

The fact that the Queen turned neither to Monsieur nor to Condé, the natural protectors of her children, shows how much her understanding had already matured. The Duc de Beaufort was a handsome, witless young man who was convinced that he had captivated Anne with his fair hair and handsome moustache. He would be loyal because he took it for granted that he would have influence over the Regent. The new King and his brother were put into his charge, the gates of Saint-Germain closed and the Swiss guards took up arms. Louis-Dieudonné must have had the impression not so much of ascending the throne as of confronting great dangers.

Another memory that was to remain with him for the rest of his life was of sitting on a pyramid of cushions decorated with fleurs-de-lys to preside over the session of the Parlement that broke his father's will and bestowed unlimited power on his mother. The partial coup d'état which had followed the death of Henry IV was now elevated to a tradition. 'At that time, the custom which confers the regency on the mothers of kings seemed to the French a law almost as fundamental as that which debars women from the crown.'[2]

Six months previously the Queen had grovelled before Richelieu. When she returned to the Louvre, she found herself more powerful than the Cardinal had ever been, the equal of Blanche of Castile and Catherine de Médicis. For the moment, she was not sure whom she would appoint to rule in her name. Richelieu's old enemies were in no doubt that they were celebrating their victory. But Anne of Austria summoned only one of the former companions of her evil days, Lord Montagu, once the friend of her beloved Buckingham. He told her that Mazarin was in every way the opposite of Cardinal Richelieu, and pointed out that no one would serve her as faithfully as a man risen from nowhere and who depended entirely on her support. Mazarin was not considered a true prince of the Church; he had no strong links with any of the great families, the nobility or the Parlement; he did not even have a country, and was not at home in any language. Self-interest would prevent him from betraying the woman on whom he was utterly dependent.

So, on 18 May, Cardinal Mazarin was confirmed in the office of First Minister, to the consternation of France and the world. He immediately exercised 'that dominion which a shrewd man was liable to have over a woman born with enough weakness to be ruled and enough firmness to persist in her choice.'[3]

It was one of history's turning-points. On the eve of the Battle of Rocroi, at a time when France was on the verge of stamping her mark on Europe, the fate of the Kingdom lay in the hands of a Spaniard who had only yesterday been in league with an enemy nation, and a Sicilian adventurer moulded by the intrigues of papal Rome.

[4]

The Childhood of a Living God

AT the age of four years and eight months, Louis XIV, King of France and Navarre, was not merely the master but also the owner of the goods and bodies of nineteen million men, given into his power by a decree of the Almighty. In the Parlement, the Avocat Général, Omer Talon, went on his knees to tell him: 'Sire, your Majesty's seat represents the throne of the Living God to us. The orders of the realm render honour and respect to yourself as to a visible divinity.' While still in petticoats, the heir of Charlemagne, Saint Louis and Henry IV was the hub and centre of an entire world. Whether or not he ever said: 'l'État c'est moi,' the State actually did depend upon the sturdy, fair-haired child with the lack-lustre eyes. Without him, everything would be called into question. No man could claim to be his equal, or even to be comparable to him. The entire world observed his every gesture and action and strove to interpret his thinking. An impassioned devotion enveloped the young King, who was dressed in gold-embroidered robes on every ceremonial occasion and put on display like the Blessed Sacrament.

The obverse of all this was that Louis XIII's eldest son came into the greatest inheritance in the world at an age when he was unable to defend it with his own hand, an age at which death was apt to cut down prince and commoner alike. He was beset by the malicious hopes of his own immediate family, while resplendent noblemen and red-robed magistrates sought, under cover of their oaths of loyalty, to seize every opportunity his weakness might afford them. The young King realized very early that his mother and godfather were the sole protectors of his birthright, the only people who would defend him and his younger brother Philippe against the uncle, cousins, familiars and dignitaries who hungered for what was his. The paradox of his kingship was that the continuation of a national policy and the preservation of French unity, menaced by the anarchic spirit of the French themselves, should have been defended by two foreigners.

Living god and tribal idol, or fragile being hemmed in by appalling ambitions – both these images are at variance with a third, that of an unhappy, uncared-for child, deprived of affection and sometimes of the necessities of life. Anne of Austria idolized her son and almost always treated him with a tenderness that Louis XIII never received. But her youth had been spent in misery and servitude, and now she was free, all-powerful and still beautiful. She was savouring her belated revenge, and Louis XIV found himself neglected and forgotten.

The entire court was enjoying the pleasures which flourished again during the early years of the Regency. Louis was left to the domestics, the servants of the chambermaids (who were ladies of quality and had their own domestics). Accorded no respect, no bows or curtseys, the god amused himself by playing footman to a chambermaid's daughter. As soon as he was out of the public eye, the splendid robes were replaced by threadbare doublets and stockings full of holes. He took his outings in a ramshackle carriage and wore the same dressing-gown for so long that in the end it came above his knees.

A further blow to his feelings was his reputation for being a gloomy, awkward child, with an 'idiotic' expression, while everyone remarked on his lively, handsome brother. The two sons of France shared between them the characteristics of their ancestry.* With his blue eyes, fair hair and round face, Louis recalled his mother's Austro-Flemish ancestry. He also had the vigour of Henry IV and the Albrets, and the precocious gravity, self-control and powers of dissimulation of Louis XIII. Philippe had the pleasing qualities of Henry IV and Anne of Austria: he was a laughing, playful, talkative, expansive, affectionate boy. Louis hardly ever laughed.

In the mornings, Anne was woken up between ten and eleven and prayed at great length before summoning the woman who slept at the foot of her bed. Her sons were then brought to her and remained at her side during the ceremony of the *lever* and until after breakfast, which consisted of soup, cutlets and sausages. The King handed her her shift and watched as she dressed her hair and showed off the perfection of her hands. Then prayers, dinner, visits in town, the Council, the court circle, supper and merrymaking absorbed the Queen until well past midnight.

Louis and Philippe did not return to her side except when some solemn occasion required it. Then they would be on display, sumptuously dressed and already stately and hieratic. Once back in their apartments, however, the velvet and plumes were put away and they again became children starved of attention and practically left to their own devices.

Anne lost no time in getting rid of Mme de Lansac, who had been so

---

* Only a quarter of Louis' blood was French. Out of sixteen quarterings (great-great-grandparents), he numbered six Habsburgs, two Jagellons (Hungary), one Wittelsbach (Bavaria), one Médicis (Italy), and one Alvarez de Toledo (Spain). He was descended six times over from Jeanne the Mad of Spain, daughter of Ferdinand and Isabella, and had more Valois blood than Bourbon.

devoted to Louis XIII. In her place, she appointed a loyal friend of her youth, Mme de Sénecé – a grateful act but not a wise one, for the new governess was so concerned with the honours due to her position that she forgot her duties. As for the assistant governess, Mme de Lassalle, she was only interested in her pupils' games: with black plumes in her hat and a sword at her side, she formed the children of honour into a company and put them through manoeuvres.

On 7 October 1643 the Regent left the Louvre for the splendours of the nearby Palais Cardinal, bequeathed by Richelieu to Louis XIII and renamed the Palais Royal. Here the little King discovered his world, peopled by beings who combined pride with servility, its pomp and circumstance the backdrop for intrigues, amours, conspiracies, obscure tragedies and history-making deeds.

First there was Louis' formidable family, headed by his uncle, Gaston of Orléans, on whom Parlement had conferred the empty title of Chief of the Councils and Armies of the Regency. In spite of all his scrapes, defeats and humiliations, he was still an optimist, hands in pockets, hat tilted at a rakish angle. Only thirty-five years old, Gaston had many likeable traits and even a few qualities, but, as Cardinal de Retz was to point out, weakness ruled his emotions through fear and his mind through indecision. Although he 'thought of everything and desired nothing,' he cannot have lost all hope of mounting the throne to which he had been heir for so long. Nevertheless, he displayed strong affection towards the Queen, and 'an infinitely tender love' towards the King, so much so that 'he was often seen with tears in his eyes.' This was overdoing things, and the boy, sensing that his uncle's reverence concealed a host of ulterior motives as well as genuine anxiety, never put aside his own grave, haughty, enigmatic mask. He was similarly wary of Monsieur le Prince, an ugly, coarse, arrogant man, and also of his son, the Duc d'Enghien, god of battles – Monsieur le Duc. The hero's aquiline face, 'huge, bulging eyes, hooked nose and thin gaunt features with their obstinate mouth and receding chin' inspired neither fear nor sympathy in Louis.

Monsieur's elder daughter (by his second wife Marie of Bourbon), Anne-Marie-Louise of Orléans, Duchesse de Montpensier, who was to become known as La Grande Mademoiselle, was eleven years older than her cousin, but persisted in calling him 'my little husband', clinging to a careless promise which Anne had made before becoming Regent and which only she herself took seriously. The plain-looking cousin and her half-sisters aroused no more than bored distrust in the little King.

With the whole court in ferment, no one was likely to take much notice of a five-year-old king. The last of the outcasts, Anne's greatest friends, had returned – Mme de Chevreuse and Marie de Hautefort. La Porte was released from the Bastille to take up his old post as valet de chambre. He received a warm welcome from Anne: 'Here is the poor boy who suffered so much on my behalf and to whom I owe everything I have become.'

Not a few of these former exiles expected to influence the frivolous woman they had left behind them. They were all the more disconcerted to find a Regent so unlike the recent conspirator, and made up their minds to get rid of the author of this deplorable transformation. Mme de Chevreuse told Anne that it was a mortal sin to love a cardinal. The aggressively virtuous Marie de Hautefort spoke far more bluntly. The Queen blushed, then burst out laughing, saying: 'The Cardinal does not like women. He comes from a country with quite a different inclination.'

None of this prevented La Porte from respectfully informing her that the kind of talk that was circulating about herself and his Eminence ought to make her 'look to herself.' The Bishops of Lisieux and of Limoges, and Vincent de Paul in person came to add their own warnings. They were scandalized that her Majesty should hold conversations with her Minister 'alone' at the end of a suite of rooms, out of earshot of her courtiers (though not out of their sight).

When the Queen paid no heed, the opposition fell back on the traditional resource of conspiracy and formed a cabal around Anne's former favourites and the Duc de Beaufort. They were known as the *Importants* because of their doctrinaire attitudes. While battle was being joined between the women of the Condé and Rohan families (Mme de Chevreuse was a Rohan), Beaufort and his friends plotted to assassinate Mazarin. The Queen promptly acted as her husband would have done. Beaufort was arrested, and first Mme de Chevreuse, then Marie de Hautefort were banished from court. It was just as frightening as the executions of Richelieu's time, and the Queen was able to resume her dolce vita.

By another irony of fate, Anne was gaining victories over her brother, the King of Spain, greater than anything known since the Battle of Marignan in 1515. Voltaire points out that after Rocroi, 'the respect in which Europe had held the armies of Spain turned towards those of France.' Enghien took Thionville and Syrck, then turned on the Emperor's forces and crushed them at Freiburg and Nördlingen (1645). These great battles were terribly costly. The nobility was decimated, and during the summer months the court was continually in mourning, with no gentleman to be seen there under the age of sixty. The lamentations mingled with the Te Deums, but roused no fear of war in the little King, whose favourite toys were swords, pistols and miniature cannon.

With rare exceptions, a man's early religious training leaves an indelible mark on him, even if he disowns it in later life. Consequently, it is worthwhile analysing the Catholic upbringing with which Louis kept faith throughout his reign. This is a crucial issue, which did much to determine the development of his character and reign, as well as of Europe in the seventeenth century.

In religion his mother was his teacher and example. Anne had lost none of her passionate Spanish faith. 'She fasted on all the proper days and throughout Lent, in spite of her hearty appetite. She went regularly to communion on Sundays and feast days. On the eve of high feast days, she would go to Val-de-Grâce and remain there for some days, secluded from all the world.'[1] On Good Fridays, she was in retreat from five in the morning onwards. However, it would never have occurred to her to reinforce her convictions through study. We are told that 'she did not like reading and knew next to nothing.' Louis adopted her simple faith and refrained, like her, from investigating its sources. He never opened a Bible or a theological work. The settlement of religious problems was not a matter for kings: their function was to enforce the solutions which the Church dictated and for which the Church must take responsibility. Anne of Austria reprimanded the Jansenists severely because they raised questions in which the laity, and women in particular, had no business to meddle. As for religious tolerance, it remained a repellent idea. Only a 'free thinker' could envisage the cohabitation of truth with falsehood.

As he grew older, Louis XIV discovered other reasons for defending Catholicism, the source of royal power (at least according to Bossuet, the famous preacher who was to become preceptor to Louis' eldest son). He also learned that correct public observance could absolve a multitude of sins, and never permitted any deviation in that respect. Another significant factor was that Anne instilled in her son the fear of certain 'crimes' against God. She thus gave the budding despot a salutary counter-balance which was lacking in the dictators of modern times and in the Caesars of Imperial Rome.

By the time Louis was seven years old and was removed from the care of women, he was already devout, grave, polite, well-spoken and instinctively non-committal. The time had come to teach him the métier of kingship.

Bewildered by their failure following the death of Louis XIII, the opposition set out to influence the young monarch's mind. Already he had heard the chambermaids sing songs vilifying the first minister. Without hesitation, Anne appointed Mazarin 'superintendent of the government and conduct of the King.' The resulting furore and the scandalized indignation of the upper nobility were to lead historians, influenced by the virulent pens of Charlotte Elizabeth and the writer Saint-Simon, to accuse the 'knave of Sicily' of prolonging Louis' infancy, preventing him from learning, inculcating 'pestiferous' maxims and dragging the King down to his own level by means of the most arrant flattery.

There is some substance in the accusation of flattery, for Louis himself testified that his tutor would sometimes agree with him before he had spoken. The rest is sheer polemic. Both Queen and Cardinal were unstinting in their duty and affection towards the King.* True, they did not give Louis a general education, or culture: not being intellectuals, they attached little importance to books. However, he at least learned Italian and Spanish, and, since Mazarin enveloped his pupil in a network of spies, he also learned to guard his every word and confide in nobody.

Under the Cardinal's direction, a tutor, a preceptor, an assistant preceptor and a host of teachers were appointed to introduce the boy to 'all the sciences', from mathematics to the guitar. In his memoirs, Saint-Simon heaps abuse on His Majesty's Governor, the Marquis de Villeroy, whom he describes as priding himself 'on always holding the chamberpot for ministers while they were in power, then up-ending it over their heads as soon as they lost their footing.' It is fairer to say that, although Villeroy was too easy on his pupil, he had the distinction of being a good man. The King loved and honoured him as long as he lived (until 1685), and perhaps excessively, for Villeroy's son inherited the affection earned by his father, which consequently lay at the root of a number of later catastrophes.

Saint-Simon's contempt for Hardouin de Beaumont de Péréfixe, the King's preceptor and a future Archbishop of Paris, has no sounder foundation, although the Abbé admittedly had the compliance of a courtier. In any case the two dignitaries exerted no more than a minor influence on the royal child. Another character, far beneath them in rank, was to acquire a much greater power. La Porte relates in his memoirs:

> I was the first [man] to sleep in his Majesty's bedchamber. . . . What hurt him most was that I could not tell him the fairy tales that the women used to send him to sleep.
>
> I told this to the Queen one day, and said that if her Majesty was agreeable I would read to him out of some good book . . . I told her that I did not think anything could be more suitable than the history of France and that I would point out the bad kings to him so as to make him want to be different from them. The Queen thought it a very good idea . . . I read to him [Mézeray's *History of France*] every night as if it were a story, to such effect that the King was pleased, and gave good promise of resembling the nobler of his ancestors, *flying into a great rage when it was suggested to him that he might turn out to be a second Louis the Sluggard,* for I used to attack his defects quite often, as the Queen had ordered me to do.

La Porte won the affection and trust of his young master, and the boy used to come to him for refuge when he was feeling unhappy:

> When he wanted to sleep, he used to want me to lay my head on the pillow next to his. And if he woke during the night he would get up and come and sleep by me.

There is no disputing the devotion and good intentions of the valet de chambre. Unhappily, it was more than human nature could endure for the man who had done and risked so much on his Queen's behalf to see her

---

* In the case of Mazarin, there was an exception which we shall encounter later.

under the thumb of a newcomer and an adventurer. He hated Mazarin and fought him with all his resources. He 'struck little blows against him', especially in the course of his reading from history, when he used to castigate the *maires du palais* who wielded power under the Merovingian puppet kings. A child is always painfully jealous of a stranger who has power over his mother. La Porte made it his business to turn this reflex into an aversion.

One day an unthinking remark proved the success of the undertaking. Seeing the Cardinal pass by on the terrace of the Château de Compiègne with a large following, his Majesty exclaimed: 'Look, it's the Grand Turk!' On another occasion, at Saint-Germain, he again commented that the Cardinal 'makes a lot of noise when he goes by, I think there are more than five hundred people in his suite.'

These processions infuriated him, and when he eventually had his own court even the princes of the blood had to give them up. One of the most striking aspects of La Porte's campaign was his basic complaint that Louis 'was not adequately brought up to be the master'. In fact, the faithful valet de chambre could have spared his lamentations, and Saint-Simon his 'tears'. Louis XIV was and remained the only member of his line since Henry IV not to be crushed by the memory of his early years. In the midst of so many people whose task it was to serve him, he was singularly free, grew up like some wild plant and drew his own conclusions from events. He escaped the neuroses of a Louis XIII, who had been continually brutalized, was never kissed by his mother and had to put up with the consistent favouritism bestowed on his younger brother. Although he inherited his father's shyness, he did not remain oppressed and paralysed as Louis XV and XVI were to be. Above all, he was not reared in hot-house conditions and could judge the outside world through his own eyes.

From the age of seven onwards, Louis was conscious of belonging to a race apart, but knew that a perpetual threat loomed over him and that he could have no real friends or confidants. He detested the Cardinal, but put up with his presence as a necessity. He was proud, but rarely showed it; flew into a rage if a prince or member of the Parlement showed disrespect, but had a strange humility which distressed fervent monarchists like La Porte. He flung himself into his childish games, but often gave evidence of a precocious, enigmatic gravity which never ceased to disconcert his mother. Already the court could discern the impassive mask, slow movements, indecipherable gaze, restrained voice and measured speech which the ambassadors were still admiring seventy years later, on the eve of his death.

31

[5]

Encounter with Revolution

In 1645 his Majesty held another ceremonial session, or *lit de justice,* in the Parlement, this time in order to raise money. The monarchy decked itself out in all its glory, as if to impress a money-lender. There was a great display of Swiss guards, musketeers and light horse, and the session was attended by all the princes, peers, marshals and ministers. Perched on his pile of cushions, Louis greeted the assembly, darted a quick glance at his mother, then announced: 'Gentlemen, I have come here to speak to you about my affairs. My Chancellor will inform you of my wishes.'

The Chancellor then presented the needs of the State, and for the first time Louis heard mention of the financial confusion which had dogged his father and was to be a perpetual thorn in his own flesh. In calling Richelieu to power and supporting him through thick and thin, Louis XIII had opted for an ambitious policy intended to make France the first kingdom of Christendom. This involved enormous military and diplomatic exertions, inordinate expenditure and, consequently, misery for the common people. Almost every year Richelieu had had to increase the already intolerable burden of taxes, provoking riots in most of the provinces, followed by cruel repressions. The saving grace of Gaston of Orléans and his fellow-conspirators was that, while they were certainly striving to further their own ends, they did want to re-establish (although to benefit Spain) a peace thanks to which the people would at last have a breathing space. In 1645 a peace favourable to France still required fresh sacrifices.

The Chancellor told the Parlement as much, reminding the assembly of 'the great and famous victories that have been gained over our enemies, the Queen's desire for peace and the need to squeeze it out of the Spaniards by continued conquests.' After a weighty harangue from the First President, Mathieu Molé, the Avocat Général, Talon, 'spoke out boldly: he pictured to the Queen the people ruined by war and went on his knees to crave mercy on their behalf, in a pathetic and touching manner . . .'

Louis was making his first acquaintance with one of the groups who wished to limit his powers, for although Omer Talon was an honest man he had his own axe to grind. A breeze of revolution was sweeping Europe in the 1640s.

32

Naples, Portugal and Catalonia had risen in revolt and the English Parliament was making war on its King. This example had been tempting the Parlement of Paris ever since the monarchy had had to call on it as arbitrator following the death of Louis xiii. The younger officials of the Parlement wanted to reform the state finances and administration. The boldest of them aspired to give France a constitutional charter.

The Parlement took every opportunity to plead the cause of the poor, and was popular in consequence, but its position was based upon three anomalies. The counsellors' function was judicial, not legislative. Since they had purchased their posts,* they could not be considered as representing anybody but themselves, in spite of their claims. They derived their authority from their legal knowledge, austerity and censorious attitudes towards the abuses of court. The sad truth is that when these 'fathers of the people' referred to 'freedoms', what they primarily had in mind was the protection of their own privileges. Furthermore, in order to offset the cost of their posts, they sold justice shamelessly. It was such an ancient custom that it never entered anybody's mind to complain.

The Parlement therefore had no foundations, either legal or moral, on which to set itself up as a reforming body. This did not prevent it from attempting to constrict the régime by starving it of money, since it was part of the Parlement's official function to register fiscal edicts. In the eyes of Anne of Austria, her first duty was to pass Louis xiii's heritage and authority on to her son intact. Consequently she could not tolerate this kind of tutelage, and the conflict between the Crown and its magistrates went from bad to worse.

Mazarin, who had successfully dealt with the nobility, had to come to terms with the Parlement. In his absorption with the great European enterprise, in which he was close to success, he did not pay sufficient heed to domestic policy and misjudged the strength of public opinion. He would say: 'Let the French get used to my ways, if they will, for I shall not get used to theirs. Once the King and Queen are on my side, every Frenchman will be my friend, and if I were to fall out of favour with them I would have nothing more to do with the French, for I would not remain in France.'

The French, for their part, were undoubtedly longing to have nothing more to do with Mazarin. The credit for military victories went to Enghien and to Marshal Turenne. The subtle diplomatic moves on which the future of the continent depended were only of interest to specialists. To the general public, this 'versatile, intelligent monster' who was not even French but was almost single-handedly engaged in defending the country's essential interests, was a swindler, a coward and a thief.

---

* Only Henry iii had the courage temporarily to supress the system of purchasing official posts inaugurated by Francis i. Henry iv made things even worse by allowing magistrates to bequeath their posts to their heirs, subject to the payment of a fee known as the Paulette.

The death of the Prince de Condé gave rise to a further danger. His son, the Duc d'Enghien, victor of Rocroi, became the new Prince de Condé, Grand Master of France and Governor of Burgundy, Berry and Champagne. He also angled for the office of admiral, in order to concentrate all the armed forces of the realm under his own command, and was proposing to conquer Franche-Comté but then to retain it under his personal sovereignty. Condé was insanely proud, boundlessly ambitious and a prey to savage passions, yet also highly intelligent and cultured. He might well have breathed new life into feudalism and made it even more dangerous to the Crown than in the days of the civil wars. Fortunately, Condé under-estimated the 'knave of Sicily'. Mazarin tickled his vanity by appointing him viceroy of Catalonia and sent him off to his first failure at the impregnable fortress of Lérida.

At the same time, it occurred to the Cardinal that he could stifle a good deal of discontent by displaying the royal idol. At the age of eight, clad in gold and mounted on a white horse, Louis reviewed his forces. He also began to dance in public. He became vain and masterful, and was no longer neglected as he had been a short time previously. Louis' cousin, the Prince of Wales (the future Charles II), visited him at Fontainebleau. They were both crammed so full of their own importance and the danger of a misplaced word that they played together in complete silence!

The far-seeing Cardinal decided that it was time to begin preparing for the future and sent to Italy for three of his nieces – one Martinozzi and two Mancinis – and for his nephew, Paul Mancini. While Mlle Martinozzi's fine features and fair hair were much admired, the dark Mancinis went unsung. Mme de Motteville said of the younger girl: 'Her eyes were small but lively, and one could hope that at fifteen they might acquire some charm.'

As for the boy, few people guessed at first what plans the Cardinal was making for his future. It was the century of royal favourites. Buckingham in England, Lerma and Olivarez in Spain, Concini, Luynes and Richelieu himself, thanks to his hold on Marie de Médicis, all had ruled in that capacity. It was only natural to assume that Louis XIV in his turn would have a chosen friend who would automatically become a rival to the First Minister, but a friend tied to that Minister by family bonds would be a different matter. If he could win Louis' friendship, he would dispose the King favourably towards the man whom he would eventually be in a position to succeed. This was the rôle which Mazarin intended for his promising young nephew. Sharp-eyed observers were soon remarking on the attempts to cut Louis off from his usual companions in order to encourage his intimacy with Paul Mancini.

At this juncture, Louis' brother Philippe, the little Duc d'Anjou, went down with dysentery. This meant that the court had to take account of the possibility that Gaston might become heir presumptive once again. 'But everybody put a cheerful face on things, though for different motives: the Queen, who would have been in despair at the loss of that Prince, pretended to be gay, while the Duc d'Orléans, who would not have been inconsolable, was so afraid of betraying any cheerful signs that he did not dare speak or laugh about anything at all.'[1]

Anjou recovered, and the Queen and Mazarin breathed again, but not for long. On 10 November 1647 the King developed smallpox. At first it took its usual course, while the young women of the court avoided the Palais Royal, trembling for their looks. But on the eleventh day the fever increased and the child lost consciousness. While the Queen knelt, sobbing, at the foot of the bed, next to her the Duc d'Orléans composed his features to hide the jumble of emotions which, according to the magistrate Olivier d'Ormesson, became overtly cheerful the following day. At a supper attended by Gaston and his favourite, the Abbé de La Rivière, a toast was drunk to Gaston I and the distribution of high offices was considered. There was even some mention of kidnapping the Duc d'Anjou. Meanwhile, the members of the Parlement were considering a possible new Regency in which the Queen would be joined by Monsieur and Condé, as well as preparing a text which would exclude foreigners from ministerial office. Mazarin tried to parry the thrust by bringing La Rivière over to his own side.

On the fourteenth day Louis seemed on the point of death, but the crisis faded at midnight, when the smallpox erupted, the disease resumed its normal course and the fever abated. The ordeal cost Louis his good looks. At Christmas the dismayed court found its little angel replaced by a little boy with a blotchy complexion and swollen cheeks spotted with red.

Not long afterwards, it was the turn of the exhausted Queen to come close to death. The consequences, had she not recovered, would have been catastrophic for her children. In the fifth year of the reign of Louis XIV, Europe was in an unprecedented situation. Spain had been bled white and stripped of a number of provinces, and although determined to continue the struggle was no more able to pull herself together than was the Austrian Emperor, who had been forced to negotiate on disastrous terms. On the other hand France, the victor, with the power to remodel Europe as she wished, was drifting towards anarchy and civil war.

Numerous events in the reigns of Louis XIV, Louis XV and Louis XVI paved the way for the Revolution of 1789, but however significant they may be, they should not be seen as the actual sources of the Revolution. All the pre-conditions for the disintegration of the Ancien Régime were already assembled by the beginning of 1648.

The creation of twelve posts of counsellor and the other magistrates' fear 'of seeing their own devalued' were the high-minded reasons that determined the Parlement to take a firm line. The rejection of a new financial edict led to a new *lit de justice* on 15 January. Omer Talon attacking its underlying principle, asked the young King:

Is it not a moral illusion and a political contradiction to believe that edicts which, by the laws of the realm, may not be executed until they have been presented and debated in the sovereign courts, should be taken as confirmed once your Majesty has had them read, and their titles published, in his presence?

Then, adopting a revolutionary style:

You, Sire, are our sovereign liege. Your Majesty owes his power to the Almighty and is accountable for his actions, other than to God, only to his own conscience, but his *gloire* demands that we should be free men, not slaves ... For ten years, Sire, the countryside has been ravaged, the peasants are reduced to sleeping on straw and their furniture is being sold to pay taxes they cannot afford ...

He turned towards the Queen:

Reflect, Madame, in your heart of hearts, if you will, on the misery of the people. This evening, alone in your oratory, consider how any servant of the kingdom might be grieved, bitter and dismayed at the sight of all his goods being distrained without his having committed a single crime. Think also, Madame, of the calamitous state of the provinces, where neither the hope of peace, nor the honour of successful battles, nor the glory of conquered provinces can feed those who are without bread and do not number palms and laurels among the ordinary fruits of the earth.

The nine-year-old King, who hoarded everything in his memory, would undoubtedly remember his mother's indignation at this slur on the royal prerogatives. The Parlement had long been the refuge of a conservative, die-hard clique. These magistrates, whose posts represented the bourgeois equivalent of the great feudal fiefs and who auctioned their verdicts unashamedly, formed a caste whose primary concern was to increase its privileges at the expense of the central authority. If they had genuinely wished to improve the lot of their fellow countrymen, they could have set an example by making justice free and humane. Since this was not part of their intentions, Louis, given the perspective of his own position, was bound to see their pleas on behalf of the people as manoeuvres to facilitate subversion. On that day of 15 January 1648 the high principles and notions of freedom aired by Omer Talon were irretrievably discredited by the hypocrisy of their advocates. Mme de Motteville expressed the feelings of those who were close to the King when she wrote: 'The bourgeois were all infected by love of the public good, which they identified with their own particular good.'

Events now moved quickly, and there was an extraordinary anticipation of the occurrences of 1789. When Parlement referred to the *lit de justice* as a 'meaningless formality', the Queen struck back by suspending the Paulette. This hit the counsellors in their most vulnerable spot, and they turned to the Grand Conseil (the court competent to rule on matters – generally ecclesiastical – which were removed from the jurisdiction of the ordinary courts), the Cour des Comptes (audit court) and the Cour des Aides (the court dealing with matters involving indirect taxation), urging them to issue a joint proclamation on the reform of the state. Mazarin summoned representatives of all four sovereign courts and forbade them to put their plan into effect. The edict was issued, and then broken in the King's Council. The Parlement counter-attacked by calling an assembly of the four courts in the teeth of a royal veto: it took place on 16 June, amid popular acclamation.

The exasperated Queen accused Mazarin of cowardice and seriously considered replacing him with her old stand-by, Chateauneuf (another piece of evidence against the marriage theory). According to Broussel, a counsellor of the Parlement, Mazarin was hard put to it to convince her that 'the condition of France was such that it was no longer possible to take drastic measures without risking a major uprising.'

This time the sovereign courts received the royal authorization to assemble, and between 30 June and 10 July they voted on a constitution whose twenty-seven articles shook the kingdom to its foundations. Its principles were democratic – freedom of the individual and of property; no prisoner to be detained without interrogation for more than twenty-four hours; a ban on the creation of any new tax or office without a vote in the Parlement. But these admirable measures were accompanied by others whose effect was to prevent the successful conclusion of the war by abolishing a quarter of the tax-load and to dismantle the administration by abolishing intendants, the delegates who exercised certain powers of inspection in the provinces on the King's behalf.

Mazarin's aim was to buy time. He initiated long talks with the magistrates and showered them with compliments. But the atmosphere was not conciliatory.

> Un vent de Fronde
> S'est levé ce matin,
> Je crois qu'il gronde
> Contre le Mazarin.*

The mood of the Fronde had spread to the nobility, the bourgeoisie and the people alike. Three months before the signature of the Treaty of Westphalia and the removal of the threat from Germany, a general move was afoot to drive its chief architect out of France and create an upheaval in which each individual hoped to grab something for himself. One consummate master of

---

* 'A wind of Fronde/has arisen this morning./I think it is blowing/against Mazarin.' The word *fronde* literally means 'sling' or 'catapult'. – Tr.

dissent was fanning the flames and spreading them: he was Paul de Gondi de Retz, coadjutor to the Archbishop of Paris, the only French bishop ever to have caused a civil war without even invoking the pretext of religion. 'Like a pestiferous fly, he flew from prince to nobleman, from merchant to magistrate and beggar, by way of the common people and the clergy. Wherever he settled, there arose passions and disorders which were to profit no one, not even himself, but were to bring the country to the verge of ruin.'[2]

The monarchy's sole remaining prop was the army and its illustrious leader, Condé, who had the proud pleasure of hearing the entreaties of the Regent and First Minister of the realm before crushing the Spanish forces at Lens in a decisive battle that opened the way towards peace. When the little King heard the news he exclaimed: 'The gentlemen in the Parlement will be quite put out!' This remark contains the seeds of the policy which he was later to pursue towards those who were disappointed by the good fortune of their country.

Anne set about the same policy, but prematurely. Following the victory Te Deum at Notre-Dame, she had four members of the Parlement arrested, among them Broussel, the man who made 'greater gains out of his reputation for incorruptibility than he would have made out of being corrupted.'[3] She thus made the mistake of forgetting one of Richelieu's maxims: 'let that great sleeping dog [the Parlement] lie.' Broussel's arrest was all the provocation needed to set Paris in an uproar. Marshal La Meilleraie, a veteran of the Thirty Years War, was given the task of restoring order and narrowly escaped being murdered, along with his guards. He was rescued through the intervention of Gondi, making his bid as saviour of the nation, in cape and surplice. When they went to the Palais Royal to report on the gravity of the situation, the Queen exclaimed angrily: 'There is rebellion even in supposing that the people might rebel. Free Broussel? I would rather strangle him with my own hands!'

Mazarin calmed her down and finally empowered Gondi to announce to the people that the counsellors would be restored to them the following day. After further violent street-demonstrations, the coadjutor returned to the palace, only to be dismissed by Anne, with a suggestion that he should 'stick to his prayers'. Next day (27 August), the embittered priest touched off a riot reminiscent of the 'Journées des Barricades' which took place in the time of the League.* There was now no option but to release the prisoners, and order was restored.

Henry III had escaped from Paris and preserved the monarchy: Anne resolved to do likewise. The King and Mazarin reached Rueil on 12

---

* Formed by Henry, Duc de Guise, in 1576, aimed at suppressing Protestant influence in France and against King Henry III. The Journées des Barricades on 1 and 12 May 1588 forced Henry III to leave Paris. – Tr.

September, in the nick of time, for their passage through the gates had started a riot. The Queen joined them openly the following day.

In the palace that had once belonged to Richelieu, Condé arbitrated between the Crown and the Parlement, and it was the latter who emerged victorious. At Saint-Germain, on 22 October, the Queen wept as she gave her sanction to a solemn Declaration of Reform. Henceforward it was to be a strictly constitutional monarch who would reign in France. The Parlement registered the Declaration on 24 October. That same day the Treaties of Westphalia were signed in Münster and Osnabrück. The Emperor's power in Germany was gone and the face of Europe altered. Alsace was now a French province, but nobody seemed to be paying much attention in Paris, where the Queen returned, determined not to stand by her word.

Another conflagration soon broke out, but this time there was an admixture of farce. By a Machiavellian stroke, Mazarin had channelled sums of money intended for the troops into Condé's pocket. Condé did not forgive the Parlement for the resulting protests. A further comic episode concerned the promise of a cardinalcy to the Abbé de La Rivière and to the Prince de Conti, Condé's brother, at the same time. Condé, who did not intend to share any of the paternal inheritance with his younger brother, was most anxious for him to join the Church. Conti was an unstable, unprepossessing little hunchback. He was in love with his sister, the Duchesse de Longueville, and the priesthood was far removed from his ambitions. As for Mme de Longueville, innocent pleasures did not excite her and the Fronde offered spicier alternatives. She enrolled Conti in the rebellion, which seemed destined to be led by Gaston once again as a result of La Rivière's frustration in the matter of the cardinal's hat.

Both sides were now preparing for war. While Gondi was handing out their parts to Conti, Bouillon, Longueville, La Rochefoucauld and other lords of the Fronde, Condé was positioning the army of Flanders to surround Paris. Anne had decided that from now on she would speak to her people through the cannon's mouth.

On the evening of 5 January 1649 the Regent calmly held court, then shared the Twelfth Night cake with Louis, and a few ladies of the Court. The King joined the others in crying 'The Queen drinks!' then went to bed.

At three in the morning Villeroy roused Louis, dressed him and took him and Philippe to one of the coaches drawn up outside the gates of the Palais Royal. Anne joined them, accompanied by a few dignitaries, and they drove to Cours-la-Reine, just outside the city walls, where they waited. Mazarin arrived soon afterward, and meanwhile the princes were being woken up by emissaries inviting them to join their Majesties. All of them obeyed except Mme de Longueville, who began her preparations to govern Paris. Her absence did not disturb Anne, and the royal household reached Saint-Germain without difficulty – a Saint-Germain where there were no beds, furniture, linen or valets, for the Queen had been careful not to have the Château prepared for visitors for fear of betraying her plans. Nevertheless, Mazarin had taken the precaution of having three camp beds sent ahead, and these were used by the Queen and her sons, while the princes and courtiers slept on straw. Within a few hours the price of straw had risen astronomically.

The Prince de Conti also acted his part cleverly. He followed the court, then returned surreptitiously to Paris with the Duc de Longueville. Such was the prestige of the royal blood that the presence of this unbalanced cripple was enough to dispel the despair and terror which had seized the people of Paris. He was appointed Commander-in-Chief of the Fronde, and the most powerful of his many lieutenants was the Duc de Beaufort, who had escaped from Vincennes. The 'King of Les Halles', worshipped by the mob for his fair hair and down-to-earth speech, was as handsome as his leader was ugly, but displayed an equal lack of common sense. The only brains among the rebel nobility belonged to Gondi and to Mmes de Longueville and Chevreuse. The Duc de La Rochefoucauld was bent only on serving his beloved Longueville and winning court honours.

The Parlement refused Anne's summons to assemble at Montargis, some sixty miles south of Paris, and Condé embarked on the siege and blockade of Paris.

At Saint-Germain the initial gaiety at the impromptu nature of the situation gave way to discomfort and apprehension. The crown diamonds had to be pawned and the pages dismissed because there was nothing to feed them on. Louis himself often went short and, in spite of his youth, was not amused by the nocturnal escape, the royal household camping among bales of straw, the departure of the servants and the defection of close relatives and peers of the realm. The impression left on his mind was one of shameful sacrilege and treason.

In February he learned of the execution of his uncle, Charles I of England, and heard his mother's oft-repeated words: 'This is a blow to make kings tremble!'

⌈6⌉

The Lessons of Adversity

THE flight from Paris marked the outbreak, or rather the resumption, of civil war, for in the space of less than forty years this was the *ninth* onslaught on the royal authority by the heirs of feudalism. Essentially it was again the great nobles who bore the real responsibility for the adventure, with the Parlement playing the rôle of sorcerer's apprentice. It had no wish for a monarchic collapse, which would have dragged down the Parlement as it did in 1789, but found itself a prisoner of its doughty defenders and its own rabble-rousing. Incapable of evaluating the situation, and stirred up by broadsides and scurrilous songs, the common people believed that they were moving towards happier times.

Historians have sometimes attempted to justify the nobility on the grounds that it took the lead in the struggle against absolutism. In fact, its greed, unruliness and lack of national feeling* were the very sources from which absolutism drew its strength. For Louis, the Fronde, with its street riots and palace cabals, violence and treachery, coups d'état and acts of vengence, was the ordeal that set the pattern for his subsequent way of thinking, character and behaviour. It brought home to him a double lesson, human and political, proving that Frenchmen both high and low were hard to control and that the ancient throne of the Capetians rested on fragile foundations, and also teaching him about poverty and adversity.

The Fronde has often been depicted as a kind of Shakespearean drama, in which lavish ballets, comic-opera idylls, farce and burlesque mingle with tragedy, melodrama and horror. It produced an extraordinary mélange of bons mots, satires, beautiful women disguised as generals, fêtes, pillage, battles, massacres, amorous and murderous follies and the confused repercussions of permutated couplings – Mme de Longueville and Turenne, Mme de Longueville and La Rochefoucauld, Mme de Longueville and Nemours, Mme de Montbazon and Beaufort, Mme de Châtillon and Condé, Mme de Châtillon and Nemours, Mlle de Chevreuse and Gondi, Mlle de Chevreuse and Conti. It contained the spectacle of the Queen-Regent playing the

---

* Compare the French nobility, ever ready to open the gates to the enemy, with that of England or Spain.

coquette to suborn a bishop (Gondi), a half-madwoman (the Princess de Condé) stirring provinces into rebellion, and a hot-headed girl (Mademoiselle) capturing a town and changing the outcome of a battle.

Alongside the wit, independence of mind and gallantry, this bout of delirium produced atrocities and sufferings that exceeded all bounds save those of twentieth-century wars. While the Parisians were hunting down the King's servants like wild beasts, Condé was killing 'any man who dared to stand against him', throwing prisoners into the Seine or stripping them naked to die of exposure. The soldiers, particularly the German mercenaries, looted churches, raped even ten-year-old girls, burned, ravaged and tortured the peasantry. Their idea of a good joke was to roast children in the oven. In some regions there was no harvest for five years. The devastation spread inexorably, famine and death were everywhere, and bodies went unburied. Wild oats were gathered to make 'mud-bread', and dogs'–sometimes even human–carcasses were eaten. The young King did not forget these horrors, which were to have a direct influence on his own system of government.

The rebels' first step was to seek support from abroad. Turenne, the renowned Marshal of the Thirty Years War, had joined the Fronde because of his infatuation with Mme de Longueville, and Gondi planned to crush Condé between the forces of his former companion in arms and those of Paris and Spain. A representative of the Spanish King appeared before the Parlement, under the protection of Conti, to ask it not to register the Treaty of Westphalia. At this point, the life's work of Louis XIII and Richelieu was almost nullified: France was only saved from reverting to the conditions of the Hundred Years War by the eight hundred thousand livres that Mazarin borrowed from Condé and distributed to Turenne's troops to keep them loyal.

This dramatic turn of events demoralized the rebels, and peace was signed. The Parlement retained its gains, the constitution of 1648 remained in force and the guilty parties were amnestied. The Queen, theoretically the victor, suffered a considerable diminution in her power and prestige. Mazarin became the object of general execration. 'The only victor was Condé . . . The Queen's absolute authority was now subject to the convenience, caprice and ambition of the impetuous, violent man of whom it was well said by the Duchesse de Nemours that he would rather win battles than hearts.[1]

On 18 August 1649 the King and his mother marvelled at the general rejoicing which greeted their return to Paris, but almost immediately they had to face trouble from another quarter – the demands of Condé. Louis cannot have failed to observe the outrageous insolence of his cousin, who pulled Mazarin's beard, insulted him, and once even boxed his ears. On these occasions the Cardinal went to unbelievable extremes of lowliness and humility. He agreed to all Condé's demands, even when he was asked to grant Ls Rochefoucauld the right to drive his carriage into the courtyard of the Louvre and his wife the privilege of the *tabouret* (the right to remain seated in the Queen's presence). These were exorbitant privileges, for they were customarily given only to *ducs et pairs* and Mme de Longueville's lover was neither, since his father was still alive. Mazarin was the victor in this episode, however, since it set the entire nobility against Condé and his protégé.

The Prince was now bloated with pride and arrogance, and one act of folly came hard on the heels of another. He took it into his head to give the Queen a lover,* the Marquis de Jarzé. Anne of Austria, whose every word was dictated by Mazarin, gave this coxcomb a severe rebuff, upon which Condé flew into a rage and demanded that the Queen should make his candidate a public reparation, failing which 'there would be trouble'. The shame of these and other incidents partly explains Louis xiv's subsequent harshness towards members of the Condé family.

Anne and Mazarin had submitted to these indignities, but they had sworn to destroy Condé and did not baulk at reaching an agreement with the Frondeurs for that purpose. The Duchesse de Chevreuse and her daughter, Gondi's mistress, arranged meetings between Anne of Austria and Gondi in the cloister of Saint-Honoré in Paris, where Gondi sold his friends' loyalty, including that of Gaston of Orléans, at a high price. He managed to regain for Chateauneuf his former post as Guardian of the Seals, and accepted with a great show of unwillingness the promise of a cardinal's hat for himself.

It was essential not to rouse Condé's suspicions. On 16 January 1650 Mazarin wrote to him:

> I promise M. le Prince, according to the good pleasure of the King and the Queen-Regent, his mother, that I shall never swerve from his interests and that I shall always be devoted to him come what may, and beg his Highness to think of me as his very humble servant and to favour me with his protection, which I shall earn with all the obedience he can desire of me.[2]

Condé's arrest had already been timed to follow two days later. That morning (18 January) Anne of Austria took Louis into her oratory, and both of them were at their prayers while Guitaut arrested Condé, Conti and de Longueville and took them to Vincennes. Mother and son did not stir until they were informed that the operation had been successful. The Queen then ordered the doors to be opened so that she could receive the compliments of the court. Paris was ablaze with rejoicing.

Unhappily, Mazarin's plan was only half-successful. Condé's mother and

---

* In the sense in which that word was used by Corneille and the circle headed by the great literary hostess, the Marquise de Rambouillet. Jarzé acted the bashful lover in front of the court.

wife, Mme de Longueville, La Rochefoucauld, Bouillon and Turenne slipped through the net and out of Paris, determined to revive the civil war.

On 1 February the eleven-year-old Louis embarked on his first campaign. It was against his own subjects, to be precise his cousin, Mme de Longueville, who was trying to stir up Normandy against him. For three weeks the King and his mother moved through the province to nip incipient risings in the bud. The Duc de Vendôme, an illegitimate son of Henry IV, had equal success in Burgundy, where Condé was military Governor, but the Prince's officers made a stand at Bellegarde. Vendôme put the town under siege and Louis came to carry out a solemn inspection of his troops. The rebels on the walls recognized him and cheered. Then they opened fire. An officer standing quite close to Louis fell. These shots would not be forgotten either.

Meanwhile, the other plotters' activities, this time involving Spain, were culminating in an attempted invasion, which was halted at the Battle of Rethel in the Ardennes, and in a serious rebellion started by Condé's wife, Richelieu's own niece, and backed by Bouillon and La Rochefoucauld, in the province of Guyenne (formerly Aquitaine). The King, the Queen and the entire court – Gaston excepted – accompanied the army which set out to crush the new uprising. On the way, Anne ordered La Rochefoucauld's Château at Verteuil to be razed to the ground. Negotiation proved fruitless and Marshal La Meilleraie attacked Bordeaux, but was beaten off. Siege warfare had to be resumed, but with the approach of October the Aquitainians had more important things on their minds than making war on their sovereign, and they opened negotiations. Representatives of the Bordeaux Parlement told Condé's wife: 'Don't worry, Madame, we shall fight again after the vine-harvest.'

War was still raging in the north, and the Spanish were drawing near to the capital, leaving behind them a terrible trail of havoc. The people held Mazarin responsible, and their hatred of the Cardinal reached fever-pitch. At the same time, Condé's cause found a new champion in Anne of Gonzaga, wife of Edward of Bavaria and a woman who combined beauty with remarkable skill in negotiation. While she was exerting her charms to win over the leaders of the first Fronde, Mazarin returned to Paris and made the glaring error of destroying Gondi's hopes of becoming a cardinal. The coadjutor declared: 'I am vexed to find myself involuntarily reduced to a position in which my only choices are to be a party leader or a cardinal.'

Anne of Gonzaga seized the opportunity to strike a bizarre bargain with Gondi: she would obtain the cardinal's hat, which was in the gift of her sister, the Queen of Poland, in return for Gondi ceding his mistress, Mlle de Chevreuse, to the Prince de Conti. The marriage of the dwarf and the ambitious young beauty would also mark the unification of the two Frondes. Gondi, who had influence over Gaston, managed to dispel his fears and uncertainties and persuaded him to become the leader of yet another conspiracy.

The Parlement opened hostilities by remonstrating with the Queen about the imprisonment of the princes. On 20 January 1651 Mathieu Molé, the President, presented these grievances at the Palais Royal, pointing out that they could only cause further disorders. Anne gave him an abrupt reply and dismissed him angrily. When they were alone again, Louis exclaimed: 'Mother, if I had not been afraid of causing you trouble I would have had the President silenced and thrown out three times over!' He was twelve years old at that time.

In these crucial days, Mazarin lost much of his flexibility and self-control through nervous exhaustion. When he compared the Parlement and the nobility to the English regicides, he gave Gaston the pretext for breaking with the Council, whereupon the Parlement voted for the release of the princes and the dismissal of the First Minister, and the mob hanged Mazarin in effigy.

During a secret meeting that evening, the Queen and Mazarin told Louis of the critical state of his affairs and disclosed their plans for the first time. Mazarin then put on a musketeer's uniform and left Paris for Saint-Germain, taking with him the Crown diamonds. His scanty following included the secretary of Le Tellier, one of the Crown ministers: he was to be responsible for establishing a secret link between the Cardinal and his collaborators in Paris. This secretary, then aged thirty-two, was Jean-Baptiste Colbert.

Gondi and Chateauneuf realized at once that the Queen was preparing to join Mazarin, and asked Gaston to order the gates of Paris to be closed. When his timidity prevented him from making up his mind, his wife signed for him. A whole league of women had formed against the Cardinal, which would be a remarkable development if the Italian had really possessed that power and authority over the fair sex which are generally ascribed to him. In answer to these Furies' summons, friends of the princes sprang to horse, the bourgeois militias assembled and the populace became a mob.

The King was already dressed, booted and ready to leave when his mother made him get into bed, fully clothed, while she hurriedly changed into night attire. Stirred up by Gondi, the crowd was soon banging on the palace gates, shouting that they wanted to make sure that the King was inside. Anne of Austria was neither as indecisive as Louis XVI nor as timid as Nicholas II (it must be remembered that Mazarin was not at her side). She gave orders for the gates to be opened and the people to be given access to the King's bedroom, and Louis XIV had to pretend to be asleep while sullen-faced men and women filed past his bed and even drew back the curtain. The sight of the King allayed their suspicions, and they walked softly and went out in good order, but nothing could erase the resentment they had roused in his mind.

Anne played her part to perfection, and even asked two of them to stay at the King's side, chatting with them gaily until daybreak. Next day the monarchy was imprisoned in the Palais Royal as it was to be imprisoned in the Tuileries in 1789.

[7]

Folly and Anarchy

MAZARIN's reaction when he found that he had been outwitted was immediate. He hurried to Le Havre, where the princes had been transferred, released them, dined them and flung himself at their feet. According to La Grande Mademoiselle, he even kissed Condé's boot! Then he spent a few weeks roaming aimlessly around Normandy and Picardy before reaching his decision to leave France.

The Parlement ordered his property to be confiscated. The fifty-four thousand volumes in his library were ransacked, his houses auctioned and his fine collections shared out among creditors, most of whom had no claim on him. His great wealth was a public scandal, and Mazarin had certainly missed no opportunity to amass it, but altruism was hardly to be expected from a man in his position, any more than from Richelieu or Sully. Louis XIII's Minister had started his career with next to nothing, but that austere King had not objected when his income finally reached the fabulous amount of three million livres. What disgusted people about Mazarin was not his greed, which was matched by that of the princes, but the way he had embarked on often sordid dealings, not with the off-hand of a nobleman but with a haste and eagerness that bespoke the starveling emigrant.

The Cardinal had not resigned himself to exile without leaving his personal interests in reliable hands. Racking his brains for a man he could trust, he remembered the harsh, ruthless fidelity of Colbert, who had almost wrecked his own career by upholding the cause of his employer, Le Tellier, against his Eminence in person. Mazarin had been furious at first, but he was a shrewd judge of character and had come to value this son of a Rheims draper as he valued few other men. Now he offered Colbert the delicate mission he had in mind. Colbert took his time before replying, which he did with feigned modesty but respectfully stating his requirements, so that the bargaining was still going on after Mazarin had crossed the frontier.[1]

With the perversity that characterizes all these events, it was to Spain that Mazarin owed his safe passage through the territory of the Elector of Cologne. He took up residence in Bruhl, where an emissary of the King of Spain came to ask him to name his price for entering His Majesty's service. The Cardinal did not even have French nationality: if he had gone over to the enemy camp, he would only have been following a precedent created by the princes, and with greater justification. Nevertheless he refused with dignity, saying: 'I shall end my days serving France in my thoughts and wishes if I cannot do it otherwise.'

Mazarin was still worried about his material welfare, however, and Colbert knew it. He dictated his terms, which were that he must be accredited to the Queen with no supervision from the Cardinal, and wrote to Mazarin:

A single person, to be chosen by Yr Eminence, must have the management of all your affairs, and, besides possessing integrity, experience and devotion to the service of Yr Eminence, that person must not be one of those base-hearted men who would run and hide in a well rather than even be suspected of a connection with yourself. This person must go about with his head high, making no secret of his mission. Further, Yr Eminence must honour him with his utmost confidence and must not hold him to blame for any vexing contingencies that may delay or ruin, wholly or partially, any of the affairs entrusted to his discretion. The man must speak out and must have judgement enough only to involve the Queen in important matters and only to make her intervene when those matters shall be of grave consequence.[2]

Mazarin accepted all these conditions, knowing that once the agreement was signed he would be assured of Colbert's complete devotion, but not suspecting that he was paving the way for his successor. He continued to govern the kingdom from Bruhl, where he lived in some style. When the Queen received his instructions she followed them to the letter and apologized when she failed.

Some of the Frondeurs discovered what was afoot and bitterly upbraided the Regent, 'to the point of telling her that it was believed that the Cardinal had cast a spell on her, or that she had married him'.[3] The unruffled Queen merely replied 'that the Cardinal had affection for the state, for the King and for herself.' This decided Anne of Gonzaga that it would be prudent to arrive at a measure of agreement, and she made contact with the exiled minister. She was to play a masterly double game between Condé and Mazarin.

Gaston of Orléans had seen his dream come true at last. After so many failures, power and the royal family's fate were in his grasp. 'Every person of quality had gone over from the Queen to Monsieur, and no longer saw her.' An official of the Palais Royal, Montglat, says of the Queen's servants that it was 'so remote from their thoughts to remove the King from Paris that, far from agreeing to it, most of them would have warned Monsieur and joined him in preventing it.'

Gaston was urged by his followers to shut his sister-in-law in the Val-de-Grâce, take his nephew into his own custody and have himself proclaimed regent, but the perpetual conspirator did not have the stuff of a statesman or even the resolution of a party leader. His opportunity had already slipped by when he went to Saint Denis with Beaufort and Gondi to welcome the released princes. They embraced one another as if the events of the previous year had been forgotten, then Condé made his triumphal entry into Paris, walking in procession past the same bonfires that had lighted his way to prison. He went to the Palais du Luxembourg to pay a courtesy call on Monsieur and chattily made his peace with his cousin, Mademoiselle, who had hated him because his victories put the house of Orléans in the shade.

Anne-Marie-Louise of Orléans was now twenty-four years old. Her beauty, marred by smallpox and an over-large nose, hardly justified the ravings of the poets. As for her mind, the kind-hearted Mme de Motteville said that 'it was not used to thinking,' and she herself confessed that she 'never got things right.' Nevertheless, she was the first peer and the richest person in the kingdom. She was so infatuated with her own grandeur that her behaviour throughout her life betrayed a kind of dizziness. Having already been close to marrying two emperors, three kings and an impressive number of princes, she was still a virgin at an age when this state seemed hardly credible. The truth is that she inherited from her father a muddling indecisiveness that was only aggravated by her own fantasies and romanticizing, so that the idea of a hero took a powerful enough hold on her imagination to dull the glitter of crowns. Condé's wife was in bad health, and if he were to become a widower the victor of Rocroi would be an attractive match. These fantasies were to have disastrous consequences for France.

Nobody could do enough for Condé now: people were begging him to usurp, if not the throne itself, then at least its prerogatives – a miscalculation, for M. le Prince, like many another warrior, dreaded the game of politics. Though unwilling to bow to anyone else's command, he had no desire to shoulder the burden of government. Dynastic scruples also restrained him, but none of these factors would have weighed heavily enough to prevent him staging a coup d'état had it not been for yet another woman's influence.

Condé had been in love since adolescence with his cousin, Isabelle de Montmorency-Bouteville, who had become first the wife, then not long afterward the widow, of the Duc de Châtillon, killed in the siege of Paris in 1649. 'Circe', as she was known in the literary circles of the Précieuses, had been as effective a force as Anne of Gonzaga at the time of the rapprochement between the two Frondes, when she did not hesitate to use her beauty to ensnare the more obstinate officials of the Parlement, and enrolled her acknowledged lover, the Duc de Nemours, under the standard of the princes.

Without abandoning this gallant lord who had served her so well, she accepted Condé's advances, announcing her feat to the world by having her portrait painted, magnificently costumed, with her hand resting on the head of a lion that the artist endowed with Condé's features. There had always been a fierce rivalry between the two cousins, the fair Longueville and the dark Châtillon. With Anne de Longueville pressing her brother to extremes, Isabelle de Châtillon preached moderation.

At all events, a week after his return the choice was no longer his. Mazarin's departure was already dissolving the coalition that had been cemented by the common hatred of the 'red tyrant'. The nobility had no intention of sharing power with the Parlement, which it intended to reduce to the status of a mere tribunal. The representatives of the Parlement asked for an Estates General* to be convened, and the Queen, delighted to be able to sow seeds of dissension in this way, promised to convene them on 8 September, the day on which Louis' majority was to be proclaimed.

In the ensuing uproar, some spoke of throwing the First President into the Seine and the Parlement mobilized the bourgeois militia. Meanwhile the Queen was buying Condé's loyalty yet again by giving him the Governorship of Guyenne. Conti was to become Governor of Provence, Longueville of Normandy. When the treaty was sealed, under the discreet patronage of Mme de Châtillon, Anne of Austria dismissed Chateauneuf, appointed Chavigny to the Council and entrusted the Seals to Mathieu Molé, whom Gaston could not abide.

Monsieur interpreted this independent gesture as an insult. He called a meeting of the leaders of the Fronde at which Gondi suggested sending the captain of His Highness's guard to Molé to demand his resignation, while he himself would rouse the people of Paris. M. le Prince treated this proposal with derision, saying: 'I feel enough of a coward as it is for all these outbreaks of rioting and sedition, and I confess to having no great liking for chamber-pot warfare.' The meeting broke up in disarray, and next morning the Duchesse de Chevreuse was informed that the Prince de Conti was not to marry her daughter. It was the decisive break between the two Frondes. Much later, the defeated rebels, reconciled once again, were to hold lengthy post-mortems on the origins of the astounding decision that sealed their defeat. No one would admit to being responsible.

Whatever the cause, its effects came quickly. Gondi advised Monsieur to reach agreement with Anne of Austria, and ostensibly withdrew to a monastery. Anne was quite content to set her brother-in-law at logger-heads with Condé by sacrificing Molé. The little King had assisted her during this critical time by 'fondling' his uncle and cousin in the most natural-seeming manner. Now it looked as if she was back in control. Mazarin was not deceived, however, and made the Queen initiate fresh talks with Gondi and resume their secret meetings, in spite of her reluctance. This time, a formal request was sent to Rome for the

* The assembly of clergy, nobility and commoners, whom the King could summon to discuss important matters. Its role was purely consultative – Tr.

coadjutor's red hat. Mazarin had given his consent, subject to a payment of two hundred thousand livres.

When Condé was informed, he remembered the upshot of the same alliance the previous year. Convinced of his imminent arrest, the hero panicked and fled to Saint-Maur on 5 July, much to everyone's amusement. Then, in order to restore his prestige, he demanded the dismissal of the 'Mazarin' ministers, Le Tellier, Servien and Lionne. Anne obeyed Mazarin's instructions to give way to the Prince's request, somewhat to the confusion of his supporters. There were stormy discussions at Saint-Maur, in which Mme de Châtillon unfortunately took little part, so that Mme de Longueville, bent on revenge, managed to persuade her brother to stand up against the Queen.

On 23 July Condé made a flamboyant re-entry into Paris, with a retinue that was more like an army. He did not make the customary courtesy visit and behaved so threateningly that Anne contemplated appointing Gondi or Chateauneuf as First Minister so as to provide herself with a protector. On 31 July 1651 the King, returning from his daily bathe in the Seine, encountered Condé and his men on the Cours-la-Reine. Instead of leaving his coach, the Prince merely inclined his head, an insult that turned Louis white with rage. Two days later, in the Parlement, Molé publicly rebuked Condé, who climbed down by declaring that the encounter had been none of his doing and that he thought the weather unsuited for his Majesty's bathe. This incident made him realize how much his power over the magistrates was declining, and he began to prepare for civil war.

No twist of fortune seemed impossible in this kingdom of madmen, and nobody was surprised when Gondi emerged as the champion of the Crown and drew up a royal declaration against Condé. The declaration produced scenes in the Parlement that almost degenerated into pitched battle. La Rochefoucauld jammed Gondi's head between two doors and ordered two of his friends to stab the traitor, but the coadjutor just managed to escape. The Parlement now beseeched the Regent to restore peace by making two new proclamations when the King attained his majority: the first was to recognize Condé's innocence, the second to broadcast Mazarin's guilt and confirm his exile. Anne accepted. Although the Cardinal had urged her to give way to Condé, he seems not to have approved the text which alludes to him personally and which betrays the hand of Gondi:

> It is in just punishment for his crimes that the said Cardinal has been banished from the kingdom ... the King ... renews the express bans and prohibitions on the said Cardinal Mazarin, his allies and domestics ever returning to the kingdom and territories of France, on pain of being hunted down as criminals guilty of lèse-majesté and disturbers of the public peace.

The unanimous verdict of historians has been that this whole performance was a sham, played up to the hilt as part of the final act of the Regency. But to Mazarin it meant disgrace and ruin, and it does seem possible that Anne, always responsive to intelligence, was under the sway of Gondi at the time.

'I renounce everything,' Mazarin wrote to the Duc de Mercoeur, 'and all I ask of the Queen, with tears of blood, is my honour. I have given good enough service to herself, the King and the state to make this request with head unbowed.' This letter would surely have been a strange one indeed, had it been the Queen's husband who signed it.

Louis XIII (Varin – Louvre)

Anne of Austria (Rubens – Louvre)

Versailles under Louis XIII (engraving by F. Thorigny)

Louis XIV as a child (attributed to Nicolas Mignard)

[8]

Bléneau

LOUIS was approaching his thirteenth birthday, the age at which French kings had been considered fit to govern in person since the time of Charles V. His ordeals had matured him, and he was quite aware of the power that would soon be vested in him. Now he gave his mother a rude demonstration of it. Since childhood, the grandson of Henry IV had shown an interest in women which his father had lacked. At the age of nine, he was seeking out the dazzling Mme de Châtillon, and Paris was singing:

> Châtillon, gardez vos appâts,
> Si vous êtes prête,
> le Roi ne l'est pas.*

In 1651, that interest came to bear on a lady of Mademoiselle's entourage, the Comtesse de Frontenac. Louis got into the habit of riding out with his cousin, who had no doubt that she herself was the object of his inclination and fell once again to dreaming about the throne of France. The Queen was more perceptive. Her fear of the scheming Mme de Frontenac led her to forbid Louis' excursions, and after some tearful scenes the King complied.

His coming of age was proclaimed on 7 September 1651. In the morning the Queen, the princes of the blood, the *ducs et pairs* and marshals came to kiss his hand. Only Condé was absent. He sent through Conti a letter of apology which was not opened. 'Either I or M. le Prince must perish,' the angry Queen exclaimed.

An immense cavalcade made its way from the Palais Royal to the Parlement, where the young monarch announced: 'Gentlemen, I have come to tell you that in accordance with the law of my state I wish to take its government upon myself, and I hope that through the goodness of God I shall do so with piety and justice.' When the Queen had relinquished her powers as Regent to Louis, he kissed her and said: 'Madame, I thank you for the care you have been pleased to bestow on my education and on the administration of my realm. I beg you to continue to give me your wise

---

* Châtillon, preserve your charms. / You may be ready, / but the King is not.

counsels, and it is my wish that you should be the head of my Council after myself.' Every listener was impressed by his seriousness, measured tone and precocious majesty.

Louis' first step was to form a ministry in which Molé took over the Seals again and Chateauneuf finally occupied the post he had been coveting for twenty years. In fact, the Queen was keeping a promise to Gondi by this arrangement, which she never had reason to regret, since Chateauneuf proved himself completely loyal and displayed statesmanlike qualities that only added to Mazarin's apprehension.

By now Condé had left Paris and was in league with Spain, although it was only after much thought that, goaded by Mme de Longueville, Conti, Nemours and La Rochefoucauld, he rejected a last compromise offered in the King's name. He told them: 'Since it is war you want, war it must be. But remember at least that I draw my sword against my will and that I shall perhaps be the last to sheathe it again.'

Guyenne, Saintonge, Aunis, Poitou, Anjou and Berry rose in revolt. It was the beginning of the last civil war of the Ancien Régime, inexorable, unpardonable and shameful. The court has often been accused of contributing to its outbreak, and it is true that Anne of Austria was as warlike (though for better motives) as Mme de Longueville, and hoped for a quick and radical solution. Up to the last minute Mazarin begged her to explore every possibility of a compromise, and the opening of hostilities coincided with the decline of his influence. In the royal camp, Gondi was undoubtedly more responsible than the exiled minister.

Once again the King and his mother accompanied the small army sent to crush the rebellion. This time Louis was in high spirits. The expedition provided the court with a cast-iron excuse for cutting its moorings and getting out of the clutches of the Parisians. Nobody dreamed that the King would be virtually banished from his own capital for a whole year.

During the first few weeks, the course of events ran in the Crown's favour. Chateauneuf manoeuvred cleverly, Condé lost his nerve, and the war would have fizzled out had not Mazarin regained his ascendancy over Anne of Austria. Away from the Queen, Gondi's influence waned. Alone, free, and at the head of a victorious army, she grew to miss the exile, and eventually wrote to him restoring her own confidence and his former power. A 'very civil' letter from Louis XIV accompanied his mother's: from that moment onward he put aside his bias against the Cardinal and recognized his worth, showing remarkable maturity for a boy of that age.

Marshal d'Hocquincourt brought Mazarin eight thousand men, whom the Cardinal paid out of his own pocket – justification enough, perhaps, for the 200,000 livres he squeezed out of Gondi. The soldiers wore Mazarin's badge, a green sash, just as Mme de Longueville's men wore cream-coloured sashes, harking back to the medieval chaos in which every nobleman had his own private army.

Chateauneuf had the courage to explain to the Queen that Mazarin's return would revive and unify the dying Frondes, and Anne's faith wavered. This news reached Mazarin, who immediately gave out that he was going to 'rescue' the King and entered France at the head of his army. It was certainly the gravest error that can be laid at his door, for the effect was to galvanize the old Fronde. The Parlement put a price on the hated Minister's head and Monsieur reluctantly concluded an alliance with Condé.

Gaston's change of heart had grave repercussions. In spite of his many recantations, he had retained the prestige of his royal birth and was master of the capital, the Parlement and a section of the nobility. A confrontation with such an adversary could well have proved fatal to the monarchy had not one distinguished rebel, Turenne, rallied to the royal flag almost simultaneously, bringing with him his brother, the Duc de Bouillon.

Looking at the portraits of Turenne, the almost bourgeois face of a serious, meditative man, a realist, to all appearances a stranger to passion, it seems hardly credible that such a person could have betrayed King and country out of infatuation for Mme de Longueville. Now he returned to his allegiance, and in the ensuing year the fate of the French monarchy was to hang on his military genius and sang-froid. Despite his high ambitions and great family pride,* Turenne's realism, logic and simplicity were a welcome contrast to the haughty, unbalanced arrogance of Condé. Between these two successful warriors, Gaston and the Parlement found themselves in a quandary. The magistrates who had made Mazarin an outlaw refused to finance an army to stop him. Instead, a few Counsellors went to beg him unavailingly to turn back, and the Cardinal marched through France with his army to the Court, where he received a welcome well calculated to salve his recent wound. Anne was radiant, the King had forgotten his childhood impressions, Chateauneuf deferred gracefully and the 'knave of Sicily' came back into his own.

Unfortunately, France was not yet prepared to accept him and fell headlong into civil war, much to the delight of the King of Spain, who proceeded to reconquer Catalonia without more ado. A Spanish army under the command of Nemours crossed the Seine at Mantes, near Paris, and joined the forces of Gaston, which were commanded by Beaufort. For the first time in twenty years Philip IV was reaping the reward of his long-term policy of support for the great rebel lords.

Detesting Mazarin, and eager to contribute to his downfall, the Pope finally gave Gondi the red hat, but the new status of Cardinal de Retz deprived him of his popularity and nullified his power as a trouble-maker. At the same

---

* He aspired to the office of Constable and claimed the rank of Prince – much to Saint-Simon's retrospective rage, because his family had ruled Sedan.

time, the Paris Fronde was paralysed by dissensions between the two brothers-in-law, Nemours and Beaufort. Their centre of operations, Bordeaux, became the scene of a rivalry that provided a group of terrorists, the Ormée, with an opportunity to exercise an appalling dictatorship. In Guyenne and Normandy alike, the bourgeoisie were sick of the Fronde and longing for the return of the King's peace.

Chavigny begged Condé to make peace between the demented brothers-in-law, and the victor of Rocroi rode almost unaccompanied from Agen to Châtillon, where he eventually took command of the rebel army. Meanwhile, Mademoiselle had decided to win her own laurels. She went post-haste to Orléans, chief of her father's dependencies, scaled the walls, had herself popularly acclaimed, intimidated the municipal magistrates and ordered the gates to be shut in the King's face. Her gift to the young King whose throne she had hoped to share was the mortification of having to retreat before a woman and the risk of defeat and capture by Condé.

Mazarin knew nothing of the King's expedition, nor did he have the strength to unify the command shared between Turenne and Hocquincourt, who were on no better terms than Nemours and Beaufort. Having defeated the latter at Jargeau, they crossed the Loire. Hocquincourt's contingent positioned, or rather dispersed itself around Bléneau, while Turenne's encamped at Briare, five miles from Gien, the temporary residence of Louis and the court. During the night of 6–7 April 1652 Condé surprised Hocquincourt and cut his troops to pieces. Discerning the order of battle by the distant light of burning buildings, Turenne spoke with his usual unshakeable calm: 'Ah, M le Prince has arrived. It is he who commands that army.'

Turenne's words started a panic in Gien. He had four thousand men, as against Condé's twelve thousand. A single charge, and surely the Fronde must capture the King and shatter the monarchy. In the face of that threat, the Queen's nerve broke and she burst into tears, while the equally demoralized Mazarin recommended cutting the bridges over the Loire and decamping to Bourges. It was Turenne who saved the situation. He insisted that the King would lose his crown if he fled, and that they must keep their heads and stake everything on one throw. He won his point.

Turenne stationed his meagre forces on a plain facing the forest that the enemy must cross in order to reach Gien. Marshes stretched between plain and forest, and across them ran a narrow causeway, within range of Turenne's artillery. When Condé's cavalry moved onto the causeway, they took the brunt of Turenne's charge and were forced to retreat. The artillery opened fire to add to the confusion as the Frondeurs tried to gather their forces. Condé rallied again, but could not pass. At nightfall he had to withdraw towards Châtillon.

Only a few hundred men were killed at Bléneau, a handful compared with all the famous and murderous battles of Louis xiv's reign, and yet it was perhaps the most vital. A different outcome might have removed him from the throne, thus transforming the future both of France and Europe.

Unable to capture the King, Condé took the capital. The easily intimidated Gaston capitulated and de Retz shut himself in his cloister. The Parlement was in two minds. President Bailleul dared to inform Condé that the sovereign court 'could not but regret the coming of a man who had just drawn his sword against his King,' yet it was hard to oppose both Condé and Mazarin at the same time. Nevertheless, finally realizing the extent of their own responsibility for the situation, they entertained hopes of a rapprochement with the court. These were quickly dashed when the princes stirred up the populace and rioting and looting became rife. Magistrates were molested, and one day Colbert, who was known to be Mazarin's man, was attacked, robbed and beaten. Having thus destroyed the prospects of agreement between Crown and Parlement, the princes tried to come to terms on their own account. Mme de Châtillon worked on her lover to adopt this course, so that all he demanded was power for himself and huge gratuities for each of his lieutenants.

On 28 April the King received Condé's emissaries. At thirteen and a half, Louis was no longer a child. A few weeks before, he had dumbfounded a delegation from the Parlement by tearing up their demands without reading them. This time, his Majesty informed the Frondeurs that they must take up their errand with Mazarin and led them firmly, despite their protests, into his Minister's presence.

No decision was reached. Mazarin's sole aim was to give Turenne time to strengthen his forces. The Marshal's success over Condé at Étampes, southwest of Paris, put paid to the negotiations, whereupon the Frondeurs appealed to the Duc de Lorraine. His armed bands committed terrible excesses, and Mazarin had to turn to another woman, the Duchesse de Chevreuse, still eager to avenge her slighted daughter. She secured Lorraine's withdrawal in return for raising the siege of Étampes in such a manner as to make it appear a victory. The war dragged on.

Realizing that only his own departure would enable any decision to be reached, Mazarin suggested that the Queen should offer to dismiss him a second time, subject to a number of conditions which would restore the royal authority. In spite of the resistance of the princes and the howls of the mob, the Parlement accepted, and Mazarin prepared to make a false exit. True, he was counting on a triumphant return once order had been re-established, but he was still running a heavy risk. After the bitter experience of the previous autumn, he no longer trusted Anne's constancy. From now on his aim would be to win the permanent confidence of Louis.

The author of the Treaty of Westphalia had lost none of his opportunist mentality, nor forgotten the habits of the little Italian courts. As he had intended, the King was showing every evidence of a lively friendship for the brilliant Paul Mancini, seeming to prefer him to all his other companions. Perhaps the time had come for the nephew to become the favourite, thus safeguarding his uncle's position.

On midsummer Eve the court was at Melun, and Mazarin offered his Majesty a little fête to which he invited Paul Mancini and other young people. The King stayed very late, and there now occurred the scabrous incident of which La Porte saw proof when he gave Louis his bath, and which led to the valet's disgrace the following year, guilty of having informed the Queen.* The strange escapade ended there. Paul Mancini died on the field nine days later, and the King's extraordinary physical and moral equilibrium suffered no harm. La Porte noted only a little 'sadness' which quickly evaporated. Louis XIV was never to have a favourite.

---

* This is borne out by La Porte's memoirs and his letter to Anne of Austria in 1664. Written at that date, it would have gravely endangered its author if it had not contained the truth. Nor was it a manoeuvre against Mazarin, who had been dead for three years.

[9]

The Cannon of the Bastille

AT DAYBREAK on 2 July 1652, while the terrified Parisians sheltered behind their impregnable wall, Louis XIV and Mazarin made their way to the hill of Charonne, overlooking Paris, to watch the last great battle in the feudal style, in which Condé's forces confronted the royalist troops of Marshals Turenne and La Ferté at one of the gates of Paris, the Porte Saint-Antoine, not far from the Bastille. While Turenne waited for La Ferté's cannon to destroy the enemy fortifications, the King and his tutor grew impatient, so the attack was finally mounted without artillery. This gigantic hand-to-hand battle between fellow countrymen, many of whom were linked by ties of kinship, thus took on an archaic form.

By lunch-time, when a truce was called, the issue was still inconclusive, but Paul Mancini had been fatally wounded, thus ending a career that might well have left its mark on history. Two hours later La Rochefoucauld was out of action with a serious eye-injury. La Ferté's artillery had at last been brought into play and was scything down the Frondeurs, who had their backs to the Porte Saint-Antoine. But it was too early for rejoicing. At the crucial moment the monarchy collided with the lunatic heroism of Mademoiselle – henceforward to be known as La Grande Mademoiselle. She had wrung out of her wretched father orders vague enough to enable her to terrorize the municipal magistrates and gain entrance to the Bastille. The Porte Saint-Antoine opened, and the Prince's defeated army was saved.

While he thanked his cousin, Condé wept for La Rochefoucauld and Nemours, whom he believed dead. His face was thick with dust, his hair dishevelled, his shirt and collar daubed with blood, although he had not been wounded. His armour was heavily dented and he held his sword in his hand, having lost the scabbard. He lost no time in rejoining his men as they passed through the gate in a disorderly mass under the enemy roundshot.

The retreat was slow, and the King's hopes rose again when Turenne's cavalry fell upon the rearguard of the Frondeurs. Then suddenly the towers of the Bastille were wreathed in smoke. Mazarin shouted with joy. There were many of his own men among the rebels, and he felt sure that the guns of the fortress were joining the fray on Turenne's side. He was still under that illusion, and communicating it to Louis, when the salvoes halted their troops' charge.

Gaston's daughter was firing the cannon herself from the height of the towers. She behaved 'on that occasion in a manner quite out of the ordinary and such as has never been allowed a person of my condition,' as her own memoirs put it. Directing her conquering gaze through a telescope, the virgin warrior spied Charonne and the little knot of people on it, realized at once who they were and ordered the cannon to be turned on the hill. The shot fell practically at the feet of Louis xiv and the Cardinal, who did his best to conceal his mortification. 'That cannon has killed her husband,' he said.

It had done more than that. The old fortress, which in 1789 was to become the symbol of the expiring monarchy, in 1652 spelled the end of the political power of the great lords. Louis xiv had just received a second shock as powerful as when the Palais Royal was invaded the year before. He now nursed the same grudge against the princes and the high nobility that he already harboured against the common people of Paris. To his dying day, the salvoes of La Grande Mademoiselle and the mob's foray into the child's bed-chamber would remain vividly printed on his heart.

Condé thought that he had conquered the capital, but found it in enormous confusion. The Fronde had splintered into small factions. There was the 'inert Fronde' of Cardinal de Retz, cowering in Notre-Dame, the Orleanist Fronde, still under Gaston's control, the royalist Fronde, which wanted the King without Mazarin, and Condé's Fronde, weak in comparison with its rivals. Condé was urged to take over the Government, but did not hamper himself with any subtleties of method.

The *prévôt des marchands* (as the mayor of Paris was then known) had decided to hold a meeting at the Hôtel de Ville on 4 July to take measures to protect the Parisians against public disturbances. Six officials of the Parlement and six bourgeois had been summoned from each *quartier*, together with numerous parish priests – about four hundred men in all. The day after the battle, Condé set about devising a plan to force this assembly to give him power. He dressed eight hundred soldiers as workmen and sent them to the Place de Grève, with a crowd of well-paid roughnecks. When they were in place, Gaston and Condé went to the assembly, objected to the *procureur*'s* suggestion of 'begging the King to give his people peace and to come back without Cardinal Mazarin,' and walked out. On the steps of the Hôtel de Ville, Condé shouted to his men: 'They are for Mazarin, do what you like with them.' As soon as the princes had left, the disguised soldiers stormed the Hôtel de Ville, set fire to the gates and forced the stairway, in spite of heroic

* The venal office of *procureur* to the royal courts of the Ancien Régime carried responsibilities comparable to those of a modern counsel. – Tr.

resistance from the town watch. They burst into the town hall and drove out the assembled dignitaries. Anybody they caught was robbed of his last sou, and about thirty were killed. Most of these men had played a part in formulating the 'Constitution' of 1648 and in the first Fronde.

In a terrorized Paris, Gaston became Lieutenant Général of the Kingdom, Condé Generalissimo, Beaufort Governor of Paris and old Broussel *prévôt des marchands*. It was a true revolutionary government, lacking only faith and real enthusiasm. The King's entourage was demoralized. Mazarin was prostrate at the death of his nephew. Mme de Châtillon and President Nesmond were persevering with their efforts to keep negotiations going, but they were nullified by a kind of fatalism. All parties were weakened and penniless.

Foodstuffs were being taxed by both the King and his enemies. Mother Angélique Arnaud, Abbess of Port-Royal, wrote: 'We see nothing but poor people who come and tell us that they have not eaten for two or three days ... Such is the barbarity of the soldiery that the Turks could do no worse ... France is completely devastated; there is not one province which is not suffering to the utmost ...' In spite of this, the famous Jansenist complained, 'the Cours-la-Reine and the Tuileries are as crowded as before, banquets and other extravagances go on as usual, nor does the dreadful spectacle of calamity which fills the streets, murder rife in the streets and at the gates, and the high cost of everything touch their hearts or bring home to them the wrath of God.'

As if tormented by remorse, Condé's friends seemed to be losing their reason. Beaufort killed his brother-in-law Nemours in a duel, and Condé himself came to blows with the Comte de Rieux in Gaston's presence. Meanwhile the Spanish were besieging Dunkirk and advancing towards the Aisne. 1652 was one of France's most disastrous years.

The threat from Spain completed the court's discomfiture. Again the Council advised the King to retreat, this time to Lyons; again Turenne objected and took charge. Between July and November he was the *de facto* Head of State.

First of all, having succeeded in frightening an enemy far superior in numbers, he checked the Spanish advance, and they reached no further than Laon. The King then moved to Pontoise and convoked the Parlement, which refused to obey as long as Mazarin remained in France. Nevertheless, several magistrates fled from Paris and formed a group around First President Molé. The conventions of farce were still operating: the embryonic assembly demonstrated its loyalty in its own turn by demanding the Cardinal's departure, except that now it was the wily Italian himself who dictated this course, with the ready cooperation of Louis.

Mazarin was only bowing to the inevitable. He appointed Le Tellier and Servien to represent him in the Council, then withdrew to Bouillon, an estate belonging to Turenne's brother, who was a party to the proceedings. Lastly, by a public manifesto singing the exile's praises, Mazarin was in effect dismissed without losing his ministerial title.

The Pontoise Parlement now summoned the Parlement of Paris to join it, failing which its members' offices were to be revoked. This threat jolted the counsellors. Condé was ill, and Gaston was overwhelmed by the death of his young son, the Duc de Valois, which Anne of Austria represented to him as the expression of the wrath of Heaven. The populace, delighted to be rid of Mazarin, clamoured for peace and hooted the Frondeurs.

De Retz thought that his chance had come to play the mediator or even to take the place of his rival. Under pretext of receiving the cardinal's biretta, he went in solemn procession to' Compiègne, where the court was now in residence, and at the end of the ceremony which created him a member of the Sacred College he spoke to the King as one authority to another: 'Sire, all your Majesty's subjects can represent their needs to him, but only the Church has the right to speak to you about your duties.' He went on to evoke the memory of Henry IV, and requested a general amnesty and His Majesty's return to Paris. Louis, annoyed by this 'overweening and intolerably bold' remark, recalled that in the days of the League the Parisians 'drove out those who oppressed their liberty.' The former coadjutor had wrecked his own plan.

Realizing that he was on the point of being ousted by the people, Condé tried a final appeal to arms. At his instigation, Spain paid the Duc de Lorraine money enough to make that fierce and greedy prince forget his promise and re-enter France at the head of eleven thousand men. In spite of the labyrinthine negotiations that Mazarin handled personally, he was unable to prevent the Duc from joining forces with Condé at Juvisy, near Paris. With destiny in the balance once more, it was again Turenne who decided the issue by taking up station at Villeneuve-le-Roi, avoiding battles and keeping the enemy at arm's length for close to a month – a month which nonetheless turned the outskirts of Paris into a desert and enabled Spain to capture Dunkirk and Gravelines.

Charles of Lorraine was not a reckless man. Seeing that fortune was not smiling on the Fronde, he resumed negotiations with the court and asked how much his withdrawal was worth. He had left it too long: the Duc's extortions had succeeded in converting the French to monarchism, and he was shown the door. Without stopping to press his point, he set off again for Flanders, taking with him the defeated Condé, who proceeded to put his sword at the service of the King of Spain. His temperament was much akin to that of the Renaissance *condottieri*. The thousands of Frenchmen who had died in vain did not trouble his conscience. He was less attracted to the career of a loyal soldier than to the adventures of a vagrant mercenary killer.

On the day of Condé's departure, representatives of the bourgeois militia and guilds went to the King and begged him to come back to his city. The only remaining obstacle to the monarchy was Gaston of Orléans. On 21 October the King returned to Paris at last, on horseback and accompanied by Charles II, the exiled King of England, and his brother the Duke of York, who had fought under Turenne's command. The populace cheered him as it had upon his coming of age, and as it had cheered Condé and the Duc de Lorraine. Louis took up residence at the Louvre, 'having had his mind made up by his vexatious adventures at the Palais Royale that private houses without moats were not for him.'[1]

The Queen's circle gathered there that same evening, while in the Palais du Luxembourg Gaston blustered about making a stand at Les Halles, the capital's market place, and putting up the barricades. Beaufort, taking him at his word, offered to go and evict Louis from the Louvre. Monsieur thanked him, ordered him to come back at dawn with his men and dismissed him. Then he set about preparing for his escape, but was interrupted by the arrival of his daughter, whom the King had expelled from the Tuileries. 'What,' she cried, 'you are abandoning M. le Prince and M. de Lorraine?' Her father's answer was to reproach her bitterly for her exploits and to suggest that she leave Paris without delay. 'Where am I supposed to go?' she asked him. 'Wherever you like!' Gaston set out for Limours, not far from Paris, Mademoiselle for Saint-Fargeau in the province of Franche-Comté.

The *lit de justice* which took place on 22 October was utterly different from those which had preceded the rebellion. A hundred Swiss guards occupied the chamber, to the beat of drums, before the arrival of the King and his entourage. After praising Their Majesties' clemency, the Chancellor read out a declaration of general amnesty, then the list of those who were excluded from it, among them Beaufort, La Rouchefoucauld, Rohan, Broussel and Mme de Châtillon, but not Cardinal de Retz. Another proclamation forbade the Parlement to consort with 'the princes or great lords of the state,' or to have anything to do with affairs of state or the direction of finance. Thus the magistrates were reduced to their strict judicial function for the next sixty years, and constitutional monarchy was buried along with their political aspirations. Now the excesses committed in the name of pseudo-democracy were to set the stage for the abuses of royal absolutism.

The most dangerous of the Fronde's leaders, its one statesman and the only man still capable of undermining the King's authority, was covered by the amnesty. De Retz had waited on his Majesty at the gate of the Louvre on 21 October, and conveyed to him the compliments of the Church. But the court did not feel safe while he remained free to conspire. Le Tellier and Servien pressed for his arrest, and the decision was taken. Several weeks were to elapse before it could be put into effect.

De Retz hardly ever left Notre-Dame, and there was no question of getting him out by force. When he appeared at the Louvre on the morning of 19 December, probably to investigate which way the wind was blowing, he gave Louis an unexpected opportunity. With everything depending on him, the fourteen-year-old King played his part just as Louis XIII had played his own at the time of Concini's execution. Forewarned of the Cardinal's presence, he showed no sign of hesitation and said: 'I must act like a king now.' He behaved in a most charming manner towards de Retz, displaying perfect good humour. Just like a child, he chattered about a play he had seen. Then, as he moved from one courtier to M. d'Aumont, captain of the guard, and whispered his orders for the Cardinal's arrest. A few moments later he left, still talking gaily, and let fall the sentence which was the agreed signal – 'Especially when there is nobody on stage.'

The sequel was over in a flash, and the idol of the people who had driven the King out of his capital found himself in Vincennes, like Condé and Beaufort before him. Informed that his order had been carried out, Louis gravely told his Jesuit confessor, Father Paulin: 'I have just had Cardinal de Retz arrested here.' Those who witnessed the scene were struck not so much by the event as by Louis' coolness and dissimulation. Even before his adolescence, Louis XIV had shed all trace of the boy he had once been. In large measure, this was the result of the cannon of the Bastille.

[10]

The Lord's Anointed

IT was during the winter of 1652-3 that Anne of Austria and Mazarin exchanged the partially encoded letters which many commentators have seen as proof of their liaison. They show Mazarin often adopting the dry, imperious, tetchy tone of a masterful husband, Anne that of a submissive, troubled woman in the grip of physical passion ('Adieu, I am worn out, Mazarin well knows why.') In the absence of concrete facts, one can only suggest that the Queen's weariness could have been caused by affairs of state, or some other factor quite unconnected with her emotional state of mind.

It would be just as logical to attribute it to other worries, if only because of its very directness, even assuming that it is indeed an avowal of passion. Then too, this short and hasty letter does not seem consistent with the slow progression of carnal images that can grip even the most upright women as they bend over their writing desks. Perhaps the Queen is merely fatigued by a long session in Council, or a prolonged intrigue . . . Personally . . . what most surprises me is an avowal of this nature written *in French* (the Queen wrote French with difficulty, and Mazarin was barely conversant and usually spoke to the Queen in Spanish). In loving, as in dying, women know only their mother-tongue.[1]

There is another reason for doubt, and a powerful one. These letters often mention the King, referring to him as *le Confident*: 'The *Confident* sends you his regards . . . the *Confident* is not writing . . . but asks me to tell you that he yields to no one in his affection.' It is unthinkable that Louis would have been so 'confident' about an affair between his mother and his godfather, bearing in mind his filial love, his former jealousy and his formidable dynastic pride. A boy of fourteen, brought up as the King had been, is not capable of such broad and indulgent understanding, and would not have written to his mother's unacknowledgeable husband: 'When you are back, you will see that your absence has not altered the affection I have always borne you.'

Except in Guyenne, where the Fronde was to drag on for a few months more, order reigned at last. Voltaire states:

The tranquillity of the realm was the result of Cardinal Mazarin's banishment, yet hardly had the universal outcry driven him out than the King called him back. He was

65

surprised to find himself back in Paris supreme and untroubled. Louis XIV received him as a father, and the people as a master. A banquet was given in his honour at the Hôtel de Ville, and he threw money to the populace, but it is said that in the midst of his joy at such a change of fortune he showed his contempt for the fickleness or rather the folly of the Parisians.

Mazarin's contempt did not stop at the Parisians. Richelieu respected his enemies, and consequently arranged for them to die. Mazarin preferred to corrupt and debase his adversaries: he married off his niece, Anne-Marie Martinozzi, to the Prince de Conti. The Cardinal now set himself three goals: to win the war which Condé's betrayal was to prolong for several years more; to rebuild his immense fortune; and to fulfil his duty as superintendent of the King's education. He paid no attention to the people's crying social needs and abandoned the economy to the mercy of a few dozen tax-farmers. Fouquet, the Superintendent of Finance, embarked on large-scale manipulations that were highly profitable to himself and the Cardinal at the country's expense. After his ordeals, Mazarin did not draw the line at any transaction likely to stock his personal treasury. He appointed Colbert, on whom he completely relied, to manage his private interests – a task strewn with temptations. Colbert accumulated a fortune that would have been considered scandalous in a different age. In his role as teacher of kingship, Mazarin showed admirable devotion, which scarcely justified the hostility of Racine or the slurs of Saint-Simon. He could easily have brought up his pupil 'in a long infancy' and incited him to laziness, loose living and pleasure, though not to the coarseness and mental inertia that the favourites of Marie de Médicis had tried to inculcate in his father.

There has been an exaggerated insistence on the indolence and apathy of Louis XIV at this time, and the voluptuous sluggishness suggested by Nocret's portrait of Louis, now in the Prado. The fact is that the King's trials had not been for nothing, and in 1653 'the prodigious machine for governing men which Louis XIV was to become . . . was already more than half completed'.[2] He had already discovered for himself that he must be wary of everything and committed to nothing, prize few men highly and guard his heart against love and hate alike. Louis' tutor taught him how to turn his profound reserve and composure to his own ends, which were those of the state. But the young King refined the formula to a certain degree. He replaced the cynical realism of the adventurer with the Olympian majesty and pitiless serenity of the demigod.

The historian Lavisse has referred to the King's 'inadequate and *corrupting*' political training, yet if he had really been corrupted, Louis must easily have become either a monster or an ineffectual pleasure-seeker. The atrocities committed by the most lucid of autocrats, from Tiberius to Stalin, are well-known. The Sun King's immutability, whether in the face of Boileau's hyperboles or of Fénelon's anathema, proves on the contrary that his moral armour was strongly forged. His gravest errors never suggest the impulsiveness of an unbalanced mind.

After his return Mazarin displayed his sure grasp of essentials by never condescending to use the cajoling charm that was the foundation of his career on Anne of Austria, but he certainly lavished it on his godson. His culture, refinement and expertise in the art of embellishing life were extremely rare in France, where the Précieuses and the Hôtel de Rambouillet had by no means eliminated 'barbarism'. Louis came under the spell of the fastidious luxury (acquired at his own expense) and the objets d'art, jewels, mirrors, monkeys, clowns and actors with which the pleasure-loving Cardinal surrounded himself. He acquired a life-long taste for display, elegance and fine manners, nor did he hesitate to refer in his memoirs to 'that Minister ... who loved me and whom I loved.' No other man ever received such a tribute from the King.

Mazarin made no great effort to repair the gaps in the young monarch's academic education, and Louis was to blush for it later, saying 'that it was a kind of disgrace to return to study so late'. Between the time he woke up and his *lever,* already quite a solemn ceremony, the King studied under the guidance of his preceptor. After the *lever* he spent some time in physical pursuits – riding, arms-drill and exercises with the pike. He then went to the Cardinal's room, which was directly above his own. A secretary of state might be shown in to work with the First Minister, and the grave, attentive pupil would observe the mechanism of government, listen to political maxims or be taught secrets forbidden to the common ear. Often he attended the Council, where Mazarin began gradually to increase the importance of the questions dealt with in the presence of his Majesty. The pragmatic Cardinal was a believer in the apprentice system. The King did homework in the afternoon, transcribing and commenting on what he remembered of the morning's lesson.

It was an age in which any king of France had to be a soldier. He could lose a great deal of prestige if, like the King of Spain, he always stayed clear of the field of battle. Louis had already participated in campaigns during the civil war. In July 1653 he faced the new Spanish invasion led by Condé.

Henry IV had charged at the head of his troops and risked his life hundreds of times. Louis XIII in his turn exposed himself to danger and looked on himself as the effective commander of his armies. By a twist of irony, it was not Louis who inherited the military vocation of his ancestors but his brother Philippe, the chattering, effeminate boy whom Anne of Austria called 'my little daughter'. Philippe had the makings of a great commander, while Louis was only to follow operations as a spectator, in spite of Turenne's lessons. From that time on, Louis joined his armies every spring.

Meanwhile Anne of Austria was considering her son's education in the art of love. After much thought she asked her head chambermaid to teach the King, in the words of Charlotte Elizabeth, 'how ladies must be treated.' The lady was noted as much for her 'lechery' as for her ugliness, and was nicknamed *Cateau la Borgnesse* – 'One-eyed Cateau'. She gave a good account of herself, and the Queen was reassured as to the continuation of the royal line. The handsome Hôtel de Beauvais still bears witness to her gratitude, and the chambermaid's husband, Pierre Beauvais, a former ribbon merchant, became a King's Counsellor and a baron. It was a gardener's daughter who was later to have the honour of revealing the charms of youth to the demigod.

Rancour and pride are commonly reputed to have been the mainsprings of Louis xiv's behaviour. We are already familiar with the grudges which Louis stored up at the time of the Fronde. It is time to investigate the extent and nature of his pride.

Lavisse has condemned 'the religion, the obsession with *gloire,* the legacy of the past weighing on what was after all quite an ordinary man, lacking the resources to counterbalance this powerful and onerous fatality.' Yet in the time of Corneille and the Grand Condé, at the end of a revolution shot through with lordly follies, it is difficult to imagine a prosaic, modest monarch, or one who had no taste for the epic style. France might have been better off with such a man, but would not have put up with him for long. A Louis xiv of that stamp would have had the same fate as Louis xvi, who really did not care for vainglory or renown. Louis accepted the 'legacy of the past' from boyhood in a manner which would be astonishing in a truly 'ordinary' man.

His entourage has been accused of conditioning him to regard himself as a living god. Again, this is an over-simplification. The courtiers were not the only people who worked on his mind in this way. Omer Talon himself, whom historians have singled out for his revolutionary bravery, honoured and respected him as a visible deity. The great majority of Frenchmen considered him as such and required him to feel the same, believing that order and unity depended on it. The successor of Saint Louis would not have been fulfilling the high hopes of his subjects if he had experienced the doubts that were to prove so fatal to his descendants. True, Louis xiv suffered from superhuman pride and some of its consequences were deplorable, but one cannot wonder at it or blame the young King. Fénelon was to be the first man to teach humility to princes. We shall see what came of his lessons.

Exaggerated conclusions as to Louis' character have been drawn from incidents such as Louis taking the part of the sun in a ballet. The sun had been part of the iconology of the House of France for a long time, and the first Sun King had been Charles vi.

There was one precept of Mazarin's that did produce grave consequences: that it was not the duty of kings to know anything of the emotions of the masses, and that kindness, clemency and pity might at times be instruments of government but would become shameful weaknesses if they came from the heart. The great nobles in general and the Bourbons in particular were not notable for tenderheartedness. Louis' heart was sensitive, as was seen at the time of the Mancini affair and the death of Mazarin. Subsequently, however, faithful to his master's teaching, once the sovereign came to full power he schooled himself to be cold and impassive, in spite of various appearances to the contrary and a rare propensity for shedding tears. He evinced neither malice nor bloodthirstiness. Instead, behind the refined manner, noble speech and even temper he kept an inner steadfastness which shattered all who attempted to breach it. His pride was of the nature of his position, but he lacked the compensation of human warmth.

The King's face at the end of his sixteenth year, still handsome in spite of the traces left by smallpox, indicates the stage the boy had reached. While the upper part remains childish, with a shy caressing gaze, the nose and the set mouth, at once hard and sensual, reveal a man who is not to be trifled with. This is the King who was consecrated at Rheims and raised once and for all above the level of common humanity. The Lord's Anointed, clothed in sacerdotal dignity, was God's representative in his realm. Only to God did Louis owe any account of the power which it was a crime for a Frenchman to evade, and he remained fully conscious of that prerogative until his dying day.

Two months after his consecration at Rheims, Louis was present at the siege of Stenay and saw Turenne relieve Arras, under siege by Condé. Every year the interminable war posed the same problems. On 20 March 1655 a *lit de justice* created new taxes – as usual. Yet the spirit of the Fronde still lived, and de Retz had escaped and reached Rome, where he was soon busily intriguing against France.

On 13 April the King was informed that the Parlement wanted to re-open discussions on edicts it had already registered. If it was Mazarin who advised on the ensuing coup de théâtre, he had nothing to do with the way Louis played his part. The Parlement was petrified by the sudden appearance of its King, booted and spurred, and speaking in a tone that no one had heard him adopt before. He pointed a finger at the counsellors, whom he had still not forgiven, and told them:

Everybody knows what troubles your assemblies have stirred up in my state and what dangerous effects they have produced. I have been informed that you still intend to prolong them, on the pretext of debarring edicts which have already been read and published in my presence. I have come here expressly to forbid you to continue, and to forbid you, Mister President, to grant or to suffer any resumption of these debates. . . .

There was general consternation at the revelation of this unsuspected new character, and even Mazarin was apprehensive. He disavowed his pupil, as it were, and restored calm by paying heavy indemnities to the principal magistrates. The King retreated into himself, as if regretting that he had shown his hand prematurely.

[11]

Pangs of Youth

THE fate of Europe depended on the outcome of the perennial rivalry between Condé and Turenne, the two greatest commanders of the century. 'They were admired in their retreats as in their victories . . . [and] their talents halted the progress of both monarchies in turn. But the chaotic state of the finances of France and Spain was a still greater obstacle to their success.'[1]

Condé's aim was to break through to Paris and revive the revolution. Several times he thought that his opportunity had come, notably after his victory at Valenciennes, but he was grossly in error. Spain had no intention of letting him get his hands on the kingdom, whose domestic divisions it preferred to maintain. While the King of Spain could always find some great French lord or lady ready to turn traitor, Mazarin could never find any equivalent in Spain. For instance, Mme de Châtillon made Hocquincourt change sides, and he would have opened the gates of Péronne to Condé had it not been for Mazarin's quick intervention.

At the same time, both kingdoms had the same long-term need for peace and quiet. Mazarin entered into secret negotiations with Madrid, but his Catholic Majesty wanted Condé to return with no stain on his honour and a powerful governorship - in other words, to have the means to resume the civil war whenever he pleased. It was scarcely possible to make such concessions to the hothead who wrote: 'If I could raise all France in revolt, I would do so with all my heart as soon as I was in a position to win everybody over to my side, and anybody who doubts it is sorely mistaken.'

Since the two adversaries were deadlocked, it was inevitable that they should look for an ally to turn the scales. With the Austrian Emperor a non-starter ever since the Treaty of Westphalia, they turned to England, which had been neutralized by the revolution twenty-five years before. This was an act of desperation on both Louis' and Philip's part, a true abjuration of faith, for this was the country, restored to prosperity and power, of the regicide Cromwell. The man who had put Charles I on the block spent some time savouring the pleasures of being courted by the principal monarchs of the West, as well as by Condé. The Council of Madrid offered him Calais, Mazarin Dunkirk - both of which must first

71

be captured. Thus the Protector had to choose between the keys of France and of Flanders.

In the event, Mazarin proved bolder than the Spanish minister Don Luis de Haro, even though the latter did not have to reckon with the same opposition at home: in France, an alliance with the English heretic responsible for the execution of Henry IV's son-in-law might easily have inflamed the passions of 1648 against the 'knave of Sicily'. In Maurice Schumann's judgement: 'Mazarin demonstrated brilliantly that he had learned from Richelieu the basic law of the century, which was that religious fervour must be subordinate to political interest. But the rapprochement with Cromwell had no precedent to recommend it. Far from tending in that direction, the course of events was running counter: nobody believed in it or wanted it, and it had to be wrung out in the teeth of appearance, sentiment, facts, individuals and Cromwell himself . . . Mazarin grappled with the task, sustained it, and won because the perfect simplicity of his perspective raised him clear of the maze of memories and encumbrances.'[2]

When the Protector finally chose sides, he did so cautiously, starting with a simple treaty on freedom of trade. The two powers agreed to open their ports to each other and to leave each other's shipping in peace. Cromwell insisted on the King of France addressing him in correspondence as 'brother', and his secretary signed the draft treaty prior to Louis XIV's representative. It was a triumph for the upstarts. Hoping to break the agreement, the unfortunate Charles II asked Mazarin for the hand of one of his nieces, and the former servant of the Colonnas disdainfully refused to ally himself with the Stuarts!

None of this was done without the King's knowledge, but he was a seventeen-year-old king. Nature was demanding its due, and opportunities were close to hand. For friendship and flirtations, Louis had the Mancini girls, three of whom – Olympe, Marie and Hortense, the most beautiful – had hopes of a fine marriage. The youngest, Marie-Anne, was still a child. It was Olympe who emerged victorious. For a time, the King sought out her company, but it was a perfectly chaste idyll. The 'Mazarinette' did not want to compromise her chances of becoming a princess, which she achieved in 1657 when she married Eugène de Savoie-Carignan, Comte de Soissons. Louis did not seem grieved.

Olympe was later to grant the King as a wife what she had refused him as a maid. Meanwhile, the young man fell for the fair hair and blue eyes of Mlle de La Motte d'Argencourt, but his mother was apprehensive of the girl's attractions. She at once showed the luckless youth 'the danger he was in of offending God . . . and how far he had strayed from the path of innocence and virtue.' There ensued the touching spectacle of Louis XIV, already capable of arresting de Retz and frightening the Parlement, trembling before his mother and his confessor. The King gave way, but it was an ephemeral victory. He met his sweetheart again at a ball, went hot and cold, and trembled. At this point the Cardinal intervened. He slandered Mlle de La Motte shamelessly, and accused her of having another lover, as well as of broadcasting Louis' confidences and making fun of him. Louis was deeply hurt and did not want to see his betrayer again, so that Mme de La Motte, fearing a fall from grace, sent her unfortunate daughter into a convent from which she was never to emerge. Among the many victims of raison d'état in the Grand Siècle, one of the least known and most pitiable is Mlle de La Motte, who was too pretty.

Louis turned for consolation to the almost sisterly friendship of the least attractive of the Mancini girls. Mme de Motteville has drawn a ferocious pen-portrait of Marie:

> She was so thin, and her arms and neck so long and skinny, that it was not possible to praise her on that score. She was all brown hair and yellow skin; her eyes, which were large and dark, had as yet no sparkle and seemed hard; her mouth was big and straight, and apart from her very fine teeth, one might consequently say that she was altogether ugly.

Louis did not care. In his eyes, Marie had other merits.

> She entertained him, excited him ... She made him ashamed of his literary ignorance and plied him with heroic literature. When he had not seen her for a whole day, always lively, always ready to bear the brunt of the conversation, eyes shining, smiling to show off her handsome teeth, he felt a vague discomfort. But all this was only badinage and companionship ... She could not be his mistress, for none of Mazarin's nieces indulged in amorous escapades before they married ... He could not be her husband, since the marriage of a king was the preserve of policy and his country's interest. Cut off from any future, therefore, and resolved not to feel for each other a violent and quite useless affection that would have marred their relationship ... they contented themselves with the pleasure of spending time together and the joy of the next meeting ... His previous adventures and misadventures had left him with painful memories, and he had been in danger of developing a deep mistrust of women: this one was giving him a different impression.[3]

While he was still suffering the pangs of adolescence, there arose a possibility of the King becoming an emperor too. Mazarin had had it in mind since before the death of Ferdinand III. He had calculated that the Electors and German princes could be bought for three million livres, and had given Colbert the task of borrowing that fabulous sum in his own name. When Ferdinand died (on 1 April 1657) he modified his plans and insinuated behind his master's candidature another project that was realized after the election of Leopold I.

Out of concern for their common security, seven sovereign princes, including the King of Sweden, had formed the League of the Rhine. France joined the League in order to maintain the Treaties of Westphalia, which the Emperor had to guarantee in his turn. As Maurice Schumann put it: 'At the very moment of taking root in Alsace, France once and for all renounced acting like a member of the German body politic and turned away from the creed of hegemony in favour of a nationalist policy. At the same time she induced the German princes to rise above their religious differences.' This continuing precedence of politics over religion was brilliantly exemplified when the Anglo-French agreement became an alliance. The treaty was hard on France. Not only did it promise Dunkirk to England, but also it obliged the King to banish his cousins, the sons of Charles I, from his territories. Catholic Europe raised an uproar, and Mazarin left it to fizzle out like all the others. Nothing mattered now that victory and peace were at last in reach.

One English fleet burned galleons near the Canaries, another blockaded Dunkirk, and six thousand veterans, the Ironsides who had established the Commonwealth in England, went to reinforce Turenne. Their pay devolved on France, giving rise to inevitable conflicts which Mazarin had to allay.

The outcome of the war was decided when Condé and Don Juan of Austria tried to raise the siege of Dunkirk. Louis took part in the siege, although he was not permitted to expose himself to danger when Turenne won his finest victory, the Battle of the Dunes, on 14 June 1658. Eleven days later the King made his entry into Dunkirk, then departed, leaving the town in English hands and thereby suffering deep grief and humiliation.

Subsequently he was present at the fall of Bergues, near Dunkirk, then went on to the encampment near Mardyck. He had over-exerted himself, vapours were drifting out of the corpse-crammed cemeteries and rations were bad. On 30 June Louis suffered a fainting fit. He was rushed to Calais, where the fever overtook him. Four doctors bled him generously, purged him and assailed him with blistering ointments. On 4 July they began to fear for his life.

The heir to the throne was the young Monsieur, Philippe, Duc d'Anjou. Haunted by the memory of Gaston's cabals and the rebellions of so many other princes, Anne and Mazarin had always regarded this boy as dangerous. With the Fronde defeated, he was now the only Frenchman in a position to bring down the fine structure that was at last rising out of the debris of civil war. From his earliest years, he had been brought up to defer to his brother, but this was not enough, and they had gone out of their way to reduce him to impotence by giving him an education that indulged and encouraged his potential vices and left his virtues dormant. Safe in the knowledge that they were serving the state well, his own mother and the Cardinal congratulated themselves on having breathed the soul of a shallow hermaphrodite into a brave, witty, impetuous and charming child. His debasement – already evident, and a safeguard to the Crown – now suddenly threatened to become its downfall.

Philippe's nature was of a rare kind in that savage court. He burst into tears when he heard of his brother's peril. Others were ambitious for him, however. Anne of Gonzaga, the most rouée of all the women of the Fronde, judged the moment ripe for seducing him. Afterwards, and following the highest traditions of the civil war, she hatched a plot: once Louis was out of the way, the new king would be taken to Boulogne, Mazarin would be arrested and his property confiscated. Cardinal de Retz would then come into his own. A number of former Frondeurs and a few ladies and counsellors entered the cabal.

Philippe had no liking for Mazarin, and in other circumstances he might well have supported a palace revolution. For the time being, it hardly entered his mind, for all his energies were devoted to comforting his anguished mother. Mazarin, equally grieved, did not relax his precautions. On his orders, Colbert was ascertaining the 'good order' of Vincennes and the Bastille and stationing guards round His Eminence's palaces.

The King received the sacraments during the night of 6–7 July. By the 8th he was considered beyond help, and many courtiers went to pay homage to Monsieur. As a last resort, a doctor named du Sausoi was summoned from Abbeville. He recommended a little-known remedy, emetic wine, which was administered to His Majesty. On 10 July the fever abated. The Faculty were dumbfounded. Anxious to minimize du Sausoi's part, Valot, the official physician, proclaimed that a miracle had saved the King.

Monsieur was sincerely delighted, but had cause bitterly to regret the situation in which he involuntarily found himself when Anne of Gonzaga's well-laid plans were discovered not long afterwards. She herself emerged unscathed, but her fellow-plotters were banished from court or exiled. As for Philippe, Louis' affection for him had always been fairly contemptuous; from now on it was tinged with suspicion. Philippe also had to suffer the renewed hostility of Mazarin, who missed no opportunity to deplore his disorderly life.* Nevertheless, the Cardinal, well aware of the potential power of a scion of the royal line, thought it best to find some way of keeping Monsieur happy. He therefore bought the beautiful villa of Saint-Cloud, where Henry III had been assassinated. Philippe forgot his troubles and bent his energies on beautifying his 'rural paradise.'

Louis profited from the lesson. For forty years he showered presents on his brother, while at the same time contriving to debase him and to remove all sense of purpose from his existence.

* According to Primi Visconti, Philippe Mancini, the youngest of the nephews, was the first to debauch Monsieur.

[12]

'You Weep, but I Leave'

WHILE Mazarin remained with the army, Anne of Austria brought her son back to Paris by slow stages. On the way, Louis' entourage, seeking to amuse him, told him that during his illness Marie Mancini had been utterly overwhelmed with grief. It was the first time that Louis had captured a girl's heart. He was moved, but did not show it. When he saw her again, no fond words appear to have been exchanged between them. That would have involved taking a very grave step down a dead-end track. The young man continued to ask Olympe for the favours she had been granting him since her marriage, under her husband's approving eye. All the same, keen observers noted certain changes in his relationship with the two sisters.

Queen Christina of Sweden arrived on a visit. She was a slightly misshapen, ugly woman, whimsical, lascivious and scholarly, who had renounced her crown as someone might take off an uncomfortable hat. One evening she plumped herself down between the King and Marie Mancini and told Louis: 'If I were in your place I would marry somebody I loved.'

The court moved from Paris to Fontainebleau, and Gaston and La Grande Mademoiselle went with it, having bought their peace at the expense of their pride. Gaston was profuse in his apologies and willing to swallow any slight from the King or his mother, for what he had in mind was nothing less than to marry Louis to Mlle d'Orléans, eldest of his daughters by his second wife.

Louis was the biggest catch in Europe, and every court dreamed of such an alliance. The Queen of Portugal was trying to bribe Mazarin to favour her daughter. The Duchess Regent of Savoy, Louis XIII's sister, offered her own daughter, Princess Marguerite, and called attention to the strategic importance of the Alpine passes to France. The Anglo-French treaty had not stopped Charles I's widow from pleading the cause of her daughter, the same Princess Henrietta whom Louis had thought too thin.

The Queen and Mazarin discouraged no one, but their real hope was to end the war by celebrating the union of Louis and the Infanta Maria Theresa of Austria, first princess of Europe and eldest daughter of Philip IV of Spain, who cherished the same ambition. Twenty-three years of war and the inordinate pride of Spain even in defeat stood in the way of a reconciliation and peace.

76

Perhaps the obstacles would never have been overcome had the masters of Europe at that time not been moderate, patient, reasonable men, with no passion for glory and violence.

Velasquez has left us the image of a tall, pale, fair-haired Philip IV that evokes a hot-house plant rooted in solitude and boredom. This indolent intellectual was undoubtedly the most humane of all the princes of his line. To compensate for his scant success as a monarch, he had turned to mysticism, hunting, courtship and literature. He wrote plays, translated lengthy works by the historian Guicciardini, beautified Madrid, corresponded with the religious visionary Maria d'Agreda and patronized the arts. His succession was by no means the least of Philip's worries. Although he had had innumerable children, only the daughters had reached adulthood. The Infantes had died young.

It has been argued that Mazarin never sought to unite the Spanish empire with France, and certainly that kind of megalomania would have been the negation of his political tenets. Equally, he could not ignore the problem. If the King of France had no desire to collect his uncle's twenty-three crowns, neither was he anxious to see them adorning other monarchs' heads. The Spaniards could not imagine becoming the subjects of their hereditary enemy, but Philip loved his daughter, and the idea that she might reign simultaneously over the two realms was never far from his thoughts. Philip IV, his sister (Anne of Austria) and their ministers all had the same thing in mind, but it could not be made public for fear of setting Europe in uproar, and this further complicated the approaching negotiations.

At this point Cromwell died, thus destroying Spain's highest hopes, for the Protector, having obtained Dunkirk, had been considering reversing the alliances so as to acquire Calais too. England now retreated into her domestic conflicts, and France and Spain remained at daggers drawn. Were they to continue their unwanted duel because each was loth to take the first step?

To set the wheels in motion, Mazarin employed a ruse: he entered into matrimonial negotiations with the Regent of Savoy, Madame Royale (so called in memory of her father, Henry IV), and in November 1658 the court embarked on the slow, uncomfortable journey to Lyons, while Madame Royale, her daughter and their entourage set out from Turin for the same destination.

The progress of the royal party was magnificent and gay. There were salutes from cannon, speeches and *lits de justice* in big towns such as Dijon, which were squeezed for money as the party passed through. La Grande Mademoiselle noted: 'The King seemed as cheerful as could be, and spoke of nothing but his marriage, like a man well pleased to be wed.' But he was 'always at Mlle de Mancini's side, talking to her as gallantly as might be ... He had got into the habit of travelling on horseback with Mlle de Mancini....'

The Cardinal did not share Louis' carefree mood, as he awaited the arrival of some agent bearing a message from the King of Spain. No one came, but a decisive development was taking place in Madrid: when Philip IV was informed of the French King's journey and its barely disguised objective, he so far exceeded himself as to strike the table and raise his voice, exclaiming: 'That cannot be, and it shall not be!'

Louis duly arrived at Lyons and met the princesses of Savoy.

'Well?' Anne of Austria asked him when he rode back to her carriage.

'She is much smaller than the Marquise de Villeroy,' the young sovereign answered cheerfully, 'she has a most charming figure, her complexion is [he refrained from saying 'black' or 'dark'] olive. It suits her well. She has beautiful eyes, and I find her to my liking.'

'I am very glad to hear it,' the Queen sighed.

Marie Mancini was not. She whispered to Louis: 'Aren't you ashamed that they want to give you such an ugly woman?'

In the course of a ball that evening, Colbert was informed that a foreigner with no passport was asking to see him in private. First Colbert went out, then Mazarin. An hour later he went to the Queen's apartments.

'I bring the news you least expected,' he told her.

'It is the Infanta, then,' Anne cried.

'As you say, the Infanta is yours.'

Philip IV had taken the lure. He sent neither monk nor merchant, but one of his chief ministers, Don Antonio Pimentel. Now it fell to the Queen to break the news to her sister-in-law. Madame Royale wept copiously, accepted some magnificent jewellery by way of compensation and obtained a promise that if the Spanish negotiations should break down the King would return to Marguerite.

Terrified at the sight of La Grande Mademoiselle, who had been mentioned as a possible bride, the young Duke of Savoy wanted to leave without more ado. This did not suit the French, who wanted the arrival of the deus ex machina to remain a close secret, and Madame Royale was finally persuaded to stay a few days more before taking away her daughter, whose dignified manner throughout the transaction was greatly admired.

The unsuspecting Marie thought that she had won. There was a strange development when they set out on the return journey. All those who might have embarrassed them – the Queen, the Cardinal, Olympe and Hortense – borrowed boats or carriages, enabling the lovers to ride side by side. That journey was certainly Louis XIV's only experience of simple happiness as an ordinary man. Marie wore a black velvet jerkin and a matching bonnet trimmed with feathers. Love and pride had made her especially beautiful and she was brimming with wit and high spirits. The people who came to greet the King admired the couple and were already building them up into a legend. At the end of the day they would play the guitar, laugh, touch and hold hands.

Back in Paris, Mme de Venel, the pious governess of the 'Mazarinettes', was the only person who occasionally disturbed the charmed existence of which Marie was to write: 'Never was time spent more agreeably. It would take a whole volume to describe the gallant adventures that accompanied our meals.' They sang and danced to airs composed by a buffoon named Baptiste to whom the King took a great liking: he was the future Lully.

On normal evenings, Louis stayed late with the Mancini girls, much too late for the peace of mind of their governess, who would curtsey him out of one door only for him to come back by another, amid loud protests. The King got his own back by giving her a box containing not sweetmeats but a dozen mice. Still the chaperone stood inexorably between Marie and himself.

Another kind of gift gave rise to a great deal of gossip when his Majesty offered Mlle Mancini a pearl necklace that had belonged to the unfortunate dowager of England. In spite of his avarice, the Cardinal paid for it without complaining overmuch, for Marie was now a key pawn in France's game. Mazarin was involved in tough secret negotiations with Pimentel. They never mentioned the Infanta, but she was always in their minds, and the fact that Louis was obviously smitten with another woman put the Cardinal in a powerful bargaining position.

Hugues de Lionne, the Secretary of State for Foreign Affairs, announced the successful outcome of the negotiations when he received the King and Queen at his home in Berry. There was an immediate stir when the Cardinal was seen arriving at this little fête with the Spanish minister. The court realized what was happening and fell over itself to make Pimentel welcome. Better still, not long afterward, and before there had been any lull in the war, Don Juan of Austria, Philip IV's natural son and Governor of the Low Countries, paid a visit to his aunt at the Louvre. Anne's welcome was almost maternal. Such civilized proceedings would be inconceivable today.

It fell to a woman named Capitor, a buffoon in Don Juan's entourage, to commit a deliberate diplomatic 'blunder' by her noisy chatter about the Spanish marriage, and she did so well that Marie had a set-to with her and managed to have her removed. The question was now apparently settled. Official negotiations were due to take place at Saint-Jean-de-Luz, and the court was informed of its imminent departure to Bayonne.

In fact, Capitor had succeeded in giving Louis second thoughts. He had been mulling things over in his mind ever since the breakdown of the Savoy engagement several months before. It was the classic Cornelian dilemma of love and duty, so familiar to seventeenth-century princes. Louis XIII had endured it before giving up Louise de La Fayette; Condé, too, when he married Richelieu's unstable niece instead of the beautiful Marthe du Vigean.

Louis XIV was of a different generation from that of Corneille. At the age of twenty, Italian pliancy impressed him more than Spanish austerity, and he preferred happiness and human feeling to raison d'état. In the course of Louis' long life, it was a unique irregularity, a deliberate breach of duty. Thanks to this lapse, we know that the Sun King could be human and vulnerable, just as the much-criticized creation of Versailles proves that he was an artist.

When Louis asked Mazarin for the hand of his niece 'because he knew of no better means of adequately rewarding his long and outstanding services,' the Cardinal was quite naturally stunned, tempted and afraid. It was his turn to confront the Cornelian dilemma.

Through all the controversies that have raged on the subject of his attitude, no one has shown that the trembling lover ever received an answer from him. Did Mazarin advise Louis to speak to the Queen, or did he undertake to do so himself? The aggressive remark reported by Mme de Motteville, who quotes Anne as threatening her Minister with civil war, is an obvious fabrication, but it does convey the Queen's reaction to this 'treachery'. The prospect of a new kind of Fronde was unquestionably raised. Anne detested the Mancini girl, and it was her dream to see her native and adoptive countries reconciled: both motives could only exacerbate the indignation to which she gave rein with her son, accusing him of insulting Spain and reviving the war for the sake of an unprecedented misalliance.

When Louis remained obdurate, Mazarin was unable to refuse the Queen's demand that he should ask his niece to give up her impossible romance of her own accord. The resulting interview clinched the issue. Marie had no love for her uncle, and her cunning, haughty behaviour testified to her confidence in her power. The Cardinal realized that if he let her marry Louis, not only would his own handiwork be destroyed and his papal aspirations dashed by the resultant Spanish resentment, but also he would soon cease to be ruler of France. He changed his tack at once, and informed the impudent girl, who was also his ward, that she and her young sisters were to be removed forthwith to Brouage, a remote village near La Rochelle. There, Mme de Venel would keep a close watch on her during the court's journey.

Marie did not deign to protest, but ran to Louis with her tidings. The King hastened to his mother, and found Mazarin there ahead of him. He begged, wept, fell on his knees, reducing Anne to such a state of confusion that she almost relented. Mazarin reminded Louis first of all about the overriding importance of the marriage negotiations, then adopted the tone of the sage adviser and refused 'to permit the King to do anything so contrary to his *gloire.*' Finally he switched to theatrical eloquence and swore 'that he would stab his niece rather than advance her by means of so great a betrayal.'

Louis went back to Marie and swore that he would never change, but added that it was better to come to terms and gain time. Perhaps the peace would not be signed. They wept in each other's arms.

Mazarin had laid the foundations of the most famous treaties of the century. Now he concluded another with Louis, who was compensated for the departure of his beloved by being allowed to write to her: 'You will give her your news and my niece will have the honour of giving you hers.' Louis pressed his demands, and obtained a formal promise that he would see Marie at least once when he went to Bayonne. The following day (22 June 1659) he led Mlle Mancini to her coach. He remained leaning at the door for a long time, not troubling to hide his tears. 'Ah, Sire,' the proud girl told him, 'you are King, you weep, but I leave.'

Louis went to Chantilly to conceal his grief. He rode in the woods for hours on end and fell to writing love letters as soon as he returned.

[13]

The Politics of Love

CARDINAL MAZARIN's long cortège had set out for the River Bidassoa to meet the Spanish plenipotentiary, Don Luis de Haro. The future of a continent was about to be settled, and yet it was not provinces, nations or armies that were uppermost in the minds of the two ministers. All their calculations were being falsified by Louis and Marie.

Mazarin caught up with his niece at Fontainebleau, where he found her ill and feverish. He took her with him, only to find at every halting-place a musketeer bearing a letter for his Eminence that contained another sealed missive addressed to Mlle Mancini. The harassed soldiers had orders not to leave without a reply. Innumerable letters were exchanged in this manner, although unfortunately none have survived. On the other hand we do possess those which testify to the distress of *les Anges* and *la Mer,* the code words for the Queen and Mazarin.

Anne of Austria behaved with the utmost tenderness towards her son without managing to cool his state of mind. Doctor Valot noted: 'His Majesty is feverish, cannot sleep and is losing a great deal of weight.' Meanwhile Mazarin was writing to his pupil in a tone that was both moving and – coming from such a cynic – surprising:

I beg you, for the sake of your *gloire,* your honour, the service of God and the good of your realm to try with all your heart not to make this journey to Bayonne with a bad grace, for you would be guilty in the sight of God and men if you were not to go there with the purpose that reason, honour and interest demand.

Louis XIV unfortunately had neither honour nor interest in mind.

From Poitiers, where they had parted with their uncle, the Mancini girls went on to Brouage. Marie was kept under close surveillance there, and she and Hortense led a solitary existence during which she read and re-read the King's letters, passed on to her by the governor, Colbert du Terron, a relation of Colbert. Mazarin had given his faithful steward the job of conveying her answers in person.

The Cardinal had no way of knowing the contents of this correspondence, and the uncertainty was undermining his already shaky health. His style now foreshadowed that of the great preachers: 'God has established kings to watch over the good, security and peace of their subjects, not to sacrifice that good and that peace to their personal passions . . . With your good qualities, you can become a great king should you so choose.' As a desperate resort, he presented Louis with an ultimatum: either he gave his minister definite instructions to proceed or not with the marriage arrangements, or the Cardinal would break off the negotiations, return his possessions to the King and retire *with his nieces* to Italy, even if only 'to a desert island'. He got his answer. He was to proceed with the negotiations and Louis and his mother would set out on their way.

Louis was surrendering, but under protest. Mindful of Mazarin's promise that he would meet Marie again, he announced his intention of seeing the Mancini girls at La Rochelle. Anne prevented this scandal at the last minute by summoning them to the halting place of Saint-Jean-d'Angély, where the King arrived three hours ahead of his entourage. He and Marie spent a long time together, and Hortense was to write: 'Nothing could match the passion displayed by the King or the tenderness with which he begged Marie's forgiveness for all she had suffered because of him.' Anne of Austria greeted the girl so graciously that she summoned up courage to ask permission to follow the court to Bordeaux. The Queen consented, providing that the Cardinal agreed.

The lovers remained together until two in the morning and parted in a daze, counting on meeting again at Bordeaux. They were forgetting that his Eminence must first agree.

That same day (15 August 1659) Mazarin was setting foot on the Isle of Pheasants on the Bidassoa River, from the French bank, Don Luis de Haro from the Spanish. The Cardinal had a guard of a hundred horsemen and two hundred foot-soldiers, and was escorted by a host of gentlemen and five hundred liveried attendants. The Spaniards were few in number, sombrely dressed and without a trace of ostentation. Their disdainful simplicity was a painful lesson for the upstart Cardinal.

To prevent clashes between the proud susceptibility of Spain and the aggressive irony of France, an enormous palisade divided the island. Nevertheless, the conference got off to a bad start when the mention of Condé brought the nascent vision of peace into stark contrast with the very incarnation of war and its horrors. The King of Spain wanted a principality or high office for his ally, and when Mazarin bridled at the thought of rewarding treason Don Luis de Haro remarked that it was 'quite usual for Frenchmen to commit similar crimes and to obtain not just pardons but advantages.' Mazarin lost his temper, threatened to withdraw, and the negotiations came perilously close to breaking down.

They had just been resumed, although when Mazarin was informed of the meeting at Saint-Jean-d'Angély he forgot all caution and psychological insight and sent the King eighteen pages of angry reproaches:

You spend your time reading her letters and writing your own. And what defeats my comprehension is that you resort to every imaginable expedient to inflame your passion when you are on the eve of being married.

Then he made the grave mistake of pronouncing a bitter indictment against his niece:

She is inordinately ambitious, contrary and quick-tempered, despises everybody, behaves without restraint and is prepared for every kind of excess . . . In fact you know as well as I do that she has a thousand failings and not a single quality that might make her worthy of the honour of your good will.

The nobility of his final sentence might well produce the opposite of the intended effect:

I vow that nothing will prevent me from dying of chagrin if a person so near to myself causes you more misery and danger than I have rendered you service since the first day I began to serve you.

Louis merely replied: 'Do as you wish. If you abandon the affairs of state plenty of others will willingly assume them.'

This was revolution, the posthumous victory of the Fronde, a threat to all that had been achieved since Richelieu. Mazarin determined to stake everything on pursuing the negotiations, and the Spaniards, probably aware of what was happening, adopted a more conciliatory tone. An unofficial intermediary told the Cardinal that he would not be snubbed if he brought up the subject of the Infanta, he did so – and Don Luis de Haro smilingly acquiesced. He even talked of celebrating the marriage as early as October, and Mazarin wrote to the Queen: 'I am ashamed to say things to Don Luis about the marriage which are not in accordance with the truth.'

His letters to the King had become quite subservient. Louis was informed about the clauses in the treaty and in the marriage contract, and they confronted him with a choice that few men have ever had to make: he must show either that he was a monarch of his own era or that he was an individualist before his time. As it happened, it was not Louis who decided, but Marie. The girl had been banking on either a breakdown in the talks or a split between King and Cardinal. Information reached her about the agreement immediately it was concluded, perhaps from Louis, who often passed on Mazarin's homilies, perhaps from her uncle himself. In the event, Marie had enough of her family's shrewdness to bow to the inevitable.

The King would not have the fortitude to destroy all this for love. If some miracle gave it to him today, he would repent tomorrow. The whole world,

'Monsieur' (Philippe I, Duc
d'Orléans, brother of Louis
XIV – engraving)

Cardinal Mazarin (engraving
by Nanteuil)

BOURBON-CON
(LOUIS II), LE GRAN
1621-1686

Le Grand Condé
(Juste d'Egmont –
Musée Condé,
Chantilly)

Henri de la Tour
d'Auvergne,
Vicomte de
Turenne
(engraving by
Nanteuil)

Louis included, would soon join in condemnation of the brazen girl who would have rekindled the war, insulted the Habsburgs and discredited the Bourbons. Having realized this, Marie had only one desire – to break with Louis before he deserted her. On 3 September she informed the King that she would write him no more letters and begged him to write none to her. She was submitting completely to her uncle's will.

Mazarin received a similar declaration, which was confirmed by Mme de Venel. He did not doubt Marie's good faith for a moment. Louis remained in doubt, however, and wrote to her again. He even sent her his little dog Friponne. When he had to face the truth, he felt all the bitterness, grief and rage of a rejected lover. So, as France approached her highest peak of power and was on the point to wresting the hegemony over Christendom from the House of Austria, the young man who would consequently become the first sovereign of Europe abandoned himself to despair and the minister who had engineered this unprecedented victory was exhausted by effort and anxiety.

Mazarin's relationship with his pupil changed. He was bound to wonder how much longer Louis would endure a tutelage whose yoke could be so crushing, and this question plagued him continually during the final talks on the treaty of the Pyrenees. Some day he might have to follow Marie's example and leave of his own accord, but when that time came he must be in a position to mount the throne of St Peter.

Like most disappointed lovers, Louis now wanted to marry as soon as possible – in October, since October had been mentioned. Mazarin preferred to have a longer breathing-space and sent the Duc de Gramont to Madrid to make a formal request for the hand of the Infanta. 'I believe the *Confident* would be well pleased with a postponement,' he wrote to Anne, 'for I tell you that if he goes into this marriage in his present state of mind he and the Infanta will be unhappy, and you and I inconsolable.'

Louis asked Marie to burn his letters and did the same with hers. He went back to Olympe, and it was decided that he would spend the season visiting his provinces in the Midi. The court stayed at Toulouse, Auch, Beaucaire and Aix, while the Mancini girls continued their melancholy residence at Brouage. In January they were finally allowed to return to the Louvre. In the midst of the negotiations, Mazarin had found a husband for his formidable niece: a Colonna was anxious to be allied with his great uncle's former chamberlain, and he was accepted only as a way out.

Marie was by no means enthusiastic. She would have preferred Prince Charles of Lorraine, so as to remain in France. Just as there was no lack of candidates for the task of whispering in Louis' ear that she had got over their affair, so Marie herself was being told that he was finding his own distractions. The peace of Europe was still dependent on their tragi-comedy, for although the Treaty of the Pyrenees had been signed, it would not come into effect until after the marriage. This gave the Cardinal's enemies and even some of his friends the occasion for bitter criticism.

Turenne bewailed the fact that France had not extended her territories as far as the River Scheldt. Many criticized the restoration of Lorraine to its Duc and the evacuation of Saint-Omer, Ypres, Menin, Oudenarde and a number of other towns. Voltaire was further of the opinion that Mazarin had been too conciliatory, in spite of the annexation of Roussillon, the Cerdagne, Artois, Marienbourg, Thionville, Gravelines, Montmédy, Landrecies and Avesnes, this last paying for Condé's amnesty and return to grace.

Later the Cardinal was to be accused, on the contrary, of having brought down vengeance upon France through his inordinate greed. It is certainly true that while the Infanta was renouncing her claim to the Spanish inheritance, she did so subject to the payment of a dowry of 500,000 écus of gold, which her father's pauperized kingdom would never be able to meet. Mazarin had the Low Countries and Franche-Comté in mind, but Spain would not hear of dismemberment, and in Philip IV's present state of health (he was being treated by suckling on a wet-nurse) it was impossible to ignore the question of his succession.

Don Luis de Haro was quite aware that he could not pay the 500,000 écus. Consequently it is not fanciful to imagine a kind of tacit agreement between the two ministers to let the future take care of the various possibilities. This was later to enable the young and fiery monarch to interpret the treaty differently from the declining Cardinal.

Mazarin did not think of Spain as a beaten enemy. Like Richelieu, he had every intention of placing the French monarchy in the vanguard of Christendom, but he was steeped in the tradition of the Papacy and the Empire and did not share the Bourbon spirit of supremacy or the hegemonic ambitions of his predecessor. Richelieu had dreamed of 'humbling' the House of Austria before an all-powerful France, whereas Mazarin envisaged a Christian alliance in which France would be pre-eminent but not predominant. With one eye on the papal tiara, he was striving to unite the Mediterranean and Catholic nations while at the same time preserving the English alliance. The King of France would thus become the arbiter of a Europe finally at peace.*

At this juncture, Louis XIV hardly seemed worthy of such a grand design. He was still preoccupied with Marie, not the treaty. When he heard of her impending return to Paris he wanted to go there too. Fortunately, Marseilles chose that moment to stage an uprising, and the King had to wait for it to end.

When Marshal de Gramont, the French ambassador extraordinary, and his

---

* In the eighteenth century, Dubois and Fleury were the heirs of Mazarin's policy. The Revolution resumed and strengthened that of Richelieu.

suite arrived in Madrid, they were somewhat awed by the icy majesty of Habsburg etiquette. One witness noted: 'The audiences given by the king of France are pitiful compared with those of the king of Spain.' The remark was conveyed to Louis, and subsequently bore rich fruit.

At the Spanish Palace, the French were barely able to conceal their astonishment as they passed through room after room lined with shimmering lords and ladies standing silent and motionless. At last, in the final chamber, as in an innermost sanctum, Philip IV appeared before them, clad in black, standing beneath a canopy of cloth of gold. Upright as a statue, his eye did not flicker as he listened to de Gramont's speech, and he did not say a word in reply. The French nobles bowed as if to a holy relic before being conducted to the chamber where they met the young Queen* and her step-daughter the Infanta, then aged twenty-one. Maria was slightly built, with a rosy complexion, long face, somewhat heavy cheeks, blue eyes, full lips and poor teeth, the entire effect set off by magnificent fair hair. The two princesses stood on a dais, lost in immense, stiff robes, like strange ships under sail. Neither of them stirred, spoke or smiled. Gramont kissed the hem of their robes and then withdrew in silence, too unnerved to deliver his prepared address. Later he was permitted to watch the Queen as she dined in solitary state, attended by two ladies in white who served her on their knees.

Maria Theresa had had a perfect upbringing. A person of royal blood can love only a person of royal blood: the Infanta was convinced of the universality of this principle, and there was consequently no question of her being jealous of a Mancini. She had known since childhood that it was her destiny to become Queen of France, and was certain that Louis, in his turn, had loved and hoped for herself alone. The ambassador was much impressed. Only one drawback occurred to him: the future Queen of France could not speak a word of French.

Gramont was informed that Maria Theresa expected to keep her confessor, her female dwarf and Molina, her favourite maid. These were grave demands. The problems that had arisen from the presence of La Galigaï† in the Louvre were well known. But the Infanta did not have the character of a Médicis; she would be absolutely subservient to her husband. Gramont gave way.

It remained for him to take his leave, and he was eager to be the bearer of a sentimental message from the Infanta. When he asked for one, Maria Theresa only recited in a singsong voice: 'Tell the Queen, my Lady and my aunt, that I shall always be at her feet.' Gramont invested her words with every possible meaning in his report to Louis, and went into ecstasies about her rosy skin and golden hair. The King heard him out gloomily. He kept quite aloof from

---

* She was twenty-four years old and her husband's own niece (the daughter of his sister).

† Leonora Galigaï was married to Concini, favourite of Marie de Médicis. She was beheaded and burned as a witch in 1617. – Tr.

the excitement of his mother, Mazarin and even Colbert, who were busy redecorating palaces, renewing uniforms, ordering gifts and devising sumptuous costumes for the young couple. Louis only glanced at the loaded chests and remarked that it was 'a financier's trousseau!' But he was finally to have his own household, that is, his own court. Until that time, he had been content to be the principal ornament of his mother's.

On 27 January 1660, after loitering in the arms of the still beautiful Duchesse de Châtillon, Condé arrived at Aix and paid Their Majesties his first call since his narrow failure to capture them. He was received with cool civility. The King gave his cousin the choice of attending his marriage or returning to Paris. 'Monsieur le Héros' was tactful enough to accept the latter alternative. He was being let off lightly. His uncle Richelieu would not have left Condé's head on his shoulders. Blood and vengeance were not in Mazarin's scheme of things.

The former rebel was partly ruined, although Spain had promised to pay him the colossal sum of 1,400,000 livres. But he still had his mansion in Paris, his château at Saint-Maur and his estate at Chantilly. His son received the governorship of Burgundy and the title of Grand Master of France. Condé quickly retrieved his fortunes and embarked on his magnificent restoration of Chantilly, while biding his time to win the King's favour.

Meanwhile, on 2 February Gaston died. His silver plate had to be pawned to pay for his funeral, but the people mourned a prince who had talked so much about alleviating their hardships and had caused them so many. Louis felt no emotion. His brother took the title of Duc d'Orléans, receiving, in addition to that Duchy, those of Valois and Chartres, as well as innumerable seigneuries.

The face of the world was changing. At the time of the treaty, Charles of England had been to the Pyrenees and had not succeeded in being received by the ministers either of his uncle of Spain or his cousin of France. Suddenly the rumour spread that he was to be restored to his throne. It had been bad strategy to refuse him a Mancini alliance and to insult his favourite sister.

With the first signs of spring, the King of Spain and his daughter set out for the frontier. The proxy marriage was to take place at Fontarabia, where Don Luis de Haro would represent the husband. The marriage proper was to be solemnized by the Bishop of Bayonne at Saint-Jean-de-Luz.

The Spanish party halted at San Sebastian, the French at Saint-Jean-de-Luz. Each wanted a glimpse of the other, with the exception of Louis xiv, who was forbidden to see his bride-to-be before the proxy marriage. The Spaniards enjoyed a refined revenge with their disdain for the Frenchmen, ludicrously decked out in trimmings, plumes, ribbons and jewellery.

Days went by while the two ministers argued about various details of the treaty. Louis sent the Infanta a letter, but her father would not allow it to be delivered. She sent compliments to Anne of Austria, adding under her breath: 'What I say about the Queen can also be understood for the King.' Eventually the negotiations were concluded and the date for the proxy marriage fixed. On 3 June 1660 Philip IV entered the church with his daughter at his left hand. He was looking very pale, and dressed in grey and silver. The 'Mirror of Portugal', a huge diamond, gleamed in his hat next to 'La Pelegrina', the biggest pearl in the world. The Infanta was wearing a simple dress of white wool, almost unadorned, much to the consternation of the French. They thought her small, but gentle and gracious. On the other hand they found her attendants dry, black, and dressed to look like poles stuck into barrels.

Philip led his daughter to the altar. When the moment came, Maria Theresa made a deep curtsey to her father and murmured, 'Yes.' Then she stretched out her arm to Don Luis de Haro, who made the same ritual gesture towards her. In the same movement, without lowering her arm, the Princess held out her hand to her father. Philip kissed it, and the candle-light now revealed the sight of the unbending, statuesque King shedding tears.

The following day Anne of Austria arrived at the Isle of Pheasants to meet the brother whom she had not seen for forty-five years and her unknown daughter-in-law. The meeting took place in the conference chamber, whose floor was covered with two carpets that did not touch; the gap represented the frontier, a forbidden line, since no monarch was allowed to leave his realm. Anne reached the edge of her own carpet and reached out to embrace her brother, but Philip IV recoiled, shocked by such improper familiarity.

At this point there was a knock at the door, and a gentleman entered to tell the King of Spain that a 'stranger' was asking for admittance. Everybody affected surprise. The Cardinal and Don Luis went to open the door, stood to either side of it and continued their conversation, taking good care to leave enough space between them for the 'stranger' to be visible: it was Louis XIV, incognito. Maria Theresa saw him and went very pale. Philip IV looked him up and down and told his sister: 'Here is a handsome son-in-law. We shall have grandchildren.' Impatient for some reaction from her daughter-in-law, Anne asked: 'What is your opinion of that stranger?' – an indecorous question, which Philip forbade his daughter to answer, quietly observing that it was 'not the time to say.' This disappointed the French, but the artful Philip of Orléans found a way round the difficulty. 'Sister,' he asked, 'what is your opinion of that door?' Maria Theresa blushed, smiled, and finally whispered: 'The door seems to me to be very handsome and very good.'

Philip IV and his daughter returned to Fontarabia by boat, and Louis XIV rode along with them on the French bank of the river, hat in hand. The King of Spain did not turn his head, and Maria Theresa dared not do more than steal furtive glances. In the evening she received the King's gift of pearls and a casket full of costly treasures. The Frenchman who brought them looked for signs of pleasure, but she remained as impassive as an idol and passed the casket to her lady-in-waiting – unopened.

Three days later the two Kings met on the Isle of Pheasants with all due ceremony. Kneeling opposite each other at a table, their right hands on two identical gospels, their left hands holding two identical crucifixes, they swore mutual peace, alliance and eternal friendship (the friendship was to last less than two years, the peace about seven). The solemn parting took place the following day. Anne, Philip iv, Louis xiv and his brother all wept. As for Maria Theresa, after kneeling three times for her father's blessing, she almost fainted. Later, the Princess withdrew, then reappeared wearing French-style clothes: a pink satin robe embroidered with gold and silver and encrusted with gems set in gold. The party proceeded to Saint-Jean-de-Luz, and the Princess dined privately in the house reserved for her and Anne of Austria. On 8 June the entire day was taken up with rehearsals for a sumptuous wedding.

On 9 June 1660 the ground between the royal residences and the church was spread with rich carpets and the whole processional route was lined with white and gold-painted pillars, loaded with garlands. The procession walked through an immense concourse of onlookers, to the deafening peal of bells. At its head was the Prince de Conti, followed by Cardinal Mazarin in ermine cape and flowing purple train. At a distance, in solitary state, came the King, dressed in gold brocade veiled with black, solemn and majestic. Next followed Maria Theresa, flanked by the Duc d'Orléans at her right hand and her *chevalier d'honneur*, M. de Bernaville, at her left. Over her robe of silver brocade she was wearing a forty-foot mantle of violet velvet strewn with fleurs-de-lys. It was supported by two ladies, while a third carried the train and another two held the crown that enclosed her fine blonde hair. Beneath her long, black veils, embroidered in silver, the Queen Mother still looked beautiful. The rear of the procession was brought up by La Grande Mademoiselle.

At the church, the couple sat under a velvet canopy decorated with fleurs-de-lys and plumes. Anne of Austria took up her station on a dais draped in black velvet and topped by a canopy of the same material. The Bishop of Bayonne administered the nuptial blessing.

After the ceremony the King, the two Queens and Monsieur dined together. Louis and Maria Theresa went out onto the balcony to receive the acclamations of the people and threw them handfuls of money. Immediately after supper Louis announced his intention of going to bed. Maria Theresa suffered a momentary qualm, and said that it was too early, but quickly collected herself. The young couple were spared the centuries-old custom of consummating royal marriages publicly. The Queen Mother drew the curtains over the bed, after kissing them and giving them her blessing.

From that time onward, Maria Theresa displayed the same naïve, touching and irksome devotion towards her husband that she maintained throughout her life. Unfortunately, she spoke no French, and Louis little Spanish: there could be no question of sparkling conversation, as with Marie Mancini.

The King announced that the Queen and he would share the same lodgings during the journey back to Paris, and Louis went out of his way to behave irreproachably towards his gentle, ardent wife. Events might have taken a different course had Maria Theresa inherited the head and heart of her mother, Elizabeth of France, who had been Philip iv's strongest support and finest minister. Unhappily, she bore no such resemblance to that great Queen, and any hopes her husband might have had of a companion capable of shouldering part of his heavy burden were quickly dashed. Mentally, as well as physically, the new Queen was subnormal. Beside the King, whom she loved submissively, jealously and absurdly (when he made love to her she would clap her hands at her *lever* the following morning so that the entire court should know), her ruling passions were for cakes and sweets, domestic animals and her dwarf buffoons. Out of the tangle of heredities, it may be that a few drops of Arab blood, mingled with that of the House of Aragon, had gained the ascendancy. Nevertheless, Louis gave the impression of being a happy man when he set out on the triumphal return journey to Paris after a year's absence. After travelling through all parts of his realm in times of rebellion, hardship, famine and war, he was now revisiting them amid general rejoicing and with the blessings of an undivided people who greeted him as the harbinger of order and peace.

Moving from one celebration to the next, they reached Saintes on 27 June. The King announced that the Queens and court were to go on to Saint-Jean-d'Angély, while he himself would pay a visit to his port of La Rochelle. Anne and Mazarin were at their wits' end. Louis had never been more imperious, and the purpose of his unexpected detour was all too apparent. The Cardinal offered to accompany his Majesty and introduce him to the province. Louis refused point-blank. Only Philippe Mancini and two other gentlemen were to go with him.

The visit to La Rochelle and to a few ships was brief and unceremonious. On 28 June the King went to spend the night at Brouage, the true object of the expedition. When he arrived, love, remembrance and grief drove all the constraints of reason and gloire out of his still vulnerable heart. Late into the night, he wandered by the sea, sobbing as if his heart was breaking. When he returned he wanted to sleep in the same room, even the same bed that his

91

beloved had occupied. The following day he rejoined the court at Saint-Jean-d'Angély.

The pilgrimage to Brouage was no last tribute to human frailty: having rediscovered the depth of his passion, Louis had no intention of consummating his sacrifice outright. If he brought Marie's brother with him, it was so that Philippe might send her a description of his reactions. What more touching way of reviving their love? How could Marie fail to be moved? She had the example of her sister Olympe, who had withheld herself before her marriage only to give way after it.

The Queen Mother and the Cardinal saw through his plan and resolved to block it once and for all during the last stages of the journey. Although they lacked their former ascendancy over the King and could no longer use raison d'état, the story of Mlle de La Motte d'Argencourt showed what must be done. They resorted to the same slanders as before. Louis was told that Marie was in love with Prince Charles of Lorraine, and that on the very evening when he was weeping at Brouage, she had flaunted her presence with Charles in the Tuileries, as was her daily custom. Louis could not forgive this unfaithfulness. When they eventually met again at Fontainebleau, he crushed the girl with his disdain. 'I had not reckoned with the coldness and indifference that his Majesty showed towards me,' Marie wrote in her memoirs. 'I confess that they mortally surprised and grieved me.'

Until the time of Mme de Maintenon, the women whom Louis loved paid dearly for the distinction of having pleased him. Marie never recovered from the blow and lived on for fifty years in all the confusion and incoherence of a ruined life. To Louis, on the other hand, the ordeal was beneficial. Almost without his knowledge, Marie had released him from the shyness and inhibitions of adolescence, stimulated his mind and roused his curiosity and imagination – had, so to speak, emancipated him. And he was indebted to her for another lesson. He realized now how much it cost to stifle the voice of reason so as to listen to that of love. From now on, he would know better.

[14]

France in 1660

ON 26 August 1660 Louis XIV re-entered Paris amid unbelievable pomp, as if to celebrate the apotheosis of the monarchy and the assumption of absolute power. The man who exercised this power, the First Minister, did not even have the strength to take his place in the procession. Only his retinue took part as he stood watching beside the Queen Mother from the balcony of the Hôtel de Beauvais.

One serious fissure marred Mazarin's diplomatic edifice. Three months before Charles II had returned to England amid the almost universal joy of subjects delighted to be emerging from the Puritan theocracy. Their new-found loyalty rounded against Cromwell's allies and their insults forced the French ambassador to leave.

Fortunately, the Stuarts still needed Bourbon gold to throw off the tutelage of Parliament, and it was at this point that Anne of Gonzaga took the stage again. Thanks to this famous intriguer, the two dynasties were reconciled and the Queen Mother of France asked the Queen Mother of England for the hand of Princess Henrietta on behalf of Monsieur. La Grande Mademoiselle recounts how the King made jokes at his brother's expense:

> The King would say to Monsieur that he need be in no hurry to go and marry the bones of the Holy Innocents. It is true that the future Madame was very thin: at the same time there is no gainsaying that she was very agreeable. She showed such good grace in all her actions, and was so honourable that anybody who had anything to do with her was pleased with her. She had discovered the secret of making people praise her for her fine carriage, although she was hunch-backed, and even Monsieur did not notice it until after they were married.

In any case, the Princess's physical defects had nothing to do with the matter in hand. The main thing was to restore the balance of Europe and keep France as its arbiter.

After half a century of civil and foreign wars, what kind of kingdom was it that was about to pass out of the hands of a brilliant adventurer into those of a young man convinced of his own divine right?

More populated, richer and better armed than her neighbours, France dominated the continent. She faced a conquered House of Austria, a giant but debilitated Spain and an Emperor now being drawn towards the Adriatic and the Balkans. The League of the Rhine was under her protection, Sweden was her ally and the Italian states were small fry. England and above all Holland were mistresses of the seas, but France was neutralizing the former by playing on her financial needs, and cultivating the traditional friendship of the latter. For the first time since the advent of the Capetian kings, the country did not have a single declared enemy.

The kingdom was vulnerable to the north and east. Lorraine was forbidden troops and fortifications, but then Lorraine was 'ringed' only by Lille, Besançon and Strasbourg. The yawning gaps through which foreign armies had invaded so many times remained open. The vice in which Emperor Charles v and his heirs had done their best to crush France could still function: all it needed was a slight resurgence of energy in Madrid and Vienna.

Similarly, any weakness in the régime would suffice to revive the revolutionary spirit that was dispersed and stunned, but not destroyed. Socially, the Fronde had produced and accentuated the same effects that had ensued from the wars of religion. The higher nobility was having to renounce its powers once and for all. Gone were the times when feudal seigneurs could extend their authority over the countryside, exercise sovereign powers of justice and threaten and even declare war on the monarchy. The lunacy of the Fronde, coming on the heels of so many others, had deprived this class of the means of playing a political role. No dukes were to head a French government again until the nineteenth century.* The only prospects for the impoverished nobles who emerged from the Fronde were to serve in the armies, to shine at court or to bury themselves in their mortgaged châteaux.

The defeat of the Parlement had also been that of the upper bourgeoisie, but did not slow down its rise. Once again civil disturbance, which puts a premium on liquid assets and devalues property, had brought the middle classes new wealth, honours and positions. Mazarin had not troubled to curb abuses, and those which derived from the buying and selling of official posts were going from bad to worse, while litigants continued to be able to purchase verdicts.

Nevertheless, this pernicious system of buying office conferred one outstanding advantage: it opened a back door into the otherwise impenetrable society in which each man's rank was determined by birth. To amass enough money to buy a post that would make its holder an *officier*, the equivalent of a civil servant, and a gentleman – this was the goal of the bourgeoisie, and in particular the merchants, whose calling was not held in such high esteem as in

* Except for the Duc d'Aiguillon under Louis xv. Choiseul is not an exception. He received his his ducal title by way of reward, when he had been in office for some time.

England and Italy. In France, neither fame nor status existed outside the military (literary prestige was in its formative stage). Monsieur Jourdain, Molière's immortal bourgeois who had grown fat on the disorders of his country, fretted at the idea of being condemned to the company of his equals, and contemplated making his début in society.

Trade was in the hands of as many as 124 guilds. At their head were those who did no manual work and were therefore worthy of municipal office – drapers, grocers, haberdashers, furriers, hosiers, gold- and silversmiths. Next on the scale came the physicians, then the surgeons, recognizable from afar by reason of their distinctive garb. On the bottom rung came the artisans. To be a 'mechanic' and work with one's own hands was so far beneath consideration that it nullified all hope of purchasing a post. Nevertheless, even at this lowest level, to ply a trade constituted a kind of privilege.

The artisan in need of assistance could appeal to his *confrérie*. The contributions he paid went to help the needy and to organize the *frairies*, tremendous popular celebrations. His life was a hard one, continually threatened by the worst scourges of nature and politics – epidemics, famines, floods and civil wars – which he had to endure stoically. The artisan was accorded no recognition; no philosopher or writer would ever dream of singing his praises. At least he did not suffer the depredations of the tax collector or military service. If guild discipline was strict, there were fields where it did not operate. The artistic industries were outside it, as were glass-blowing, lace-making, silk hosiery, banking, exchange and the occupations with the title of supplier to the King.

The bulk of the King's subjects were peasants, eking their days out in continual labour that benefited them only minimally, and easy prey to the exactions of the tax-collector, the extortions of civil servants, the avarice of money-lenders, the ravages of campaigning troops and the abuses of their seigneurs. They were nameless men whose toil and sweat made possible the greatness of the realm, indispensable creatures burdened not only with feeding the privileged but underwriting their extravagances. They could hope for neither gratitude nor respect, indeed they were considered stupid, cunning, ill-natured and dirty. Vincent de Paul, himself of peasant stock, called them 'savage tribes.'

They had nevertheless made considerable progress towards land-ownership. In spite of the vast ecclesiastical estates and bond service, small-holdings existed and were spreading. The villein was master of any property he could pay for, and he could pass it on to his eldest son or share it out among his children like La Fontaine's labourer. There were very few other countries where he might have enjoyed such freedom.

At the base of the social system were millions of human beings who were generally illiterate, never went far from their soil and knew nothing of the world to whose evolution they were being sacrificed. At the apex was a brilliant society in which luxury, culture and wit could flourish. The Fronde had closed the Hôtel de Rambouillet, the 'paradise of refinement and gallantry', but its work had had time to come to fruition. The uncouth aristocracy of Henry IV's era had evolved into an urbane society, and writers and thinkers had won the esteem of the public.

In 1660 the court had not regained the position as a centre of influence that it had had under the Valois, and the salons that had given birth to styles of living and thinking no longer existed. It was a transitional period for society as much as for literature and the arts. The great century of Descartes, Pascal, Corneille and Le Nain was drawing to a close. The course of the second cycle was unforeseeable.

Since the wars of religion, the Church of France had renewed itself through devout humanism, mysticism, humility before God and above all the spirit of charity incarnated by Vincent de Paul. The Jansenist movement was growing, and had already alarmed Richelieu with its ascetic doctrine that salvation could only be attained through divine grace of which nobody could be assured, and because of its social influence. First the Sorbonne, then the Pope had come out against the new doctrine, war had broken out between Jansenists and Jesuits, and all France had joined in. Mazarin was soon to advise Louis XIV 'not to put up with the Jansenist sect any longer, nor even their name.'

On the other hand, the Protestant problem seemed to be settled. The Calvinists no longer constituted a state within a state, nor even a political party, but they retained freedom of worship and conscience by virtue of the Edict of Nantes promulgated by Henri IV in 1598. During the Fronde, they had been staunch loyalists. The mere fact of their existence was no obstacle to the French dream of total national unity, and many Protestants were in favour of that unity. They still had scruples, of course, and the theologians were applying themselves to diminishing the differences between the two faiths. Numerous conversions were occurring, not all of them from disinterested motives, and the higher nobility, which had been almost entirely Protestant at the end of the sixteenth century, was gradually returning to the Catholic Church.

The attitude of the Crown to the reformed churches was changing. Although he had often argued against them, Louis XIII had never hindered them in the practice of their religion. On his death-bed, he had merely enjoined the Protestant nobility to undergo conversion. Whether the change is to be ascribed to Anne of Austria's Spanish attitudes or to the Roman upbringing of Mazarin, this tolerance was waning. Louis XIV had been taught that the Reformation was brought about by certain abuses in the Church, long suppressed thanks to the Council of Trent. The obstinacy of the heretics, who had done themselves considerable damage through their attitude, was consequently explicable only in terms either of a blindness that must be cured or of a mask for subversive ideas.

In 1660 Mazarin made up his mind to dissolve the Company of the Saint-Sacrement, originally founded by the Duc de Ventadour in 1627. Its members assisted the needy and opposed heresy, free-thinking and moral laxity with an intolerant, inquisitional ardour not unlike that of the English Puritans. It was not the excesses of their 'pious zeal' that disquieted the Cardinal but the power with which their numbers and their organization as a secret society invested them. Even dissolved, the Company retained a sometimes insidious, sometimes direct influence: the group of free-thinkers centred in the Temple district of Paris was compelled to be on its guard.

The frequent witchcraft trials that had disgraced the two previous reigns were becoming rare, although the fires were not yet extinguished. As late as 1663 Morin, a demented wretch who thought that he was the Messiah, was burned at the stake.

France was a nation of paradoxes. Freedom of the individual was unknown, but a host of collective freedoms checked the power of the central authority. The state subjected to the despotism of a king who could say (if indeed he said it) 'L'État c'est moi', was nevertheless a breached citadel. Even the civil servants were not dependent on it, since their posts, once purchased, permitted no advancement, transfer or revocation.

The sovereign was bound to respect the basic laws regarding justice, property and the succession to the throne. With that reservation, his powers were theoretically unlimited. In fact, they were continually coming up against customs, franchises and privileges: it was impossible to expropriate a man, to tax the poultry that the Parisians imported from their country houses, to levy a tobacco tax in Bayonne or to claim mortgage dues against inhabitants of Perpignan. The local assemblies assessed and levied taxes, floated loans and made the decisions about public works. The municipalities were powerful. Voltaire was to write: 'A man who travels in France changes laws as often as he changes post-horses.'

The King and his ministers were constantly encountering the same kind of difficulties that the American federal government met in its clashes with state legislatures in the nineteenth century. The economy was subject to so many constraints, with such variegated exceptions, that anarchy prevailed. There were often customs barriers between provinces. The idea of free circulation of grain advocated by the capital aroused indignation in other quarters, where famine and its terrible consequences seemed preferable to so evil a practice. Yet in spite of all this, the centralization and unity of the realm was unparalleled in Europe.

Paris was the wonder of every foreign visitor and remained what Montaigne described as 'the glory of France, one of the world's most handsome ornaments.' Yet Sauval could write: 'No town is more muddy or more filthy. Its filth is black and stinking, with an unbearable stench that is offensive and noticeable for several leagues around.' Fifteen thousand horses and eight hundred carriages caused inextricable jams in the streets, which were now and then traversed by herds of animals and which ran with fetid rivulets. The infamous district known as the Cour des Miracles, north of the Halles, was still the refuge of a half-starved, dangerous population of habitual law-breakers. Vagabonds and beggars made up seven per cent of the city's inhabitants.

There was a further contrast between the power of France and the penury of her treasury. The state owed some five million livres to Fouquet, who had been the supreme superintendent of finance since 1659. He was now leading a life of ostentatious arrogance, buying and fortifying the isle of Belle-Isle, off the Breton coast, building the château of Vaux-le-Vicomte, some twenty-five miles from Paris, and setting himself up as a patron of the arts. This juggler was still providing the money necessary to Mazarin's enterprises, but at an outrageous cost. Colbert hated him because he both disapproved of his conduct and coveted his post. At the time of the Treaty of the Pyrenees, he was drawing up an implacable report against Fouquet, denouncing: '. . . the appalling profits and overbearing manner of the administrators; the exorbitant commissions of the tax farmers; the financial expedients and scandalous profits of the treasury book-keepers; the embezzlement of public funds; sharp practices and the purchase of old unredeemed bills on the treasury at three or four per cent of their nominal value, which are then reassigned against solvent funds and repaid in full.'

Colbert advised relieving Fouquet of his post and arraigning him before a court of justice. Mazarin's only response was to order him to make his peace with the superintendent, and the triumphant Fouquet had his own praises sung by the poets he patronized, while the wealth of France continued to be frittered away solely for the benefit of ministers and tax farmers.

It is at this point that a puzzling contradiction emerges. In 1630 Gaston of Orléans had written to Louis xiii:

Only a third of your subjects in the country eat normal food, another third live only on bread and roots, the rest are not merely reduced to begging but languish in such lamentable want that half of them actually die of hunger while the other half subsist on nothing but acorns, plants and the like, as animals do. And the least pitiable of these eat only the bran and blood that they collect out of the runnels from butchers' shops.

In 1694 Fénelon was to write to Louis xiv: 'Your people are dying of hunger . . . All France is nothing more than a great, ravaged hospital, devastated and without supplies.'

The same complaint was repeated hundreds of times between these two letters. Yet these same Frenchmen, nine-tenths of whom were said to be suffering without respite, were to gain the hegemony of Europe, hold its combined forces at bay, win several wars, annex five provinces, transform the structure of their country, rebuild their towns, construct palaces, fortify frontiers, give birth to countless geniuses and impose their style and culture on the western world. Either the laws of economics are nonsensical, or else this phenomenon never happened. France could not have become predominant in war, culture and splendour while the majority of her sons were foundering in poverty.

These facts must be taken into consideration before we accept unreservedly the evidence of rebellious princes, embittered diarists, hostile prelates, administrators whose first concern was to prevent their provinces from being too heavily taxed and, above all, taxpayers who were perpetually acting out a comedy of penury. Certainly there was terrible destitution, principally due to the passage of armies, natural calamities and famines against which no remedy could be found. The effects of the bad harvests of 1661 and 1662 took on the proportions of a national disaster. But La Fontaine's rich ploughman and singing cobbler were by no means exceptional.

Louis le Nain's peasant models were sturdy women and delightful children. The youth tuning his violin to entertain the *Repas du Paysan* is no pathetic figure. If the setting does not evoke opulence, neither is it in the least squalid. The clothing is necessarily wretched, since it is one of those clues that might give away to the tax-collectors the existence of the écus that will be dug up one day to buy a field or a mill from the dandy impatient to convert them into velvet and gilt.

In fact, the average Frenchman's purchasing power remained at an adequate level: the lowliest labourer earned the daily equivalent, after being fed, of 3·8 lb of corn during the Fronde and 6·1 lb at the end of Louis xiv's reign. The race was growing and multiplying. With nineteen million inhabitants, France far outnumbered her neighbours. Life-expectancy was greater among peasants and artisans than at court, perhaps because they were less exposed to the physicians. With the exception of the Dutch and English, there was not a commoner in Europe who did not have reason to envy the subjects of the Bourbons.

There is one indication which is not ambiguous. After the continual ordeals they had undergone since the death of Henry iv, the French had every right to demand a rest. Instead, they seethed with energy, created, argued and thought of glory and conquests. They would obey a strong hand readily, but would soon unseat their master if they sensed that he was unworthy. Louis xiv knew it, and he never forgot it.

[15]

Armed Vigil

WITH his romantic crisis at an end, Louis went back into his shell and became Mazarin's pupil once again. Convinced of Marie's unfaithfulness, he forgot his resentment of the Minister whose lessons were still indispensable to him. The face he showed to the court during the autumn of 1660 gave fresh proof of his powers of self-control and dissimulation. Batista Nani, the Venetian ambassador, wrote to the Senate of the Republic:

His favourite exercises are military, and he finds his main diversion in the company of his three hundred mounted musketeers ... His Majesty is their captain. He rides at their head, instructs them in discipline and makes them perform exercises and form squadrons. For the rest, hunting, dancing, balls and gambling, to which his Majesty is more than moderately addicted, are his favourite pastimes ... He is eager for information about affairs, but considers himself as yet too young and inexperienced to direct them ... No one has seen him in a rage or heard him complain or lie, even in jest. *He affects the utmost indifference towards everybody, to such a degree that even among his familiars none can boast of any evidence of partiality or trust. This quality, which is rarely encountered in a prince, is quite astounding in a monarch in the flower of youth* ... The young King reveres his mother ... He is completely in love with his wife[!]. He loves his brother most tenderly, but all his affection seems to go to the Cardinal ... It must be confessed that there is a profound sympathy and submission of spirit and intelligence which incline a great prince to depend on the genius of a particular man ... He sees him several times a day ... As soon as he has finished dressing he goes to see the Cardinal ... These visits are made without ceremony and in a quite familiar manner. The Cardinal does not go to meet him and does not see him out. If he is busy, the King is content to wait ... Generally the interview lasts for several hours, in the course of which the Cardinal brings him up to date with everything, instructs him and moulds him. Thus his Majesty knows everything from a good source.

Mazarin was behaving like a real monarch. It was he whom the court followed wherever he chose to go. No one had free access to him, and if anybody was so inept a courtier as to ask a favour of the King direct, he was lost. The Cardinal did not allow the Queen Mother to have anything to do with affairs, treated her disrespectfully and did not conceal his impatience with her. Never before had Mazarin given such free rein to his love of luxury and wealth. Power and riches were his weapons against the fear of approaching death, since his health was declining at a frightening rate. Racked by gout and gravel, he was also suffering from hydrothorax.

In this condition, the Cardinal pacified the north of Europe and made France the guarantor of the Peace of Oliva (3 May 1660), which restored the equilibrium between Sweden, Poland and Denmark. Concerned about Turkish victories in Transylvania, he also sent troops to Crete to reinforce the Venetians. It seems possible that at that time he was considering a resumption of the policy that France had abandoned since the time of Francis I, of forming a coalition of Christian nations to oppose Islam. If this sceptic really was entertaining an idea so contrary to the principles of the Valois, Henry IV and Richelieu, the explanation is indubitably to be found in his papal ambitions.

On 26 October 1660 an event occurred that seemed to have nothing to do with these vast designs. Monsieur's players – Molière and his company – who had recently been installed in the Palais Royal, performed in the Cardinal's apartments at the Louvre. The King was present, but incognito, leaning on the back of his minister's armchair.

At the end of the performance of *L'Étourdi* and *Les Précieuses Ridicules*, which were still enjoying great success after a whole year, Molière was summoned before his Majesty and his Eminence, who presented him with a gift of three thousand livres: even if he was the director of a company, an actor was still a man to whom one gave tips when he had pleased. The next day Louis told Mazarin: 'This man Molière suits me, he is amusing and clearsighted' – not a bad judgement on a new author who was overturning established ideas, coming from a young man so ignorant of literature. In his own turn, the Cardinal told Colbert, through whose agency the court had already shown favour to the former protégé of the Prince de Conti: 'Molière must continue to receive favours. He shows promise of a comic genius which could be very useful if certain circumstances arose.' Mazarin was taking a long view, but his illness was proceeding apace.

Shortly afterwards Princess Henrietta returned from London with a dowry voted by Parliament. In the space of a few months yesterday's Cinderella had given way to a young girl who, while not beautiful in the ordinary sense, was nevertheless captivating and enchanting. No one was immune to that charm, not even Monsieur, until the moment when he discovered the promiscuity of the girl whom Charles II called 'Minette'.

While the younger members of the court were celebrating, the doctors had joined in consultation and agreed that they were powerless to save Mazarin. Their principal, Quénaud, took him the news.

'How long have I left to live?' the sick man asked.

'Two months at least.'

'It is enough.'

On 6 February 1661 a raging fire broke out at the Louvre, not far from Mazarin's apartments, forcing him to flee in the middle of the night. This event shook him considerably. He was taken to Vincennes, where he was joined on 11 February by the King and his mother.

During the following days, master and disciple were closeted together for long periods. Louis absorbed these final lessons eagerly and was later to dictate a memorandum, albeit an incomplete one, in which Mazarin's political testament was summarized under ten headings. The Cardinal enjoined the King 'to maintain the Church, as being its eldest son,' although not without keeping an eye on its members; to treat the nobility with trust and kindness; to keep the magistrates 'within the bounds of their power'; to lighten taxation; to convince all his subjects that the monarch was the sole master, the sole dispenser of favours, and thus to suppress the office of First Minister; to forestall divisions among the members of the Council; to punish any individual whatsoever who took the slightest political initiative without his own sanction; not to permit scandal or impiety at court.

Louis xiv did not follow this last precept, nor did he show any trust in the nobility, and he only toyed with the idea of reducing taxes. All the other counsels became articles of faith for him, so that in 1686 the Venetian ambassador, Venier, could write: 'One might say that Mazarin is still alive, that he reigns from the depths of his tomb as once he reigned from his cabinet.'

Never were there more intrigues and expectations in any court than during the last days of Cardinal Mazarin. Women with a claim to beauty flattered themselves that they would hold sway over a twenty-two-year-old prince whom love had already seduced to the point of offering his crown to his mistress; young courtiers believed that they would revive the rule of favourites; each minister hoped for the first position; not one of them thought that a king brought up remote from affairs would dare to take the burden of government upon himself.[1]

Fouquet enjoyed the Queen Mother's protection and believed that he would be the Cardinal's successor. He was reckoning without Colbert, who was determined to bar his path and to try his own luck. Louis was preparing himself in silence, apparently deaf to these rumours. He had already been tempted on many occasions to take over the government. Now his hand was being forced by the unexpected suddenness of the event.

To Louis' great surprise, Mazarin informed him that he was making him the sole beneficiary of his estate – the largest known fortune. Although hitherto restricted to an allowance, Louis' was a royal response; he refused. A monarch did not receive goods from one of his servants, above all when he had allowed that servant to amass them by closing his eyes to his methods.

Mazarin, moved to tears even though he was on bad terms with his family, gave thanks to God, to the King, and especially to Colbert, who had anticipated his Majesty's reaction and hit on this method of reconciling the worldly and spiritual interests of his patron. Colbert received his reward in one of their final interviews, Mazarin warmly commended him to the King and abandoned Fouquet.

Colbert was no stranger to Louis and had even played a part in his love affair, receiving Marie Mancini's letters at the time of her exile at Brouage and conveying them by his own hand. A kind of complicity already existed between the two, which fore-ordained that the austere financier would find himself saddled with taking care of his master's mistresses and bastards.

Now that he was free to do as he pleased with his wealth, the Cardinal shared it out among his nephews and nieces, reserving the greater portion for Hortense. Nevertheless, he gave a great many jewels to the royal family. Condé and Turenne received a diamond apiece.

On 28 February Hortense married the Duc de La Meilleraie. Mazarin had arranged the contract between Marie and Constable Colonna. He would dearly have loved to see the marriage take place before his death, but the signatures were a long time arriving from Italy.

The King, bored at Vincennes when he was not with the Cardinal, yielded to the temptation of spending evenings at the Palais Mazarin, where the Mancinis were staying. He and Marie now had the meeting that he had been avoiding since their encounter at Fontainebleau. It seems that everything was explained and that their affair almost came to life again. Louis suggested that Marie should marry a French nobleman instead of the Constable, but Marie refused. After having almost been a queen, she did not want to become a favourite, and the King seems not to have insisted unduly, perhaps sensing that he would be running the risk of tarnishing the brilliance of his accession to full power.

On 3 March the Cardinal took a turn for the worse. Anne of Austria could hear his groans from her own apartment. Still she did not show any signs of grief that would accord with the feelings expressed in her letter of 30 June the previous year ('To the last breath, Anne is yours'). In fact she showed no evidence of grief at all, although her son's was intense.

Mazarin was to be a man of surprises until his final breath. People had always jeered at his cowardice, yet now Mme de Motteville, who detested him, had to testify that 'he looked upon death with such steadfastness that he told M. Joly (his confessor) that he had qualms about not fearing it enough.' On 7 March he took his leave of Louis and Anne of Austria. The King was in tears when he left. That evening he summoned the Council for the first time, but hardly spoke a word. They admired his regal bearing without in the least suspecting what was going on in his mind. Each of the ministers watched unavailingly for a sign to found his hopes on. Only one, Le Tellier, wondered whether the King was proposing to govern in person.

The day of 8 March was an armed vigil. Thanks to his memoirs,[2] we know what thoughts passed through the mind of the young sovereign:

> I never stopped testing myself in private, confiding in no one, reasoning alone and in myself about all the events that arose, full of hope and joy when I sometimes found that my first thoughts were the same as the final conclusions of clever and accomplished people, and fundamentally convinced that I had not been placed and preserved on the throne with so great a passion to do well without being provided with the means.

Louis XIV's decision to take control was almost as grave as if he had mounted a coup d'état. The monarchy had not governed France for half a century. Louis XIII had always seemed to efface himself behind Richelieu. Further back, Henry IV had been an exception. The last Valois had been under the thumb of their mother, Catherine de Médicis. Henry II was pliable, and at the age of twenty Francis I thought only of battles and left a free hand to his mother, Louise of Savoy. No French King had taken power at his accession for two hundred years, since Louis XI, a man of mature years and inured to the game of politics. It was the same story in other countries. Neither the Empire since Charles VI, Spain since Philip II nor England since Elizabeth I had had a sovereign capable of imposing his own exclusive prestige and authority and of identifying his person with the achievements of a reign.

Louis' main motive in running his own affairs was probably the love of *gloire* that consumed him like one of Corneille's characters:

> In my heart I valued above all else, more than life itself, a high reputation ... A governing and overriding passion for greatness and *gloire* stifles all others in [kings]. The love of *gloire* has the same subtleties and, if I may put it so, the same timidities as the most tender passions.

Following Mazarin's advice, Louis was determined not to appoint a First Minister, 'there being nothing more shameful than the spectacle of all the functions on one side, and the mere title of king on the other.' He weighed up his new responsibilities: 'In the high rank that we hold, the slightest errors always have troublesome consequences.' At the same time, his feet were still firmly on the ground: 'The function of kings consists mainly in letting good sense take its course.' But the conviction of the dogmatic quality of his authority gave him unshakeable self-assurance:

> [God] who has given kings to men wished them to be respected as His lieutenants, reserving to Himself alone the right to examine their conduct ... There is no maxim more established by Christianity than this humble submission of subjects towards those who are placed over them.

When the time came near the King fell asleep at the Queen's side without betraying the slightest sign of anxiety. He had given his instructions to Pierrette Dufour, his former nurse, now the Queen's chambermaid, who slept, according to custom, in the same room. When Pierrette heard the King stir in the early morning, she approached and silently gave him the pre-arranged sign. Mazarin had died between two and three o'clock in the morning.

Taking care not to wake the Queen, Louis got up, dressed and went to the Cardinal's apartment. He seemed overwhelmed, and ordered the court to observe full mourning, an honour strictly reserved for members of the royal family. Some writers have tried to see this as proof of the secret marriage, but the opposite seems more likely: if the marriage had really taken place, Louis would have taken care not to provide that kind of confirmation.

Immediately after dining Louis set out for Paris, having instructed his ministers to come to the Louvre at seven the following morning. He shared his mother's carriage, since the pregnant Maria Theresa was travelling by sedan chair. He still showed his grief, which caused the Queen Mother some irritation. According to Mme de Motteville, Anne of Austria 'was the first to tell those who kept harping on the death of the Cardinal *that he must no longer be mentioned.*' It was Anne's revenge for the self-effacement that her creature had forced on her. Since Mazarin had existed only thanks to the Queen, it was for the Queen to consign him back to oblivion.

Part Two

The Rising Sun
[1661-80]

[1]

Dictatorship by Divine Right

At seven o'clock on the morning of 10 March 1661, Chancellor Séguier and the ministers and secretaries of state gathered around the armchair of his Majesty, who remained standing. The eight men looked into his face with feelings that ranged from curiosity to fear: it was a grave and inscrutable face and the large, drooping nose and jutting, tight-lipped mouth, apparently incapable of smiling, accentuated the underlying cold, enigmatic, self-willed quality of mind.

The King addressed Séguier in what was to become his characteristic tone, that of a man 'master of himself and of the universe':

Monsieur, I have called you together with my ministers and secretaries of state to tell you that up to the present I have been pleased to leave the government of my affairs to the late Cardinal. It is time for me to govern them myself. You will assist me with your advice *when I ask for it*. Outside the normal course of state business, which I do not intend to change, I request and command you, Mister Chancellor, to seal no orders except at my command and without having discussed them with me, unless a secretary of state brings them to you on my behalf. And you, my secretaries of state, I order you to sign nothing, not even a safe-conduct or a passport, without my command . . . And you, Mister Superintendent Fouquet . . . I request you to make use of Colbert, whom the late Cardinal commended to me. As for Lionne [Secretary of State for Foreign Affairs], he is assured of my regard and I am satisfied with his services.

Incredulous amazement greeted these words. No one dreamed that a new and revolutionary phase in the history of France and the world was beginning. Until the early twentieth century, men always thought of revolutions as movements originating among the people and intended, at least in theory, to liberate or serve them. The meaning of the abrupt change that took place in 1661 has thus been distorted. In the eyes of an historian who has observed authoritarian revolutions in our own times, some of them originating at the summit, it stands out far more clearly. When Louis xiv made up his mind to rule, he was not behaving like the respectable heir of an ancestral monarchic tradition, but as an individual, as a Caesar might have done following a plebiscite, perhaps a coup d'état. Although born out of the lessons of Mazarin, the concept was an original one, implying the establishment of a dictatorship such as France had never experienced, and which is not to be confused with modern dictatorships.

The modern dictator, usually thrown up by a mass movement, must constantly maintain and increase his popularity by means of spectacular achievements; at the height of his power he remains dependent on the turn of fortune. The dictator by divine right need not be concerned about his position, his reverses or the whims of public opinion. This allows him the serenity and patience of those who participate in things eternal.

In the bitterness of his exile the Comte de Chambord, legitimist claimant to the French throne from 1843 to 1883, would remark of Louis XIV, with some truth, that he had been the first of the Bonapartes. Like Napoleon, Louis wanted to hold in his grasp not only the government but also the multifarious aspects of the nation's life, from court protocol to troop movements and theological controversies. No marriage of any importance, no plan for a new road was to be decided without his approval. It was the ascendancy of one man over an entire country, to the point where their identities would merge and their separation would not be imaginable without perplexity or distress.

Here the analogies stop. Napoleon put his finger on the essential difference when he said that whereas the kings, his enemies, had no reason to fear the return home after losing a battle, he himself was in no position to run that risk. Not one person dreamed of supplanting the divine right despot whose grip would choke factions, annihilate parties and erase the ideological divisions so dear to the French – and all this through a generally accepted discipline, not through violence.

Certainly Louis had excellent channels of information, and even created the modern police, but his authority was never backed up by the kind of police terror that has operated under twentieth-century totalitarian régimes. Then too, in the twentieth century there have been dictators who were a prey to their own passions, fury and exaltations, sometimes close to hysteria. During an existence that was always exposed to the public gaze, Louis XIV lost his composure only five times in fifty-four years.

From the beginning of his assumption of full power, the King applied himself unflaggingly to affairs. He set himself a strict time-table which gradually became as immutable as a law of nature. He devoted six to eight hours daily to work:

... informed about everything, listening to the least of my subjects, knowing at any time the numbers and quality of my troops and the state of my strongholds, unceasingly giving my instructions upon every requirement, dealing directly with ministers from abroad, receiving and reading dispatches, making some of the replies myself, regulating the income and expenditure of my State and keeping my affairs secret as no other man has done before me.

Government gave Louis a profound pleasure: 'I do not know what other pleasure we would not give up for this one . . . I felt an enjoyment difficult to express.' From the first, he was able to dominate his ministers. They were quite overawed by his natural majesty, inimitable courtesy and inscrutability, the manner of listening gravely then giving his decision with a single word. Often he would go into minute detail about some matter, without a moment's warning, 'when [the minister] least expected it, so that he should realize that I might do the same in other contexts at any time.'

The historian Pierre Gaxotte has called Louis' reign the dictatorship of work. It was also that of secrecy. The King drew an impenetrable veil over his own feelings and intentions, and intended to protect the affairs of state in the same way. He made it clear that indiscretion was an unforgivable crime in his eyes, and ministers and other civil servants soon became as secretive as himself. There is a complete antithesis between methods of governments involving the obligation to give daily explanations – whether true or false – to public opinion, and the mystery of Louis' procedures. Not that the accompanying inconvenience of these procedures escaped the King:

I have devoted some thought to the position, in this respect hard and rigorous, of kings who owe a public accounting for all their actions to all the world and to all centuries, yet cannot do so in their own times without violating their greatest interests and revealing the secret of their conduct.

This was one of the reasons that led him to have his 'memoirs for the instruction of the Dauphin' drawn up: 'I shall not be displeased if you have here the means to redress history, should it misinterpret or misjudge.'

Nicolas Fouquet, the most brilliant and intelligent of Louis' ministers, misjudged completely. He was sure that the urge to work hard would soon give way to the attractions of pleasure, and was quite determined to do everything in his power to allow the King to drown in them. Having succumbed to his own system, the corrupter believed himself capable of corrupting the King. Louis had had a fairly dull youth, under the rod of a miserly teacher. The superintendent's intention was to 'spoil' him in the literal sense, whereupon affairs would devolve quite naturally upon himself.

Colbert's appointment as Intendant of Finances was not enough to put Fouquet on his guard. His spies may well have discovered that the King and Mazarin's confidential assistant were working together every evening, but he was blinded by his own cynical contempt for others. Colbert, on the other hand, had quickly realized what kind of man Louis xiv was, and his insight made his fortune. The complicity that had grown up between them at the time of the Mancini affair took on a different dimension now that the draper's son was secretly unravelling Fouquet's accounts and bringing his malversations to the King's attention.

Although Louis XIV and Colbert were utterly dissimilar, their cooperation was necessary for the achievement of a grand design, and they valued one another at their true worth. Louis realized that the low-born, sombre clerk, crabbed, unattractive and morose, would be the ideal instrument of his own authority. Colbert's iron exterior concealed a flexibility that enabled him quickly to adjust to his new master. The servant of Mazarin had been obliged to involve himself (at no small personal gain) in shady deals and projects; the servant of Louis XIV was to gain favour by virtue of his integrity, intransigence, loyalty to the service of the state and above all his refusal to accept the least advantage that did not stem from the King.

Louis took two months to come to his decision. By the beginning of May he was determined to bring down Fouquet as soon as the collection of taxes would not be endangered by his fall.

Marie Mancini married Colonna in the Louvre and set out for Italy, after seeing Louis lean over her carriage door to say his final farewell. Her place was taken by Henrietta of England, whose marriage to Monsieur was celebrated almost at the same time.

Since the moment of her betrothal, Madame, as Henrietta now became, had been playing havoc with men's hearts and captivating their minds. Age was going out of fashion at court, which still numbered not more than one or two hundred people, and it was the reign of youth – proud, turbulent, debauched, cruel and Rabelaisian. Maria Theresa could hold no sway over this society, which found its true Queen in Madame. At the end of April, when his brother and sister-in-law joined him at Fontainebleau, it was the King's turn to be overwhelmed. The ugly, poverty-stricken cousin, so insignificant only a short while before, was truly the only companion worthy of him. Mignard consecrated the apotheosis of 'Minette' when he audaciously painted her as a mythological shepherdess sitting by the side of Apollo-Louis under the protection of Love.

The King's relationship with Marie Mancini had been exemplarily chaste for two years. The innocence of Mignard's two sitters was less certain: Monsieur was jealous, and the three Queens, Maria Theresa, Anne and Henrietta of France, indignant. Louise de La Vallière, the most reticent of Henrietta's maids of honour, was slightly built, rather lame and moderately pretty. She was appointed to divert suspicion, but it happened that she was in love with the King, who was moved by her artless, disinterested affection. Within a few days she had supplanted the haughty Stuart, who took her revenge by embarking on an affair with the Comte de Guiche, her husband's special favourite, so that the passion of Louis and Louise and the war between Monsieur and Madame broke out simultaneously.

All this was to Louis' advantage. The ill feeling between his brother and sister-in-law, cunningly inflamed, but kept alight by the follies of one or the other, was to enable him to hold the balance and to play at being the god of a household which might have caused him problems in more normal circumstances.[1] As for Louise, who was sincere, pure and totally lacking in ambition, it was a near-miracle that a King should have found this awed little girl for a mistress. Louis himself was fascinated to find himself adored, not as a sovereign, but as a lover. Marie had enslaved and dominated him. Louise was at his feet, gratifying his vanity without jeopardizing the smallest fraction of his liberty.

As soon as he got wind of the affair, Fouquet sent an obliging friend, Mme du Plessis-Bellièvre, to offer Mlle de La Vallière twenty thousand pistoles on his behalf and promise that she need want for nothing from now on. The gentle child bridled and replied that 'two hundred thousand livres would not make her take a wrong step.'

The story reached the King's ears, and he was outraged. It was not to be endured that a subject should offer to protect the King's mistress. The superintendent was working like a beaver for his own downfall. He sold his high judicial office of Procureur Général to the Parlement, which had made him practically invulnerable, and decided to invite his Majesty to a sumptuous entertainment at his château of Vaux, with the idea of impressing the young man into taking the full measure of his minister's power, wealth and *gloire*.

Louis XIV did indeed take their measure when he crossed the threshold of Vaux. The splendour of the gardens, fountains, illuminations, ballets and feasting proved that Fouquet had built up his own opulent state within the state. The humiliated Louis compared all this luxury, amassed at his own expense, with his own archaic and dilapidated châteaux. If Anne of Austria had not restrained him he would have interrupted the fête by putting the master of the house under arrest.

Yet this was not the main consequence of the visit to Vaux. Even as Louis was feeling insulted, he was also receiving an indelible impression from the poetry of the gardens and the orderly enchantments that laid mythology under tribute to art. He swore to himself that he would recreate them on a scale worthy of a King of France, and that henceforward the geniuses of the age, from Molière to the landscape gardener Le Nôtre, would be in his own employ, not that of a shady financier. The revolution that was to sweep through Europe and transform the way of life of the powerful and the leisured was conceived on that evening of 17 August 1661.

Louis' hatred of Fouquet now fused with Colbert's. It was the first instance of the implacable resolve with which the King could pursue a man who fell from grace. Neither time, circumstance nor the punishment of its hapless object ever quenched his resentment. Fouquet had been ill enough advised to try to provide himself with a territorial base by fortifying Belle-Isle and the

Breton coast, and Louis made up his mind to overthrow him in the very province where he felt most secure. The court was transferred to Nantes, where the King presided over a meeting of the Council on the morning of 5 September. After its conclusion he took his leave of Fouquet, smiling to allay any nascent suspicions, and soon afterward M. d'Artagnan, commander of a brigade of musketeers, arrested Nicolas Fouquet. As he was being conducted to a barred carriage, the prisoner asked his captor 'not to attract attention', thus demonstrating his utter lack of understanding of Louis, who wanted precisely such attention, as a way of telling the world that the time had come for him to take charge of his own affairs.

The government was now reconstituted, and Villeroy was appointed president of a modified Council of Finances on which Colbert sat as a mere intendant. The post of Controller General was not to be created for him until 1665, after the abolition of the post of Superintendent.

The High Council which dealt with important affairs was made up of men whom the King summoned to his counsels without their receiving any official appointment, and this alone conferred the title of minister on them. Louis reduced the number of ministers from twenty-four to three – Le Tellier, Lionne and Colbert. The Chancellor also attended the Council, and the secretaries of state confined themselves to making reports and noting down decisions. Among these secretaries was Le Tellier's son, Louvois, reversioner to the post of Secretary for War.

Ministerial specialization did not exist, but the Chancellor supervised justice, foreign affairs were the domain of Lionne, war of Le Tellier. With his obsessive appetite for work, Colbert took over almost all the others, from finance to the police: he controlled trade, public works, labour, the colonies, the navy, fine arts and the King's household.

Like his master, Colbert had a Cartesian bent, and his first move was to set about transforming the administration into a monarchic bureaucracy, unified and centralized. No other country possessed such an organization: leaving aristocratic governors to represent the King's splendour in the provinces, he concentrated the real power into the hands of administrators sprung from the common people. To the horror of the aristocracy Louis XIV, who held that the very fact of his function removed such a man from his original class, ennobled most of the principal clerks; ministers, as holders of a fraction of the supreme authority, had to be addressed as 'Monseigneur' and accorded the same precedence as a prince. The service of the King bestowed rights equal to those of birth.

Louis did not summon a single member of his family, or any duke or nobleman, to his Council, and Anne of Austria was so hurt that she announced her retirement to Val-de-Grâce. Her son restrained her, as she had hoped, but did not give way either on the political question or in the matter of his amours. In any case, Maria Theresa was still convinced that only a princess could touch the heart of a king; she had stilled her fears of Madame, and could not imagine a La Vallière. On 1 November 1661 she gave birth to the Grand Dauphin. When he saw his son the King forgot his dignity, rushed to the window and shouted to the crowd: 'The Queen has had a boy!'

The new-born child was an insurance for the future and saved his father from the uncertainties that had weakened Richelieu's position for so long. The Dauphin was the finishing touch to an apparently indestructible edifice.

A grave diplomatic incident in London, almost coinciding with a crisis brought about by the ruinous effects of a bad harvest, was now to put the King to the test. The long-standing dispute between the Kings of France and Spain over the matter of precedence came to a head between their ambassadors at a ceremony in England. The Spanish servants of the Baron of Vatteville, supported by the populace, killed the carriage-horses belonging to the Comte d'Estrade and his men were injured and put to rout.

Louis did not consult anybody. In spite of Lionne's fears, he dismissed the Spanish ambassador in Paris, recalled his own from Madrid, together with d'Estrade, and demanded that Charles II punish those responsible and that Philip IV make a reparation that would sanction the primacy of France: 'Truly I would have taken so just a grievance to the furthest extremes, and even in that evil I would have accounted as good the subject of a legitimate war in which I might acquire honour.' An astonished Europe discovered the existence of an absolutely new diplomatic system. Louis XIV replaced the mercurial resilience of Mazarin with an implacable hauteur and calculated brutality that allowed him to negotiate subsequently with an artfulness worthy of his master.

The King of Spain was forced to humble himself and put his seal on the hegemony of the Bourbons – all without a shot being fired. An ambassador extraordinary came to the Louvre and assured Louis, in the presence of leading members of the court and the entire diplomatic corps, of Philip IV's regrets. He promised in the name of his king 'that the Spanish ambassadors and ministers would no longer vie with those of France.' This resounding success marked the beginning of a policy of prestige whose aggressive imperialist character may be repugnant, but which corresponded exactly to the nation's aspirations.

Some months later, following a similar incident in Rome, Louis XIV threatened to send an army into Italy and the Parlement summonsed the Pope (de Retz's protector) and seized the papal state of Avignon. Alexander VII did not dare even to mention excommunication, whereas his predecessors would not have hesitated. He gave way completely, and the King took the opportunity to gain the gratitude of the Dukes of Parma and Modena by having certain lands restored to them.

Having spared neither the Supreme Pontiff nor his own father-in-law, he had no cause to be any less uncompromising towards the impoverished Charles ii of England. At Louis' command, the French fleet refused to salute the British flag before their own was saluted, a tribute claimed by England as the due of her maritime superiority. Henceforward, Europe knew who was 'the greatest king in the world.' France was lost in admiration.

Meanwhile, the country was still in the grip of a famine which seemed as if it must surely start a chain-reaction of disasters. On Colbert's advice, Louis again took a revolutionary, one might even say a socialist step:

> I compelled the most prosperous provinces to relieve the others [a drastic innovation], and private individuals to open their shops and put their provisions on sale at fair prices. I sent out orders in all directions to obtain as much grain as possible by sea from Danzig and other foreign lands; I had it purchased at my own expense and I distributed it free, the greater part to the common people of the towns . . . I had the rest sold to those who could afford it, but at a very modest price, from which the profit, if there was any, went towards the relief of the poor, who by that means derived from the more wealthy a voluntary, natural and tangible assistance.

Even more socialist was his attitude to the bourgeois, who had taken advantage of the crisis to acquire government bonds at low prices and were now receiving exorbitant interest. The bonds were bought back 'by paying the same price which [the holder] had paid and deducting from this basic sum whatever he had received in dividends over and above the legitimate interest.'

By these means, the state and the towns were relieved of an enormous burden. It was the King in person who, mindful of Mazarin's last advice, reduced the *tailles,* the direct taxes that were crushing the peasants. The revenue from these fell from fifty-three to thirty-nine million livres, collectors' commissions were cut, and a special court proceeded ruthlessly against corrupt financiers. The wealth of businessmen, their relations and heirs, was investigated. For the first time since Sully, the state finances were put in order, but unlike Henry iv, Louis did not leave it to a single minister to manage his wealth:

> I had already subjected myself to signing in person all the warrants that were issued for the smallest expenses of the State. I decided that this was not enough, and chose to take the trouble of writing in a little book which I always kept by me, on one side the monthly income I ought to be receiving, on the other all the sums disbursed on my own orders in that month . . . The weightiest matters are nearly always brought about by means of the most trivial, and what would be baseness in a prince were he acting sheerly out of love of money becomes eminence and loftiness when his ultimate object is the welfare of his subjects, the execution of an infinity of grand designs, and his own splendour and magnificence.

The first year of Louis' personal rule had yielded significant achievements. In 1662, on the occasion of the famous Fête de Carrousel, the King took to himself the symbol that is still linked with his name:

I chose to assume the form of the sun, because of the unique quality of the radiance that surrounds it; the light it imparts to the other stars, which compose a kind of court; the fair and equal share of that light that it gives to all the various climates of the world; the good it does in every place, ceaselessly producing joy and activity on every side; the untiring motion in which it yet seems always tranquil; and that constant, invariable course from which it never deviates or diverges – assuredly the most vivid and beautiful image of a great monarch. Those who saw me ruling with a degree of ease, unhampered by the many cares that royalty has to assume, persuaded me to add the globe of the earth, and for a motto *Nec Pluribus Impar*: by which they meant, agreeably flattering the ambitions of a young king, that, equal in myself to so many things, I would certainly yet be equal to ruling other empires.

[2]

Idol of the Nation

LOUIS XIV's enterprise could not have succeeded had it not been in harmony with the unanimous will both of the élite and the masses. The French were clamouring for stability and order, but Louis held a still more powerful card: he was the absolute personification of a nation at the height of its powers, bursting with energy, young, and no less infatuated with grandeur and gloire than the King himself. Louis XIII, a morose and stoical monarch, had been venerated at a distance. The people had execrated Richelieu and despised Mazarin. It was a blessing, even a deliverance, suddenly to see the supreme authority incarnated in this proud, high-minded, handsome boy. France fell in love with her King.

The nobility and the masses were not tamed overnight: they yielded to a wave of enthusiasm and infatuation, and their obedience stemmed from a state of mind rather than any compulsion. It is no distortion to compare Louis' popularity with that which in our own age deifies a champion or star. He had already accumulated too much bitter experience to have any illusions about the durability of this miracle, and consequently was all the more able to turn it to advantage. The turbulence, ambition and treachery of the upper nobility remained his abiding concern.

The King conceived the bold plan of taming these wild beasts, shutting them in the gilded cage of the court and transforming their minor wars into futile rivalries. He would corrupt them with gambling, cripple them with pleasure, make their fortunes and the future of their families dependent not on the fear they inspired but on their skill in pleasing, and eventually remove them from public life so as to devote them exclusively to the army and to the *domestic* service of their master. Louis could never have put his scheme into effect had not his prestige dazzled an arrogant nobility raised in a seditious tradition.

The process worked with startling speed. Soon a look, a smile or a royal expression were enough to make or break a man, a word could freeze or burn, and the least sensitive of people fell ill because they had *displeased*.

The King required the continual attendance of his gentlemen and compelled them to desert their lands and châteaux for the uncomfortable

118

apartments of his own residences. He created a situation in which absence constituted the worst of all misfortunes, and the great trembled at the prospect of exile (to their own estates!) when their fathers had not quailed even before Richelieu and the scaffold.

Etiquette was one of the main cogs of the machine. It had existed in France long before Louis xiv, for Henry iii had drawn up the first code in 1585, but now it became an instrument whose intricacy and complexity are almost unimaginable today. The idea did not originate in Spain, as has often been claimed. It went back to the dukes of Burgundy, ancestors of the Habsburgs and therefore of Louis xiv. In the fifteenth century Philip the Good had wanted to surround the throne with the kind of ritual and ceremonial that would place it above ordinary men. Philip ii of Spain had developed this technique so far that he had transformed the monarch into a kind of oriental idol.

Louis xiv did not intend to be inaccessible, still less invisible. Petitioners could speak to him more easily than to ministers, and petitions were handed to him directly. No barrier prevented the humblest of his subjects from watching him strolling in his gardens. Nevertheless the King wanted to raise himself to such an exalted plane that the smallest service to his person would assume a quasi-sacramental character. The princes alone had the honour of handing him his shirt or his napkin. The post of *porte-coton*, the official who handed the King a napkin when he was on the way to relieve himself, conferred nobility. Primi Visconti wrote:

> The *petit coucher* is the moment when the King, after disrobing and bidding his courtiers goodnight, has donned his bed-robe and is installed on his night-commode. The only persons allowed to be present are those who have the office of gentleman of the Bedchamber or letters patent which cost as much as 60,000 crowns and which many people would buy for 100,000. Thus you may see what value this nation sets on all that comes from the King, even the most repugnant things. It is true that the King is very considerate, and puts himself in that position more through ceremony than necessity.

This is not to be interpreted as extravagance or megalomania; apart from the fact that the sale of posts at court enabled a substantial tax to be levied on vanity, the King felt better assured of public law and order when his gentlemen were arguing over his candle-holder instead of fomenting political plots. His glittering, dissolute court intoxicated with fine distinctions of precedence and plied with attentions by the most assiduous of masters, was closely watched. The King had placed spies everywhere, and no letter could remain secret. Every morning Louis was kept informed not only about the actions but also the thoughts of his family, mistresses and courtiers. He intended to keep unceasing guard against the machinations of others and his own feelings:

One must guard against oneself, beware of one's inclinations, always be on guard against one's nature ... The heart of a prince is assaulted like a stronghold ... Abandoning our heart, let us remain master of our mind, let us separate the tenderness of the lover from the resolve of the sovereign, and may the beauty which creates our pleasures never have the freedom to speak to us about our affairs or about those who serve us in them.

He loved the artless Louise de La Vallière in this manner. Their liaison was dangerous and insecure, for the court was not yet as submissive as it eventually became. A faction was forming against the intolerable cripple, numbering as its most prominent members Anne of Austria, Madame, the Comtesse de Soissons, the Comte de Guiche (son of Marshal Gramont) and the Comte de Vardes. The latter was a treacherous double-dealer who succeeded in winning the trust of all, and then worked with all his ingenuity for their downfall.

The first quarrel between the two lovers erupted when Louise tried to conceal the liaison between Madame and Guiche from Louis. When the King did not unbend by evening, as he had sworn always to do, his unhappy mistress fled to the convent of Chaillot. Louis pursued her at a gallop, found her half dead, and brought her back. Madame refused to allow the object of such a scandal back into her service. Louis had to beg, then threaten, before Henrietta agreed to 'treat her as one of your women' – an insult that the King never forgave.

Olympe, Vardes and Guiche now had the idea of fabricating a letter written in Spanish and signed by Philip IV to inform the Queen how badly she was being treated, and this was how Maria Theresa learned that it was not only princesses who could move kings' hearts. A great commotion ensued. 'What are you grumbling about, Madame,' the King replied, indifferent to his wife's grievances, 'do I not sleep with you every night?'

Intoxicated by this success, Vardes then proceeded to hatch a whole brood of intrigues, one of which involved turning over to Louis some extremely compromising letters written by Guiche, and in order to save her lover Madame disclosed the secret of the Spanish letter to her brother-in-law. Louis realized that he was not yet master in his own house, and struck hard: Vardes was jailed, then exiled, as were Olympe and Guiche. Although the intrigues soon resumed, there were no more cabals.

By 1662 Colbert's management had already begun to revive the economy and replenish the treasury. The King set about using this advantage with remarkable guile and caution. The surrender of Dunkirk to the English had never stopped being a thorn in his flesh. Charles II was a poor man and a spendthrift. He took the bait which was artfully dangled in front of him, and offered of his own accord to cede the stronghold on payment of five million livres. The King got it for three and a half million, and the outcry from the indignant English was to no avail.

Lorraine was acquired by the Treaty of Montmartre (6 February 1662) on no less advantageous terms. Duke Charles IV ceded it against payment of a revenue of seven hundred thousand livres and an annuity of one hundred thousand crowns. France's gold also preserved her eastern frontier, for the King paid substantial subsidies to the German princes, particularly those in the League of the Rhine. A twenty-five-year alliance with the Dutch guaranteed the sea frontier, where in any case the fighting between the English and the Dutch fleets had been neutralizing both. Later, Louis apologized for having carried out a bourgeois policy of acquisition rather than conquest. Had he always followed such a policy, he would have spared Europe a great deal of misery, but the French would have despised him as they despised Louis-Philippe.

The year ended with the greatest theatrical success since *Le Cid,* Molière's somewhat sacrilegious *L'École des femmes.* A great reign was decidedly under way.

Now a sudden outbreak of whooping-cough struck first Maria Theresa, then the King, whom his doctors brought to the edge of the grave. The Catholic *dévots* and the resuscitated Company of the Saint-Sacrement saw their chance at once. They obtained the execution of a sentence passed on the visionary Morin, who was burned alive, and they attacked Molière violently. Louis XIV himself underwent a total change. He ordained that in the event of his death the Regency was to go, not to Anne of Austria or Monsieur, but to the Company's leader, the Prince de Conti, whose 'sanctity' was now as aggressive as his former vices and disloyalty. Fortunately, the King's illness abated. One morning he felt in good heart once more, and fathered a child on La Vallière.

Clergy and court had got out of hand. Now Louis gave them grounds for repentance. The master forbade the removal of Protestant children from their parents and gave Molière permission to ridicule his detractors. Richelieu had had the idea of using men of letters for political purposes, and after him Fouquet. Colbert developed it so much that he can be regarded as the earliest minister of propaganda. The King knew the importance of the creators of renown. He approved a list of pensions established on Colbert's orders, which ranged from the King's historiographer, Mézeray (three thousand livres), to a young beginner, Racine (six hundred). These annuities, presented in silk purses, were not total losses: the beneficiaries tacitly agreed to become 'heralds of the King's virtues'. They vied with each other in hyperbole, and since most of them had talent, and some of them genius, they gave the Sun King the radiance demanded by his name.

This does not mean that Louis XIV became a patron of letters only for the sake of his own prestige. True he was no intellectual and had no particular love of writers and artists – except in the case of Lully perhaps, for Louis loved music. But he had a near-infallible instinct for recognizing distinction, and he also had an aesthetic sense. He was fully aware of what he was doing when he accorded his favour and support to the men who made up the Grand Siècle. Nor would he or they have seen any discrepancy between the creations of the spirit and the designs of the monarch. The idea of a separation between official art and a contemporary, misunderstood avant garde would have struck them as ridiculous. With the exception of men like La Fontaine, too friendly with Fouquet, or La Bruyère, too involved with the Condé family, all the great writers gravitated towards the throne. There is no instance of a plight such as that of Diderot in the eighteenth century, obliged to sell his library to a foreign empress, still less of that familiar spectacle of the nineteenth century, the genius held in contempt and suspicion by society.

The Academy, placed under the royal protection and with its headquarters at the Louvre, now took on the importance it still possesses. If Louis xv had acted like his grandfather towards the writers of his own time, posterity would have quite a different image of him. The King did not permit men of letters to meddle in politics, but was quite prepared to implicate them himself, sometimes without their knowledge. He became godfather to Molière's child in order to scotch scandalous rumours,* while using him as a weapon against the unruly younger element at court, in whom something of the Fronde still breathed (*La Critique de l'Ecole des Femmes*), and against the dangerous bigotry of the Company of the Saint-Sacrement (*Tartuffe*).

Louis' prestige, freedom of action and audacity were unrivalled at that time, yet he did not dare to risk public indignation by publishing the birth of a bastard 'of the blood', a tradition that had fallen into disuse since the time of Henry iv. La Vallière's son Charles was delivered secretly, in a pavilion of the Palais Royal, under the watchful protection of Colbert himself, who also looked after the favourite, took away the newborn baby, made arrangements for his baptism and put him in the care of foster parents.

---

* Molière was accused of having married his own daughter, Armande Béjart.

[3]

Embellishing the Kingdom

LOUIS' grandmother, Marie de Médicis, had been the most prodigal Queen France ever had. Perhaps it was from her that he inherited his inordinate love of display and collector's mania. He wanted to take over the role that had been played by Spain and Italy since the Renaissance as the model of western civilization. He was fortunate enough to have a galaxy of incomparable artists at his disposal, yet, far from taking his inspiration from them, Louis managed to impart to them his own vision of nature and beauty.

In a famous and venomous passage, Saint-Simon decries Louis XIV, but cannot withhold his tribute: 'Born with a less than mediocre mind, but a mind capable of moulding, polishing and refining itself, of borrowing from others without imitation and without strain . . .' A less than mediocre mind would have had difficulty in borrowing from others without strain, and would have been absolutely incapable of managing it without imitation.

Louis had never received a single lesson in the arts, but he developed a taste that was both precise and distinct. That taste may be criticized by some for its nouveau riche ostentation, and it is regrettable that the admirable realist school of painters such as Georges de La Tour and Le Nain should have been over-shadowed by the bombast and rhetoric of Lebrun. But it cannot be gainsaid that Louis XIV inspired the creation of a style, that this style was adopted in every court and that it became the symbol of France's greatness.

Louis' ambition far outweighed that of his forerunners. Not content merely to bring back the splendours of the Valois and to transform towns and châteaux, the Sun King set out radically to change his subjects' way of life and its setting. His success was to earn him furious censures from the traditionalists of the Fénelon/Saint-Simon school, as well as from the eighteenth-century *philosophes* and their disciples. Yet there is a credit side. The larger towns now finally emerged from the medieval conditions that had been offering stubborn resistance to the incursions of the Renaissance. Monumental new fortifications reduced the old fortresses to the status of curiosities. The countryside changed, and sometimes even the climate. Many pestilential marshes disappeared. Trees, water, plains, hills and even virgin forest were turned into astounding scenic set-pieces.

The alteration was equally marked inside the home. Fénelon waxed indignant at the idea of common people owning a bed apiece when the entire family would formerly have made do with one. For half a century, light had been struggling to dissipate the darkness which enveloped most houses. Now it suddenly broke in, by day through great windows, by night thanks to abundant supplies of candles. Even the Paris streets were lit. Mirrors became plentiful, and light came with them. Flowers served to create a thousand ephemeral masterpieces. Water, fire, and even the most commonplace object might provide themes for the inspiration of artists.

Only hygiene was forgotten. The stench and squalor that had taken possession of France under Henry IV remained untouched during his grandson's reign. In Paris there were continual epidemics. These, in addition to unhappy childhood memories of street rioting, contributed to the eventual departure of the King, who had all the Bourbon craving for the open air.

Colbert had to plead and argue to have the benefits of urban redevelopment extended to the capital, where he did his best to improve standards of cleanliness, but the colossal achievements carried out during his ministry and for some time afterwards were not due to him alone. Voltaire and many others have censured Louis XIV for having sacrificed Paris to his châteaux, yet no age had ever seen such a growth of streets, squares, boulevards, *quais,* palaces, gardens and triumphal arches in so few years.[1] The King himself selected the plan for the Louvre Colonnade, but it is true that certain works, even the extensions to the Louvre, were not completed and that Louis XIV took no creative pleasure in developing Paris.

Ever since the fête at Vaux, he had wanted a residence worthy of him, and in 1661 he appointed the architect Le Vau to improve on the little 'card castle' built by Louis XIII at Versailles. Surprisingly, he refused to touch his father's work, perhaps in order to conceal the immensity of the project he had conceived. After 1663 Colbert was distressed to see Versailles absorbing excessive sums, and his thrifty mind boggled as he noted: 'His Majesty has laid down that everybody to whom he gives apartments [at Versailles] should be provided with furniture. He is having everybody fed and all the rooms equipped even down to wood and candles, *which has never been the practice in royal houses.'* In earlier times, gentlemen who stayed with the King had done so at their own expense, but they had hardly ever remained at court for more than three months. Louis' intention was to keep them there and to make them feel their subjection, but also to surfeit them with a continual round of fêtes, spectacles, hunts and a host of other diversions.

---

* The Louvre Colonnade, the Tuileries Gardens, the Galerie d'Apollon, the Invalides, the Place des Victoires and the Place Louis-le-Grand (Place Vendôme), the Porte Saint-Denis and Porte Saint-Martin, the Salpêtrière, the Collège des Quatre-Nations, the Pont-Royal, the Observatoire, the Gobelins, the Val-de-Grâce, the Champs-Élysées, the boulevards, etc.

Colbert may be excused for a feeling that was shared by almost all his contemporaries. Amid the tides of adulation breaking at the feet of the Sun King, it is hard to find any in praise of the construction of Versailles. Fortunately, Louis paid no heed. He sensed that this work would make him the equal of the great builders of antiquity, and he put all his creative power into it. Not one grove or parterre was designed without his examining and sometimes modifying the plans. The genius of the landscape gardener Le Nôtre, Mansart, the sculptor Coysevox and Lebrun does not alter the verdict. Versailles was built to reflect a certain image of royalty, and made to its master's measure. Louis xv never succeeded in adapting it to his own.

Long before its completion, the work gave rise to the most violent disapproval. People whispered that it could never be finished, and exaggerated the expense as fancy dictated. Preachers railed against this delirium of splendour. The King was pouring millions into a desert. Versailles was bleeding the nation dry. In subsequent centuries the opponents of the monarchy have delighted in composing infinite variations on this theme. The luxury of the court was contrasted with the squalor of the wars, and they mourned the workmen and soldiers who died accidentally or as victims of diseases contracted in the service of the new pharaoh.

This invective has lost much of its edge in our own time. We know that in a liberal century the requirements of industrialism reduced the proletariat to a condition quite as arduous as that of Louis xiv's workmen. We know that Versailles cost about as much as a modern aircraft carrier,* and that it brings in a considerable annual income as one of the wonders of the world. We also know that it was copied in every country in Europe and was an outstanding factor in the prestige of France. There was a death-toll of two hundred and twenty-seven during the twenty or so years of the building of Versailles. However deplorable, this figure does not begin to compare with, say, the losses from mining accidents today. An era that devotes incalculable sums to armaments that are obsolete within a few years has lost the right to condemn an extravagance that produced the masterpiece of a civilization.

---

* About 65 million livres. Obviously the annual expenditure of the nation at this time must be taken into account, but the burden of Louis xiv's great works was never so heavy as that which we now carry through scientific progress in the military sphere. All these buildings together cost about 95 millions, *spread out over half a century*. The debt left by Louis after so many ruinous wars amounted to three thousand millions.

[4]

From *Tartuffe* to the
Fouquet Affair

THE Venetian ambassadors Grimani and Sagredo wrote the following account of the Louis XIV of the years 1664–5:

His constitution is sturdy and his appearance majestic; his face is at once open and imposing, his manner courteous and serious ... He evinces partiality to no one, and no one can presume on receiving it; he does not let anybody jest with him, nor does he jest with others ... As he applies himself to work with extraordinary zeal ... he fatigues his mind too much and occasionally falls prey to violent headaches. These troubles are accompanied by a certain weakness of the stomach, and he is also subject to dizzy spells and vapours. Hence ... he has recourse to purges, baths and repeated blood-lettings ... As for his mental qualities, his Majesty has natural wisdom and an extremely lucid intelligence. He greets any and everybody with immense good will, and in his every action mingles kindness and gravity with a grace that captures every heart! ... *There is nonetheless a side of his character that is a subject of discontent with many Frenchmen ... it is his concern for accumulating money, the thrift he has introduced into all fields. Moreover, the King's avarice is widely acknowledged ...*

The King's heart is constantly ablaze with two consuming subjects: one is jealousy of his own greatness, which rules out any favourite ... the other is the desire to surpass, with acts of true magnificence, the finest examples that present themselves for his emulation ... But his soul glows with a feeling of humanity. The King loathes all severe and, *a fortiori*, cruel actions ... His Majesty proceeds with the utmost wisdom in all the affairs of the realm. He can obviously keep a tight curb on his tongue, and never lets slip an unconsidered word.

This was the Louis who had the proud and unprecedented pleasure of seeing the Pope's nephew, Cardinal Chigi, bearing his uncle's apologies over the incident of the Corsican guard and assuring him that a pyramid would be raised in Rome to commemorate the event. It is said that Molière took advantage of the occasion to submit *Tartuffe* to the Legate. The same Louis, in his beloved Versailles, scorned to conceal his feelings any longer and gave the fabulous 'Fête of the Enchanted Island' on behalf of a blushing La Vallière.

The enchantment lasted from 5–14 May 1664, or rather until the 12th, for that day offered something other than pleasing allegories. There was a performance of a three-act *Tartuffe* compared with which the version that has

come down to us is a pantomime: in his petition to the King in 1667, Molière
wrote:

My play, Sire, has been unable to enjoy your Majesty's favour here. I have produced
it to no avail under the title of *L'Imposteur* and disguised the character under the
trappings of a man of the world: no matter that I gave him a little hat, long hair, a big
cape, a sword and lace . . . and painstakingly cut out anything that I judged liable to
furnish the shadow of a pretext to the famous originals of the portrait I wished to
draw; all that has gone for nothing.

So the Tartuffe of 1664, without the trappings of a man of the world,
without long hair and cape, probably wore ecclesiastical garb, and moreover
bore a striking likeness to 'famous originals'. At all events, immediately
after the first performance the King 'forbade the piece to be performed in
public until it was complete.' He may have been yielding to the complaints of
his mother, who had been gravely ill since the previous year, or to the fury of
the *dévot* party, but it seems that the volte-face was premeditated and that he
wanted to fire a warning shot at the Catholic zealots without driving them to
extremes. The hapless Molière knew nothing of all this.

Louis XIV enjoyed being disconcerting. His ultimate intentions towards the
dévots and the Church are puzzling. He inflicted fearful affronts on the Pope,
encouraged Molière to launch his fireship, and at the same time took steps
against the Jansenists by having the nuns of Port-Royal dispersed, then
against the Protestants, who were henceforward compelled to pay annuities to
any of their children who went over to Catholicism.

His foreign policy was equally rich in contrasts. French troops under the
command of the Comte de Coligny reinforced the Imperial armies which were
opposing the Turks and played a glorious part in the battle of St Gotthard, at
which Montecucculi halted the Ottoman invasion in 1664. Could this mean
that the King was abandoning the policy of his ancestors and following that
laid down by Mazarin shortly before his death: a coalition with the House of
Austria to create a new Christendom? The truth was that he simply wanted
France's presence to be felt everywhere, and he proved this when other
'volunteers' entered the service of Portugal to fight Spain. Louis XIV was
applying Henry IV's empiricism with almost cynical offhandedness.

The Fouquet trial, which opened on 14 November 1664, disclosed a more
sinister side of the King's character. The judicial inquiry had been going on
for three years, and its principal effect had been to turn an initially hostile
public opinion in favour of the accused. This was due to the shrewd, proud
stand taken by the former superintendent, to the efforts of his friends, who
from Mme de Sévigné to La Fontaine had spared no pains on his behalf, to
the surviving spirit of the Fronde in the Parlement, but above all to the fierce
hatred of Colbert, who was determined to have Fouquet's head.

Although not usually a bloodthirsty man, Louis too wanted that head, so as to give a terrible object lesson to bad servants of the Crown. On the other hand, he had ordered that the memory of Mazarin was not to receive the slightest blemish, an arduous requirement in view of the close collaboration between the two. So he allowed Colbert to make an outrageous mockery of justice. Nothing was omitted: high-handedness, misappropriation of documents, of which more than a thousand mysteriously vanished, erasures, judicial inventories transformed into police operations, a refusal for two years to allow lawyers to the accused and brutal pressures on the judges. This procedure succeeded in transfiguring a megalomaniac swindler into a martyr.

The affair was entrusted to a court whose members had been selected with great care, but even so its president, Lamoignon, and the prosecutor, Talong, had to be replaced as too circumspect for the King's liking. As for the recorder, Lefèvre d'Ormesson, Colbert tried first of all to win him over with favours, and when that approach failed, took a tougher line, deprived Ormesson of the intendancy of Soissons and tried to intimidate his father, an old counsellor of state. Louis never forgave Ormesson, whose career was ruined. The King could personally admire the integrity of a judge, but he could not allow that quality to stand in the way of raison d'état.

At the opening of the trial, the members of the court were sharply divided into two camps, and the *fouquettistes* shone with the reflected glory of the Frondeurs of 1648. Fouquet was putting new life into the opposition. He was so brilliant in his own defence that Colbert came close to stopping the trial, but Ormesson still proceeded to declare Fouquet guilty 'in fact and in law' of corrupt practices and embezzlement, and to request banishment and the confiscation of his property, not the death penalty. Thirteen judges concurred with Ormesson, nine voted for death – a severe setback for the King and his minister.

Louis XIV has been strongly criticized for not having complied with the sentence, but it would have been singularly imprudent to send abroad (with all his secrets) a man who had become so dangerous. Fouquet disappeared into the cells of the fortress of Pignerol, and never emerged. Later, he became one of the candidates for the true identity of the 'Man in the Iron Mask'. The theory does not stand up to examination.

The Fouquet trial is a prototype of cases that have become common in the twentieth century, in which the passion of those who mete out justice and their contempt for its forms almost constitute extenuating circumstances for the guilty.

[5]

National Self-Sufficiency

THE Fouquet trial made Colbert unpopular, and the gigantic task he had set himself far more difficult. The minister had just received the account of the country's resources on which his experts had been working since 1663. Backed by their evidence, he set out to initiate a thoroughgoing policy of Cartesian mercantilism.

Louis XIV had never studied political economy and was certainly unware that mercantilism represented a system of unification, monetary protectionism and a concept of society that implied seeing the supreme authority of the state as an end in itself. However, his reason readily took to the idea of state control of the economy, his pride was stirred by the possibility of French self-sufficiency and his ambition by the prospect of an obedient, willing nation devoting all its energies towards expanding the power of the monarch. He already knew that the first condition of power was prosperity, the second complete independence from the banking and trading nations, particularly the Low Countries.

Colbert therefore had a free hand. The ruthless penalties inflicted on dishonest tax-farmers and the considerable increase in the yield of general tax-farms had replenished the public coffers. In 1664 the King quadrupled the *aides*, indirect taxes that applied to everybody. If in addition we take into account the vast sums contributed by the clergy in the course of the reign and the income from the sale of public offices, it becomes clear that the common people certainly did not bear the whole burden of Louis XIV's expenditure.

The King and Colbert often disagreed over this expenditure: 'One must save five sous on *unnecessary* things and throw away millions when your *gloire* is at stake. . . .' Yet Louis was by no means a spendthrift. These disagreements concerned the necessity of certain kinds of extravagance. The King had a keen sense of the value of publicity. Buildings, fêtes and lavishness did not serve only as amusements for himself; they must also capture the people's imagination. One of Louis' continuing concerns was to obtain results at the lowest possible cost – hence the poor quality of the raw materials for Versailles and many of the unjust accusations levelled at Colbert. Ultimately the King's policy proved ruinous, but it achieved its ends. From that time onwards,

France became the model of the western world, and remained such even when the world condemned her. To such effect, according to the ambassador Saint-Aulaire, that Louis XIV carries the responsibility for the spread of the French Revolution in Europe.

Since the days of Francis I, the King of France had been 'emperor in his own estates.' Colbert made up his mind to extend the formula to the economy, which meant maximizing production and exports, reducing imports and starting or developing industries to manufacture at home the finest products of foreign countries. Specialists were brought in, sometimes at great cost, from Germany, Holland, Flanders and Venice; middle-men were eliminated; factories were built and their products assigned trade-names controlled by law – Gobelins carpets, Saint-Etienne steel, Saint-Gobain glass and a host of others. As early as 1668 an apprehensive report from the Venetian ambassador set the seal on Colbert's success: 'Whatever is best from every part of the world is now being manufactured in France.'

A heavy price had to be paid in restrictions. Standardization of products dates from this period, and was ensured by more than five hundred edicts. One of them fixed the size and quality of cloth; another dealt with dyeing, and numbered 377 clauses. The law was enforced by legions of clerks, assisted by the guilds. No artisan had the right to work if he was not affiliated to one of them.

While French goods flowed out on a tide of fashion, the door was shut in the face of foreign exports by raising tariff barriers to a considerable (1664) then a near-prohibitive (1667) level. The entire nation was jolted into activity, work became virtually compulsory, the birth-rate was stimulated by benefits granted to large families, and a clean sweep was made of the numerous unemployed, notably the beggars, some of whom found themselves prisoners at the General Hospital built in 1657 while the rest were compelled to work.

The machine came into prominence, and the workman was tied to it – a revolution that amazed contemporaries just as the kolkhozes amazed the bourgeois in the twentieth century. In fact Stalinist Russia provides the best point of comparison with that prodigious effort. The worker toiled, bound by a rigid schedule, with no hope of diversion other than holy mass and under threat of cruel punishments, but he shared the country's glorious ideal.

Production was pointless without efficient distribution. Roads were built, the Canal des Deux-Mers was dug between the Mediterranean and the Atlantic, ports such as Sète on the Mediterranean were created and ship-builders were given special incentives. This was not enough, for the need was for ships capable of competing with the maritime powers, but Louis shrugged off Colbert's nautical visions. Perhaps his instinct restrained him from entertaining the overreaching ambition of simultaneous supremacy over both Europe and the ocean.

Colbert knew that to get what he wanted he must appeal to the eye of his master. During the work on the Grand Canal at Versailles he ordered nine different kinds of boat from Rouen, and laid a small galley on the stocks at Versailles itself, arming it with thirty-two cannon after its successful launching. Soon a small armada, gilded and decked out with rich materials and damask sails, was flying his Majesty's colours, adding to the splendours of the château. The Republic of Venice augmented the fleet with the gift of two ornate gondolas. Finally, in 1673, a bizarre vessel appeared, devoid of mast or sail and propelled 'by means of a kind of capstan that turned wheels placed at the side.'

Won over, but not captivated (he never visited his dockyards), the King ceased his opposition to Colbert's 'mania' (1665). Four years later he appointed him Secretary for the Navy. At that time, France had about twenty warships: when Colbert died she had 276, and the number of galleys designed specially for the Mediterranean had increased from six to thirty. A fleet of that size required a large number of men. Colbert introduced naval conscription to provide crews, and turned to the courts for galley-slaves. The fate of these wretches is notorious, manacled to their benches, rowing until death relieved them, under the lash which imparted its rhythm to the vessel. Since ships' complements had to be frequently renewed, the intendants put heavy pressure on the judges and apologized when they were unable to provide enough victims. Tax evaders and Protestants found guilty of failure to salute a procession were chained alongside real criminals. The galleys were the concentration camps of the Grand Siècle, precursors of the Soviet labour camps.

Colbert's bureaucratic, socializing despotism might well have transformed France into an ultra-centralized kingdom, suppressing individualism and obsessed with productivity, where everything from philosophical speculation to the creations of its craftsmen would have been state-controlled. Once again Louis XIV instinctively perceived the danger. Colbert was never able to go as far as the totalitarian régimes of our own era.

He did at least succeed in uprooting the remnants of feudal tyranny. In the rugged lands of Auvergne, Forez and Velay, the Fronde had brought about the rebirth of a new medievalism, bizarre, temperamental and ferocious. One notorious squire kept a man shut in his wardrobe, able neither to sit nor to stand. Another made his ten-year-old son kill his enemies by repeated childish blows. A gentleman of Forez who considered himself supreme on his own lands murdered three bailiffs who came to serve a summons.

Colbert would have liked Louis XIV to undertake in person a grandiose punitive expedition against these princelings in the manner of his ancestors. Failing this, he tried to transfer the task from the jurisdiction of the local

Parlements to that of the Council. He did not succeed, and it was the parliamentary commissions who administered the *Grands Jours*.*

Even as he was clipping the wings of the nobility, Louis remained aware that he could not do without them in time of war. Nevertheless, a number of harsh examples were made, and no one dared to flout the royal authority again. Every knee was forced to bend before his representatives, the intendants, clerk-dictators whose actions sometimes prefigured those of the National Convention of Revolutionary times.

Colbert miscalculated with the companies he set up to wrest the monopoly of foreign trade from the Low Countries. Although the King and the princes bought shares in the French companies of the West and East Indies, Senegal and the Levant, and there was a campaign to persuade the big investors that trading did not mean losing caste, their reaction was unenthusiastic, and the general public remained apathetic. He had no better luck with his attempts to discourage the production of wine, which lowered the workers' productive potential, and also failed to enforce free domestic trade in wheat (the export of cereals was forbidden).

On the other hand, one of his innovations has become a universal commonplace. In 1667 he gave Nicolas de La Reynie, one of the greatest administrators of the reign, the job of organizing a police force. In the space of thirty years La Reynie did much to make Paris safe, lit the streets, improved public hygiene, organized the control of epidemics and the distribution of regular food supplies. He created the first police information service on crime and criminals, the economic police and the policing of public morals, gambling, entertainment and traffic, and made the criminal police unprecedentedly efficient. He also instituted censorship of books, printing and newspapers, and introduced public opinion surveys. He never lost favour with Louis, who held him in high esteem.

Colbert's position was not so stable. Even before the outbreak of the great struggle between himself and his supporters on the one hand and Le Tellier and Louvois on the other, there were several occasions when it looked as if he was in disgrace. His relations with the King, who was twenty years his junior, were often difficult. Louis would let him argue, even lose his temper, and kept him in check by creating misgivings that he could dispel when it suited him.

Louis xiv was exactly the opposite of those brilliantly intuitive leaders who give objectives to their subordinates and leave them to devise ways to achieve them. Matters came to him 'digested . . . after being prepared in advance by those concerned, then by the secretaries and finally by the minister making the report.'[1] The King never made a decision without knowing all the facts and possible solutions of the question before him: of course the minister could

---

* The extraordinary sessions of justice held in provinces where civil disorder was rife and the usual procedures could be blocked by wealth or family influence. – Tr.

present them in accordance with his own views. When a technical problem arose on which he had no special knowledge, the King might give a free hand to Colbert, but he never allowed his minister to dictate to him over 'important issues'.

For the information of the Dauphin, Louis dictated: 'It is for us, my son, to choose what is actually to be done. And I make so bold as to tell you that provided we do not lack sense and courage, this choice is one which no other could make better than ourselves.'

[6]

The Science of Tears

THE first serious quarrel between the King and his mother arose out of her growing animosity to La Vallière. Louis sulked, the old Queen once again talked of retiring to Val-de-Grâce, and to avoid a scandal, Louis had to pay her a visit. The scene was typical of the way he behaved towards his family in delicate situations. He wept floods of tears, which came easily to him, and words of affection and repentance poured out. Anne accused him of being 'drunk with his own grandeur, and setting no bounds either on his desires or on his vengeance.' The King redoubled his tears, and when he saw that his mother was finally melting, told her: 'I know my fault and sometimes it brings me pain and shame. I have done what I could to restrain myself from offending God and giving way to my passions, but I am bound to admit that they have become stronger than reason, I can no longer resist their violence and *I do not even feel the desire to do so.*'

Seeing her son so unhappy, and anxious to be reconciled, Anne consented to receive the favourite at her gaming-table, with the result that Maria Theresa had a miscarriage that almost killed her. While Louise would gladly have avoided such clashes, the King was intent not only on pleasing her but on enforcing his authority over his family, even as he plied them with endearments and attentions.

Shortly afterwards, La Vallière became pregnant again. Madame took advantage of her condition to push her bosom friend Cathérine de Gramont, Princess de Monaco, into the King's arms. For a few months Louis remained infatuated with this veteran of innumerable adventures, much to the annoyance of her previous lover, young Puyguilhem,* who went so far as to assault Mme de Monaco.[1] The King put up with his escapades for some time before running out of patience and clapping Puyguilhem in the Bastille. He still had the last word, however. 'What might have ruined him saved him. . . . He let his beard grow in prison, and being an excellent and as yet unrecognized actor, convinced the King of his despair and at the same time his passion for him.'[2]

The youthful follies of a seething court were now in striking contrast

* The future Lauzun, see p. 143.

134

with the long illness of the Queen Mother, who had been in the grip of cancer since 1663. On the one hand fêtes, love affairs and intrigues: on the other, the religious and funereal machinery that was set in motion each time an apparently fatal crisis occurred. Anne faced death with characteristic courage and piety, but it is difficult to know what to make of Louis xiv during the thirteen months of his mother's painful last illness. He displayed violent grief, appropriated the large pearls that the Queen had intended to leave to the daughter of Monsieur, and fled Saint-Germain to amuse himself at Versailles with La Vallière, successfully delivered of a second son (who died a few months later) and victorious over Mme de Monaco.

Philip iv of Spain died before his sister (17 September 1665), to the great grief of Maria Theresa. Louis let his tears mingle with his wife's, then immediately fell to calculating how to take advantage of the event. He wore mourning while still attending balls. Pearls and diamonds created a magnificent effect against the violet cloth.

In early January 1666 there were several grand fêtes. On the 18th the Queen received the last rites. Her two sons and Maria Theresa watched over her, and on the evening of 19 January the dying woman emerged from a coma and sat up. Louis broke down and was prevailed upon to withdraw, and that was the last time he saw his mother.

Anne of Austria died on 20 January 1666, between four and five o'clock in the morning, and Louis wept throughout the night. Monsieur, crazed with grief, took several days to emerge from Saint-Cloud. When the two brothers met again they wept in unison, and the King promised, in a wave of tenderness, that Philippe's young son, the Duc de Valois,* would be brought up with the Dauphin. Subsequently he dictated a cynical commentary on this encounter for the benefit of his successor:

Although the time when I told him these things and the frame of mind I was in leave no grounds for doubting that they were suggested by a pure urge of friendship, yet it is certain that after thinking this speech over with an open mind, I could have devised no subtler method both of doing my brother an honour for which he was obliged to me and at the same time of taking the most precious pledge he could give me as surety for his conduct.

The death of Anne of Austria brought great changes. The King felt released from his final chains. With his mother gone, he could tower above all other human beings and live the life of a god on Olympus. The confirmation came immediately, when he 'declared' his mistress, whom the wretched Queen had to welcome among the ladies who lived close to her.

La Vallière was pregnant again, and Maria Theresa scolded her for presenting herself in such a condition. Louis was furious. He decided that by

---

* Born in 1664. He died at the age of two.

way of recompense Louise must give a supper for the principal ladies at court. Madame stubbornly refused to attend, and the King's revenge took the form of stirring up more troubles between her and her husband. The royal family was a long way from the stately harmony so dear to its head.

[7]

Mars and Venus

LOUIS XIV's ideas on the subject of war cannot be viewed fairly through modern eyes. From his earliest years, he had known that his reign and his own importance would be judged according to how well he waged war. Since the Treaty of the Pyrenees, he had known that his father-in-law's death would be the signal. Nevertheless, he made no haste when the time came. Observing him during his preparations, one wonders whether to admire his Machiavellian assurance or to marvel at the ease with which he misread the character of some of the parties involved.

Nothing could be done without the friendly neutrality of England, then engaged in a war with the Dutch, the allies of France. Under the terms of the 1662 treaty the King was obliged to declare war on Charles II (on 26 January 1666). He promised the United Provinces that he would make no move in the Spanish Netherlands without them, and would help them to break through into the Thames, but the feeble strength of his fleet absolved him from participation in the raid that took Ruyter as far as London. To make up for it, he sent a force of six thousand men to the Rhine, where they arrested the bishop of Münster, a warrior prelate in the pay of the English, thereby retaining the friendship of the Dutch at small expense while England was suffering defeat, plague and the Great Fire of London. The indigence and extravagance that bound her king to Louis XIV may be counted as a further calamity.

The secret contacts between the two cousins had been pursued since 1661 through Madame. When the quarrel over La Vallière prevented her from maintaining that role in 1666, her mother, Queen Henrietta, took her place: a new pact was concluded guaranteeing France against surprises from the English side.

Meanwhile, a curious transaction had been going on between Louis XIV and the Emperor of Austria, Leopold. The chancellories had never in their wildest dreams imagined that after losing so many sons, Philip IV would leave one to succeed him. The birth of the Infante Don Carlos in 1661 had not altered their expectations. He was a rachitic weakling already likely to rejoin his brothers, or so it seemed. The weakling had since become King Charles II, but it was doubtful whether he could survive much longer.

137

Louis and his brother-in-law* were certain that he could not, and signed a treaty of partition: France would get the Low Countries and Franche-Comté, the Emperor the rest of the Spanish possessions.

No sooner had Leopold signed the document than he repented it; at least he demanded that no court should know of it, that the usual duplicate copy should not be made, and that the sole document in existence should be locked in a metal casket to which the Emperor would have one key and the King the other. This casket was to be placed in the hands of the Grand Duke of Florence. To that end, the Emperor handed it over to the French ambassador in Vienna, and the King sent sixteen of his guards to the gates of Vienna to escort the courier, for fear that the Emperor might change his mind and have the casket seized on the way.[1]

The result was that the precious casket arrived, not in Florence, but in Paris. A few subsidies easily stifled Leopold's complaints. Further sums guaranteed the abstention of the German princes.

During this time Louis xiv, the natural protector of his young brother-in-law Charles ii, was declaring himself as such to the Regent, Marie-Anne of Austria, and negotiating a Franco-Spanish commercial treaty. He was also mobilizing his armies. Louvois thus had his first chance to display his talent for organization, while Turenne drew up plans for a campaign against Flanders. When preparations were complete, Louis unearthed a 'right of devolution' by virtue of which he claimed Flanders, Franche-Comté, Brabant and Luxembourg in the name of his wife, whose dowry had never been paid.

France and Spain fought at first 'with bankers' figures and lawyers' arguments', a final artifice designed to postpone everything until spring, the season of battles. The French nobility, to whom eight years of peace had seemed an unbearably long time, did not stop to ask whether Louis' real duty lay in protecting the inheritance of an orphan, as head of the family, or in taking advantage of an exceptional turn of events to cut the invasion routes by closing the country to the north and east. After equipping themselves at great expense, they rushed to the King's side, and he manoeuvred his troops in front of the ladies.

The pregnancies of his wife and mistress seemed to be His Majesty's sole concerns. Two daughters were born. The little Princess was to die at the age of five. Louis, anxious not to expose himself to the perils of war without providing for his natural child and her mother, had little Anne-Marie of Bourbon solemnly legitimized in the Parlement, in the tradition of Henry iv, while La Vallière became a Duchess. The court wondered if this excessive honour might not presage a break.

On 31 March 1667 Louis signed the treaty with Portugal which was the last step in his diplomatic arrangements, on 1 May he reassured the uneasy Spaniards, and on the 8th he began his campaign – not a war, which was not

* Leopold had married the second daughter of Philip iv.

even declared, but a simple family matter: the King was setting off to take possession of the lands belonging to his wife. The expedition was a military stroll, punctuated by a few sieges. Lille was the only place where the Spanish put up any serious resistance. The King, with great white ostrich-feathers nodding over his head, mixed with the soldiers in the trenches and proved his courage, if not his military genius. When the bravery of Monsieur fired the enthusiasm of the troops, Louis was most put out.

The King soon granted himself a fortnight's leave and rejoined the court at Compiègne, leaving Turenne to continue operations. It was here that he became the surreptitious lover of the Marquise de Montespan. The victory of this opulent blonde had in common with the conquest of Flanders the fact that each brought to a successful conclusion a campaign in which no pains had been spared. Dissatisfied with the moderate fortune of Montespan, Françoise-Athénaïs de Rochechouart-Mortemart had long been musing on the career of a royal favourite. One step at a time, she had become friendly with Monsieur, then with the Queen, who admired her piety and virtuous speeches, before making herself the intimate of La Vallière, which enabled her to parade her wit and beauty before the King himself. She then enlisted the support of the devil. Sorcerers and fortune-tellers, such as Lesage, La Filastre and La Voisin, gave her the means of winning Louis through black masses, spells and potions.

Louis evinced 'wonderful gaiety' after so much success. He decided to present the towns seized on her behalf to Maria Theresa, and the entire court, with the exception of La Vallière (pregnant again), left for the battlefields. The terrible confusion and numerous accidents that marked the journey did not prevent him from being extremely cheerful. Mars and Venus were conspiring for Louis' happiness. They also warred in the heart of Monsieur, who forgot some of his warlike ardour in the presence of the handsome Chevalier de Lorraine, soon to become a 'declared' favourite in his turn.

The Queen and her ladies had just arrived at La Fère from Compiègne when La Vallière appeared, pale, wasted and consumed with jealousy. She had got wind of the Montespan affair. Maria Theresa, sick with rage, gave orders that dinner was not to be served to her rival. Next day, in her carriage, Athénaïs allowed herself the pleasure of condemning the impudence of the favourite, saying: 'God preserve me from being the King's mistress!'

Lille surrendered on 27 August, after Ath, Tournai, Oudenarde, Furnes, Armentières, Courtrai and Douai. On the 31st Marshal Créqui cut the remains of the Spanish army to pieces, and terror spread as far as Antwerp. All Flanders was expected to fall into the hands of France, but the King halted the campaign. He instructed Vauban to build a citadel at Lille, based on his revolutionary principles of fortification, and returned to Saint-Germain.

In the autumn the court abandoned the Louvre for the nearby Palais des

Tuileries, where it entered on a round of pleasures. La Vallière gave birth to a son, the Comte de Vermandois, while Louis dallied with Mme de Montespan until four in the morning. Only the Queen remained in ignorance of the new affair.

The war seemed almost forgotten, but Louvois, chafing under the command of Turenne, brought Louis a plan drawn up by Condé to take Franche-Comté in the middle of winter, when an attack would be least expected. The King was impressed, and an army was secretly assembled in Burgundy while French gold was distributed inside Franche-Comté. On 2 February 1668, in spite of a terrible cold spell, his Majesty 'abandoned ladies' pleasure, and carnival for *gloire*'. The province put up a feeble resistance, and Condé conquered it in three weeks.

Europe woke up with a start. Since his enemies could not stop Louis, his allies undertook the task, and in the space of five days John de Witt, Grand Pensionary of Holland, joined his country with England and Sweden to 'curb the ambition of France'. The fuming Sun King received pressing and respectful requests from the Dutch ambassador, Van Beuning, which were equivalent to demands. Louvois advised turning a deaf ear, but Lionne and Colbert pointed out the danger of a coalition. Louis now demonstrated his astuteness and prudence by offering peace to Spain of his own accord. The plenipotentiaries met at Aix-la-Chapelle, but the real negotiations were conducted by Van Beuning at Saint-Germain.

Louis offered to restore half his conquests to Spain, and eventually got the better of the Dutchman, for while he gave back Franche-Comté he kept the Flemish stronghold, thanks to which he would be able to avenge himself on the United Provinces when the time came (the Treaty of Aix-la-Chapelle, 2 May 1668). His moderation was not to the taste of his subjects. In seven years, unanimity had already departed and the wind of the Fronde was blowing again. While the Dutch were dizzily striking a medal to celebrate the fact that they had 'halted the sun', the Marquis de Saint-Maurice, ambassador of the Duke of Savoy, was writing:

> Powerful factions are forming against the King, taking courage from the fact that he has not achieved anything outstanding, or made the famous conquests he could have made . . . It is true that the French grumble about everything, and that if they are not occupied with war they cannot keep still.

[8]

The Sun Palace

IF the years 1668–72 do not mark the apogee of the reign of Louis xiv, they are its finest moment. Neglected ports revived, ships multiplied, the French flag flew in Africa and America, the army grew as orderly as a Le Nôtre garden, and the administration functioned with unprecedented efficiency. At the same time Paris was transformed, monuments sprang up in every large town, peace reigned in the countryside, Molière's genius excelled itself, La Fontaine published his *Fables*, Racine triumphed with *Andromaque* and flopped with *Britannicus*, Bossuet spoke his first funeral orations and every courier carried some masterpiece from Mme de Sévigné. Obviously it was not Louis xiv who created so many world-famous statesmen, generals, engineers, artists, writers, preachers and philosophers, but he was the masterly conductor who created harmony among them.

In ten years the young autocrat had not suffered a single reverse or made one serious error. In certain respects he already resembled the pen-portrait that Saint-Simon drew with a blend of admiration and spleen in which a kind of unrequited love emerges:

Never did any man give with a better grace, and thus increase the value of his bounty. Never did a man sell his words, his smile, even his glances in a finer manner. He made everything precious through the discrimination and majesty which were greatly enhanced by the rarity and brevity of his words . . . Never was there a man so naturally polite, nor of such strictly measured politeness, strict by degrees, nor who better distinguished age, merit, rank . . . But above all, he had no equal with women. He never passed by the most modest coif without raising his hat, even to chambermaids . . . Nothing could match him at reviews, fêtes, and wherever an air of gallantry could be assumed because of the presence of ladies. He had derived it from the court of the Queen, his mother, and from the Comtesse de Soissons . . .. But to the least gesture, his walk, his bearing, his whole countenance, all was measured, all seemly, noble, grand, majestic and withal very natural, for habit and the incomparable and unique advantage of his whole figure made all this very easy.

Until 1670 Louis enjoyed showing off that 'figure' by dancing. He gave it up after hearing the lines from *Britannicus* that refer to Nero excelling 'in making himself a spectacle to the Romans.' This did not detract from the favoured

141

position of Baptiste, now known as Lully, composer of most of the music for the royal ballets. A formidable personality, brimming with genius and intrigue and as loose in his morals as Monsieur himself, Lully had come close to the rank of favourite; when he became director of the Opera, for which he produced twenty works in twenty-five years, no other man was able to have his work performed there. Louis had a passion for music and needed a 'tuneful background' for every moment of his life, itself so like a ballet, so that his violinists followed him everywhere.

The Sun King wanted the meanest detail to take on importance beneath his rays. 'In order to distinguish his principal courtiers, he had devised blue cloaks embroidered in gold and silver: to be allowed to wear them was a high favour for the vain, and they were almost as much in demand as the collar of the Order of Saint-Louis.'[1] The vogue for cloaks, doublets adorned with ribbons, broad shoulder-belts and lace neck-bands was to prevail all over Europe for the next twenty years, except in Spain and Poland. People prided themselves on emulating the court of Louis xiv, and began to wear the great leonine wig. Until 1670, the King had been able to indulge his vanity by displaying his own hair.

Yet this dazzling society which was already being compared to that of Augustus had its dark side. A criminal industry prospered by virtue of public superstition. Magicians made fortunes out of an extensive clientèle greedy for a glimpse of the secrets of the future and begging them to make that future favourable. Whether it was to win a heart, get rid of a rival, cover up a pregnancy or hasten a succession, they would make destiny do their bidding. Their wares were love potions and poisons, and their dens were besieged by nobles and bourgeois, princesses and courtesans. Where death might be convenient, it struck. This was a period when black masses were being celebrated over the naked body of Mme de Montespan, and when Mme de Brinvillers, the famous poisoner, was wiping out her near relations.

Louis xiv did not even suspect the existence of these horrors. At this time, people were ready to see in him 'a soul formed in the school of heaven'* in which 'the feeling of humanity shone forth.' He was anything but a tyrant, and yet in his private life he behaved in an abominable fashion. After so many years of concealed passion, he forced La Vallière to make a scandalous spectacle of herself as his official mistress, at the very moment when he was losing interest in her. Loaded with honours, but out of favour, Louise had to live for seven years alongside her victorious rival in order to preserve a few shreds of appearance – since it was a matter of a twofold adultery. The two enemies lived in the same apartment, to which a single key gave admittance. When they travelled, they shared the carriage of the heart-broken Maria

* Report of the Venetian ambassador Giustiniani.

Theresa, and onlookers asked one another whether they had seen the 'three queens'. When he returned from hunting, Louis would go and change in La Vallière's room, barely greeting her before going through to Mme de Montespan.

The Sun King believed that he had found his true companion at last in Françoise-Athénaïs, that goddess as noble as her lover, resplendent, sparkling, arrogant, mordant, exuberant, drunk with pride, sensuality and cruelty, furious in her anger, her jealousies and her hatreds, sacrilegious and bewitching. She constantly provoked the King, and defied him at bed and board alike.

M. de Montespan tried to interfere; he put on full mourning, gave his wife a thrashing and prepared a harangue larded with biblical quotations for the King's benefit. His Majesty had him arrested and packed off to his estates in Guyenne.

La Vallière too would have been delighted to disappear. One morning she fled, asked for asylum with the nuns of the Visitation of Our Lady, and rebuffed first the Comte de Lauzun* then Marshal de Bellefonds when they came to fetch her. Now it was Colbert's turn, and he brought her back to be greeted by Louis' ready tears. The entire court followed suit, and Athénaïs sobbed. Mme de Sevigné wrote: 'The King has had most tender conversations with her and Mme de Montespan,' but her cousin, the writer Bussy-Rabutin, was not taken in: 'It is in his own interest and purely out of policy that the King has made Mme de La Vallière come back.'

Despite his tears, Louis knew nothing of pity and flouted decency, convention and the laws of the Church. According to the ideas of the time, there was a kind of personal breach between religion and himself. If we are to believe the recent historian Lavisse, the son of Anne of Austria was well on the way towards becoming a free-thinker. Nevertheless, he reassured the pious by taking new measures against Protestantism, which had just been dealt a heavy blow by the conversion of Turenne.

On 18 July 1668 a prodigious fête at Versailles demonstrated that Louis was truly enacting a living myth. Molière played *Georges Dandin,* and the august audience roared with laughter at the poor cuckold who reminded them of M. de Montespan. The reflections of the fireworks in the windows filled with variously coloured statues transformed the Château into the Sun Palace.

Some months later the first son of the magnificent lovers was born. He was put in the care of the widow Scarron, née Françoise d'Aubigné, a pious young woman of good family, but fallen on such hard times that she had once been obliged to look after her aunt's turkeys. Her confessor, the Abbé Gobelin, had told her that it could not be a sin to obey the will of the King. When Louis

---

* Puyguilhem had taken this title on the death of his father, his elder brother having waived his own claim.

first met her, he found her antipathetic and 'bizarre', for she was something of a blue-stocking.

In 1670 Colbert was bold enough to defy the new favourite to whom the King had just assigned the dues from the Paris butchery trade, worth 150,000 crowns. A short time before, raison d'état would have prevailed. Now the King had changed tack. Realizing this, Colbert gave way and became a kind of steward of the whims of the Marquise.

Colbert and Louvois, the Crown's two principal servants (Lionne had just died), were now openly at each other's throat. Goaded beyond endurance by the ever-increasing expenditure of the court and by the status of his rival, Colbert made a scene with the King in front of the Council. The letter that Louis wrote to him following this incident is justly famous:

> Yesterday I had enough self-control to conceal the sorrow I felt on hearing a man like you, on whom I have lavished kindnesses, speaking to me as you did. I have had a great deal of affection for you and have shown it through my actions; I still have some now, and I believe that I am giving you quite a considerable proof of it when I tell you that I briefly restrained myself for your sake, and that I did not wish to tell you in person what I am writing to you, in order not to expose you to displeasing me further . . . Do not risk vexing me again, for, once I have heard your arguments and those of your colleagues, and have pronounced on all your claims, I do not wish to hear mention of the matter again.[2]

Colbert hastened to beg Louis' pardon, obtained it, and received a second letter, which restored things to normal by reminding him of his precise position:

> Do not believe that my friendship is diminishing. While your services continue, that is not possible. But you must render them to me as I want them, and believe that I act for the best. The preference that you believe me to be giving to others ought not to trouble you. I only wish not to do injustice and to work for the good of my service. That is what I shall do when you are all at my side.

From the heights of Olympus, the supreme master manipulated his ministers, his mistresses and the princes of the blood. He was never to give them the opportunity to oppose his will or to sway him as they might perhaps have managed to do if they had been united. It was for this reason that he fostered strife among his mistresses, the members of the Council and especially in his brother's extraordinary ménage.

⌐9⌐

The Infernal Machine

LOUIS XIV was continuing his dazzling rise, and yet already sowing the deeds of his decline. He was believed to be fully occupied with his amours, his buildings and his fêtes. In fact, he was pondering his grand design, the destruction of Dutch power. This dismaying break with traditional French policy was to alter the course of the reign. Nothing could have been less reasonable, and yet nothing was more logical. At one and the same time, he would be fighting a war of revenge, class, religion and economics. The rancour of the Sun King whom a bourgeois plutocracy had halted in his course derived as much from modern ideas as from archaic ones. If the heir of Saint Louis found it intolerable to be barred by a republic of Calvinist tradesmen, the son of the Rheims draper was no less exasperated by the arrogance of these competitors. Colbert wrote: 'Just as we have annihilated Spain on land, Holland must be annihilated at sea.' Condé saw the war as a strategic imperative. Consequently there was no one to point out the drawbacks of his undertaking to the King.

Diplomatic preparations began as early as 1668. Once again everything depended on England, where Louis sent a new ambassador, Colbert de Croissy. When Madame was informed that secret negotiations had been opened, she believed that her chance had come to win the conjugal battle that was taking on the proportions of a tragedy. She was having to put up with rages and daily harassments from Monsieur, egged on by his evil genius the Chevalier de Lorraine, who had become the effective master at the Palais Royal* and Saint-Cloud and thought himself invulnerable. In order to ruin her husband's darling, Henrietta asked her brother to request her personal mediation. Charles II told Colbert de Croissy 'that he would be well pleased to show how amenable he was to the entreaties of Madame.'

The scope of the matter broadened, and spread into the field of religion, for Louis wanted to bring England back into the Catholic fold, which would be the surest guarantee of an alliance. For his own part, Charles II saw such a development as a means of reinforcing his position, but did not dare to attempt it without the financial, and if necessary military backing of France.

* The King had given the Palais Royal to Philippe.

145

On 18 December 1669 he handed the ambassador a draft treaty that contained exorbitant financial conditions. The ensuing hard bargaining was arbitrated by the Duchesse d'Orléans.

The Chevalier de Lorraine made the mistake of discovering the secret and informing Monsieur that one of Charles II's conditions was that 'Minette' must make a journey to England. Furious at being kept in the dark, Philippe complained to his brother, and from then on Louis XIV considered the favourite a gossip – a species that he particularly despised and feared. He had him arrested at the first available pretext, in Monsieur's own apartments. Philippe fainted, then retired to Villers-Cotterêts, taking his wife with him. Colbert was appointed the go-between in a series of farcical negotiations whose outcome was that the Chevalier was released and went to Italy, where he became the lover of none other than Marie Mancini, and that Monsieur appeared at court again with a bitter grudge against his wife, considering her responsible for his friend's misfortune.

Meanwhile, the main negotiations proceeded. On 28 April 1670 the court moved to Flanders, on the pretext of visiting the recently annexed towns. An army of thirty thousand men escorted it, under the command of Lauzun (with whom La Grande Mademoiselle had recently and unexpectedly fallen in love). 'All you have seen of the splendour of Solomon cannot compare with the pomp that surrounds the King,' an officer wrote to Bussy-Rabutin.

At Lille, Madame set off for Dunkirk to embark, accompanied by a considerable entourage. Among her ladies in waiting was Louise de Kéroualle, the doll-like beauty who was to be the agent of the French alliance at the court of Charles II.

Monsieur had flatly refused to allow his wife to go to London, so Dover was the setting for the decisive interview between brother and sister. Henrietta returned triumphant, bearing with her in the form of a secret document the infernal machine that was to spark off half a century of wars, topple the Stuarts and destroy the Bourbon hegemony in Europe.

The Treaty of Dover brought Charles II the immediate advantage of large sums of money, with the expectation of more. It would enable him to keep his mistresses in style and strengthen his navy. The two sovereigns agreed 'to lay low the power of a nation that has the audacity to aspire to making itself the supreme arbiter,' and to share out its territories, with England taking the islands facing her coast. However, they stipulated that they would leave a few provinces to young William of Orange, Charles II's nephew, and revive on his behalf the title of Stadtholder held by his ancestors and abolished by the 'austere partisans of liberty', or rather by high finance. Charles was to postpone his conversion to a more auspicious date, but the English Catholics would benefit from certain measures of tolerance.

This pact became the object of an enduring hostility in Great Britain, although it also brought her the mastery of the seas. Since no one at the time could have foreseen that the French and Dutch would exhaust one another to England's gain, the Stuart really seemed to be betraying his faith and his country.

Madame disembarked on 12 June, to the salutes of cannon, trumpets and applause. Her brother-in-law was generous in his gratitude, but once again she became the butt of her husband's persecutions, for he wanted her to have the Chevalier's exile rescinded.

The court had just said its last farewell to Paris. On 26 June Henrietta spent the day at Versailles, where she had a private audience with Louis to report on her mission. Monsieur went to join them, and the sudden silence that greeted his entrance was the cause of a further, and particularly violent scene. Madame left Versailles in tears. On 29 June the King was stunned to be informed that she was dying after drinking a glass of chicory water. The court hastened to Saint-Cloud. Louis stayed at the unhappy young woman's side for a while, then they took their final leave of each other.

Madame died in the night. The King was informed at six in the morning, and wept copiously, though without losing any of his sang-froid, since after breakfast he said to Mademoiselle: 'Cousin, there is a place vacant. Do you want to take it?' Both in France and England, everybody was convinced that Madame had been poisoned, if not by Monsieur, then at least by his favourites. The affair has never been completely clarified, but it hardly seems possible today to uphold the accusation. Louis took good care not to disclose his own opinion.

The King's treatment of his brother remained unchanged. The Chevalier de Lorraine returned to favour in 1672, and remained so until his death thirty years later. The Marquis d'Effiat, suspected of having administered the poison with his own hand, also remained in favour, received the Cordon Bleu and finished his career as a member of the Regency Council under Louis xv. It is impossible to believe that the King would have treated them in that fashion if he had believed them guilty of the murder of his sister-in-law.[1]

After some hesitation, Mademoiselle declined the 'vacant place'. At forty-three years of age, she was infatuated with Lauzun and plucked up the courage to ask permission to marry him. Louis consented, but whatever his motives, he was making a mistake. A man like Lauzun, insatiable, restless and unscrupulous, could become very dangerous if he acquired the lands and wealth of a great feudal inheritance. The King soon realized this and was only too pleased to yield to the vehement protests of Monsieur and Condé (signally ungrateful to the woman who had saved him during the Fronde) and revoke his promise. Weeping profusely, he stabbed his cousin in the back.

All the same, a wedding ceremony did take place in 1671, marking the union of Philippe d'Orléans and the poor, ugly and heretical Charlotte

Elizabeth of Bavaria, daughter of the Elector Palatine. Her birth was inferior to his, but the interesting point about this ill-assorted match is that the parsimony of the bride's father was to deter him from paying the agreed dowry, like Philip IV of Spain before him, thus giving the Bourbons a claim to the succession.

If 'Liselotte' did not seem in the least impressed by the luxurious life of her new family, the court was quite taken aback by a Highness 'who had the face and loutishness of a Swiss,'[2] and the rudeness and vulgarity of a German mercenary. But the rudeness was accompanied by honesty, straightforward-ness and respect for honour and virtue, and the vulgarity by wit and shrewdness. Louis was amused by her bluntness. Liselotte became his friend, and gradually, without realizing it, fell in love with him.

None of this prevented Louis from laying up trouble for himself by recalling the Chevalier de Lorraine. To have Monsieur firmly in hand was also an element in his preparations for war. When he received the news, Philippe threw himself at his brother's feet, speechless with emotion, and Louis told him cynically: 'I want you to feel this obligation all your life, and to love him out of love for myself.' Monsieur's ecstasy was balanced by the lamentations of Mademoiselle. Lauzun had deeply offended Mme de Montespan; he was too ambitious and too bold. Much to his own surprise, he was arrested and packed off to join Fouquet in Pignerol. Both of these decrees had been unexpected: friendship had as weak a hold on the heart of the Sun King as family feeling.

Meanwhile, Colbert's gold was finding its way to the Emperor, the King of Sweden and the German princes. Only the Elector of Brandenburg refused to be bought. 'Everything that human ambition and prudence could do to prepare the destruction of a nation, Louis had done. No minor enterprise had ever been planned with such formidable preparations.'[3]

In February 1672 Louvois proudly presented to Louis the most powerful army, commanded by the greatest warriors, that the West had known since the Romans: 120,000 superbly trained men, armed with a new weapon, the bayonet, and placed under the orders of Condé, Turenne, Luxembourg and Vauban. The King's Household, where from now on young gentlemen undertook military service without pay (a great innovation), sported gold- and silver-embroidered uniforms. Nothing was accidental; these troops were to be 'at once an object of terror and of wonder for people among whom any kind of magnificence was unknown.' A hundred English ships and thirty French were taking their stations to control the 'narrow seas'.

The States-General of the United Provinces were panic-stricken. When they inquired of their ally, the King of France, whether his preparations were directed against themselves and in what respect they had offended, Louis answered 'that he would make such use of his troops as was required by his

François de Salignac de la
Mothe Fénelon (after Joseph
Vivien)

Jean Baptiste Colbert (after P.
Mignard)

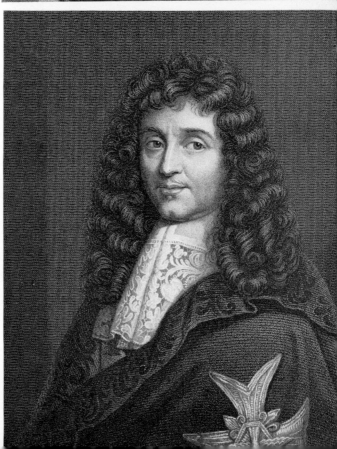

Meeting of Louis XIV and Philip IV of
Spain, 6 June 1660, concerning the
betrothal of Louis and Marie
Thérèse (Gobelin Tapestry after
Charles Lebrun – Versailles)

Marie Thérèse
(attributed to Jean
Petiot)

dignity, for which he owed account to no one.' The desperate Grand Pensionary broke the mould of the unlucky medal that showed Holland halting the sun.

[10]

The Surprises of War

At a remove of centuries, Louis' war looks like a piece of sheer folly, and its methods often reminiscent of the Fronde. The first irony came when John de Witt, hoping to conciliate the lower classes and to please Louis XIV, appointed as Captain-General the same William of Orange who was to destroy his rule and to become France's most bitter enemy (January 1672).

On 23 March Charles II, unable to resist the lure of plunder any longer, launched his squadrons against a Dutch fleet anchored off the Isle of Wight. His treachery was in vain: the fleet and the convoy it was protecting escaped almost unharmed after a running battle that lasted for two days. On 6 April Louis XIV opened hostilities. He did not deign to give his reasons to the enemy, but referred in a memorandum for posterity to 'the ingratitude and intolerable vanity of the Dutch.'[1] To modern eyes, Louis XIV emerges at this point as a warmonger, yet he was never prone to the flashes of blind aggression or the terrible love of risk that we encounter in the conquerors of antiquity, in Napoleon, and above all in Hitler. As Jacques Madaule writes: 'He loved show much more than war – sieges conducted like ballets, where ladies were invited to witness the surrender. Very cautious by nature, as far as he was able to do so the King ventured only on undertakings that were safe, even without risk.'[2]

True to his temperament, Condé proposed that the cavalry should strike at Amsterdam, gain control of the sluice-gates and seize the States-General – the right move, but its undignified audacity was too much for Louis. His Majesty left Saint-Germain on 29 April, reviewed his troops at Charleroi, and advanced sedately along the Meuse, accompanied by Louvois. The crossing of the Rhine, recounted by Boileau and painted by Van Der Meulen, took place on 12 June – a spectacular operation, carelessly handled. The young princes and many gentlemen charged blindly and suffered unnecessary losses. Seeing his nephew Longueville fall, Condé forgot his duties as Commander-in-Chief, dashed to his assistance and was wounded in the vanguard (it was the first wound in his career.) There was a period of confusion before Turenne came and took his place.

According to Boileau, Louis complained during the attack 'of his high rank, which tied him to the bank.' Later, the absurd accusation that he lacked courage became current, but it was not for the King of France to jump into the water, or to come under the first volleys of the Dutch army.

Once order had been restored, strongholds and fortresses tumbled like nine-pins. Sir Winston Churchill wrote: 'The Dutch people, faced with extermination, set their despairing hopes upon William of Orange. The great-grandson of William the Silent did not fail them. He roused and animated their tough, all-enduring courage.'[3] In reality, the young prince was retreating deep into the country, and was no longer in a position to defend Amsterdam, The Hague or Muiden, the location of the sluice-gates that held back the waters of the Zuider Zee.

Condé had wanted to send six thousand horsemen to this crucial point. Turenne sent only four thousand, and on the insistence of Louvois placed them under the command of the Marquis de Rochefort, whose wife was Louvois' mistress. Rochefort had no idea of the importance of his mission and did not over-exert himself to accomplish it. When some of his dragoons entered Muiden and were driven off, he did not dig his heels in. Louis XIV and Charles II had already lost control of the high seas, following the Battle of Sole Bay, during which Ruyter broke the power of the combined Franco-British fleets.

The King had not yet had time to work out the full implications of these events when the deputies of the States-General sent by John de Witt came to sue for peace on 22 June, much to the disgust of William of Orange. Louvois received them at Doesburg with a coarse harshness quite contrary to the traditions of diplomacy, and kept them waiting for a week for a second audience. A number of irreparable actions occurred during those seven days. The King, dealing with the Dutch like rebellious subjects, threatened sack and pillage to any town that put up resistance, and in those he had already taken he solemnly instituted the supremacy of the Catholic rite. The economic operation was taking on the aspect of a crusade.

Driven to desperation, the Dutch did not wait on the negotiations. They opened the sluices and threw themselves on the mercy of the ocean, halting the French advance in a single stroke. Louvois' amours were costing dear.

The Secretary of State was hot-headed, cruel and wildly ambitious; he played a still more fatal part when the negotiations finally got under way at the camp at Amerongen. Lionne had died the previous year, and his successor, the Jansenist Pomponne, did not have the resolution to enforce his own moderation over the intransigence of his colleague, who in any case was positively eager for the war to be prolonged.

The King set exorbitant conditions. In effect, he was demanding that the Dutch should go back to their marshes, sacrificing the belt of provinces and strongholds which in the hands of the French would have kept them in a perpetual state of siege. He also required that they submit to the ruinous tariff of 1667, pay an indemnity of twenty-five million livres, re-establish the Catholic Church, and, finally, that 'the Republic should send an embassy extraordinary each year with a gold medallion on which the engraving would read that they received their liberty from His Most Christian Majesty.'

The Dutch negotiators left and did not return. The flooding spread, engulfing Leyden, Delft, the fertile countryside, villas, palaces, the houses that had inspired so many masterpieces, and the exotic gardens and treasures that had already transformed this land into a kind of universal museum. Ruyter's invincible fleet surrounded Amsterdam, which had become an island. Although largely submerged, Holland still ruled the seas. Its flag still flew in the East Indies. Louis had won a few battles, but lost the war.

The King proceeded to examine his own conscience lucidly and logically; he paid tribute to the enemy and recognized his errors, albeit with an affected nonchalance:

> I cannot help but admire and praise the zeal and fortitude of the men who broke off the negotiations, although their advice, so salutary for their country, was most prejudicial to my service. Posterity . . . may blame this refusal [to make peace] on my ambition and my desire to avenge the injuries I had received from the Dutch. I shall not attempt to justify myself. Ambition and *gloire* are always pardonable in a young prince whom fortune has treated well.

Had he prolonged his meditation, he might perhaps have understood what was to lie at the root of two centuries of tragedies for Europe. France cannot be supreme on land and sea at once. When she forgets that law, she exposes herself to a Rosbach or a Waterloo.

The hour of William of Orange had come. On 27 June, thinking that all was lost, he had asked the States-General to allow him to negotiate with the enemy in person in order to safeguard his own lands. On 3 July he was appointed Stadtholder, but at that time he was still regarded as a protégé of the French. It was not until a few days later that, feeling Germany beginning to stir, he took on the part of a national hero. Thus began the astonishing career that was to lead him to become the victorious rival of the Sun King.

As a child, William had enjoyed neither laughter, play nor learning. Only theological discussion and the study of languages seemed to stir his mind. At the age of twenty he already was what he would always remain: taciturn, cunning, aggressively self-centred, averse to pomp, indifferent to women, firm, tenacious, impossible to discourage and burning with two exclusive passions – power and fighting.

Louis xiv made the mistake of waiting until 22 July before opening negotiations with William. The Emperor and the Elector of Brandenburg signed a treaty of defence against France and sent troops to the assistance of the United Provinces, and without consulting Madrid, the Spanish governor in Flanders put six thousand of his men at the disposal of the Prince of Orange, who was thus enabled to turn down disdainful offers. By the end of July the military stroll had been transformed conclusively into a war. The King returned to Saint-Germain, 'satisfied to have taken so many towns in the space of two months,'[4] but satisfaction was not destined to be complete.

As for William, now that he was momentarily delivered from the French danger, he set about establishing his authority by getting rid of his political adversaries. The Grand Pensionary, John de Witt, and his brother were killed in a riot at The Hague, after an iniquitous trial. Their friend Ruyter narrowly escaped the same fate. The Prince let it be known that he was 'comforted' by the abominable crime that he could have prevented if he had not been its instigator. In spite of the adulation of his admirers, that is enough to deprive him of any moral superiority over Louis XIV.

There were discordant notes among the panegyrics that greeted his Majesty's return, but Louis was unmoved. He was happy to be back with his two loves, Mme de Montespan and, above all, Versailles. Twenty-two thousand men and six hundred horses were working there, and the King made constant visits, complaining that things were not moving quickly enough. Le Vau, who had started the construction of the new palace, had died in 1670 and been succeeded by Dorbay. Sculptors and decorators were doing the initial work on the façades, and Le Nôtre was completing the great vista of the park. A one-storey pavilion, the porcelain Petit Trianon, covered with squares of blue and white Delft, had been built to amuse the favourite.

Since the King no longer wanted to live in Paris, he had to put up with staying for a while at Saint-Germain, which was transformed in its turn. Little remains of these splendid alterations. The balconies round the façades are gone, as are the hall of shells and 'the great silver vessel that sets a hundred fountains playing at will.' Of the 'hanging gardens', nothing remains but the terrace from which Louis loved to contemplate the endless perspectives that lead the eye from a somewhat over-contrived foreground down to the natural countryside.

While Louis lavished money on his buildings, he was also preparing to expand his armies and pour still more gold into England, Germany and Hungary, although this did not prevent his enemies from joining forces. France was embarking upon a long-drawn-out conflict in which the King would find compensations for his failure in Holland. On the other hand, Colbert was playing an inevitably losing game. Far from gaining the economic hegemony, France was on the brink of the financial chaos which persisted until the age of Napoleon.

[11]

The Crusade Rebounds

THE year 1673 was the worst since the Fronde. Molière died on 7 February, an opportune departure from the point of view of the King, with whom his favour was declining. Until 1672, in spite of the ban on *Tartuffe*, Molière had been well treated by his master. He had received generous compensation in 1665, when the *dévots* succeeded in halting (for two hundred years) the performance of *Don Juan*; *Tartuffe*, finally authorized in its new version, had been a success since 1669; *Le Bourgeois gentilhomme,* partly intended as a satire on the pretensions of the Turkish ambassador, had been enthusiastically received at Chambord, as had *Les Femmes savantes* at Saint-Cloud. But in 1672 Molière had fallen foul of Lully, and the Italian had gained an overwhelming advantage: no theatre except his own was to have the right to play ballet music. A bitter struggle ensued, and the King became estranged from his favourite author under the influence of his own love of music and Lully's intrigues. Molière's misfortunes came to a head when he was unable to present the première of *Le Malade imaginaire* in the presence of his Majesty. Lully had been cooperating with his other enemies to plant doubt in Louis' mind about Molière's genius.

Years later the King asked Boileau: 'Who was the greatest writer of my reign?' 'Molière, Sire.' 'I did not think so,' Louis answered thoughtfully, 'but you know more about it than I do.'

Madame and Molière were dead; La Vallière was in decline; Louvois' power was challenging Colbert's; the court had deserted Paris for good. The reign of Louis XIV was taking a new turn.

The most marked alteration was in the relationship France now had with foreign countries, where she was practically on the defensive. Marshal Luxembourg tried to seize Amsterdam when the Zuider Zee froze over, but a sudden thaw halted him and almost drowned his army. Luxembourg took a Frondeur's revenge by wreaking terrible devastation in the countryside. He especially enjoyed watching the houses of the Prince of Orange and his favourite go up in flames.

Since the Thirty Years War, defeated countries had been ravaged and held to ransom as a matter of course. Louvois conceived the idea of bringing method to these outrages. For the first time, the horrors of occupation were the product of a system, not the whims of the soldiery. The Dutch suffered cruelly, but France paid even more dearly for Louvois' administrative ferocity and the cheerful inhumanity of Luxembourg. Traditionally, she had been regarded as the natural ally and protector of small nations and the oppressed. In the time of Henry IV the peoples of Europe had looked to France: their admiration was now to be superseded by a profound hatred and resentment.

All this was done without the knowledge of Louis XIV, who was informed too late. Luxembourg was dumbfounded when he now received the letter in which Louvois blandly told him that the King had been extremely surprised:

> to see that the country is still being pillaged and exposed to the violence of the soldiery. You know as well as anybody that that is a certain way to ruin the troops and the country ... His Majesty has commanded me to inform you that he wishes you to remedy the situation so that the peasants in the country may have as much peace when they pay their taxes as they had in the time of the Dutch.

But the damage was done. The superb machine of Louis XIV's régime was suddenly rattling, losing its rhythm. There was no plan afoot to retrieve the situation, and the forces of morality were working against France. Germany's indignation at Luxembourg's ravages was equalled by the religious fury of the English when the secret clauses of the Treaty of Dover leaked out.

True to his word, Charles II had promulgated a Declaration of Indulgence on behalf of Puritans and Catholics. Parliament found such tolerance intolerable. It refused to give him a penny until the Declaration was rescinded, and passed a Test Act excluding papists from public employment. Within a few days the atmosphere was reminiscent of that of the civil war.

Louis XIV took fright. If Charles was obliged to go on his travels again, as the opposition had threatened in no uncertain terms, the English alliance and the entire war would be lost at one blow. Forgetting his crusade, Louis urged his cousin to satisfy the Commons' demands, but Charles wanted to resist. Eventually he yielded to the tears of his French mistress, poor 'Minette's' last gift, Louise de Kéroualle, recently created Duchess of Portsmouth. The Duke of York, Charles II's brother and heir to the throne, at once gave up his official posts, thus admitting his Catholic allegiance. London celebrated, Parliament granted Charles £1,200,000, and Louis had to reward Mlle de Kéroualle for her services by according her the right of *tabouret* and the French duchy of Aubigné.

Louis now thought it prudent to pension not only the King of England but also the members of the Opposition. It only remained for Colbert to find further millions. A doctrinaire Protestant, the Marquis de Ruvigny, was appointed ambassador to carry out the mission, replacing Colbert de Croissy. As for Charles, he put the government in the hands of the Earl of Danby, a declared enemy of Catholicism and France. 'The King swung steadily and smoothly with the change of the tide like a ship at anchor.'¹

Spring came – time for 'the greatest king in the world' to reassert his power. Louis decided that he would win a military victory in person. While Condé contained William of Orange, and Turenne the Imperials, he left Saint-Germain, taking with him the Queen, Louise de La Vallière and the pregnant Mme de Montespan. After Athénaïs had given birth to a daughter at Tournai, the King took leave of the ladies. He reached Courtrai, followed by a smaller cortège and a full complement of historians and poets, and put himself at the head of the army.

On 12 June Louis invested Maestricht, a key fortress that he would have done better to seize in 1672. 'Vauban,' he wrote ingenuously, 'suggested measures to me which I judged to be the best.' These consisted of employing the technique of lines of parallel trenches by which Italian engineers had enabled the Turks to enter Candia in 1669. The King had no desire to hazard his reputation, and 'enjoined great caution. He displayed greater exactitude and perseverance than he had ever done before: by his example, he accustomed to patience and toil a nation accused hitherto of possessing only the courage of impetuosity, quickly dissipated by fatigue.'²

The contemporary poet La Fare expressed the opposite view in his memoirs:

> The precautions did not have a good effect on a nation which glories recklessly not only in daring but in seeking danger. I know that this is not the function of a king, but when he wishes to lead others into such circumstances, he ought not to seem to be blatantly avoiding them, especially if he affects the reputation of a warrior and a hero.

Louis XIV, a great modern ruler, should not have aspired to the anachronistic panache of chivalry.

Maestricht yielded after eight days. Almost simultaneously, three desperate naval battles were fought between the Dutch under Ruyter and the English and French under Prince Rupert and Vice-Admiral d'Estrées. The issue was inconclusive, and Louis XIV and Colbert were accused of having instructed d'Estrées to let the English squadrons be crushed.

Thereupon the Emperor and the King of Spain, now allied with the United Provinces (on 30 August 1673), declared war on France. Leopold I was a visionary who thought that Heaven would grant revenge to the House of Austria. Crucifix in hand, he preached holy war to his army. In an extraordinary reversal of fortunes Louis XIV, now evil incarnate, saw the crusade rebound on him, uniting the Habsburgs and their former worst enemies, the heretic Netherlanders.

Turenne was unable to prevent the Emperor's army from joining forces with the Prince of Orange, who recaptured the stronghold of Naerden from the French. A minor event, it had important repercussions, for it was the Sun King's first defeat. Louis was infuriated, and inflicted a harsh punishment on Du Pas, the officer who surrendered. Soon he himself would be giving way, evacuating the occupied Dutch provinces and being snubbed by having his discreet peace feelers rejected out of hand by William, his former protégé. The hatred that France had incurred was an emotional factor entirely new to European politics. The entry of the Emperor's forces into Bonn was another blow that almost cost Louvois his job.

Louis tried to insure himself by providing the Duke of York with a Catholic wife, Princess Maria of Modena, Mazarin's great-niece. It was another mistake: an angry Parliament compelled the English King to accept Spanish mediation and to make peace. The Dutch seemed only too happy 'to accept in all humility the naval supremacy of England.' Here – yet another unforeseen factor – was a political success for Charles II.

Inferior to Louis XIV in so many respects, Charles nevertheless inherited the immense cunning of Henry IV, their mutual grandfather. He was on excellent terms with his chief minister while being opposed in principle to his ideas, creating a curious diarchy that enabled a balance to be maintained between Crown and Parliament.

In spite of the defection of England, Louis XIV continued to influence her government, since he was subsidizing both parties at once. At least, so he believed. In fact, he enabled Charles to become a dual blackmailer by demanding money from Louis so as to remain independent of the Commons, and from the Commons so as to prepare for war against Louis. Danby used to say: 'Let us make the French pay through the nose, they are getting nothing in return.' All the same, they were getting the English neutrality thanks to which this extraordinary traffic could be maintained.

There were English regiments in the pay of France, and Charles II allowed his brother-in-law to retain one of them, suggesting that the command should go to Captain John Churchill, then twenty-four years old. The Captain had a number of claims to this promotion: he was a valiant, handsome soldier, the brother of the Duke of York's mistress and the lover of the King's principal English mistress, the Duchess of Cleveland. Louis XIV gave him a gracious welcome to Versailles when he was presented, and the future Marlborough began a year's apprenticeship in the army whose supremacy he was destined to shatter.

At the beginning of 1674 the picture was gloomy. Abandoned by England and even by her German allies (Münster, Cologne), France confronted a coalition for the first time since Louis XII. There were risings against the revenue officials. What changes in less than two years! Yet Louis, although secretly always prepared for the worst, was still Le Grand Roi and was proving it by the splendour of his life. In 1674 the first coins bearing the inscription Ludovicus Magnus were struck. The Venetian ambassador, Primi Visconti, was fascinated by the sight of Louis leaving Versailles 'With his body guards, carriages, horses, courtiers, valets and a seething mass of people rushing noisily after him.' He added: 'It reminds me of the queen bee.'

It was the King's own mistakes that were about to set him back on the right track. Naval ventures and crusades were not for France. As long as her frontiers were vulnerable it was on land and against the Catholic powers that the struggle lay. Defeat in Holland compelled the country to resume the policy of Richelieu.

[12]

The Rage to Live

BY the age of thirty-five, Louis XIV no longer resembled the ideal monarch whom ambassadors had once described in such glowing terms. There was still mention of his 'beauty', although he was already beginning to be rather 'engorged with flesh', but Van Der Meulen's portrait brings out the Bourbon traits and underlines the curious contrast between small moustache and gigantic wig. The face has thickened, and the remaining traces of smallpox complete the picture of a red-cheeked, weather-beaten countryman. Before and after his eight-hour working day, Louis took physical exercise, walking, riding, hunting, playing royal tennis, displaying his skill as a marksman, all of which compensated for his excessive appetite and his physician's remedies.

The King was now showing every sign of an omnivorous greed that had been lacking two years previously: he was greedy for gloire, conquests, pleasure, sport, food and women. Charlotte Elizabeth writes: 'he was gallant, but often he took gallantry to the point of debauchery. Nothing came amiss to him as long as it was female – peasants, gardeners' daughters, ladies of quality. *They need only pretend to be in love with him.'* The traits of his character were becoming as strongly marked as those of his face. Never was Louis more self-controlled, more imbued with his own grandeur, jealous of his authority, secretive and suspicious. 'He wants to know everything,' Primi Visconti noted. 'Not much happens in the course of any day without his knowledge, there are few people whos name and habits he does not know, and once he has seen a man or heard him mentioned he remembers him always.' It was awkward to be one of those exceptions who left no trace on the royal memory, for the King, thinking that perhaps he had something against the person in question, would withhold his favour.

No private letter was safe. A staff of officials was employed secretly to open correspondence.

The promptitude and dexterity of that procedure beggars comprehension. The King saw a summary of every letter containing matter that . . . [was] deemed worthy of his personal attention . . . A word of derision about the King or the régime, a joke, in short a specious and out-of-context extract from a letter could ruin a man beyond retrieval . . . The secrecy was impenetrable, and nothing came more easily to the King than to maintain a profound silence and to dissimulate in the same way. He often took this last talent to the point of duplicity, but even then he never told a lie and prided himself on keeping his word. Which meant that he hardly ever gave it.[1]

1673 was the year in which Louis legitimized his three children by Mme de Montespan, thus proving that the twofold adultery no longer embarrassed him. It was also at this time that his aversion for their governess changed into respect, then friendship. Mme Scarron, a widow, was thirty-eight years old and at the peak of her charms. The King by now had no control over his desires and thought himself irresistible, so that it is impossible to believe that in the course of their frequent tête-a-têtes he always respected the virtue of his future wife, or that if he had suffered a rebuff he would have gone on seeking out this *déclassée,* endured her sermonizing, or bestowed on her the title of Marquise de Maintenon. Mme de Montespan did not take long to identify her protégée as an enemy, if not a rival. From 1674 onward the virtuous widow employed a diabolical strategy to alienate the King from his mistress and the children from their mother.

Even if her activities had come to light, there would have seemed no point to them. Mme de Montespan, of whom Maria Theresa said 'That whore will be my death,' had been haughtily usurping the supreme position. Beneath her golden robes and her diamonds, this full-blown goddess, insatiable in bed and at the dining- and gaming-table was, with her charms and rages, her hauteur and her laughter, her fine and ferocious manners, the true counterpart of a King obsessed with the rage to live.

The same rage also burst out in quarrels and violence. Athénaïs kept a sharp watch on her lover, and ladies of the palace replaced the Queen's maids of honour because Louis 'made free' with some of these girls.

She even called in supernatural assistance: La Voisin supplied the favourite with 'powders' that were mixed with his Majesty's food, with the cooperation of one of the royal cup-bearers. It is hardly surprising that on 1 January 1674 Louis suffered quite violent dizzy spells.

Meanwhile, on the advice of her confessor, Bossuet, Louise de La Vallière asked permission to join the Carmelites. Mme de Montespan was greatly put out, and dispatched none other than the pious Mme Scarron to talk her out of so extreme a step, but Louise persisted and at last, grudgingly, the King gave his consent.

On 19 April Louise played out a famous scene, worthy of the fabulous drama in which she had acted the most sympathetic role. The Duchesse de La Vallière took her leave of the King and prostrated herself before the Queen, imploring her forgiveness. Louis restrained his tears, but not so Maria Theresa, and the entire attendance burst out crying – among them, of course, Mme de Montespan. Two days later Louise took the nun's habit in front of a sobbing court. Bussy-Rabutin was unimpressed: 'God attracts people to himself along all kinds of roads. If one may make so bold as to say it, he would have had difficulty in attracting that penitent woman out of the arms of her lover, but jealousy has worked the miracle. . . .'

Thus Louis finally cut himself off from his youth. From then on, although he was very fond of Mlle de Blois, La Vallière's daughter, he hardly ever spoke her mother's name. Twenty-six years later, when he was informed of her death, he merely commented that 'from the day she had left him, she had been dead to him.'

[13]

Fêtes, Massacres
and Conspiracies

A NEW gateway into Paris, the Porte Saint-Martin, had been intended to commemorate the conquest of Holland. It reached completion at the moment when French troops were withdrawing from the United Provinces. To restore his prestige and demonstrate his power, Louis now went onto the offensive against the most vulnerable of his enemies, Spain. Having bought off the Swiss, who refused to allow passage to an Imperial relief force, he attacked Franche-Comté for the second time. The ceremonial of Saint-Germain continued unaltered during a series of sieges conducted by Vauban with masterly self-confidence, and in six weeks Franch-Comté was overrun. The Queen and the ladies visited Dole while it was still reeking of blood and smoke, and his Majesty went back to his châteaux well pleased with himself.

Versailles was almost complete in the first version, that is, without the great gallery and the two wings. A dazzling series of fêtes took place there during the summer. The courtiers admired the grove of the Marais d'Eau, constructed after designs by Mme de Montespan, listened to concerts under the trees of the Trianon, caroused around the fountain of the Cour de Marbre and acclaimed Racine's *Iphigénie*. Athénaïs was in her element, 'Juno thundering and triumphant.'

She was triumphant certainly, but the thunder rolled because the Queen's apartments were too luxurious. To appease her, Louis appointed a young architect, Jules Hardouin Mansart, to build the Château de Clagny; the gardens were laid out, naturally, by Le Nôtre. Twelve hundred labourers started work, and Colbert groaned yet again. Meanwhile the war was reaching frightening proportions, and a few gentlemen were hatching a republican plot, hand in glove with the Dutch and Spanish.

The affair was discovered in July. A man named Van den Enden, a Fleming who taught Latin in Paris, had rented rooms to one of his pupils, Cauzé de Nazelles, who was surprised to find his teacher receiving visits from La Tréaumont, an officer of ill repute, and from a very great lord, the Chevalier de Rohan, natural son of the Comte de Soissons* and the Princesse de

---

* Killed at La Marfée in a battle against his King (1641).

Guéménée. The student discovered that they were planning to kidnap the king and the Dauphin, spark off an uprising and a Dutch invasion of Normandy, and eventually proclaim a Republic.

Rohan, a childhood playmate of the King, was a handsome adventurer, a gambler, up to his neck in debt and a favourite with women. Displeased by his rowdy conquests, Louis xiv had put the Chevalier in the Bastille for a month. After the Dutch campaign, in which he served as a volunteer, Louvois refused to allow Rohan any compensation, although he had been wounded. Disgraced and ruined, he turned to conspiracy like his father before him, and like another of his forebears, the Duc de Rohan, a Protestant leader in the time of Louis xiii, who had planned the King's downfall and drafted a constitution providing for a popular State.

Cauzé warned Louvois, but the King would not move before receiving concrete proof, a cautious approach suggested by Colbert, whose daughter had married the Duc de Chevreuse, the Chevalier's cousin. The battle of Seneffe, which took place on 11 August 1674, brought him that proof in an unexpected manner. This battle, fought between the French forces under Condé and the coalition forces (actually including a number of Frenchmen) under William of Orange, was a fearful massacre. Eight thousand men fell on each side. Condé had three horses killed under him, and his only victory lay in remaining master of the field of battle. He sent the King a harvest of standards and the helmet of a Spaniard, the Marquis d'Affentar, which contained a statement of the sums disbursed to Rohan and La Tréaumont.[1] There could be no further reason to hesitate.

The Chevalier was arrested at Versailles as he came out of mass, and about sixty others received the same treatment, unjustly in some cases. Rohan, Van den Enden and two of their accomplices went to the scaffold on 27 November. The public were shocked by the cowardice of the princes and great nobles, none of whom dared intervene on behalf of a man who was related to all of them.

At the price of dreadful carnage, Condé had gained nothing. In a few small battles, Turenne drove two of the Emperor's generals back across the Rhine, as well as Duke Charles of Lorraine 'who spent all his life losing his states and raising troops'.[2] It was the time of year when armies usually paused for breath, but the Germanic fury was so intense that they took no account of the season, and seventy thousand Germans invaded Alsace, blockaded Breisach and Philippsburg and thought that their winter quarters were now secure.

Turenne had barely twenty thousand men at his disposal; the King wanted no chances taken, and Louvois kept giving him orders to the same effect; the winter was severe. The Marshal overrode every objection, crossed the snow-covered mountains, fell on the astonished enemy, scattered them and forced them to retreat over the Rhine again. It was these celebrated Rhine campaigns that brought Turenne's fame to its peak. Unfortunately, they also made the French the bugbear of other countries.

Turenne had invaded the Palatinate in spite of the King's prohibition and his family connection with the Elector. The murder of a few soldiers, who were left hanging from trees, provided him with the pretext for 'gobbling up the whole country.' Twenty-seven towns and villages were burned, and all Europe was scandalized. Wars were not yet ideological in the seventeenth century: in the twentieth the operation would have been considered almost lenient.

Turenne was the father of his men, which meant that he did not flinch from sacrificing populations to them, whether friendly or hostile. Nor did he flinch from the strategic necessity which led him to butcher Lorraine and even parts of Alsace. Posterity has not held it against him, yet has readily accused Louis XIV of barbarity. Nevertheless, the King did something that no modern head of state would dare; when the great chemist Poli suggested the use of poisonous bombs, Louis paid him a pension on condition that his invention remained a secret for ever.[3] It was at about the same time that he expunged from Roussillon the worst vestige of Spanish domination – the Inquisition.

[14]

Retribution

THE King's health suffered that winter. Colds and 'fluxions on the chest' were accompanied by dizzy spells, fainting and shivering. These were the most evident effect of the powders that La Voisin was still supplying to Mme de Montespan, some of which contained ingredients such as excrement and toad's spittle.

The mixtures did not prevent Louis from finding a growing pleasure in the company of Mme Scarron. This 'secret which has been working in the earth for over six months,' Mme de Sévigné wrote on 7 August 1675, ceased to be one when the humble widow became the Marquise de Maintenon. The antagonism between her and the favourite burst its bonds at the same time. 'It is a real aversion,' the letter related, 'it is bitterness, it is antipathy, it is black, it is white.'

These were no petty female squabbles. Behind them lay the long-term plan of the Church, which was determined to put an end to the disorderly life of the court and gradually to bring the King under its direct influence. The grand-daughter of the fiercely Protestant Agrippa d'Aubigné was to be the clergy's unexpected instrument.

At Easter, this policy was considered far enough advanced for a heavy blow to be dealt. In spite of her twofold adultery and dabblings in witchcraft, Mme de Montespan was a very pious, or rather a very religious woman. She was delighted to hear that a priest at Versailles, the Abbé Lécuyer, was known for being 'easy' on poor sinners, and she went to see him on Maundy Thursday. To her great consternation, she found herself dismissed from the confessional by Lécuyer, who said: 'Is that the Mme de Montespan who is scandalizing all France? Go, go, Madame, and cease your scandals. Then you shall come to throw yourself at the feet of the ministers of Jesus Christ!'

Beside herself with rage, Athénaïs hastened to the King to demand justice, maintaining that a confessor could not refuse absolution. Louis, unconvinced, sent for the Bishop of Condom, who was the Dauphin's preceptor and champion of the divine right of kings – none other than Bossuet himself. The Bishop's hopes were firmly fixed on the 'conversion' of the monarch and an end to the scandal that was doing so much damage to the magnificent orderliness of his doctrine. 'He spoke out unhesitatingly, and said not only that the confessor had the power to refuse absolution but also that in some cases it was his duty, and he made no bones about saying that this lady's case was one in which a confessor could not give absolution.'[1]

Coming in the middle of Holy Week, these words had a considerable effect on the two lovers and awoke the fear of hell in them. For the second time in his life, Louis enacted the climax of *Bérénice*, but duty alone had parted him from Marie Mancini, whereas this time that duty was being preached to him not only by a bishop but also by another woman. Mme de Montespan left the court and withdrew to Vaugirard, to the house where Mme de Maintenon looked after her children. This must surely have been the supreme penance, for that self-righteous soul made a poor job of concealing her joy. Athénaïs visited churches, prayed, wept, fasted and advertised her repentance. For his own part, the King put on a show of great religious fervour. Bossuet visited Vaugirard daily, and was eventually assured of the sincerity of the unlikely penitent.

Mme de Montespan's friends wondered why she should not come back to court. Birth and rank made it her proper place, and she could live in as Christian a manner there as anywhere else. Bossuet gave his consent, although much to the disgust of the *dévots*, who could recall their own youth, and were much better acquainted with the passions than was the good bishop. They protested that Mme de Montespan ought not to appear before the King again without due precautions being taken: they must see one another before they met in public, in order to avoid any undesirable effects of the shock of meeting.

Accordingly it was decided that His Majesty was to pay a visit to the Marquise, but that a number of 'grave and respectable' ladies should be present at the interview to silence wagging tongues. The King came in, took one look at his radiant mistress, and found his heart and senses unequal to the strain. After exchanging a few civilities, he drew her into an alcove where they whispered to each other and gushed with tears. The matrons observed them with apprehension. All at once they were frozen by the spectacle of the lovers making a brief bow and disappearing into the next room. Nine months later came the birth of a daughter whom the Regent, her eventual husband, was to dub 'Mme Lucifer.'[2]

By July Mme de Montespan was restored to all her former glory. She took precedence over duchesses, and the Queen and the royal family paid visits to her at Clagny, which according to Mme de Sévigné was now comparable to the palace of Apollo and the gardens of Armida.

During the performance of this comedy, the war had continued and the kingdom was in danger. The Emperor had summoned the famous Montecucculi, conqueror of the Turks, to the rescue, and he was threatening Alsace. Once again the destiny of France depended upon Turenne. the old warrior never gave a more clinching demonstration of this genius than during his confrontation with Montecucculi, in which both strategists attained the perfection of their art. 'Each man judged the move his adversary was going to make according to what he himself would have done in the other's place, and they were never wrong.'[3]

As if intimidated, Louis made no appearance among his armies. He knew that Turenne had decided to give battle at the time of his first visit to Clagny, when he dined alone with Mme de Montespan. The tête-à-tête was rudely interrupted when a gentleman entered to announce that the marshal had been killed by a cannon-ball near Salzbach (on 27 July 1675).

The *dèvots* immediately attributed this bad news to the resumption of sin. In the evening, as the courtiers crowded round the table where the King customarily dines, no sooner had he made his appearance than he said gravely: 'We have lost the father of the country.' Those present suddenly turned pale; nobody said a word.[4]

What followed was a rare phenomenon, especially under a despotic régime: with the exception of Louvois and his supporters, the entire nation, from prince to peasant, mourned the illustrious soldier because, in the words of Voltaire, 'the virtues and talents that were unique to himself made people forget the faults and weaknesses that he had in common with so many others.'

Turenne's death acted like a flash of lightning, revealing the frailty of the French monarchy, which had seemed to be as solid as a Roman monument. There was an undercurrent of panic in the land. Faith had been forgotten as long as the genius and good fortune of the marshal continued. Now the question was, had it been the sovereign's sceptre or Turenne's sword that had been keeping the country together?

Even when he was most flushed with success, Louis had always been aware of the precarious nature of his greatness. He showed no sign of anxiety, and even congratulated Madame gallantly when one of her relatives defeated Créqui at the battle of Künz-Saarbrücken, which was followed by a mutiny that enabled the Germans to capture Trier.

Montecucculi had crossed the Rhine and invaded Alsace following the death of his great antagonist. In Flanders, Condé, prematurely aged by gout, was on the point of giving up. The King decided to summon the nobility and their retainers, an old feudal custom forgotten for half a century. The holders of fiefs were theoretically bound to fight for their suzerain at their own expense, although the period of service was not supposed to exceed a specified annual limit. The experiment was a failure. Any gentleman with a taste for war was already under arms, and the rest were useless. This was the final bow of the chivalric system which had brought so many disasters to France. The direction of the war, now falling daily more firmly into the hands of Louvois and his officials, took an administrative turn. Only Luxembourg remained to provide some spark of genius, out of all eight of the marshals nicknamed 'M. de Turenne's small change'.

During the same period there occurred a trivial event that entailed unguessable consequences: John Churchill left the service of France, having fallen in love with a blonde beauty aged only fourteen years, Sarah Jennings, already a remarkably self-willed woman, who had succeeded in driving her own mother from the court of the Duke of York, while she herself remained with her sister, the Duchess's maid of honour.

The following year the question arose of appointing Churchill to the command of the regiment known as the Royal-Anglais. Louvois objected that the young man 'would give more satisfaction to a rich and faded mistress* than to a monarch who did not wish to number in his armies drawing-room cavaliers, dishonourable and dishonoured.' However, it is not Louvois who bears the responsibility for having thus provided the enemies of France with their greatest captain. The future Marlborough himself preferred, as his descendant put it, ' " to sport with Amaryllis in the shade" rather than lease himself as a French popinjay!'[5] He contented himself with periodic visits to Louis as the bearer of Charles II's requests for money.

Meanwhile, the realm was threatened by invasion. Condé was prevailed upon to ignore his afflictions, entrusted the army of Flanders to Luxembourg and proceeded to Alsace, where he showed a skill and prudence worthy of his former rival. The fire and daring of his youth were gone, but they would have been ill-suited to this courteous war conducted by artists solicitous of their soldiers' blood if not of the people's. Montecuccoli was forced to withdraw over the Rhine, and retired from the Imperial service.

Having thus won his final victory, Condé followed suit. He wanted his son to succeed him, and offered to become his adviser – but Louis xiv and Louvois did not want young men, least of all young princes, at the head of armies; only the renown of the Grand Condé himself had been able to make them depart from this principle. From now on M. le Héros hardly ever left Chantilly, which he had renovated beautifully and which attracted the flower of French culture. He ended his days peacefully.

When the year 1675 came to a close, France had suffered none of the disasters with which she had been threatened. All the same, there had been uprisings in Brittany, difficulty in obtaining recruits, and Vauban had written: 'Things are still going from bad to worse, and are making me tremble.'

At court, Mme de Maintenon was enjoying the first raptures of being a favourite. 'Everything is under her dominion,' Mme de Sévigné recorded, 'all her neighbour's [Montespan's] chambermaids are hers. One kneels to offer

---

* The Duchess of Cleveland, favourite of Charles II.

her the pot of paste, another brings her gloves, yet another puts her to bed. She bows to no one, and I believe that in her heart she laughs at this tyranny.'

A craze for gambling swept through the court that winter. *Hoca*, a game banned everywhere else on pain of death, enabled the winner to make twenty-eight times his stake. For some courtiers, it was their sole means of subsistence. Maria Theresa enjoyed gambling, although she never won – unlike Mme de Montespan, who could win or lose a fortune in one evening.

Conversation frequently turned to the Marquise de Brinvilliers, accused of having poisoned her father and two brothers for the inheritance. The lady had fled to Liège, but had been arrested by Desgrez, the most famous policeman of his time, when he made a romantic assignation with her. She was executed after displaying remarkable courage. Mme de Sévigné was watching from the Pont-Neuf, and remarked: 'Never has Paris seen so many people so moved and attentive.'

Messina rose against the Spaniards and asked for French assistance, which arrived in the shape of seven warships under the command of the Duc de Vivonne, Mme de Montespan's brother. In consequence, the Spaniards were reduced to begging for help from their hereditary foes, the Dutch. The French fleet commanded by Abraham Duquesne, 'better known at that time for his skill as a privateer than as a general', had to face Ruyter himself, at the head of the combined squadrons of Holland and Spain. Duquesne was victorious in two encounters, the second costing his famous opponent his life. Then he won a third battle, but it was hazardous to have designs on land and sea at the same time. France could not hold Sicily. The main effect of this demonstration of naval strength was to antagonize the English and to make their indispensable neutrality even more precarious.

In Flanders, the season of battles had come round again, and the King and Monsieur had to show themselves to their soldiers. Siege warfare was resumed under Vauban's direction, but there was a rapid change of scene when William of Orange marched to the relief of Bouchain at the head of fifty thousand men. From the height of Heurtebise, the King watched these troops taking up their somewhat disorganized battle stations. He held a horseback conference with Louvois, five marshals of France, and a few others. Marshal Lorges was in favour of giving battle. Louvois thought otherwise, and the rest followed suit. The King yielded to the majority.

He was quite right. At that stage in the war and in the state of the kingdom, a defeat would have been catastrophic. Louis never acted on impulse or trusted to chance. Public opinion condemned him, the nobility were indignant, and Saint-Simon, who was Marshal Lorges' son-in-law, called the centuries to witness the King's cowardice.

A month later Luxembourg was unable to prevent the surrender of

Philippsburg, which provided a new wave of discontent. 'But after all,' said the exasperated Louis, 'I shall still be King of France.' Whereupon the Duc de Montausier, the Dauphin's tutor, who inspired Molière's *Misanthrope*, boldly replied: 'True, Sire, you would most certainly be King of France when they had taken back Metz, Toul, Verdun, Franche-Comté and several other provinces that your predecessors managed to do without.' This reaction is instructive about the warmongering and imperialism which have brought down so many reproaches upon Louis' head. It shows that his actions did not arise solely from his own inclinations, but were deeply rooted in the national character.

The fall of Philippsburg brought about a mortal quarrel between Luxembourg and Louvois, who sent the luckless general a brutal reprimand and even threatened him with the Bastille.

At the end of the campaign, the enemy found themselves in the Vosges foothills. In spite of the fine sieges, the situation was deteriorating and its outcome was unpredictable – all the more so because of the storm that was brewing in England. 'The hatred of this nation is turning to anger,' wrote the ambassador Courtin. Charles II had managed to do without Parliament in 1676, but he was forced to call it early the following year. It was not difficult to anticipate that the Commons would insist on a break with Louis XIV. While Charles schemed and all his friends shamelessly demanded bribes from Courtin, the only person to defend the French cause was the beautiful Duchess of Portsmouth.

At Saint-Germain, Fontainebleau and Versailles, the round of fêtes and pleasures maintained its unchanging rhythm, and the workmen their industry. Louis wrote: 'The people like spectacle. In this way we hold their minds and hearts, sometimes more firmly than through rewards and benefactions.'

The amours of the King were quite another kind of spectacle. Anne de Rohan-Chabot, Princesse de Soubise, had a fine figure, red hair and very fair skin. She also had a most assiduous husband, who bestowed a child upon her almost yearly. One day the ever-watchful Mme de Montespan noticed that the Princess regularly wore a pair of emerald ear-rings when M. de Soubise was going to Paris. She had the King followed and discovered that the ear-rings were the signal for their rendezvous. Louis was extremely fond of Mme de Soubise, although their relationship was intermittent: his new mistress tended to become ugly after a few weeks of pregnancy, and she had eleven children in all, of whom at least one is supposed to have had royal blood.

An outbreak of rage from Athénaïs compelled Louis to put up a show of repentance. 'It is all smoothed over,' wrote Mme de Sévigné, '*Quanto* [Mme de Montespan] was leaning her head on her friend's shoulder in a familiar manner at the gaming table the other day. This posture was taken to mean: I am better off than ever.' In reality, Louis had by no means severed relations with the ambitious Princess, who succeeded not only in prolonging the affair but also in transforming love into friendship when the King became a *dévot*.

Mme de Soubise was no threat to the favourite, since she abhorred scandal. Not so Mme de Ludre, Charlotte Elizabeth's maid of honour and a canoness in Lorraine.* The King's infatuation with this beauty was no accident. Charlotte Elizabeth, who was unconsciously in love with her brother-in-law, enjoyed putting forward rivals to her great friend Mme de Montespan.

This occasion brought a new instance of Louis' success in taming the nobility. 'Merely on the assumption that she [Ludre] was loved by the King, all the princesses and all the duchesses got up when she approached, even in the Queen's presence, and did not sit down until she gave them a sign, just as if it had been Mme de Montespan.'[6] This was the first the Queen knew of her husband's new infidelity, but she was resigned to her fate and suffered far less than Athénaïs, who made a great fuss and accused her enemy of having a disgusting skin disease, although it was an apparently trivial incident which caused the downfall of the latest comer.

To oblige one of her lady friends, the scandalous canoness appointed her husband go-between for herself and her august lover. Indiscretion was still the crime of crimes in Louis' eyes, and he was horrified that his secret (transparent though it was) should be entrusted to an 'inconsequential scapegrace'. He broke off the affair at once, and suggested that she had better retire to a nunnery; he also offered her two hundred thousand livres, which she refused.

Bussy-Rasbutin wrote: 'If the refusal . . . makes her lover come back to her, I shall find her very clever. If not, I shall echo old Senneterre's saying that the honourable have no shoes.' Mme de Montespan, victorious once again, gave birth to a son the following year. The Church and Mme de Maintenon still had a long way to go.

* Hence the title of Madame.

[15]

Louis the Great

IMMEDIATELY after it reassembled, the new House of Commons sent Charles II an address in which it complained that 'his people were extremely angry and troubled by the evident danger that menaced his realm through the power and aggrandizement of the king of France.' The members were prepared to vote his Majesty the sum of £20,000,000 for a war with Louis XIV. Charles reminded them that it was for himself alone to decide on peace and war. He told Courtin: 'I am making myself unpopular with all my subjects for the love of the King, your master. I am resolved to keep the promise I gave him, but I beg him to humour me a little and make peace before winter comes.'

This time, Louis got off with paying Charles the exceptional sum of two million livres (very little, compared with the Commons' offer) and the gift of an abbacy to the Duchess of Portsmouth. The respite he earned enabled him to pull off a military decision, without which the interminable fighting would be settled by a stalemate. The dreams of 1672 had faded, but fortune, lately so miserly, suddenly smiled on French arms. At this happy moment Racine and Boileau were appointed historiographers to the King, much to the disapproval of Mme de Sévigné, who objected to their middle-class origins and considered Racine a pedant.

While Louis in person was taking Valenciennes and Cambrai (by courtesy of Vauban), Monsieur revealed his gifts of leadership by scoring a resounding victory over William of Orange at Cassel (April 1677). The nation was overjoyed. 'If I had won it myself, I would not be more excited,' the King wrote to Condé, but it was a lie. At Heurtebise, Louis had rejected his only opportunity of setting the seal on his *gloire* by gaining victory in a pitched battle. He was deeply embittered by the prospect of the victor's laurels going to the effeminate brother whom he treated with such affectionate contempt.

Philippe of Orléans never received another command, and the French army lost a great general at a time when it had very few left. Neither the character of Monsieur nor the situation of the monarchy in 1677 justified the fear that a son of Louis XIII might use his prestige to shake the throne. The Sun King yielded to a base jealousy for which he paid the price when the time of defeats came round.

William of Orange also resented his inability to become a great military leader. His victories were destined for a different field. Louis XIV's efforts were no longer directed against the Dutch, and he would have liked to detach them from the coalition. He made secret peace proposals, but he also committed the colossal blunder of offering the Stadtholder the hand of La Vallière's legitimized daughter; this to a Prince descended from the Stuarts through his mother, the sister of the King of England, and consequently the great-grandson of Henry IV!* William never forgave the insult, and his hatred continued to grow.

An idea now germinated in the mind of the English minister Danby, who had been playing a double game, assisting his master's financial schemes and busily encouraging the francophobia of Parliament. Although Charles II had fathered countless bastards, he had been unable to have legitimate offspring, and the heirs to the throne were therefore the Duke of York, and after him the two Princesses Mary and Anne, daughters of his first marriage. Although the Duke was a Catholic, his daughters had remained loyal to the official religion of their country. Danby had the idea of marrying the elder girl to the Prince of Orange.

The matter proceeded amid absolute secrecy, until William arrived in England unexpectedly and announced that he had come to ask for his cousin's hand in marriage. This was not at all to the liking of Charles or the Duke of York, still less of Louis XIV. They tried to parry the blow, but it was too late: England acclaimed the champion of Protestantism and the enemy of France, and applauded the engagement. There was nothing to do but to give way. The marriage that brought about one of the decisive events in the world's history took place almost without ceremony on 4 November 1677.

Louis realized at once that he had been badly outmanoeuvred. His generals were winning battles everywhere – Créqui at Freiburg, Luxembourg at Charleroi, Vauban at Saint-Ghislain – and he himself captured Ghent, then Ypres, in March 1678, but each of these conquests brought the English a step nearer to war.

John Churchill was appointed to negotiate a treaty of alliance and to prepare the ground for joint military action with the Dutch and Spaniards. As his famous descendant delicately phrased it, William of Orange was not averse to young men. He gave a splendid welcome to the handsome colonel, who was twenty-eight years old, the same age as himself, and they set about poring over the map to plot the downfall of France.

They were reckoning without Charles II. In the last analysis, it was this great politician who managed to allay both the aggressiveness of his subjects and the ambitions of the French king, although Louis XIV showed himself no less adept. He had to face the obvious fact that for England to join his enemies

---

* Because of the marriage between Charles I and Henrietta of France.

would turn the tables on him. At best he would be compelled to suffer English arbitration, as he had with the Dutch in 1668. Louis could not accept this at any price and reached an immediate decision: in the midst of his conquests, a fortnight after his entry into Ypres, he issued peace proposals in the form of an ultimatum which must be either accepted or rejected inside a month (on 9 April 1678).

The talks opened at Nimwegen, with England as mediator. Making a clean sweep of the grand design which had caused the war, and sacrificing the policy of Colbert, the King renounced the 1667 tariff, returned Maestricht to Holland and gave Spain a line of strongholds that were to serve as a protective 'barrier' against any new invasion of the United Provinces. These unexpected terms were so favourable that the States-General accepted them in spite of the Stadtholder's rage at being deprived of his vendetta. Holland thus profited from an enterprise intended to destroy her, but her naval power emerged in a weakened condition.

In Spain, the pro-French faction and its leader, Don Juan of Austria, natural son of Philip IV, had just overthrown the régime of the Queen Mother's favourites. The example of the Dutch furnished a reason for accepting Louis XIV's terms, draconian though they were. The sickly empire of Charles II of Spain was to foot the bill for the adventure: France retained Flanders and Franche-Comté.

The last to give way was the Emperor, who abandoned Freiburg and Breisach and confirmed the treaties of Westphalia. Since Charles V, the new Duke of Lorraine, refused to accept a French garrison in Nancy, Louis continued to occupy his states.

William of Orange avenged himself by an act of bloody treachery. Holland had signed the treaty on 10 August 1678, and Luxembourg was camped outside Mons. He was dining peacefully at the village of Saint-Denis, on 14 August, when the Stadtholder fell on him unawares with all his forces. Four thousand men died – a complete waste, since William did not even win this shameful battle.

At the beginning of 1679 there was peace at last, but Louis XIV remained the villain of Europe. The new state of affairs was symbolized by the marriage of the King of Spain to Louise of Orléans, eldest daughter of Monsieur. Celebrated amid a crushing burden of ceremonial, this sacrificial wedding reduced the poor Princess to tears, for she was in love with the Dauphin and had almost fainted at the sight of her husband's portrait.

The Sun King was approaching his zenith. Almost single-handed, he had repulsed a formidable coalition, triumphed on land and sea, annexed two provinces, confiscated a state (Lorraine) and laid down the law to his enemies. The world was stunned, despite the evacuation of Holland and Sicily.

Yet there were still some factors that rankled. Louis knew that the carefully planned operation undertaken in 1670 had in fact failed, that he had been coerced into negotiating and limiting his conquests by pressure from England, and that the marriage of the Prince of Orange had created a menace for the future. It was the architect of that marriage who suffered Louis' vengeance.

Montagu, the English ambassador in Paris, had been incautious enough to become the lover first of the Duchess of Cleveland, then of her daughter. Charles II's temperamental favourite managed to have him recalled, and being now out of favour he entered the pay of the French. In return for a hundred thousand crowns, he delivered proof to the House of Commons that Danby, the Protestant hostile to France, had personally signed the receipts for bribes disbursed by France. At this time, England was passing through a bout of anti-papist hysteria stirred up by the former Jesuit Titus Oates. It was into this climate of suspicion, hatred and terror that Montagu's revelations came. The Commons sent Danby to prison, and Charles II found himself even further out on a limb because Louis xiv had cut off his subsidies in retaliation for his niece's marriage.

Everywhere the brilliance of crowns was fading, when they did not actually seem about to topple. England was again on the verge of revolution. Against all expectations the King of Spain had reached the age of seventeen and had married, but because of his shaky health he had received hardly any education. He could not read or write and did not even know the location of the lands he ruled. The Emperor was faced with an uprising in Hungary and feared an attack by the Turks. Sweden was in decline. The princes of Germany and Italy hardly counted. As for the Dutch republic, it was busy licking its wounds and rebuilding its economy.

Thus there really was only one king in Europe, and the symbol of the sun did not seem exaggerated. At Versailles, ceilings, sculptures and decorative motifs celebrated the exploits of the demigod and mocked his rivals. Two allegorical groups on either side of the courtyard gates displayed, first, a grounded eagle (the Empire), second, a captive giant and a sleeping lion (the Spanish monarchy).

In 1680 the Council of Paris solemnly conferred on Louis the title of 'the Great', which some of the coinage already carried and which was inscribed on public monuments from then on. Nevertheless, it is not 'Louis the Great' but Louis xiv who is remembered, and that fact bears truer witness to his greatness. Voltaire wrote: 'To posterity, titles are meaningless: the name of a man who has achieved great things compels more respect than any epithet.'

[16]

The Onset of Middle Age

Now in his fortieth year, Louis XIV was enjoying a supremacy unmatched since the time of the Roman Caesars. Like them, he was the object of a pagan cult. The Capetian prince, inseparable from the life of the people and a true head of the family, had disappeared. While Louis XIV was quite ready to speak of his fatherly duties towards the nation, he would have been incapable of exclaiming, like Louis XIII: 'Long live my people!' He preferred his subjects' submission to their love.

Paradoxically for a sovereign so convinced of his own greatness and his quasi-divine essence, Louis' appetite for flattery was insatiable, and he was continually preoccupied with the impression he created. Foscanini, the Venetian ambassador wrote: 'He is liberal out of self-interest, magnificent in display, miserly by nature, curious out of suspicion and suspicious out of curiosity.'

Ezekiel Spanheim, ambassador of the Elector of Brandenburg, put it bluntly: 'On top of everything else, he has a jealousy or aversion, real but concealed, towards anything that may vie with him in grandeur, power, merit or whatever involves public esteem or veneration . . .' Louis XIV had come to the point often reached by famous and much praised men and women, where they are no longer satisfied with mere success but must also enjoy it exclusively. His common sense, which he himself considered essential to wise government, had not protected him. He was almost in good faith when he claimed personal credit for every happy event in his reign, and he showed dangerous contempt for the achievements of his enemies.

His childhood experiences reinforced daily fear of the slightest derogation from an authority that few men before him had wielded to such an absolute degree. The Sun King made a complete contrast with Henry IV, who had forged his easy manner, his malice and even his coarseness and lechery into instruments of government. There was an equally striking contrast between Louis and his father, a martyr to his function. He wanted to ignore the fact that he was one link in a long chain, so that while he enjoyed hearing about mythological heroes he was deaf to any mention of his ancestors.

It was extremely irritating for the King not to be able to ignore his successors in the same way. Louis XIV secretly nursed the same suspicious jealousy of the Grand Dauphin that Louis XIII had once shown to himself. No prince could have been less deserving of such feelings. Monseigneur, as the heir to the throne was now known, had inherited his mother's docility and low intelligence. All his life he remained petrified with admiration of his formidable father and stood in fear of him even while lavish proofs of 'affection' were showered upon him. The best way for Monseigneur to do someone an injury was to commend him to the royal favour. He knew it, and did not conceal it from his rare petitioners.

Louis XIV saw to it that his son's upbringing was quite the opposite of his own. Instead of a devoted mother and an affectionate and likeable tutor, the Dauphin had the repellent and misanthropic Duc de Montausier, who ruthlessly applied the same methods that had so disturbed Louis XIII. They annihilated his grandson. For a preceptor, the heir to the throne had Bossuet, Bishop of Condom and France's most learned expert in divine right. This qualification had erased the memory of his bold speeches against the King's adultery. Bossuet overwhelmed his backward pupil with such splendid lessons that the Dauphin developed a lasting horror of books, learning and history. By the age of eighteen, Monseigneur had assimilated almost none of the knowledge amassed to so little purpose, and the apathy of his mind was second only to that of his senses.

The King therefore had nothing to fear from comparison with his heir. True, there was no longer any question of his being 'beautiful'. His face was beardless now, and furrowed by lines that gave him a somewhat bitter expression, but he was still young, still the prey of overwhelming sensual appetites, and as vigorous as ever.

If possible, the King had still further refined his lofty manner, his gravity and his all-embracing métier. He could create terror or ecstasy at will, was a remarkable orator, an engaging raconteur and an unequalled stylist. Primi Visconti noted: 'In everything he says, even in the most trivial matters, it is an oracle that speaks.' The oracle himself was sparing of his pronouncements, explaining: 'A King should listen rather than speak, because it is difficult to say much without saying too much.' Since he wanted to know everything, the King listened a great deal. 'As a result of hearing sermons, poetry and speeches and reading the books dedicated to himself, he is fatigued,' Primi Visconti tells us, destroying Saint-Simon's fable of an ignorant Louis XIV.

The court now bore little resemblance to the bold, debauched, insolent and witty scene of the 1660s. Its numbers had grown from a hundred or so to thousands, and discipline was almost military. Nobody dreamed of avoiding draughts, since His Majesty enjoyed them, or of not cramming themselves when His Majesty was hungry. Even a pregnant woman could not be excused from arduous coach-rides. A small princely court on the lines of the court of

Henrietta of England was no longer conceivable. Louis intended the nobility to live under his eyes and to be governed by a clockwork organization.

The Sun King was woken up at half past seven, got up an hour later and enacted the complex rituals of the *petit* and then the *grand lever*. From ten until noon he presided over the Council (this schedule was modified during the latter part of his reign). Then he went to mass. People stood along the route and many handed him petitions as he went by. His invariable answer, only with differences of intonation, was: 'I shall see.'

In the chapel, the congregation formed a circle round the foot of the altar. Standing with their backs to the officiant, they raised fervent eyes towards the King's dais as he knelt down. La Bruyère, author of the contemporary *Caractères,* explains: 'One cannot help viewing this custom as a kind of subordination, for these people seemed to be worshipping the prince and the prince to be worshipping God.'

After mass, the King felt ready for sin. This time – one o'clock in the afternoon – was allotted to visiting one or another of his mistresses. At two o'clock he and the Queen dined together. Charlotte Elizabeth describes his appetite: 'I have often seen the King eat four plates of various soups, a whole pheasant, a partridge, a large plate of salad, two big slices of ham, mutton with gravy and garlic, a plateful of pastries and then fruit and hard-boiled eggs.' Monsieur was the only man who sometimes dined with him.

After dinner the King hunted or went for walks, then worked until eight or nine o'clock at night. He might then relax over a game of billiards or listen to music until ten o'clock, when he would sup with members of the family. At eleven he paid another visit to one of his favourites before the hour arrived for the *grand* and *petit coucher,* as solemn as the *levers.* He always spent the night with the Queen. On festive evenings the public was admitted to watch the fabulous spectacles that took place in the gardens. Providing he was respectably dressed, any Frenchman could observe his sovereign for a good part of the day.

Fashions changed according to the age of the monarch. The cascades of ribbon and lace had been replaced by the majestic coat reaching to the knees and girded with a shoulder-sash, the wig accentuated his leonine appearance, and jewels sparkled in his hat, garters and shoes. Etiquette was growing ever more rigid. The Duchess of Osnabrück, Madame's aunt, mother of the future King George I of England, had to come to court incognito because it had been impossible to reach agreement on the kind of chair to which she would be entitled if she appeared officially!

It was the second turning-point of the century, and the culmination of the classical age, now on the verge of decline. A generation was disappearing, or being transformed. Mme de Longueville and La Rochefoucauld followed Turenne to the grave, Condé was living in retirement, La Grande Mademoiselle was nothing more than a pathetic, love-sick woman, Corneille had not written anything for a long time and Racine had given up the theatre and was devoting himself to his official functions. With Lully and Boileau, Racine was better off than most of his fellow-authors. On one occasion the King gave him a gratuity of four thousand louis (roughly £40,000 or $100,000 today).

Louis' policy for the nobility was bearing fruit. The obligation to live and gamble on a grand scale diverted their ambitions away from power and towards money. The first misalliances were beginning to take place, and lords quarrelled over the daughters of financiers. Chevaliers of the Order of the Saint-Esprit no longer had scruples about sitting at the same gaming-table as millionaire butchers.

Morals had never been worse. Bussy Rabutin wrote:

> The easy virtue of all the ladies had made their charms so contemptible to the young men that they were hardly looked at any more. Debauchery held sway more than anywhere else in the world, and although the King had often expressed his utter horror of that kind of pleasure, this was the only matter in which he was unable to have his way . . . Most persons of quality were of that character, but so were the princes, which vexed the King unconscionably.[1]

The 'persons of that character' went so far as to form a fraternity whose prospective members had to swear, if they were married, that it was purely a question of convenience. The Grand Dauphin himself was enrolled for a short time.[2] These gay young men were frantic drinkers, roamed around Paris at night breaking street-lights and tearing down crosses, stabbed a wafer-seller who refused to let himself be assaulted and erupted into 'wild actions' against prostitutes.

When La Reynie told him about these occurrences, the King frowned, but took little positive action. He was probably less than displeased to see the wreck of families that had caused his predecessors so much anxiety. The ladies did not have the influence they had wielded in the time of Francis I and during the Fronde, and which they still exercised in England, but their charms continued to work on Louis for a time.

Those of Mme de Montespan were fading, however. The mother of eight children (including one son by her husband), with an appetite as hearty as the King's, she was growing immense, and the magic powders were not potent enough to conceal it from her lover. It was at this moment that Angélique de Fontanges arrived from Auvergne, officially to become one of Madame's maids of honour, but with every intention of obeying her parents' instructions to become Louis' mistress. She was silly and provincial, but her beauty, youth and freshness produced the desired effect. One night, escorted by a few guards, the King was led by a devious route to the Palais Royal, then occupied by Monsieur and Madame. One of Mlle de Fontanges' companions opened the door to her apartment, and Louis the Great made yet another conquest.

It did not take Mme de Montespan long to find out, and her bitter reaction had no effect. It was the beginning of March. On the 12th La Voisin was arrested. Her colleagues La Vigoureux and Marie Bosse were already in custody. Fate was conspiring against Athénaïs. Mme d'Osnabrück noticed her 'gloomy affliction' and 'neglected' appearance.

The final break in this legendary liaison took place in April. La Vallière had received a ducal title as a parting gift; Athénaïs was appointed to the highest post a woman could occupy at court, that of Superintendent of the Queen's Household. Its present incumbent was the Comtesse de Soissons, and Colbert explained to her how obliged the King would be if she would resign – subject to a payment of two hundred thousand crowns. Olympe did not put up much of a fight, partly because the arrest of La Voisin was causing her grave concern. Mme de Montespan spoke of retiring to the Abbey of Fontevrault, but was dissuaded: Louis did not want a repetition of the scenes that had marked the departure of La Vallière.

Mlle de Fontanges was given the apartment next to the King's cabinet, and a little room linked to her lover's by a hidden staircase. Before the court, Louis at first pretended not to know her, but soon the new favourite was to be seen at the royal mass kneeling on the right-hand dais, while her supplanted rival occupied the position on the King's left. Mme de Maintenon wrote to her confessor: 'I ask you to pray and have prayers said for the King, who is on the brink of a very steep precipice.'

Louis was not unused to such positions, and never suffered from vertigo. His love affairs did not make him forget his position as head of the family, and while he pandered to the whims of Mlle de Fontanges he was also busy arranging marriages for his son and the eldest of his natural daughters. Mlle de Blois, a charming young girl, had fallen head over heels in love with the young Prince de Conti when she was only thirteen and a half. Conti's response was just as ardent, and Louis xiv, delighted to be able to transform a legitimized into an authentic princess, endowed his daughter as if she were marrying a king. Love matches were a rare occurrence among the high nobility.

Monseigneur was not so fortunate. The fiancée who had been chosen for him was Christina of Bavaria, who according to the Marquise de Maintenon's niece, Mme de Caylus, was 'not only ugly but disagreeable', and was judged by Mme de Sévigné to be 'very indifferently good-looking', although she added: 'Her wit, teeth and figure are praised.'

There was great agitation at court during the last weeks of 1679. Conti's marriage was celebrated, Angélique de Fontanges was delivered of a stillborn

Louis XIV (J. Gole)

Mme de Montespan
(Mignard)

Mlle de la Vallière
(lithograph by Delpech)

child, and the approaching marriage of Monseigneur was provoking a great deal of embarrassment and a number of sensations. The embarrassment was caused by the Prince's indifference to women. Things were explained to him in the plainest possible terms but to no avail, as he pretended not to understand a word. At the last minute Mme de Rochefort, Louvois' mistress, made the supreme sacrifice and gave him 'a lesson behind closed doors which succeeded to perfection.' In this manner she gave the House of France some compensation for her husband's costly mistake during the war in Holland.

The sensations at court were unrelated, but equally astonishing. Mme de Maintenon was appointed second tirewoman to the future Dauphine, which publicized her favoured position, and the Foreign Minister Pomponne, guilty of an act of negligence in the matter of the marriage, fell beneath a combined assault from Colbert and Louvois.

These great state servants were also changing. If their master had not kept a tight rein on them, they would have created a new kind of feudalism. They had counties, marquisates and Cordons Bleus, they had amassed enormous wealth, married their daughters to dukes and appointed their sons and relatives to strategic offices of state. Magnificent châteaux advertised their prestige as heads of two rival dynasties, two parties between which Louis maintained a careful balance.

Both ministers wanted to control foreign policy. They combined to crush Pomponne, and Colbert then manoeuvred to outwit the Louvois clan and have his brother, Colbert de Croissy, appointed to the secretaryship. Pomponne retained his salary, and the Colberts paid him seven hundred thousand livres (over £500,000 today), which was the King's valuation of his post.

Apart from Fouquet and, later, Chamillart (Controller-General of Finance and Secretary of State for War), Pomponne was the only minister dismissed by Louis xiv in fifty-four years. In his memoirs the King, after explaining his reasons, concluded haughtily: 'Everything that passed through his hands lost the force and greatness that a man must have in executing the orders of a King of France, who is no common man.'

[17]

Pride and Distrust

AFTER signing the peace, Louis took two important decisions, one of them reflecting his pride, the other his distrust. Revealing a project which he had kept secret for seventeen years, he gave orders for Versailles to be extended by the addition of two wings capable of housing the entire court together with numerous attendant personnel. The gardens and the town itself were to be enlarged and embellished in proportion. His purpose was to impress the whole world and publicize the power of France.

The second decision was less sensational. The King was aware of what General de Gaulle has called the 'frightful infirmity' of his frontiers, so vulnerable that a single serious defeat could put Paris and France at the mercy of an invader. He instructed Vauban to provide a defensive chain of fortresses. This project was more prosaic, but no less admirable than the erection of fabulous palaces. As a result, the invasions that had ravaged the country since the Hundred Years War did not touch the soil of France again – with one brief exception – until the Revolution.

Vauban's counterpart in the sphere of civil magnificence was Jules Hardouin Mansart, who had already revealed his talent at Clagny. When he studied the memorandum in which Mansart proposed the lateral extension of the Château and the transformation of the terrace into a vaulted gallery, the King signed it proudly: 'Let it be done in accordance with our greatness.'

Versailles now became the site of a building operation on a scale unprecedented since Roman times. As many as thirty-six thousand men worked there during the next ten years. Mansart also transformed the Orangery, dug the Pièce d'Eau des Suisses, peopled the gardens with statues and created the Fountain of Neptune, the Place d'Armes, the two Stables and the Grand Commun, but he did nothing without first submitting his plans to the King, who often made alterations.

During this period, Le Brun assumed a task capable of exhausting several men and several lifetimes. The *premier peintre* devised and designed all the decorations for Versailles – paintings and tapestries, furnishings and woodwork, vases and doorlocks. He too was subject to the strict supervision of the

182

master, whose vision he interpreted, as did Mansart and Le Nôtre. That vision flew in the face of general censure and consternation. Primi Visconti was shocked:

Knowing nothing of architecture, he has no idea of what to do and what not to do, and the result is that owing to the great amounts of earth that have to be moved the atmosphere there is unhealthy. Furthermore, the putrid waters infect this atmosphere, so much so that in August everybody fell ill . . . excepting only the King and myself, I believe. Yet the King is set on remaining . . . Moreover, this countryside is barren, there is only sand and unhealthy marshland. *If Versailles were to be abandoned for as little as two years, only traces would remain.*

From La Palatine to Mme de Sévigné, with Saint-Simon yet to add his voice, everybody embroidered on the same theme. Louis paid no attention.

All the same, it did occur to him that he would like to escape now and then from the imposing grandeur of Versailles, and he cast his eye around for a pleasant site for a rural retreat. Saint-Simon tells us: 'On the other side of Louveciennes [south-west of Paris] he found a deep narrow dell with steep sides, made unapproachable by marshes and cramped by a sorry-looking village on the slope of one of these hillsides, which was called Marly. This enclosure, with no view and no means of providing one, constituted its only merit.'

On this unpromising site Louis created a vast open-air salon dedicated to Neptune. Between 'walls and pilasters of verdure', water held dominion in the pools, jets, waterfalls, allegorical figures and groups of ornamental fountains; it leapt in the great cascade of the Tapis Vert. As to the buildings, these consisted of one lodge standing apart, and twelve smaller ones, six on either side. The main lodge was decorated with frescoes and had Corinthian columns, trophies and heraldic figures. The King was soon spending several days a week there, with a marked relaxation of protocol, in the company of a few privileged persons. An invitation to Marly became the ultimate sign of favour.

Louis xiv was certainly not indifferent to the cost of these projects, but he was determined to erect proof of his greatness for other countries and before history. Colbert, who was left to find the means while having hardly any say in the expenditure, exclaimed: 'As regards expenditure, although it has nothing whatever to do with me, I beg Your Majesty to let me tell him that whether in peace or in war he has never looked into the state of his finances so as to determine his spending, which is so extraordinary that it must surely be unprecedented.' The King, however, was quite capable of appeasing his formidable servant and reviving his enthusiasm.

The year 1679 was a profitable one for the Contrôleur Général, who received a gratuity of 400,000 livres and had his brother made Secretary of

State for Foreign Affairs. A third success did not turn out so well: his son Colbert d'Ormoy was put in charge of the royal buildings, under his father's supervision. D'Ormoy did not have the calibre expected by a despot used to finding genius in the men who carried out his wishes.

Early in 1680 Colbert was consumed with anxiety yet again. He sent His Majesty an alarming memorandum: the deficit for the year that had just ended amounted to fifty-five millions. This would have to be charged against the coming year, although the expected receipts for that fiscal period were not more than seventy millions. It was no use raising the interest-rate on state borrowing (five, ten, soon perhaps fifteen per cent), because takers were becoming hard to find. If he did not reduce his scale of living, the Sun King was in danger of bankruptcy. 'I know, Sire, that the part I play in this matter is not a pleasant one.'

Louis XIV concurred with Colbert's self-assessment. Aware that he was accomplishing a great and misunderstood task, knowing nothing of financial priorities, or perhaps despising them, brooking no opposition to his 'good pleasure' and reinforced in these sentiments by Louvois, the King was growing tired of a minister who no longer met his requirements without demur.

At the same time as losing the King's friendship, Colbert was also becoming a target of mounting resentment among a populace whom, as he himself confessed, he did not spare. Those peasant notables, the tax-collectors, were responsible. When they did not wring enough out of the poor (real or pretended), their goods were forfeit and they could even be thrown into prison. On the other hand, the higher echelons, the tax-farmers whose abuses had been savagely punished in 1661, had become wealthier and more powerful than in Fouquet's time. They received exorbitant privileges because it was essentially on them that the treasury depended. As in totalitarian states, only the end was important, and any means were acceptable.

The haughty extravagance of the Sun King has been one of the principal grievances levelled against him down the years. Today there is a school of thought that holds, with some justification, that he was making a long-term investment of the money of the French people. They were not gilt-edged investments, but then what fruits came of the bourgeois wisdom of the subscribers to Imperial Russian loans?

Monseigneur was married at Châlons in March 1680. Referring to his daughter-in-law, Louis had confided to the Queen: 'The first impression is not good!' He nevertheless lavished gifts and favours on the new Dauphine, and gave her so much jewellery that Maria Theresa was jealous. Early in the following month, still more pearls and stones embellished Angélique de Fontanges when she was made a Duchess, with a pension of twenty thousand écus. His Majesty went in solemn procession to pay her his compliments, followed by the entire court.

Mme de Montespan thought that she would explode with spite, and like a second Medea threatened to rend the King's children limb from limb before his eyes. During the outbursts of his former mistress, his one consolation was Mme Scarron, who was daily advancing in his esteem and good graces. The more Mme de Montespan's rages alienated him, the more the other's kindness brought her closer to his heart.[1]

Appalled by the Fontanges affair, the Church put its last hopes in Françoise d'Aubigné and prevented her from making the slightest error. Heaven – or perhaps hell, in the person of the witches – all at once brought her invaluable support. Angélique had a miscarriage, then suffered 'a very persistent and disagreeable loss of blood' – which the uncharitable Mme de Sévigné called 'being wounded in the King's service.'

When the unfortunate girl grew bloated, feverish and almost ugly, there was talk of poisoning. In any case, the King's passion abated. Mme de Montespan now made a final effort, and tried to arouse the King's interest in her pretty niece, Mme de Nevers. She failed, because times had changed. A moral revolution was under way and the living god was on the point of finding the road to Damascus that had been prepared for him for so long.

Part Three

Heaven and Ocean
[1680-9]

[1]

From Scandal to Hypocrisy

A PERIOD of less than a decade, from 1680 to 1689, contains most of the events that altered the course of Louis XIV's reign, the destiny of France and, a century later, the face of the world.

The prologue had been enacted discreetly on 21 September 1677, when an anonymous note found in the confessional of a church in the Rue Saint-Antoine drew attention to a plot against the King's life. In the ensuing enquiry, a great many priests were induced to disclose that they had heard people admit to being poisoners in the secrecy of the confessional. A year later La Reynie, the chief of police, announced the results of his investigation: 'People's lives are literally for sale. It is close to being the sole remedy used to settle family problems. Impieties, sacrilege and abominations are virtually commonplace in and around Paris and in the provinces.'

The police began to arrest traffickers in black magic, but all this was still a matter of routine until Louvois saw a way of getting his own back on Colbert for his recent defeats. He sent for the dossiers, and began addressing almost daily reports to the King.

Louis was horrified to discover what chaos and monstrosities lay beneath the surface of the land that he had dedicated to order, greatness and beauty. It would have been quite in character for him to have the matter hushed up, but Louvois had his own axe to grind and argued for proceeding. In any case, the scandal was assuming such proportions that it would have been extremely difficult to smother it. The King therefore announced that justice must be done. The Parlement had shown its own lack of resolution at the time of the first trials, so he set up, still at Louvois' instigation, an extraordinary tribunal called the Royal Chamber of the Arsenal, also and more generally known as the *chambre ardente,* the 'burning chamber'.

In addition to poisoners, the Chamber was to bring to book 'impiety and all vices'. Soon it was unearthing evidence of unimaginable atrocities that made the entire nation tremble. Birth, rank or genius were no protection. After the common criminals, indictments were levelled at magistrates, the higher nobility, a Marshal of France and eventually at Princesses, Mazarin's nieces the Comtesse de Soissons and the Duchesse de Bouillon.

Three cases particularly disturbed the King: those of the Comtesse, Marshal Luxembourg and Racine. Louis seems to have believed in the guilt of Olympe, accused of having poisoned her husband; he certainly knew her too well to dismiss the possibility out of hand. But she had been his mistress and friend, and she was the niece of his great teacher. The Comtesse received a message from His Majesty giving her the choice 'either of going to the Bastille the following day to suffer the hardships of prison or of leaving France forthwith'. Olympe, though protesting her innocence, fled to the Spanish Netherlands. Louis xiv had made the mistake of ignoring his own maxim that kindness is a weakness in a king. If he had kept the Comtesse de Soissons in France, together with her son Prince Eugène, then the Abbé of Savoy, he would have been spared any number of misfortunes.

Luxembourg, whom Louvois had sworn to ruin, found himself in the Bastille. Even though the tribunal acquitted him, he still had to go into exile. A year later the King realized the extent of Louvois' deception, but he was an indispensable servant of the Crown and amends had to be made to the victim without disturbing the balance of the kingdom. The Marshal was discreetly restored to favour and to his old post of captain of the guards.

Racine was accused of having poisoned the actress Du Parc in a fit of jealousy, and Louvois would have been happy to see him imprisoned also, but the tribunal did not take the matter any further. His case was an exception. Apart from the lesser nobility, the *chambre ardente* put on trial members of several distinguished families. The 'poisons affair' was dimming the radiance of Europe's most dazzling court.

La Voisin, dressed in white, was burned at the stake on 22 February 1680, after being tortured. There remained her daughter, Marguerite Monvoisin, Romani, Bertrand, Lesage, La Filastre, La Vigoureux and the worst of them all, the repulsive Abbé Guibourg. From July onwards they unanimously accused Mme de Montespan of witchcraft, sacrilege and two attempts at poisoning, one on Mlle de Fontanges, the other on the King himself.

The only evidence we have of Louis' reaction is a letter dated 2 August in which he enjoins La Reynie to do his utmost to bring the facts to light. Meanwhile Louvois flew to the rescue of Athénaïs, his old ally. Louis was persuaded to grant the Marquise a private audience.

Racine himself could not have devised the scene that was enacted on 19 August. Athénaïs, reputedly 'very attractive in tears', wept floods of them, and acted humbly at first, but her lover's haughty reproaches elicited all her suppressed passions. She threw all Louis' faults in his face – his 'barbarity', his infidelities, his monstrous selfishness. It was he who was responsible for her fall from grace, since he had driven her to despair – he and that ungrateful servant, that Scarron woman. . . .

La Filastre, one of the chief accusers, went to her death on 30 September without managing to say a word about the favourite to her politic judges. The King decided not to run any further risks, and suspended the sittings of the *chambre ardente* the same day. However, the affair dragged on until the end of 1682. Guibourg, Lesage and eight others avoided the stake. They were imprisoned in the citadel at Bescançon, whose officers were instructed to see that they let slip no '*sottises*' concerning Mme de Montespan.

In the meantime, the unhappy Angélique de Fontanges had died, in her twentieth year. Contrary to the usual account, Louis was very grieved. It was universally agreed that she had been poisoned. Bussy-Rabutin relates: 'The King's suffering was so acute that he could not prevent himself from letting it show, and it is certain that he would have taken a resounding vengeance on Mme de Montespan if he had not had powerful motives for concealing his resentment.'[1]

The crimes laid at Mme de Montespan's door were originally believed without question, but it seems to be generally accepted today that the murder attempts and the participation in human sacrifices were invented by rogues who hoped to prolong their lives by causing an enormous scandal. All the same, the marquise had been an assiduous client of La Voisin and her kind since 1666. Her superstition went hand in hand with her piety, and she practised numerous magical rites and sacrileges in order first to win, then to keep the King's heart. Even if she did not have the absurd temptation to kill her lover, she certainly made him ill by administering foul concoctions which were supposed to quicken a fading love.

Louis xiv seems to have reached similar conclusions. Nothing was more calculated to cut him to the quick than criminal activities that sullied his own majesty and enabled foreign pamphleteers to sling mud at his *gloire*. The ground was threatening to open under his feet and engulf his old age. A peril of this magnitude enhanced the effects of the exhortations of preachers and the homilies of Mme de Maintenon.

Still only forty-two years old and exceptionally vigorous, Louis now came to a heroic resolve: he renounced pleasure, or rather variety in pleasure, and decided to conform to the requirements of the Church. It would be an outward show, however, for his pious adviser, the supposed author of the miracle, was also secretly resigned to making it possible, and 'sacrificed herself to the pleasures of the flesh'.

This was a *tartuferie* worthy of Molière, performed for the edification of the world and the state's well-being. The King restored his good graces to the Queen and behaved like an exemplary husband. 'She soon realized to whom she was obliged for this. She was moved to tears by the marks of affection that the King gave her, and would exclaim in a kind of ecstasy: "God has raised up Mme de Maintenon to restore the King's heart to me!" '[2]

Maria Theresa gave Françoise a diamond-encrusted portrait of herself, but, as Mme de Sévigné tells us, 'this lady de Maintenon or *de Maintenant* spends every evening with His Majesty between eight and ten o'clock. M. de Chamarande conducts her thither, and then back in full view of the universe'. It never occurred to the 'universe' that a woman of forty-five could have any physical attraction for the conqueror of so many beauties in full bloom. Yet this attraction was still active twenty-five years later, as is proved by the correspondence between the Marquise and the Bishop of Chartres.

Françoise d'Aubigné took the same care to conceal her new power that others had taken to display it. 'It is certain that as far as dress, ornament and manners were concerned there was no indication of her true status,' Primi Visconti wrote. Mme de Sévigné was deceived: 'The King has discovered a completely new land: friendship without constraint and without chicanery. He seems enchanted by it.'

Never did Mme de Maintenon invoke Heaven so frequently or evince so much fervour. In her, hypocrisy reached its zenith, even if it was in a good cause. She wrote to her sister-in-law:

My dearest child, I ask God daily to lead you in his holy paths. Worldly people do not make such wishes. *I make them in the midst of the court where one only has to exist to hate the world and its pleasures.* I realize here that God alone can fill the void in the heart of man. Believe me, my daughter, all the things that you imagine to be so delightful and that you perhaps envy me are only vanity and affliction of spirit.

But she admitted to her confessor, the Abbé Gobelin: 'I am in good health and I am content – too much so for my salvation, for I do not know what my cross is.' In another letter to her agile guide, who held that it was no sin to obey the King, she wrote: 'It is hardly ever for any deed that I reproach myself, but for very human motives: great vanity, great freedom of thought and judgement, and a restraint in my speech that is based only on human caution.' The saintly lady founded an 'Association of Ladies of Charity' at Versailles and converted those of her relations who had stood by Protestantism: 'I am everlastingly to be seen leading some Huguenot to church.'

Mme de Montespan affected a serenity she did not feel: 'All is peaceful here, the King only comes to my chamber after mass and after supper. It is much better to see each other seldom with tenderness than often with tears.' His Majesty was still paying regular visits to the former client of La Voisin. Nothing must be allowed to put the public on the scent of the dreadful secret.

Mme de Maintenon had 'free and cordial conversations' with Mme de Montespan, but she continued to insure for the future. The Duc du Maine, eldest son of the twofold adultery, looked on her as his true mother, and her all-embracing affection for the crippled child who owed her his life was not entirely disinterested. She was just as preoccupied with his 'establishment' as Mme de Montespan: the Duke must have a fortune worthy of a legitimized royal son. No one knows whether it was the sacred or the profane favourite who had the idea of 'blackmailing' La Grande Mademoiselle. At all events, it was the former who obtained the King's agreement and the latter who did the dirty work. On 2 February 1681, in Mme de Montespan's apartment and in the presence of Colbert, Mademoiselle formally ceded the county of Eu and the principality of Dombes to the Duc du Maine. In return, she expected the release of Lauzun and permission to marry him. She waited for a long time.

The prisoner of Pignerol did not make his bow to the King until March 1682, and even then there was no question of the grand wedding on which the fifty-five-year-old maid had set her heart. It brought her no happiness when she later received permission to celebrate it in secret.

An appreciable change was taking place in the atmosphere around the monarch. It became a crime to talk during mass, and piety was the first duty, although many courtiers became atheists again as soon as they got to Paris. Pomp and circumstance did not disappear – on the contrary, fête still followed fête – and gambling fever did not abate, but a sham Puritanism stiffened people's backs, starched their remarks and cast a chill over gaiety and wit. The court 'was sweating hypocrisy' and it was not virtue but tedium that took over. Peopled by 'men without friendship and without charity, ever distrustful, ever on their guard,' it was, thundered the Jesuit preacher Bourdaloue, 'the centre of the world's corruption.'

In 1682 a new scandal broke, and Louis mounted his only outright assault on 'Italian morals'. Suddenly, the practices he had long ignored, scorned or even used to further his own policies took on the proportions of a crime. The scapegoat was not one of the hardened rakes who turned their corruption to their own profit, but a fifteen-year-old boy who had got himself in the toils of the Chevalier de Lorraine and his brother the Comte de Marsan, the King's own son by Louise de La Vallière, the Comte de Vermandois.

Louis XIV questioned Vermandois and got even more than he had bargained for. Not only were a host of lords unmasked but also the Grand Dauphin in person. Marsan was spared, as was his nephew, the Comte de Brionne, but the King expelled the Prince de Turenne and at least seven other leading figures of the court. Vermandois was treated like a leper and found no consolation or support from anybody but Madame. Soon afterwards, desperate to buy his return to favour, he insisted on joining the army, although he was unfit, and died soon afterward. He was sixteen years old.

It may well be that the King's indignation stemmed not so much from morality as from raison d'état. There was a smell of subversion about so many gentlemen grouped so closely around two Princes. Subversion was as dangerous and inadmissible as it can be under the dictatorships of our own time.

⌈2⌉

La Raison du Plus Fort

THE Treaty of Nimwegen allayed neither Louis' pride nor his suspicions. His fame, as well as the security of the realm, demanded greater conquests. In spite of Vauban's fortresses, there were still many breaches in the nation's defensive wall, and the King's legitimate concern to provide against this threat was combined with his expansionist ambitions and his formidable appetite for *gloire*. Bossuet told Louis XIV : 'The Prince's *gloire* is the support and adornment of the entire State . . . While he sustains his *gloire* he sustains the public welfare.'

The Sun King preferred this doctrine to that of another preacher, Father Mascaron, who had been bold enough to proclaim in a forthright sermon 'that a hero was a thief who did at the head of an army what robbers do on their own'. That was how Europe viewed the creation at Metz, Breisach and Besançon of the 'Chambers of Reunion' whose task was to exhume ancient feudal deeds by virtue of which numerous territories were held to belong to those annexed by France since the Treaty of Westphalia.

While Colbert de Croissy advocated moderation in the exercise of this policy of 'gnawing and encroaching', Louvois kept spurring Louis on to greater excesses. In fact, the King took personal charge of foreign affairs during this crucial period, and applied his own methods: at the same time as striking blows intended to astonish the world, he cautiously strengthened his rear, avoided provoking the Dutch and signed treaties with Brandenburg and Bavaria (hence the Dauphin's marriage).

Louis' most potent argument lay in the fact that his armies stayed on a war footing when other powers had disbanded their own. *La raison du plus fort. . . .** But the argument was covered by a legalistic smokescreen, and lawyers dug as far back as Charlemagne to proclaim as French a great many lands in a great many different hands, among them those of the King of Spain, the Emperor, the King of Sweden and the Prince of Orange. It was a novel kind of conquest.

There was no documentary basis on which to neutralize Strasbourg, which had allowed France's enemies to cross the Rhine on three occasions, but the

---

* . . . *est toujours la meilleure.* – 'The argument of the strongest is always best' – the moral of La Fontaine's fable *The Wolf and the Lamb*. – Tr.

drawback was not insuperable. French gold undermined the town's defences from the inside, and when Louvois arrived at its gates with thirty thousand men and eighty cannon there was nothing to do but capitulate.

That same day (on 30 September 1681) another French army headed by Marshal de Catinat was occupying the key stronghold of Casale, purchased from the Duke of Mantua. Mattioli, the negotiator of the agreement, was playing a double game and had warned the Spaniards, who were incapable of putting up opposition in any case. He was hauled off to take Lauzun's place in Pignerol and was later identified with the Man in the Iron Mask, a riddle that was never solved.

In a single day, Louis had secured control of the Rhine and the Po. On 23 October, accompanied by the Queen and the entire court, he made a solemn entrance into Strasbourg as cannon roared out a triple salute. Louvois and Vauban showed him the site that had already been marked down for the construction of the citadel. Several German princes came to greet him as if he were their sovereign. He returned to Saint-Germain after a six-week journey, and one of his first actions was to legitimize the last two children of Mme de Montespan, who became Mlle de Blois and the Comte de Toulouse.

At the moment of asserting his power in Germany and Italy, he was also giving a striking demonstration in the Mediterranean. Colbert had expanded the navy 'beyond the hopes of the French and the fears of Europe.'[1] France had more seamen than England, the ports of Brest and Toulon had been created, Le Havre and Dunkirk fortified and 'nature subdued' at Rochefort. The corsairs of Algiers provided a golden opportunity to make this power felt as far away as Africa.

Bernard Renaud, the sailor and engineer discovered by Colbert, proposed sending a squadron to bombard Algiers. 'It had not occurred to anybody that mortars did not need to be placed on dry land, and the proposal was shouted down. Renaud suffered the opposition and jeering that any inventor must expect, but his persistence, together with the eloquence that usually comes to men deeply impressed by their own inventions, determined the King to allow a test of this novelty.'[2] Five days after Louis' entry into Strasbourg, his bombs flattened and burned half of Algiers. France had the sorry distinction of being the originator of this step forward in the art of mass-destruction.

One blow followed another, and a wave of panic and rage swept through Europe. The Emperor, Spain, Holland and even Sweden, which had been cheated out of the duchy of Zweibrücken, signed a treaty of coalition against France. William tried to rekindle the war, but Louis xiv had taken his precautions and was supporting the Czech and Hungarian rebels as well as discreetly egging on the Sultan to attack Leopold i.

The Turks had been hesitating for several years. If they had made up their minds before the Treaty of Nimwegen, when the Habsburg Empire was still having to resist France, they would probably have altered the future of Europe. At last they decided to respond to an appeal from Count Imre Thököly, leader of the Hungarian insurgents. The French ambassador led them to understand that they would not have to contend with Louis xiv if they were to conquer Austria.

Certain of the impotence of the Habsburgs, Louis took advantage of it to demand from the Spaniards jurisdiction over Alost, 'forgotten' in the recent treaty. When he received no satisfaction, he laid siege to Luxembourg.

Two hundred thousand Turks invaded the Austrian states, the Emperor retreated to Linz, then to Passau, and it seemed as if nothing could withstand the hurricane. Christendom turned to Louis xiv, who magnanimously raised the blockade of Luxembourg, but put pressure on the Imperial Diet assembled at Ratisbon to ratify his annexations. As long as the Turks were on the move, Louis felt that he was close to achieving his highest ambitions. His army, massed on the Rhine, would be the only possible defence for Germany if Austria fell. In exchange, Louis counted on seeing his son proclaimed King of the Romans – that is, on transferring the imperial dignity to the House of Bourbon. Thus the Habsburgs would have lost everything in the East, while the Spanish monarchy would be at the mercy of the French. The heir of Francis i would finally prevail over the descendants of Charles v.

Not content with supporting Hungarian Protestants and encouraging infidels, the newly 'converted' Louis was also involved in a violent dispute with the Pope.

Relations between the Holy See and the French monarchy had been strained ever since Henry iv had dealt at the time of his conversion not with Rome, but with the French clergy. Out of their agreement sprang Gallicanism, a national religion that was very quick to take offence. Not only was the King the temporal representative of God, he could also refuse to allow a new dogma into his kingdom, supplanted the Inquisition in suppressing heresies and slurs on the faith, evaluated theological doctrine and accepted or rejected papal bulls. The opportunities for clashes were innumerable.

Matters became even worse with the accession of Pope Innocent xi Odescalchi in 1673. Louis xiv wanted to extend the *régale temporelle** throughout his kingdom. He also claimed the right to nominate the abbesses of women's religious communities – a new departure. Innocent xi denied him the right, and even threatened to excommunicate Louis when he took no notice. Louis was unmoved. Apart from two Jansenists, the French bishops were on his side, quoting the example of Saint Louis, who had stood up to the Pope but had

---

* The royal right to collect the revenues of a diocese during the interval between the death of a bishop and the nomination of his successor. Louis did not benefit from the *régale* in provinces annexed since the Concordat of 1516.

been canonized nonetheless. The Gallicanism of the bishops was considerably more moderate than that of the jurists of the Parlement, who would not have drawn the line at schism.

On the suggestion of Harlay de Champvallon, Archbishop of Paris, the King called an assembly of carefuly selected prelates in Paris. Bossuet, now Bishop of Meaux, was summoned, but took the stance of a moderate, opposing the intrigues of Harlay and the double game played by the Jesuits – Gallicans in Paris and Ultramontanists in Rome. He succeeded so well that he displeased the King without pleasing the Pope. On the other hand, his opponents showed so much zeal that Louis had to restrain them.

Eventually, Harlay obtained a vote in favour of the famous Four Articles of 1682, which limited the Pope's influence to the ecclesiastical sphere, subjected that influence to the 'established constitutions of the Gallican Church', asserted the predominance of church councils over popes, and declared that 'the decrees of the Pope in matters of faith are not irrevocable as long as the consent of the Church has not confirmed them.'

Other nations were outraged by the tyranny which was making the universal Church bow down like the Berbers and crushing countries in no condition to resist. Yet recent history has to some extent mitigated the excesses of the Sun King. Since the seventeenth century, the world has endured other autocrats, other triumphant aggressors and far more terrible atrocities. In spite of the brutality and occasional ferocity of Louvois, his master's reign did not witness the reduction of nations to slavery, the uprooting of populations, massive deportations, genocide or scientifically organized massacres. Compared to the invaders of modern times, it may be said that Louis XIV abused his power with moderation.

[3]

The Triumph of Equivocation

ON 6 May 1682 Versailles at last became the seat of the monarchy and the government. It is difficult to image what the new capital looked like. Here was the largest building site since the Romans, full of dust, noise, debris and 'pestilence'. And here too was the temple of the sun, with its profusion of gold and gilt. Contrasts abounded. Marbles, tapestries, chandeliers of crystal and precious stones, fine carpets, the paintings that later made up the first endowment of the Louvre, mirrors, Boulle cabinets, silver-gilt furniture, porcelain and intricately-wrought consoles decorated icy, evil-smelling, draughty rooms. The chimneys drew appallingly badly and produced less heat than smoke, mingled in autumn with a fog 'so dense and clinging that one could discern nothing but vague shadows as one moved about.' On some winter evenings, water and wine froze at the royal table.

From the first, Mme de Maintenon received apartments that opened onto the top of the Queen's staircase and were on the same level as the King's. In spite of the allegorical figures and gilded ceilings, she never felt at home there. She could not even obtain shutters, because they would have spoiled the harmony of the façade.

Louis XIV was unperturbed by these grievances. He was creating a prodigious museum and inviting the world to marvel at it. People came flocking from at home and abroad. Twice daily, a coach service brought the people of Paris. Any properly dressed visitor might walk through the gardens and galleries, and be present while their Majesties supped and gambled. In a single day, there were as many as six thousand sightseers. It was a continual fair, a throng that included every walk of life, thieves and beggars among them. Sometimes the King had to give up his walk because of the crowd. No statesman in any modern democracy or people's democracy would accept such a way of life.

None of this affected the pomp of ceremonial occasions. The Ambassadors' Staircase had been devised not just to dazzle the men who mounted it but also to cramp their style a little. The ambassadors hardly had time to draw breath as they climbed the stairs, embarked on a long journey from salon to salon, escorted by ever more richly attired and eminent personages, and eventually entered the Chamber of Apollo, where a silver throne nearly eight feet high stood on a platform draped with a Persian carpet woven on a gold background. Louis XIV sat, surrounded by the princes of the blood and dressed in black velvet encrusted with diamonds that sparkled in the light of innumerable candles, the true image of the Sun King.

'I am just back from Versailles,' wrote Mme de Sévigné, 'and I am enchanted by it. Everything is great, everything magnificent, and the music and dancing are quite perfect.' This is one of the few contemporary verdicts in favour of the masterpiece conceived as the reflection of one man's ideal of monarchy.

It was a truly revolutionary achievement to establish and concentrate the power of the state at Versailles. Contrary to the opinion of the time, Louis' decision to leave Paris was correct. The city was inconvenient, unhealthy and riotous, making the monarchy vulnerable to the whims of the populace, as the Fronde had proved conclusively. As soon as it had won its independence, the United States took the precaution of installing its administrative centre far away from the larger cities, and has had no cause to regret the decision. The error made by the Sun King was in breaking with the nomadic tradition of his ancestors.

For seven centuries the Capetians had looked after their lands, according to circumstances, from the town, village, fortress or camp where it seemed most appropriate to fight, pacify, give justice and above all to exhibit to the people the figure-head that symbolized the nation. Between 1619 and 1622 Louis XIII had made no less than eighteen journeys. Except for the coronation, a journey to Cherbourg and the flight to Varennes, Louis XIV never left the Ile-de-France.

Louis XIV put an end to the French monarchy's practice of remaining in constant touch with its subjects. Gradually he ceased to know his people, and in the long run he became a stranger to them.

On 6 August 1682 such a future could not yet be imagined. The Dauphine gave birth at ten that evening to a new Prince, Louis, Duc de Bourgogne. In a tumult of illuminations, bonfires, pealing bells and thundering cannon, France was delirious with joy. That birth marked the zenith of the dynasty that had been identified with France for seven hundred years.

In the spring of 1683 Louis decided to make a visit to Franche-Comté and Alsace, keeping an eye on the Turkish advance in Austria at the same time. The entire court accompanied him on this journey, during which he held several spectacular reviews meant to overawe his enemies and inspected Vauban's new fortifications, which had cost so little compared with Versailles. Louis returned on 30 June, well satisfied, but the Queen was exhausted. Since she was officially her tireless husband's sole companion, he took her with him everywhere, forcing her to lead a life that undermined her constitution.

Colbert was in no better health. Gout, gravel, stomach pains possibly due to attempted poisoning and above all the strain of a thankless task were reducing him at the age of sixty-four to a weary old man. His increasing ill-humour was taxing the patience of Louis, who told him cruelly at the end of the journey: 'I have just seen the finest and best-maintained fortresses in the world. How is it that we are spending such staggering amounts on Versailles and seeing next to nothing brought to completion?'

Colbert, deeply wounded, explained that specialist craftsmen, artists and gardeners cost more than soldiers pressed into constructing fortresses. When he tried using cheaper labour, His Majesty was most put out by the resulting bad workmanship. The court was beginning to entertain hopes of the downfall of its *bête noire* when its attention was absorbed by a far more important event. The Queen developed an abscess under her arm, and died of it very suddenly on 30 July, 'through the offices of the doctors,' wrote Charlotte Elizabeth. Louis' response was: 'This is the only trouble she has ever caused me!'

After Mme de Maintenon had paid her respects to the dead sovereign, 'she wanted to go back to her apartment, but M. de La Rochefoucauld took her by the arm and pushed her towards Louis, saying: "This is not the time to leave the King, he has need of you." '[1] They left together for Saint-Cloud.

The entire court, headed by Mme de Montespan, now agreed that the King must marry again. The dead were soon forgotten at Versailles. Maria Theresa had attracted little notice while she was alive, and was hardly missed when she died. Nevertheless, her death posed a difficult question. The King was a widower and already a grandfather at the age of forty-five. If he took a second wife, he would risk producing children whose jealousy of the Dauphin's offspring might eventually provoke a return to the disruptive rivalries of former times.

Mme de Maintenon provided the only way out of the impasse, and this unthinkable conclusion all at once became part of the logical order of things. One of her biographers[2] has written that if ever there was a marriage of reason, this was it. Yet passion too played its part.

Like the correspondence of Louis and Marie Mancini, that of Louis and Françoise d'Aubigné was completely destroyed by the recipients, but a secret of such magnitude could not remain hidden. The King's behaviour betrayed him on several occasions, notably at the camp at Compiègne in 1698, and we have the Marquise's revealing letters to her confessor and the astonishing complaint, coming from a woman of fifty: 'It would be difficult to realize in advance how far husbands' authority can go. They make one submit to near-impossible things.'

Louis loved Françoise, with mind and with body, longer than any mature woman would dare to expect. His heart was another matter. Since the departure of Marie Mancini, no woman, neither the submissive La Vallière nor the tempestuous Athénaïs, seems ever to have won it.

The King arrived at his decision and communicated it to Mme de Maintenon with extraordinary speed. Two revealing letters are dated 7 August, a week after the Queen's death. On that day Mme de Maintenon wrote to her brother: 'The matter that prevents you from seeing me is so advantageous and so glorious that it should cause you nothing but joy.' And to her friend Mme de Brinon, the appalling remark in which the mask momentarily slips: 'I hope that I shall gain some reward out of my affliction.'

Born in the prison where her father was jailed for debt; brought up practically as a servant in the house of the relative who converted her to Catholicism; shuttled back and forth between France and the remote West Indies; forced at the age of sixteen to marry the poet Scarron, a paralytic; a charming hostess to the brilliant and dissolute society out of which her household made its living; the intimate friend of a courtesan, Ninon de Lenclos, who thought her 'gauche in love'; promoted to the high office of governess of the royal bastards; finally the Church's ambassador to the court of the Sun King: everybody knew about these stages in Françoise d'Aubigné's meteoric career, and yet her piety, her loves, her character and behaviour were by no means an open book.

In spite of the accusations and defences, portraits, studies and commentaries, the mystery has not been entirely dispelled to this day. Michelet, the nineteenth-century liberal historian whose authority, when he writes about this period, is somewhat undermined by his feelings, has nonetheless left an incomparable description of Mignard's portrait of Mme de Maintenon in the hour of her triumph:

... skilfully shrouded, revealing only what she wanted to reveal. She is magnificently gowned with coquettish prudery in rich black, covered with lace (is it in mourning for the Queen?). Everything is ambiguous. She is looking and yet not looking. She holds a rose, not too rosy, slightly overblown, its semi-violet tints in perfect harmony with the black. She sits in state and governs (as a queen? a governess?) ... Her head is quite small, but rounded and resolute. Not at all classical. In her youth, she was called *La Belle Indienne*, but she must have been pretty rather than beautiful, a miniature Creole with tiny features ... This is not an open face. It reveals nothing of kindness, tender intimacy or equable temper. Rather, the suggestion is of a restless, active mind that will say both yes and no. There is warmth in her gaze, but it is hard, with a dry heat rarely encountered in women. Altogether, it is a twofold face. It is the portrait of *equivocation*.

When the King confided his intentions to Louvois, the Minister threw himself weeping at his feet and begged him to consider what a stain Louis the

Great would be casting on his *gloire* by marrying the widow Scarron. He succeeded only in incurring the hatred of the Marquise.

No one knows whether the King ever envisaged an official, 'declared' marriage, or what date the union was legitimized. 1683, 1684, 1686, even 1697 have been suggested as the date when Harlay de Champvallon performed the ceremony in a room at Versailles, in front of Louvois, Father La Chaise, His Majesty's confessor, Bontemps, the *valet de chambre*, and the Marquis de Montchevreuil.

October 1683 seems the most likely date. It is the only effective explanation of the tears shed by the Marquise that summer, her vapours, terror, and fits of pride and ill-concealed rejoicing. Many writers have attributed her wild behaviour to the sudden requirement for this mother of the Church to please Louis' senses at the same time as watching over his salvation – but this was nothing new. The humble creature in charge of Louis' bastards had probably been yielding to the ardours of the Sun since 1673.

The revolution was seen to have occurred when Mme de Maintenon remained seated in the presence of the Princesses and took her place in chapel on the Queen's dais. Yet it took the court a long time to admit the inadmissible, and ten years later it was still wondering whether the King was 'both lover, and husband'. Europe asked itself that question while her confessor was calling the *dévote* to order: 'What grace, to do out of pure virtue what other women do without merit out of passion!'

After an initial period of caution and timidity, Françoise steadily gained confidence. She succeeded by devious means in creating bad blood between the King and Louvois as well as between the King and Madame, whose letters are full of insulting references to 'the great man's filth' and accuse Mme de Maintenon of being an incendiary and a poisoner. The former governess did not shrink even from setting son against mother, and used the Duc du Maine to dislodge La Montespan from her last position of strength. Mme de Maintenon obtained what no woman before her had ever managed. By slow degrees, she acquired influence over policy without losing the attentions of an assiduous husband. All this with eyes still lowered, the modesty of a nun and the authority of a moralist.

Louis worked with his ministers in her presence, and she was still bemoaning the exigencies of her ageing lover to her confessor *at the age of seventy*. His constancy was no more to her liking than were the enchanted castles, wars, hunts, splendour and fresh air that were indispensable to Louis XIV. She would probably have shirked her mission in the long run if the clergy, finally in command of his Majesty's soul, had not constantly recalled her to duty. 'Your bedroom,' wrote the Bishop of Chartres, 'is the domestic church to which God leads him in order to uphold and sanctify him without his knowledge . . . God has placed in your hands the interests of Church and State and the salvation of a great King.'

Mme de Maintenon never imposed any strain on the treasury, and when she retired to lead the life of an abbess after the King's death she took nothing with her. Nevertheless, she was and remained as unpopular as the most ruinous and vilified of Louis' favourites. Although she stood guard to the end on the dignity of the demigod, the intolerant, hypocritical and bigoted atmosphere which she engendered around him did the King untold damage.

Her reign as a secret wife did not escape hurts and disappointments. For years the King tantalized her, governing in her presence, asking her opinion about everything and then almost teasingly rejecting her smallest requests, so that she had to retire behind her curtains to sob for her frustrated ambitions. Then she discovered that there were more devious ways to attain her aims, but it was not until she was approaching seventy-five that she won the right to admit almost inadvertently: 'It is I who must be approached and through whom everything passes . . .'

Louis XIV had come to the point of submitting to the will of a virago whose tastes had nothing in common with his own. It was a far cry from the passage in his own memoirs in which he had insisted: 'Once give a woman the freedom to speak to you about important affairs, and she is certain to lead you astray.'

[4]

The Ides of September

SEPTEMBER 1683 saw events whose disastrous consequences changed the character of Louis XIV's reign.

Colbert had taken to his bed at the end of August, and in an attempt to restore their relations to their former closeness, Louis wrote to his minister 'to command him not to overtax his strength and to take care of himself'. Colbert did not say a word when the letter was read out, and when Mme Colbert asked if he did not wish to answer the King, he told her: 'It is to the King of Kings that I must think of answering.'[1]

Louis still continued to send for news of his progress. On 2 September he was informed by Seignelay that his father was dying, and sent an immediate reply that exploded all rumours of Colbert's disgrace: 'I am most upset by the condition of your father ... I am still hoping that God will not see fit to remove him from this world when he is so necessary to the welfare of the state. I desire this with all my heart, because of the special friendship I bear him as well as yourself and all his family.' Colbert died on 6 September.

Of all France's great and unpopular ministers, from Sully, Richelieu and Talleyrand to Poincaré, it was undoubtedly Colbert who, after Mazarin, inspired the most virulent hatred. His funeral procession had to be guarded for fear of an attack by the populace. Yet he was one of the architects of the greatness of France, even though much of his work did not survive him. His lasting achievements include towns, canals, numerous industries and monuments and the administrative system he initiated. His ordinances controlling the police, municipal sanitation, trade, the navy and a host of other subjects remained in force until the end of the Ancien Régime. But his protectionist innovations failed, his finances had reverted to chaos well prior to his death, his navy declined as quickly as it had risen, his companies collapsed and France failed to gain the economic and maritime hegemony of which he dreamed.

While Seignelay took over most of his father's functions, notably the secretaryship of the navy, finance fell into the hands of Le Pelletier, an unimaginative clerk. Louvois was the real beneficiary. He emerged victorious in the struggle for the superintendency of public works, and remained at liberty to apply his strength and brutality to the entire machinery of govern-ment.

While Colbert's death-knell tolled the prosperity of France, the fate of the West was being played out before Vienna, which was under siege from the Sultan's armies. A Turkish victory seemed inevitable, and Louis XIV took it sufficiently for granted to resume his war against Spain in the Low Countries. Kara Mustafa, the grand vizier, was equally overconfident, and conducted operations at his leisure, so that the King of Poland, John Sobieski, was able to intervene and raise the siege, routing the Turks on 12 September 1683. Emperor Leopold, triumphant and humiliated, regained his capital while the Te Deum was being sung in honour of the King of Poland.

The Turkish defeat was both crushing and decisive. It foreshadowed the decline of the Ottoman Empire and radically altered the balance of power in Europe. Since the time when, from his captivity in Madrid, Francis I had sent his ring to Suleiman the Magnificent, France had shaken off the hold of the House of Austria and eventually overtaken it, thanks to increasing Turkish pressure on successive emperors. Now, for the first time, the Habsburg Empire was free to bring all its power to bear in the west. The retreat of the Crescent partly nullified the effects of the Treaty of the Pyrenees, upset the balance of the opposing forces and brought the century to its major diplo-matic and military turning-point.[2]

At the same time, Louis was receiving unexpected compensation from the direction of England. Two opposing trends had given rise to representative parties, the Tories and the Whigs. The former represented rural and loyalist interests and tradition; the latter were closer to the Puritans, and their strength lay in the industrial and commercial areas. The Whigs were hostile to the Stuarts, to Catholicism and to France, and had been fostering the twin bogeys of Popery and tyranny for nine years, reducing the Crown to impotence and conducting a reign of terror. They made arrangements to assassinate the King they could not get rid of, and when the plot was discovered public opinion reacted sharply against them. Charles II found himself safely on his throne again, with a Tory reaction under way.

An apparently trivial event occurred during this period. Princess Anne, second daughter of the Duke of York and a Protestant like her elder sister, married Prince George of Denmark with the approval of Louis XIV. This enabled her to attach to her person her childhood friend and idol, Sarah Jennings, now the wife of John Churchill.

Louis XIV could not possibly know what misfortunes were in store for him as a result of the appointment of a mere 'lady-in-waiting'; he did realize, however, that for a possibly limited time Europe was at his mercy, and he hastened to press home the advantage. His armies bombarded and captured

Luxembourg and seized Courtrai and Dixmude in Flanders and Trier in Germany. All this was given out as being in accordance with the spirit, if not the letter, of the Treaty of Nimwegen.

Spain and the Emperor, who was busy chasing Turks in Hungary, had to bow the knee. The Treaty of Nimwegen became a twenty-year truce by virtue of which the French annexations were 'regularized' (Treaty of Ratisbon, 1684). In the Mediterranean, hostilities against the corsair slave-traders continued. Algiers was bombarded a second time, sued for peace and freed its Christian slaves, after paying a ransom. The same happened in Tunis.

The Genoese Republic had furnished arms and munitions to the Berbers, and was also building galleys ordered by the Spanish navy. Louis made up his mind to teach the Genoese a lesson, and Seignelay, who rivalled Louvois in ruthlessness, brutality and ambition, personally accompanied a fleet under the command of Duquesne which lobbed fourteen thousand bombs into the city. Four thousand men landed, and the Republic sued for mercy. Contrary to its laws, the Doge, Lescaro, went in person to present apologies at Versailles and to ask for clemency (on 15 May 1685).

In the meantime, Louvois had been running the royal building schemes like a military operation, sending the King memoranda about mirrors, gilding, chimneys, paint and the size of screws. Louis covered these documents with impatient annotations. Soldiers reinforced the workmen and toiled in the grip of a discipline worthy of present-day China.

The main problem was to lay on a supply of water adequate to feed the ornamental lakes and fountains. It was solved by an engineer from Liège, Renkin Sualem, an expert on pumps. Eighteen hundred workmen were employed on the 'machine of Marly', which was constructed of 14,000 cubic yards of wood, nearly 900 tons of copper and lead, 1,500 tons of iron, 2,500 pounds of rope and 1,200 pounds of grease. On 15 November 1684 the illuminated Galerie des Glaces was opened to the court, and a few months later the water of the Seine gushed out at Versailles. It was the turn of the 'haunt of snakes and frogs', as Saint-Simon called Marly, to become one of the wonders of the world.

The Sun King's works were admired by a delegation sent by the King of Siam to present gifts to Louis and negotiate a trade treaty. It was even given out that the Asian potentate was thinking of becoming a Catholic convert. His Chief Minister, the Greek son of a Cephalonian inn-keeper, was hoping to reinforce his position by obtaining the support of the French, who had just begun to establish trading centres in the Far East. As well as flattering the King's vanity, the Siamese delegation confirmed the very recent Western interest in remote countries to which the Christian civilizations had paid scant attention previously – an interest that was to jolt the harmonious and exact notions on which the universe of a Bossuet was built.

This was the moment in history when France reached the zenith of her power and magnificence. She only rediscovered it, and then fleetingly, under the First Empire. The Duc de La Feuillade laid out the Place des Victoires in Paris, and a statue was erected showing the Great King trampling shackled nations underfoot. Before that statue was unveiled, the wheel had already begun to turn.

[5]

The Interests of Heaven

Des intérêts du Ciel pourquoi vous chargez-vous? – Molière.*

IN about 1683 or 1684, the change which had been occurring gradually and as if by degrees in the King's mind and conduct became more marked and striking. He made less of a secret of the reformed life that he was beginning to lead, and no longer feared to seem what he was and openly to replace with religious practices the gallantries that had amused him hitherto.[1]

Molière's former protector had become a *dévot*. He still adhered, as he had always done, to the firm and very simple beliefs he had received from his mother, but the alteration in his behaviour as man and sovereign was far-reaching.

His conversion made no difference to his pride, egoism and taste for dominance, glitter and ostentation. Worse still, convinced, like many of his contemporaries, that an orderly life and precise observance of outward practices were a sure way to divine approval, he developed a fatal self-assurance that removed any scruples he might have had about acting in-humanely. He had been hard-hearted ever since the ordeals of his early youth. Now he grew harder still, and his feelings could only be moved on exceptional occasions.

Louis XIV had never allowed his actions to be prompted by kindness. After ordaining that soldiers were to abstain from meat on Fridays, even during campaigns, and giving his courtiers an incentive to fulfil their religious obligations by promising to show favour to the zealous, he felt permanently armoured against pity and sentimentality.

It has been said that Louis was not a *Christian* monarch because charity was foreign to his nature. The consequences of that failing cost him dearly, even though there were limits to his insensitivity and he occasionally curbed the excesses of those who acted for him. But his underlings had fallen into the habit of taking their master's tendencies to extremes. Where the King was strict, his ministers were cruel (this applies to Colbert and Seignelay, as well as Louvois); where he was known to be implacable, they often became execu-tioners.

* 'Why take Heaven's interests upon yourself?' The parallel between the religious policy of Louis XIV and this line from *Tartuffe* comes from M. Daniel-Rops.

Mme de Maintenon might have played a worthy part by standing for gentleness and mercy, but this was not in the character of the dry school-mistress. Since those early years when the Sun King had fired the young to enthusiasm and emulation, a moral rift had cut him off from the new rising generation, as was soon to be demonstrated in the course of a curious affair.

The Prince de Conti and his brilliant young brother, the Prince de La Roche-sur-Yon, were burning to fight. In spite of the King, they offered their swords to the Emperor and joined the armies that were still fighting against the Turks, taking with them Prince Eugène of Savoy, son of the Comtesse de Soissons. During their campaigns, numerous letters passed between them and the Princesse de Conti, the Marquis d'Alincourt, the Duc de La Roche-Guyon and the Marquis de Liancourt, these last two the sons of the Duc de La Rochefoucauld, the King's closest friend.

Their correspondence inevitably came to the attention of the examiners of the mail, who passed it on to Louvois. He handed it over to His Majesty – all four hundred letters. They contained remarks to the effect that the King was 'an enfeebled squire by the side of his aged mistress' and (from the Prince de La Roche-sur-Yon): 'a play-actor king for show, and a chess king for battle.'

The Princesse de Conti was severely reprimanded by her father and Mme de Maintenon, and the three gentlemen were banished. As for the Princes, their uncle, the Grand Condé, ordered them to return, and they had to throw themselves at the feet of Louis, who forgave them grudgingly. Conti died of smallpox not long afterwards, and his brother, who inherited the title, never returned to favour. The King's new-found piety had not tempered his vindictiveness.

On the other hand, it did lead him to take to heart the mission of the Gallican monarch who had sworn at his coronation to extirpate heresy. Bossuet had never ceased to remind him that: 'The King has a duty to use his authority to destroy false religions in his state.' Louis was quite determined not to put up with any interference from the Pope in his lands, and felt himself all the more obliged to be the secular arm of the Church. He was not temperamentally equipped to realize that problems of metaphysics are not solved by police methods. In fact, seventeenth-century Frenchmen were not shocked by dictatorial interventions in the spiritual realm, and the Holy See was practically alone in complaining about these infringements of its authority. It was an age when no country, whether Catholic or Protestant, made any distinction between political and religious unity. The English Catholics were second-class citizens and had just been through a period of severe persecution under the Whigs.

The wind had shifted, however. Charles II died suddenly in January 1685, and the Duke of York was able to succeed him without difficulty, under the title of James II. He retained his obedience to the Roman Church, and the delighted Louis XIV immediately sent him an unsolicited gift of 500,000 livres. All the same, when John Churchill visited Versailles to present his master's compliments, he said quite openly 'that if ever the King yielded to influences that would make him change his country's religion, he, Churchill, would no longer serve him.'

The warning went unheeded. Louis trusted in his own power. Europe was at peace and England was ruled by a Catholic. He thought that the time had come to implement the 'grand design' that had been in his mind ever since he had begun to govern in person.

The Protestant consistories had appointed the Marquis de Ruvigny as their official representative at court. One day, as he was presenting grievances to the King, he was informed in the sharp, precise style that was Louis' hallmark: 'The King my grandfather loved you, the King my father feared you – as for me, I neither fear nor love you.' Louis was unimaginative and incapable of theological doubt. He still had the facile ideas about the Reformation that his early education had instilled in him, and was under the illusion that it had arisen out of various abuses that the Church had remedied long ago. The obstinacy of heretics whose aberrations were immensely damaging to themselves was consequently no longer logical, and these lost sheep must be brought back to the fold if such they were, or punished if their conscientiousness was a cloak for minds infected with republicanism.

In 1661, he had given instructions 'to restrict the Edict of Nantes* within the narrowest confines of justice and propriety', thus giving impetus to what became known as the 'quiet persecution'. The memoirist Abbé de Choisy summed it up: 'The Courts of the Edict of Nantes had been broken; four hundred or more churches had been pulled down; Huguenots were no longer allowed to hold office in the police or finance; doctors and midwives of their faith had been taken from them.' The next step came when Protestants were compelled to pay allowances to their converted children and to receive at their deathbeds priests whose job it was to urge them to make last-minute conversions. A fund was set up to provide material assistance to Protestants who went over to Catholicism. Those who relapsed risked banishment and the confiscation of their goods. Catholics were forbidden to marry Protestants.

Louvois carried a major share of the responsibility for the change from quiet to violent persecution that began in 1681. Mme de Maintenon held no brief for lenience, nor did Harlay de Champvallon or Father La Chaise, the King's confessor. The general tenor of public opinion was no less intolerant. The General Assembly of the Clergy was interpreting that opinion when it urged the King to act like 'another Constantine'.

---

* By which Henry IV had granted freedom of worship and conscience to the Protestants in 1598. Most of the political clauses of the edict had been revoked by Richelieu in 1629.

Louis, although bent on converting the Protestants, did not intend to institute a reign of terror, but his over-zealous agents concealed from him the methods they used to achieve his ambition. The origin of the notorious *dragonnades* was a law by which all Frenchmen were obliged to provide quarters for soldiers in an emergency. The King was persuaded to enact an ordinance exempting new converts from this duty (on 11 July 1681). This mild measure enabled Louvois and his subordinates, unknown to Louis, to pack Protestant homes with soldiers who were encouraged to commit outrages. Marillac, the intendant at Poitiers, claimed thirty thousand conversions in a single year thanks to this method. He got no credit, but only because Louis finally discovered what had been going on.

Louvois wrote to Marillac revoking his own suggestions in the same icy tone he had adopted towards Luxembourg during the Dutch war: 'His Majesty has commanded me to inform you that it is his unalterable will that you call a halt to the violent acts of the cavalry and hang the first man who commits any, even if the violence has produced conversions.'

Different instructions were therefore issued: the King must be convinced that an almost spontaneous wave of mass emotion was bearing Protestants towards the Church. Floods of reports and statistics poured into Versailles. Chancellor Le Tellier, relieving his terrible son, was now using peaceful methods: the good word was to be preached by way of trials, legal quibbles and the threat of ruin. This was a matter for the provincial parlements, and there was no need for the King to be kept informed about such trifles.

Most of the Catholic population were a party to these tactics, and there were uprisings at Uzès and Nîmes when a more humane intendant authorized the reopening of Protestant churches. In Dauphiné and the Vivarais region of Languedoc it was the despairing Protestants who opened fire on the dragoons.

When Louvois ordered the Duc de Noailles, Governor of Languedoc in the name of the Duc du Maine, to devastate the country, Noailles, an accomplished courtier, improved still further on the cruelty of his commission. There were massacres in Languedoc and the Cévennes and executions at Grenoble. Nîmes, left to the mercy of the dragoons, was converted in three days, Montauban in one day. Noailles then wrote to the King that everything had gone off 'with great wisdom and discipline' and that soon there would not be a single Huguenot in his province.

By a royal proclamation of 17 June 1681, conversions of Protestant children over the age of seven were declared valid. On the face of it, there is nothing barbaric about this measure either. Although Louis was convinced that it was his duty to offer his young subjects the means of saving their souls as soon as they attained the age of reason, it was not possible altogether to conceal from him the terrible effects of proselytizing enthusiasm. His anger was aroused and he gave orders for moderation, but he valued the mirage created by his servants and more or less consciously closed his eyes to the facts.

From 1684 onwards financial considerations aggravated the persecution. The King, short of money, was only too willing to confiscate the wealth of the Protestant churches, charities and hospitals. After these communal goods, covetous eyes now alighted on the property of individuals. 'Everybody was in hot pursuit of the quarry. It was an open gulf, a mêlée into which people threw themselves so as to profit from the passing torrent.' The pious Mme de Maintenon wrote to her brother: 'Now is the time to buy the Protestants' lands, they are going for nothing.' She found nothing inconsistent in casting doubts on the sincerity of conversions that were decided 'without knowing why'.

During 1685 more and more Protestants were arrested and more acts of violence committed against them, in an atmosphere reminiscent of the wars of religion. Several bishops stood out against intolerance and protected the victims. The Archbishop of Paris had the use of force condemned in the General Assembly of the Clergy, but his true motive was to strike a blow at Louvois.

There was bitter rivalry between the prelate and the minister, each man striving to acquire the 'honour' of having eradicated heresy and so to win the King's gratitude. In addition, Harlay de Champvallon hoped that success would make the Holy See overlook his opposition and his 'scandalous commerce' with a number of women, among them the abbesses of Pontoise and Andely, according to the German diplomat Ezekiel Spanheim. It was Harlay who pressed insistently for the revocation of the Edict of Nantes, which he claimed was a dead letter. After long hesitation:

> The King raised the matter for discussion in his Council. Opinion was divided. Some advised following the same maxims as before, saying that consciences cannot be ruled by a big stick. Others, possibly in the grip of a thoughtless zeal, cried that there was nothing to fear from a handful of people who, seeing themselves despised and leaderless, would soon lose their nerve . . . and that if the master would speak earnestly and forthrightly, they would follow like sheep.[2]

On 18 October the King signed the Edict of Fontainebleau, revoking the Edict of Nantes and the Edict of Nîmes, known as the Edict of Grace, of 1629. To his way of thinking it was a strictly logical course which brought into alignment the religious dogma whose protector he was and the political dogma that he incarnated.

Although Louis xiv certainly deluded himself as to the number and especially the genuineness of the conversions, he was not deceived to the point of believing that the 'deadly conflagration' of the Reformation was extinguished. Otherwise, he would not have sent the strange missions of priests and dragoons that proceeded to scour the provinces. France was now the scene of a persecution unparalleled since medieval times. Under the last Valois kings, it had been a matter of a *war* of religion, with victims in both camps.

In spite of everything, the Protestants had not expected to suffer the kind of treatment that was meted out to them, nor the Catholics to meet such stubborn resistance. The new dragonnades far exceeded those of 1681. On several occasions Louvois advised killing as many people as possible. The soldiery were licensed to torture as many as they pleased, and the benches of the galleys were crowded with 'converted' Protestants who had celebrated their old rites or tried to escape. Three hundred thousand Huguenots fled abroad.

For some time Frederick William, Elector of Brandenburg, had been nursing the idea of attracting to his 'underdeveloped' state all kinds of persecuted minorities. After 29 October he took measures to offer asylum to the Protestants (Edict of Potsdam), and the Dutch, Swiss and English followed suit. Louis xiv's ministers were too slow to realize that precious brains and wealth were draining away.

The disturbances continued until the end of Louis' reign. Far from strengthening the unity of the realm, the Revocation brought disorder, rebellion and an undeclared civil war. Instead of rounding off the achievements of French classical civilization, it opened an appalling breach in it. As for the spirit of the Reformation, far from being stamped out, it was galvanized and embittered all over the continent and even in America.

There is no event that looks more different depending on whether it is viewed down the perspective of centuries or through the eyes of contemporaries. Moral considerations aside, it appears today as a colossal blunder, one of the great catastrophes of French history. In 1689 Vauban began to draw up the balance-sheet: the exile of a great many valuable men and expatriation of huge sums of money; the ruin of a section of French trade and the stoppage of numerous industries; 'enemy nations swelled by the addition of eight or nine thousand seamen; their armies by five or six hundred officers and ten to twelve thousand soldiers far more seasoned than their own.'

Yet all these losses are trifling by comparison with the impetus given to Prussia, the rekindling of old fanaticisms, the rebirth of the wars of religion, the triumph of William of Orange, who was invested with a prestige he could never have hoped for as the head of international Protestantism, and the provocation for half of Europe to detest the King of France.

A torrent of pamphlets poured out of Holland:

Sache, pourtant Louis, le plus traître des hommes,
Sache, cruel auteur des tourments où nous sommes,
Que ton nom, exécrable à la posterité,
Sera maudit sans fin et sans fin détesté.*

* 'Yet know, Louis, most treacherous of men, / Know, cruel author of our torments, / That your name will be hateful to posterity, / endlessly detested.'

Yet Louis' treatment of the Huguenots was the most popular act of his reign, just as the creation of Versailles was the most unpopular. Eighteen out of nineteen million Frenchmen rejoiced, and the throne basked in the almost forgotten adulation of twenty years before.

Not one tear had been shed for Colbert, and now the Revocation was applauded. Vauban, one of the few men to realize the extent of the disaster, wrote: 'Nothing would have been of greater benefit to the kingdom than this long-desired uniformity of sentiments, if it had pleased God to bless the subject of that uniformity.' Choruses of praise burst forth from the Trappist reformer the Abbé de Rancé, Racine, Fontenelle, Mme de Sévigné, the compassionate La Bruyère and the honest La Fontaine.

Bossuet condemned acts of violence and tried to forbid them in his diocese, but when he came to pronounce the funeral oration of Le Tellier, who had sealed the Edict not long before his death, he could nonetheless exclaim: 'Moved by such wonders, let us give heartfelt thanks for the piety of Louis . . . and say to this new Theodosius, this new Charlemagne . . . this is the crowning achievement and true essence of your reign.'

Only Saint-Simon, of all the great writers of the age, splendidly castigates

> . . . the appalling conspiracy that depopulated a quarter of the realm, weakened it in every part, subjected it for so long to public and avowed pillage by the dragoons, authorized the tortures that in fact led thousands of men and women to their deaths, ruined so great a community, tore countless families apart, armed relative against relative . . . made a gift of our manufactures to foreign nations . . . gave them the spectacle of such a prodigious number of people outlawed, stripped, fleeing, vagrant though guiltless of crime, seeking asylum far from their homeland.

Later, however, when the Regent considered re-establishing the Edict of Nantes and recalling the Protestants, Saint-Simon was equally vehement in his opposition.

If the question had been put to the people in a referendum, or as an electoral issue, an overwhelming majority would have come out in favour of the Revocation. This may give food for thought to a democrat, but it does not excuse Louis XIV. The sole effective justification of absolute power is that a leader is not obliged to follow the misguided masses.

[6]

Stoicism and Violence

THE physical or mental state of an autocrat can sometimes have a decisive influence on the course of history. Louis XIV had a robust constitution, but not good health. Since his attack of smallpox at the age of ten he had suffered several serious illnesses. His ideas about medicine were as conventional and as dangerous as his preconceptions about religion. A monarch, responsible for his own life to millions of people, had no right to evade his doctors. As a result he heroically endured an astounding variety of tortures.

The terrible bloodletting that left him dazed and exhausted eventually had to be discontinued. To make up for it, the court physicians, led by M. d'Aquin, put their faith in a laxative of their own invention, thanks to which the patient had to take to his commode eighteen times in one day, and had 'red stools'. His martyrdom began in 1685 with the extraction of a tooth, which provoked as abscess, then osteitis and sinusitis. Following this, M. d'Aquin recommended the extraction of all his upper teeth. This operation destroyed part of his palate and shattered his jaw. The remedy was to apply a red-hot coal to the wound. Seventeen times the King endured this torture, which was similar to that inflicted on hardened heretics. The cure was never completed, and His Majesty remained subject to a most irritating infirmity: if he did not drink with care, the fluid would emerge through his nose.

Louis did not allow his sufferings to affect his steady, majestic conduct, but new lines furrowed his countenance, the mouth became sunken, the nose seemed to swell and the expression grew bitter and almost aggressive. He became touchy, irascible and inclined to violence. It was at the time when Louis XIV was undergoing the greatest physical pain that his régime was at its most oppressive and his foreign policy at its most brutal, although Michelet's claim that his illness represented a kind of demarcation line in his reign is exaggerated.

In December 1685 the Protestants received a further blow: 'Every child aged from five to sixteen years will be removed within eight days. . .' This gave rise to atrocities, and Louvois' Neronian instincts had full rein, with competition from Seignelay, the head of the navy. At that time, the galleys were the last circle of hell.

The King's ordeals during this period were almost as cruel as his subjects'. He had developed a tumour on the knee. While the public marvelled at the Galerie des Glaces and he was setting himself up as an idol in the Place des Victoires, nature was afflicting him in the spot 'through which all men are humbled.'[1] The Sun King developed an anal fistula. Surgery was the only cure, but it was an appalling gamble which could have far-reaching consequences for France and Europe. The King ordered his condition to be kept secret, but there were too many watchful eyes on him. From the end of February 1686 the rumour that he was in mortal danger reached foreign courts, and intrigues gathered around the Dauphin.

To put his enemies off the scent, Louis presided over an unusual number of fêtes, still impassive in spite of the incisions and cauteries he had undergone. On 24 March he was unable to unveil the statue in the Place des Victoires, and the Dauphin deputized for him at the ceremony, which was overlaid by a macabre irony. The King never forgave the unfortunate La Feuillade for this setback, in spite of his good intentions and the millions he had spent.

Louvois now had an inspiration. He assembled every sufferer from fistulas in Paris and its environs at the offices of the superintendent of public building. Doctors set to work on these guinea-pigs and experimented with every imaginable treatment, but to no avail. The King's pains increased, along with his anxieties for the future. Europe was buzzing with his illness. The weak-willed Dauphin had fallen into the clutches of a group of young people singularly lacking in piety, the Princesse de Conti, her brother-in-law,* and the Duc and Grand Prieur de Vendôme, great-grandsons of Henry IV and great nephews of Mazarin.

Mme de Maintenon began to cast about for a suitable refuge in the event of some calamity. One of her protégées, Mme de Brinon, was educating a few deprived orphans of good birth, mainly officers' daughters, with the aim of preserving them from the dangers to which poverty might expose them. Mme de Maintenon asked Louis for a house where the little community could expand. Louis responded enthusiastically and Mansart was commissioned to build the school of Saint-Cyr. Within a year it was ready to receive two hundred and fifty girls and thirty-six teachers.

With Louis so ill, the Marquise had no time to lose. In June 1686 His Majesty signed the letters patent that founded the Community of Saint Louis. The inmates received a medallion bearing the effigy of the canonized king on one side, and on the obverse that of their protectress. Louis amused himself by devising the girls' outfits personally, a different one for each class.

Françoise d'Aubigné could breathe again. She now owned a refuge fit to

---

* The daughter of the King and La Vallière was now the dowager Princesse de Conti. Her brother-in-law, who was now Prince de Conti, was the former Prince de La Roche-sur-Yon.

receive her and to safeguard her reputation and dignity in the event of a second widowhood. In the meantime, she worked on the articles of the institute and submitted them to the King. It was not to be a convent, which would then be answerable to the Pope. Knowing her husband as she did, Mme de Maintenon had arranged things so as to make him the sole patron of Saint-Cyr, so that Louis, delighted, told Racine: 'Do not forget to include the foundation of Saint-Cyr in the annals of the reign.'

The school was run in the tyrannical, military spirit that was so prevalent in France at the time, even when it came to young ladies. They were completely under the control of the Marquise, who had a true vocation as a teacher, but also an authority worthy of the wife of Louis xiv. She ruled Saint-Cyr as the King ruled his people. When a candidate presented himself for the hand of one of her pupils, four of them appeared before the suitor, as in a slave market. When the gentleman had made his selection, the girl concerned was asked whether she was in agreement. If not, there was almost no other course open to her than to take the veil.

It was a solace to the King to take his mind off weighty affairs and act as a father to these orphan girls, but his pleasure was outweighed by the exasperation of finding that far from being settled, the Revocation question was becoming more complicated still. Many converts were so far gone in perversity that they were retracting on their deathbeds. Louis was scandalized, and ordered the bodies of these wretches to be drawn on hurdles. Corpses that had already been buried were exhumed in order to inflict this punishment. At Cany, in the Caux region, a zealous official organized a display of the remains of a woman named Diel: he charged an admission fee 'for looking at the body of a damned woman'.

There was worse to come. In Savoy, in a fold of the Alps, there was a small reformed community, the Vaudois, whose ancestors had suffered special persecution under Francis i. The King was persuaded that Protestant émigrés might take refuge in these mountains, and their doom was sealed. The young Duke of Savoy gave way, and French troops under the command of Catinat proceeded to a massacre worthy of a tribe of cannibals. Some played bowls with children's heads, an old man was flayed alive and a girl was pinned to the earth with a sword and then raped.

Scenes of this nature were being enacted fifty years after the publication of Descartes' *Discourse on Method*. They did not shock any of the great Cartesians who argued so passionately for moderation and reason.

In France, Louis might appear to be a champion of Catholicism, preoccupied with his own salvation, or a sick man whose last creation was destined to be a community of young ladies. In the eyes of the world, he was a devouring giant suspected of harbouring ambitions for a world monarchy, and no one doubted that he wanted to subjugate all the Christian princes and to reduce their subjects to slavery.

The truth is that whatever Louis' secret ambitions may have been, his conquests, even the most lawless, were justifiable in terms of his concern for the protection of his realm. They were also *natural* – so much so that in spite of her revolutions and subsequent defeats, France still retains them.* Compared with Napoleon, Hitler or Stalin, Louis seems almost like a rational landowner busily – and not over-scrupulously – extending and enclosing his property.

The King's contemporaries were unfamiliar with his deep-seated caution, and did not discern the sense of balance that was present even in his excesses. They saw the brutality of his methods, his insolence, his intolerable way of exalting his own victories and humiliating his adversaries. In reality, the Sun King's designs were less reprehensible than his attitudes. The most ambitious figure of the moment was not Louis, but the little Stadtholder of Holland.

William of Orange had sworn to destroy the hegemony of France, appropriate the English crown and become the arbiter of nations in his turn. On 9 July, at Augsburg, he quietly engineered the signing of a Treaty of Alliance, a League between the United Provinces, the Habsburg Emperor, the Elector of Brandenburg, a large fraction of the Empire and the Duke of Lorraine. The King of Spain and the Duke of Savoy became members not long afterwards. The Pope urged them all on and Venice encouraged them. Sweden too abandoned France, whose only remaining friends were the King (but not the people) of England, and Denmark, which was powerless. At Versailles, the courtiers sought to ridicule the Coalition of Augsburg, comparing it to La Fontaine's dragon, a fearsome but paralytic monster.

The birth in August of the Duc de Berry, the third son of Monseigneur, following that of the Duc d'Anjou in 1683, came like a pledge of the immortality of the House of France. The King was uneasy, however. He wanted to maintain the status quo and had no taste for another war.

Louis' building projects were nowhere near completion, and he ordered the construction of a marble Trianon to take the place of the porcelain Trianon. Every year he bought quantities of diamonds. This hunger for expenditure, due perhaps to his uncertain health, was not compatible with the burden that an international crisis would impose on his already over-extended finances. Such a crisis seemed all the more imminent with the Emperor scoring brilliant victories over the Turks, in which the young Prince Eugène of Savoy distinguished himself by his daring. He too hated the King of France, who after the poisons affair and the accusations levelled against

---

* With the exception of a number of towns such as Casale and Luxembourg, which were strategic strongpoints. Even the provinces that Louis restored, Lorraine, Nice and Savoy, finally returned to France.

Eugène's mother had refused the Prince the post of Colonel General of the Swiss Guard, which was the appanage of his family.

Two courses of action were now open to Louis XIV. Colbert de Croissy begged him to appease and divide his enemies by making concessions. Louvois, possibly so as to make his services indispensable, was pushing for war. The advocates of force won, but in Louis' mind it was a matter of preventing a war, not provoking one. Together with his ill-timed refusal to negotiate with the Dutch and his treatment of the Huguenots, it was the third of his fatal mistakes.

He was nagged by recurring fears of what might happen in these circumstances if the throne fell to his ineffectual son. In opting for the hazardous course, Louis was also compelling himself to risk his own life. It was secretly decided to operate. The surgeon Félix practised on Louvois' guinea-pigs for several weeks, until the King was racked by such intolerable pains that he ordered the operation to be performed on 18 November. He did not utter a single cry during the two lancings and eight incisions that the surgeon made. When the latter had finished:

the King ordered him to make a close examination to see whether more might be necessary; following which, his Majesty's wound was dressed and he ordered the First Gentleman of the Bedchamber to be admitted, telling him what had just taken place and instructing him to usher in the first arrivals. The King was bled at eleven o'clock, as a precaution, heard mass at midday, and at two o'clock thirty people watched him take some soup . . . At five o'clock he summoned the Council, which sat until seven in the evening.[2]

Louis continued to suffer agonies for the next month, but the tempo of the royal machine did not alter for a single day. It is the courtiers' minds that seem to have been thrown out of gear. About thirty of them hastened to their doctors 'urgently requesting an operation, and such was their folly that they seemed angry at being assured that there was no need for one.'

At Chantilly, the Grand Condé died. He had finally bought his way back into favour by marrying his grandson, the Duc d'Enghien, to Mlle de Nantes, Louis' daughter by Mme de Montespan. Louis had given in to his entreaties on behalf of his nephew Conti, and the headstrong young man returned to court.

On 27 December, four days after Condé's funeral, Louis' operation scar was completely healed and Louvois was able to announce 'a perfect and absolute cure'. The French people manifested the last explosion of love ever aroused by the Sun King. D'Aquin received a gift of land, a huge gratuity (about £75,000 or $180,000 in modern terms), and soon his dismissal. Mme de Maintenon wanted a man devoted to herself at the King's bedside, and M. Fagon became chief physician. His opening move was to forbid his patient to drink Champagne wine. Instead he prescribed Burgundy to combat the royal gout, which only grew worse, tying Louis to a wheel-chair.

His health remained extremely shaky for several years, and his ill-temper continued to goad him into aggressive actions. While continuing his persecution of the Huguenots (though their bodies were no longer drawn on hurdles), he turned his thunderbolts against the Pope.

The right of asylum accorded to criminals by ambassadors to the Holy See had gradually extended to the quarters where their residences were located, so that the Rome police were virtually powerless against the criminal element. Innocent XI asked the various sovereigns to give up their franchises, and they all agreed, with the exception of Louis, who pretended to be insulted. His new ambassador, the Marquis de Lavardin, entered Rome at the head of four hundred soldiers and turned the French quarter into a stronghold. The Pope now excommunicated Lavardin, with no effect other than that of demonstrating how ineffectual this once terrible weapon had become. The ambassador did not stop visiting the Supreme Pontiff, and even continued to take communion, thanks to the simple expedient of obtaining provisional absolution. The relentless defender of the Catholic Church was making its practices a laughing-stock, but Innocent XI was just as obstinate as Louis, and the conflict went on until the King had the county of Avignon occupied as he had in 1662.

His interests on the Rhine took the form of an increasingly provocative and vindictive attitude. The French occupied Hüningen and built a fort in the middle of the river to enable them to cross whenever they chose. Following the death of the Elector-Archbishop of Cologne (in June 1688), the King attempted to grant the succession to one of his men, Cardinal Fürstenberg, in the teeth of papal opposition. He also submitted a claim on behalf of the Duchesse d'Orléans for part of the estate of her father, the Elector Palatine, who had died in 1685. Not for nothing had the Bourbons made an alliance with an ugly and dowerless princess.

Since none of this was achieving its aim of intimidating and discouraging the League of Augsburg, Louis bowed to the fatal influence of Louvois. Assured of having won a crown in Heaven, he staked his terrestrial power at the moment when the storm was blowing in from the sea.

[7]
The Tide of History

RELIGIOUS feeling was running as high in England as in France, but there were also two economic considerations that set the Catholic Stuart at logger-heads with the majority of his subjects. With the rise of commercial capital-ism, these subjects' utilitarian individualism was growing stronger, and it was not compatible with the control of property, which was regarded as a public function in states ruled by an absolute monarch.

After the Reformation the belief took hold that although the Christian's slavation lies in faith, true faith is the kind that leads to achievements. It follows that man will be judged on his achievements. The businessman, like the man of God, must work for the benefit of the community. His success will prove that he has found favour in the eyes of the Lord. In spite of the Gospel, he will have satisfied two masters, God and Mammon.

The Protestant Whigs were delighted with this argument. They wanted economic hegemony for England, and for the English a greater measure of independence from government. Consequently they detested James II, a militant Catholic and friend of Jesuits, who emulated Louis XIV and could not understand the evolution of his country. The King's ambition was to restore the former rights of the Catholic Church, and it is ironic that he was working against the will of the Pope in this. Innocent XI hated Louis XIV so much that he preferred the English to remain heretics rather than become allies of France. Voltaire's summary of James II's failure cannot be improved upon:

It is sometimes a simple matter to make a religion supreme in a country . . . but in order to bring about such changes, two things are absolutely essential: a deep-laid policy and favourable conditions. James had neither. His self-esteem was wounded by the sight of so many despots in Europe and of Denmark and Sweden on the way to that condition; in short, Poland and England were the only countries where liberty of the people coexisted with royalty. Louis XIV was encouraging him to become absolute in his own land, and the Jesuits were pressing him to re-establish their religion along with their prestige. He set about it so ineptly that he succeeded only in turning people against him. To begin with, he acted as if he had already achieved what he wanted – a public reception for a Papal nuncio; Jesuits and Capuchins at court; imprisoning seven Anglican bishops when he might have won them over; removing the privileges of the City of London when he ought rather to have increased them; arrogantly overturning laws that he should have undermined in secret; finally, behaving so undiplomatically that the Roman cardinals had a joke 'that he must be excommunicated, as the man who was going to destroy what little Catholicism remained in England.'

This was how matters stood when the French refugees driven out by the Revocation brought the English hatred of their persecutor to boiling point. Parish collections were made for them and songs were written lamenting their misfortunes and promising revenge. The climate of the wars of religion had decidedly returned. 'The sense of a common cause grew across the barriers of class, race, creed and interest in the hearts of millions of men.'[1]

James II swam on energetically against the tide. His dynastic prestige was still so great that the Whigs had to contain their grievances in patience. They could afford to wait, since after his death the crown would pass to Mary, the Protestant wife of William of Orange.

Then the news broke that the Queen, Mary of Modena, childless for fourteen years, was pregnant, and she gave birth to a son not long afterwards. This Papist Prince of Wales triggered off the avalanche. The King's daughters and the entire Protestant faction cried that the country had been tricked, and it was even claimed that the child had been smuggled into the palace in a warming-pan. Seven lords wrote secretly to the Prince of Orange urging him to overthrow his father-in-law (on 30 June 1688).

William had been hoping for nothing else, but the task was a dangerous one and could not be attempted without the backing of the League of Augsburg, for Louis XIV had assembled a formidable army on his northern frontiers. The Protestant princes of Germany gave their consent, and the Elector of Brandenburg even sent troops, under the command of a Huguenot refugee, Marshal Schomberg. The Emperor and the King of Spain suffered pangs of conscience at the idea of supporting a heretic against a Catholic sovereign, but the Pope urged them on. It only remained to enlist the cooperation of the Dutch States-General, who were unwilling to send their troops to England with a French army at their gates.

Louis XIV had perceived the danger. In July and August he offered James subsidies, his fleet and thirty thousand men. The Stuart refused. He did not believe in the existence of a conspiracy and had no intention of saddling himself with a master. In any case, French intervention would ruin his chances of converting the kingdom.

The French King decided to save James in spite of himself. On 2 September he informed Holland curtly that any attack on England would be considered as an attack on France. It is at this point that one might be tempted to admit the existence of fatality, of a 'tide of history'. The Dutch were angry, but James II was infuriated and haughtily repudiated the French alliance. Louis could not believe that he was doing so out of sheer stupidity and assumed that there was some secret agreement, an intrigue between the English king and his son-in-law. In any case, it seemed pointless to support so unfriendly a monarch. If the Prince of Orange really did try to dethrone him, the way would be barred by a powerful army. James had forty thousand men at his disposal, more than Cromwell had ever had. An England in the grip of civil war would be neutralized. The real menace was in the east, for Prince Eugène had just won a final victory that put the Turks out of action and released the Imperial armies.

So Louvois reasoned, and the King was swayed. The War Minister was alarmed at the prospect of operations that would mean bringing the navy, and thus his rival Seignelay, to the fore. This fatal jealousy prevented the French fleet from intercepting William and left him an open road.

Louis XIV turned his back on Holland and faced towards Germany. On the very day when the Austrians were entering Belgrade (on 24 September 1688), he called on the Empire to change the Truce of Ratisbon into a definite Treaty, recognize his protégé Cardinal Fürstenberg as Elector of Cologne, and grant the Duc d'Orléans a share of the Palatine inheritance. The ultimatum provided for a three-month moratorium, but the French army set out for the Rhineland on 25 September.

Surprisingly, it was under the command of Monseigneur. The King must still have been feeling seriously ill and anxious for the prestige of his dynasty thus to place his successor in the spotlight. It was the first time that he had diverted the gaze of the world onto another man and put the official propaganda machine at his service.

One of his closest friends, Marshal Duras, seconded by Vauban, directed the campaign, which was fought with extreme brutality but without a declaration of war. Europe was still unused to such behaviour. To a continual chorus of praise for Monseigneur and the young Duc du Maine, who was receiving his baptism of fire, the French occupied the left bank of the Rhine and besieged Philippsburg, which fell on 22 October.

The King was hearing mass at Fontainebleau when the news arrived, and interrupted the sermon to shout it aloud. Tears were streaming down his cheeks, and naturally the entire congregation burst out crying.

The Dauphin came home in triumph. No one realized that, at this very moment, the King was exposed to the most serious peril of his reign. William of Orange had crossed the Channel and landed in England in early November. He took with him fifteen thousand troops from half a dozen nations, a microcosm of Protestant Europe, as well as the great opponent of divine right, John Locke. 'There, and there only is *Political Society*,' this philosopher of the new order had written, 'where every one of the Members hath quitted this natural Power, and resign'd it up into the hands of the Community in all cases that exclude him not from appealing for Protection to the Law established by it.' According to Locke, absolute power was incompatible with civil society, and no one ever 'dream'd of Monarchy being *jure divino,* which we never heard of among Mankind, till it was revealed to us by the Divinity of this last Age.'

Locke claimed that 'the *State of Nature* has a Law of Nature to govern it,' and equated that law with the 'Law of Reason' – a bold though moderate concept that could not coexist with James Stuart and the divine right of which his grandfather James I and Thomas Hobbes had been the principal English advocates. At the beginning, Locke's new doctrine seemed to have little chance of victory. Encamped at Exeter, William spent ten days of uncertainty before loyalties started to dissolve. Everything failed the unhappy King at the same moment, and he failed himself also. The unkindest cuts came from the Churchill household, John, his own associate, brother of his former favourite, and the indomitable Sarah. Churchill caused the army to defect, while Sarah set daughter against father by bringing Princess Anne over to William's camp.

'At last, finding himself attacked and harried by one son-in-law and abandoned by the other, having against him his two daughters and his own friends, hated even by those of his subjects who were still on his side, the King abandoned hope.'[2] His one thought was for the safety of his wife and son, who were helped to reach France by an Italian named Riva and by a Frenchman – none other than Lauzun. James tried to follow, but was hasted by the populace, taken back to London and imprisoned at Rochester. Yielding to the fears that William had done his utmost to arouse, he escaped through an 'accidentally' unlocked door, and this time succeeded in reaching asylum across the Channel, throwing the Great Seal of State into the Thames on the way.

William had conquered England without a drop of blood being shed. Many historians have seen the sombre little man as a champion of liberty, but this is an absurd description of a prince whose one ambition was absolute power. He even refused to rule jointly with Mary, saying that he had no wish to be his wife's usher, but finally had to knuckle under to the Whigs. After voting a Declaration of Rights that became the charter of English liberties, Parliament crowned William III and Mary.

A miraculous balance had been struck between prince and city, power and finance, and Locke had fortunately defined his concept of the 'Law of Nature'. Otherwise the legitimacy of the new sovereigns would have been based only on 'anti-Popery and a warming-pan'.[3] Full of bitterness, William lost all interest in the domestic affairs of England, which were run, as in Venice, by an aristocratic and mercantile oligarchy. Hardly ever resident in London, and spending half of the year on the continent, he focused all his energies on the struggle against France.

Louis XIV had suffered a serious defeat. He was now encircled by enemies, and would have to face a vast siege without any outside help. He could hardly be aware that a still more serious change was under way and that his grim opponent represented the future. William fascinated all those who were weary of absolutism, including a large fraction of the rising generation. His star was still dim, but it heralded the twilight of the Sun King. A pamphlet entitled *Les Soupirs de la France esclave qui aspire après la liberté,* published in Amsterdam in 1689, contained the message: 'France must awake and feel the weight of the frightful tyranny under which she groans, remembering the happy freedom enjoyed by all the neighbouring States under their legitimate princes and in possession of their ancient laws.'

Less than thirty years after accomplishing his own revolution, Louis XIV was already the incarnation of an old régime and a petrified order. Yet in France, none of the adversaries of despotism, the forces who would soon be forming a coherent opposition, had any aspiration towards a new order. They were calling for a return to an outdated past and the preservation of traditions linked with feudalism. The power-concentration that was the one guarantee of French independence was also their main source of discontent. Louis remained the revolutionary 'tyrant' who was enforcing a growing equality under the impersonal authority of a law whose dictates could not be swayed by individual interests or local contingencies.

The King went personally to Chatou, on the Seine, to welcome the Queen of England. Touched though he was by the misfortunes of the dethroned Princess, it was a different kind of emotion that came over him when he set eyes on her. Mary of Modena, the daughter of a Martinozzi, had something of the charm of the 'Mazarinettes'. She revived Louis' youthful memories so much that she caused Mme de Maintenon 'raging anxiety'. Mary received the same honours and treatment as a Queen of France. A purse of ten thousand gold louis spared her any material cares, and her rescuer, Lauzun, was rewarded with a ducal title in spite of the tears and rages of Mademoiselle.

Some days later James II rejoined his family. Louis treated him generously and installed him in the Château of Saint-Germain. The leaders of the Hungarian rebellion, Cardinal Fürstenberg, who now had no prospects in Cologne, and a host of other refugees gathered around Louis XIV, while Protestants from all over Europe flocked to the standards of William III. A true ideological struggle was brewing.

Completely unaware of the danger, isolated in a magic circle, the court was absorbed by quite a different matter. After suffering various qualms, Racine had taken up his pen once more to write a pious tragedy in honour of Mme de Maintenon. The young ladies of Saint-Cyr were to perform *Esther*. The cast was chosen from among girls aged less than fifteen years; only to them did

225

Mme de Maintenon dare allow the Biblical costumes, Persian robes, jewelled diadems and flowing tresses.

Louis attended the performance on 26 January 1689 and was enchanted. He returned with bishops and Jesuits, then with the deposed sovereigns of England. In the mouths of the innocents the contemporary references underlying the noble thoughts acquired a peculiar piquancy, for nothing had been overlooked – the exaltation of Françoise-Esther, the shaft loosed off at Montespan-Vashti, the menace of Louvois-Aman, even the promises of revenge for the exiles.

Meanwhile, Louvois was making Louis the executioner of the Palatinate and the object of its eternal hatred. This time the action was a defensive one. The 'cruel Aman' wanted to turn the Rhineland into a wasteland so as to prevent the Imperial troops from using it as a base from which to move against France. Like Turenne before him, Louvois had nothing but contempt for the unwritten rules of war. He unquestionably exceeded the orders wrung from Louis xiv, and some of his subordinates overstepped even Louvois' intentions, even though others did not conceal their horror at this bestial strategy. Nevertheless, the King must bear much of the responsibility, and is further discredited by his particularly odious behaviour in singling out Madame for his resentment when she grieved over the atrocities committed in her name.

Louis xiv allowed nothing, least of all individual feelings, to take precedence over raison d'état. Louis xiii had worked from a similar starting-point, but the sacrifices had been imposed primarily upon himself.

Mannheim and Heidelberg were razed and the surrounding countryside devastated, while the inhabitants scattered in search of refuge. Still Louvois was not satisfied. In the spring a new wave of destruction broke. The Minister wanted to go even further, against the wishes of the King, who was informed about the scale of the damage too late, just as he had been at the time of the dragonnades. When he found out that Louvois had taken the decision to raze Trier on his own authority, the King succumbed to one of the few bouts of anger of his reign:

> He flung himself at the firetongs and ran at his minister, who ducked. At the same time Mme de Maintenon threw herself between them and tried to take the tongs from the King, who was raging at Louvois and finished by telling him to countermand the order immediately, adding that he had better take special care in choosing his courier, because if the man did not get there in time, Louvois' head would be forfeit.[4]

Trier was saved, but the indignation of Europe was not appeased. Hatred of France lasted for generations in Germany. In this manner errors led to misfortune and misfortune to further errors.

That was for the future to reveal. In the present, the Great King shone in his fiftieth year with a glory and splendour unmatched in any previous age. Louis XIV remained the wizard of enchanted palaces, the symbol of the classical ideal and the master of a nation as powerful as all the others combined. He was still fascinating, and the Venetian ambassador wrote: 'He is feared and respected throughout the world.'

Louis XIV (Gustave Lévy after Philippe de Champagne)

Nicolas Fouquet (engraving by Nanteuil)

The Château de
Marly (Martin le
Jenne)

Mme de Maintenon (engraving)

Part Four

The Looming Shadow
[1689-98]

[1]

Splendid Isolation and 'Pure Love'

THE War of the League of Augsburg, War of Orléans (so called because of the Palatinate question), or Nine Years War, had the characteristics of a great modern conflict: a power subject to the will of one man confronting a coalition riddled with differences and contradictions; a ruthless ideological struggle and unremitting hostility that brushed aside the courtesy and consideration of former times; and the decisive importance of economic factors.

When Louvois applied to his master the motto 'Alone against all', he was flattering, not reproaching the King. Far from trembling at her own isolation, France took a fierce pride in it. She had an army of three hundred thousand men, more than any Christian prince had ever assembled.

However, the plight of the country people was lamented by La Bruyère: 'Fierce animals are to be seen, black, livid and quite burnt by the sun, tied to the earth, which they grub up and turn over with invincible stubbornness. . . At night they retreat into lairs where they live on black bread, water and roots.' ('Roots' means vegetables, at worst turnips and rapes, perhaps potatoes, which were probably already grown in certain areas.) This famous excerpt has been widely misconstrued. The wretched condition of the peasants was not due to the policy or building expenditure of Louis XIV. Since the death of Henry IV it had been described time and again, and the other nations of Europe presented an even more dismal picture. In Germany, part of the population had just been reduced to a state of slavery. In Italy, the towns were thronged with beggars from outlying areas. In Spain, the desert was encroaching on the fields.

Louis XIV did not generally show compassion, and lacked it altogether with regard to the landless classes, but no other sovereign of his era offered any example of that virtue. True, Louis put the greatness of France before the happiness of the French, but the French would have been the first to be shocked at seeing him sacrifice his prestige to their own well-being. Twentieth-century judgements are different because minds have softened along with bodies. The people of the seventeenth century bore misery in the same way as Louis XIV bore his red-hot coal.

That misery had very widespread causes:

231

... a progressive reduction in trade with Spanish America, a decline in shipments of precious metals, which fell to next to nothing in about 1650; consequently a decline in the century-long rise of prices up to 1630, overall stagnation of prices between 1630 and 1640, then a fall to rock-bottom between 1675 and 1685, and difficulties for the producer, the peasant and the artisan, who were selling at less and less remunerative prices.... But also great climatic disasters and their aftermath: bad harvests, high prices, shortages, 'mortalities' as they were then called, and disruption in the economy... The combined effect of famines and epidemics was lasting impoverishment. Two or three bad harvests could make half the inhabitants of a rural parish destitute ... Entire floating populations drifted from the poorest into the least hard-hit areas. The authorities refused entry to strangers, suspended fairs and markets and refused merchandise from outside. It was economic bedlam.[1]

Several such crises had taken place under Colbert's administration well before the beginning of the wars. Twenty-five years later things were much the same. The new calamity was the financial deficit, which had become a permanency since 1672, and was annually increasing the power and corrupt practices of the farmers general and their agents. It did not prevent the nation from sustaining the extraordinary vitality that enabled it to stand alone against the whole of Europe for a third of a century.

One point has been overlooked by the critics of Louis XIV's imperialism. The pamphlets and satires that began to flay him at this date did not denounce his aggression, but accused him, on the contrary, of being a 'braggart', a 'poltroon', of 'making war without fighting' and being 'the son of Mazarin'. They make it abundantly clear that a policy of appeasement would not have won the support of his subjects. While a well-worn tradition made them scoff at their king, the French wanted him to be glorious, considered him invincible and would not have allowed him to compromise. It was in Louis' immediate entourage, of all places, in the secrecy of private rooms at Versailles that a radically new doctrine was coming to life.

Mme de Maintenon had hated Louvois ever since his attempt to prevent her marriage, and consequently frequented the Colbert clan a great deal. She dined regularly with two of the dead man's daughters, the Duchesse de Beauvillier and the Duchesse de Chevreuse, and with their husbands, who held exceptional positions at court. They both led lives of unfeigned piety, and Louis XIV used to call Beauvillier 'one of the wisest men in my kingdom'.

Against all his principles and prejudices, Louis had summoned this nobleman to attend his Council, had made him President of the Financial Council and entrusted him with the upbringing of his grandson, the Duc de Bourgogne. He was the only figure of any importance who owed his prestige solely to his good character. The Duc de Chevreuse was inseparable from his brother-in-law and shared his favoured position, while their wives aided them with their wit, grace and modesty.

Theirs was one of the few families to which Saint-Simon paid an uncon-ditional tribute, but they did not content themselves with observing the formal, dry-as-dust official piety. The family had acquired an unusual con-fessor, a kind of mystic who had been introduced by the fathers of Saint-Sulpice. The Abbé de Salignac de La Mothe-Fénelon combined a silken suavity of manner with pre-romantic fervour and an originality of thought that was daring enough to startle but not so bold as to scandalize. Mme de Maintenon fell under his spell.

The secret wife was already paying for her good fortune. She had avoided being an acknowledged mistress only to become a slave instead. Subjected to the inexorable rhythm of a man who was a total stranger to fancy and who had probably forgotten the meaning of contradiction or resistance, she was stifling in her invisible prison, as were many other sensitive people. Perhaps the young ladies of Saint-Cyr had played their parts with too much con-viction: the performances of *Esther* had shocked the Church and precipitated stern reforms in the school regulations.

Fénelon mitigated this oppressive atmosphere. He himself had been struck by a spiritual 'love at first sight' in 1688, when he encountered a strange woman, part mystic, part mad, certainly an hysteric, who had believed herself to be with child by Jesus Christ. Mme Guyon had just come out of prison. She had been over-influenced by Father Lacombe, a disciple of the heresiarch Molinos who was arrested in Rome in 1685. 'The Molinist doctrine was one of categorical quietism. His spirituality revolved on two great themes: absolute passiveness and contemplation in complete repose of spirit. The soul must aim at a mystical death, annihilate itself in God.'[2]

Mme Guyon went further still, and declared that 'to commit the sin that one most abominates is to offer God the greatest of sacrifices.' So much audacity had led to the arrest of herself and Father Lacombe, who was shuttled from one prison to another for the next thirty years, and died insane. His associate was more fortunate and obtained her release. She wrote a number of brief treatises that became fashionable talking-points. '*Le roucoule-ment en Dieu*' (literally 'cooing in God'), 'pure love' and 'ineffable innocence, indifferent to actions', had great success among people in quest of spiritual progress and what we would call escapism.

An extraordinary relationship sprang up between Fénelon and the proph-etess of quietism. The Abbé introduced Mme Guyon to the Beauvilliers and the Chevreuses, and sent her works to Mme de Maintenon, who was cap-tivated by them. Fénelon's 'little flock' was uplifted by the comforting doctrine of quietism, and he also conquered Saint-Cyr.

In this manner, Fénelon acquired considerable influence over the King's wife and the Colbert clan. Now the gentle cleric was consumed with ambition. He dreamed of Richelieu and Mazarin, but only in order to eradicate their footmarks. Fénelon detested the policies of prestige, conquest and despotism. In an era that now appears as the apogee of the French monarchy, he wrote: 'We live under a universally despised régime.' In place of royal centralization, he would have preferred a kind of theocratic feudal republic, where power would be parcelled out in minute amounts to the seigneurs who had been vainly pursuing it since the fifteenth century by means of conspiracies, civil wars and foreign alliances.

Mme de Maintenon was not yet playing a political role, but she was already winning remarkable successes with individual appointments. The King's absolute trust in Beauvillier made him willing to accept the Duke's suggestion that Fénelon be appointed preceptor to the Duc de Bourgogne (in 1689), and it was in this fashion that he lowered his guard sufficiently to let in the man whose philosophy was destined to destroy the monarchy.

In spite of his superb intelligence system, it took Louis a long time to find out that on the eve of his confrontation with Europe he had put his grandson at the mercy of a man who was deeply hostile to himself, his system and his life's work. Fénelon's reactionary pacifism was no less formidable for being unrelated to practical possibility.

[2]

Sterile Victories

WAR broke out on all fronts in spring, and contrary to all expectation the French found themselves doing better at sea than on land. The Brandenburgers and the Dutch routed M. de Sourdis at Neuss and areas of the Rhineland rose against the occupying power. In the meantime the fleet, spurred on by Seignelay's appetite for *gloire,* sailed from Brest, landed James II in Ireland and captured seven Dutch merchantmen on the way back.

The Irish were indifferent to the dynastic struggle in England, and not interested in international affairs, but they were eager to shake off the yoke of London. James was able to rally support and formed a Catholic government with the Jesuit Innes as secretary of state. William III had made the mistake of dispersing his forces. His best troops, under the command of Churchill, now Lord Marlborough, had been sent to reinforce the polyglot army of Prince von Waldeck in the Low Countries.

Summer came, and suddenly France discovered to her amazement that things were going badly. Waldeck defeated Marshal Humières at Valcourt and Marshal Duras abandoned Mainz. There was such a dearth of recruits that Louvois was reduced to pressing young peasants into the army, greatly to the annoyance of Louis, who was not tyrant enough to regard military service as obligatory.

Since the coffers were empty, Louis was forced to send his gold and silver plate to the Mint to be melted down. The Comptroller General of Finance, Le Pelletier, was replaced by Pontchartrain, who increased the number of venal offices, even to that of supervisor of wigs. 'Every time your Majesty creates a post there is always some fool who will buy it,' the new Minister told the King. The bourgeois who spent his money in this way was no fool: he was buying the means of rising in the world. A *parvenu* and a ludicrous figure he might be, but thanks to his office he could play the gentleman, with town house, château, objets d'art, lackeys and fine clothes. And his daughter's dowry would buy his descendants into the nobility.

This social miscegenation was certainly no part of the King's intentions. Necessity drove him to do something equally distasteful when his friend Duras and Humières, the husband of one of Louvois' mistresses, proved incompetent. Not only was Louis obliged to recall the hunchback genius, former Frondeur and ravager of Holland, Marshal Luxembourg, who had been clapped into the Bastille so casually, but he was also forced to allow him to go over Louvois' head and communicate directly with himself.

Luxembourg's brilliant victory over Waldeck at Fleurus (on 1 July 1690) quickly justified his appointment as Commander of the Army of the Low Countries. Nine days later seventy-two French warships commanded by Tourville, Châteaurenaud and d'Estrées shattered the combined Dutch and English fleets at the battle of Beachy Head, thus unexpectedly gaining the naval supremacy which Louis XIV had been seeking for twenty years. These victories on land and sea might have spelled the end of the coalition, but the King's extraordinary good fortune lasted only twenty-four hours. The day after the battle of Beachy Head the army of William of Orange encountered his father-in-law's forces at the Battle of the Boyne (on 11 July).

James and his Irishmen were in an excellent position, and in spite of his courage William was a poor strategist, but the whole picture was transformed by the desperate fury of the French Protestants, who crossed the barely fordable river at three points and spread havoc among the Catholics. The Huguenot leader, Schomberg, was killed, together with his son, and William was lightly wounded in the shoulder. James had been a great leader on other occasions, and he might have retrieved the situation if he had not been overcome by the feeling of dazed resignation that dogs unlucky men. He was the first to turn tail, and his troops followed his example. It was the only battle ever won by William of Orange, and the most vital to his cause.

He owed his victory to French refugees. Michelet has sung the praises of the Huguenots who fought in the vanguard on every front, but however just their reasons may have been for hating Louis XIV, it is hard to sympathize with their extremism. The émigrés of later years have been roundly criticized for fighting to restore the King to whom they had sworn oaths of loyalty. The Protestants could not have deluded themselves that they stood any chance of overthrowing Louis XIV or obtaining another Edict of Nantes. They were continuing a very ancient tradition when they gave religion precedence over patriotism, but these victims might have remained completely blame-free rather than serving their country's enemies so effectively.*

The day after the Battle of the Boyne, a false report reached Paris of the death of William of Orange. Bonfires were lit, bells pealed and the hated enemy and sacrilegious usurper was burned in effigy. The true facts were known soon enough, but all the same, France was still mistress of the seas. Seignelay wanted Tourville to pursue the English fleet into the Thames, and he had the temerity to bring up galleys from Marseilles – the first time the

---

* With Schomberg dead, William showed them no great consideration. It never crossed his mind to negotiate on their behalf.

cliffs of Dover had seen these craft. During July and August the English awaited invasion, as they did in 1940.

If the outcome of the Battle of the Boyne had been different, or if it had taken place one or two weeks after Beachy Head, the fate of the island would have hung in the balance. As it was, the flight of James, who returned ignominiously to France, provided Louvois with excellent arguments against invasion (in addition to his unspoken opposition to anything that might bring more credit to the navy). For his own part, Tourville hung back, and eventually burned thirty merchantmen in Teignmouth Bay, destroyed the little town and returned to base. Seignelay bellowed with rage, but the King was wearying of his outbursts and did not really believe that he could master the seas. Once again he took Louvois' advice and ordered the fleet to be laid up until spring. William and England were saved. Seignelay died of grief on 3 November.

In Italy, Marshal Catinat had crushed the Duke of Savoy at Staffarda (on 18 August) and captured the county of Nice. Neither Louis xiv nor any of his predecessors had ever won so many victories in a single year. But it seemed as if some evil power was bent on making them ineffective.

[3]

Family Affairs

THE Dauphine had lost her father-in-law's affection because she had once asked a question about public affairs. Charlotte Elizabeth wrote:

She is unhappy, and although she does her best to please the King she suffers daily maltreatment at the instigation of the old woman (Mme de Maintenon). They make her eke out her life in boredom and pregnancy. Her M. le Dauphin does not care at all. He seeks diversions where he can, and debauches himself horribly.

Maria Christina caused a scandal when she sought consolation with one of her ladies-in-waiting, La Bessolla. She spent her life shut in a little room behind her apartment, with no view and no air. She also suffered from 'vapours' and, after the birth of the Duc de Berry, from continual haemorrhages. She died on 20 April 1690.

The King shed tears, set off for Marly and thought no more about it. Monseigneur also wept, and even 'cried aloud'. He was now in the same dilemma that his father had faced after the death of Maria Theresa. He had been separated from his gloomy, eccentric wife for some time, and lived almost permanently with his half-sister, the sparkling dowager Princesse de Conti, then twenty-four years old. Her maid of honour's niece, Mlle Choin, had been given a post in the household. According to Saint-Simon's malicious description, she was 'a big girl, crumpled, dark, ugly, snub-nosed, but witty and of an intriguing, cunning turn of mind,' but Charlotte Elizabeth wrote: 'Her big bosom enchanted Monseigneur.'

The Dauphin did not know where to turn. He was a widower at the age of twenty-eight, the father of three princes, and already set in ways that made life easier for a man of his amorphous, timid nature. Of course there was talk of a re-marriage even before Maria Christina's body had reached the basilica of Saint-Denis, the traditional royal burial place north of Paris. The dynastic question to which the King had found a radical solution when he became a widower was once again at issue. In a burst of lunatic bravery such as timid men can produce under pressure, Monseigneur made up his mind to build an impregnable wall round his wretched happiness. He married Mlle Choin so privately that no one at court had the slightest suspicion, then, quaking, let his step-mother into the secret.

The Marquise cannot have been happy about the prospect of a new Dauphine, and must have been delighted to hear of the Prince's misalliance. She waited for years before informing Louis, in circumstances that will be dealt with later. The method she used shows the extent of her guile and subtlety. One day the King found two letters that appeared to have got into his mail by accident – letters from Mme de Maintenon to Monseigneur in which she mentioned *his wife*. We know nothing about the King's reaction, but since he showed no evidence of anger, it is safe to assume that he felt none. He probably gave orders for absolute secrecy to be maintained, and these were carried out with remarkable success.

No immediate change was perceptible. Mlle Choin remained with the Princesse de Conti, and Monseigneur continued to spend most of his time there when he was not at the wars or wolf-hunting. According to Saint-Simon, some members of the Princesse's coterie, notably Conti and Luxembourg, noticed how self-confident Mlle Choin had become, but merely assumed that she was looking for a husband!

The man so full of his own quasi-divinity and so violently hostile to any departure from order and decorum thus became head of the most eccentric family in his kingdom. He could be seen at Marly walking beside his bastards' former governess in her sedan-chair and treating her with a respect and consideration that he had never given to the dead Queen. He never spoke to Françoise without raising his hat, and he spoke to her constantly.

In fact, the King's love was deeply selfish. He had indeed married his servant. He opened windows when she was feverish, dragged her around with him whatever her state of health and 'arranged his life without ever asking whether she might not be inconvenienced.' At six in the morning Françoise would slip away to Saint-Cyr, the only place where she enjoyed some semblance of freedom. She returned at eight and did not have a moment's rest until midnight. Louis sometimes referred to her as 'Sainte Françoise'. He also dubbed her *L'Enrhumée* because of her continual colds, deliberately drove her to tears and occasionally caused her extreme anxiety for his own amusement.

The revenge of 'Sainte Françoise' was gradually to impose a humdrum domestication on the Great King. They would sit by the fireside, she plying her needle in the depths of the red damask niche that protected her from draughts, he in an armchair, working with a minister. When the minister left, conversation flagged.

In the meantime, Louis' son was attempting to forget his misspent youth in the embraces of an empty-minded wife.

The eldest of the grandsons, the Duc de Bourgogne, who was slightly deformed, displayed a ferocity and precocious arrogance that seemed to hark back to Charles the Bold, the distant ancestor whose title he bore. Fénelon won him over, coaxed him and broke him, turning a rowdy and turbulent boy into a timid shadow – or so it seemed. Once having gained control over the boy's mind, Fénelon never lost it. He induced him to accept his own version of the ideal prince, good-natured, peace-loving, a despiser of pomp and ceremony, who would lead his naturally virtuous people back to the simplicity of the pastoral age. These were no flights of fancy from a poetic teacher, but deliberate preparation for a day when grandson was to reject grandfather.

The younger brother, Philippe, Duc d'Anjou, was seven years old in 1690, the age when boys were given into the care of men. He was not entitled to Fénelon's high-flown teachings, for his tutors' task was to keep him ignorant and sap his will, so that, like Monsieur, he would never be a nuisance to his elder brother. The little Duc de Berry was not yet a problem, but was destined for the same intellectual treatment.

Having no reason to be proud of any of them, Louis showed them little affection. On the other hand, he was not insensible to the charm of his natural daughters. The Princesse de Conti held a significant place in spite of her rebellious temperament. At the age of eighteen, Mme la Duchesse was a demon, endowed with the beauty, wit and perversity of her mother. The two young women were rivals in insolence, and privately scoffed at religion. Louis was sometimes annoyed when he read their intercepted letters, and Mme de Maintenon would then scold and elicit tearful promises. 'But what was forgiven was not forgotten.'

Françoise had become estranged from Mme la Duchesse, whom she had brought up. Her maternal instincts were focused exclusively on her former pupil, Mme de Montespan's son, the Duc du Maine, who made good use of them. He had been taking the side of his governess against his mother for a long time, and his letters to her betray his cunning, his anxiety and his dreams:

> Work for your dear child, if you find him worthy to be acknowledged . . . I would rather be useful than hobble about in front of people to whom the sight gives pain . . . Tell the King, Madame, how deeply moved I am by all that comes from him. Depict me as overwhelmed by his kindnesses. Use the strongest terms . . . I cannot fail as long as you guide me . . . You ask if I am ambitious? I am bursting with it, Madame, as well as with submission to the orders of the King.

Only the Duc du Maine presented the princely image that tallied with the ideals of the *dévote,* and he did so with a cunning that is frightening in so young a man. At first, Louis XIV displayed the same obduracy towards him as to La Vallière's son, the ill-fated Vermandois. Mme de Maintenon set about converting him, and succeeded so well that the King grew to love the cripple and to regard him as his own son, born of 'Sainte Françoise'.

There remained the youngest of the legitimized children, Mlle de Blois, who hid a determined mind behind her pretty face and timid expression, and the Comte de Toulouse, a well-behaved youth. Because they were so young, they were still living with Mme de Montespan, who put the finishing touches to the family charade by continuing to inhabit her handsome apartments and to appear at state ceremonials.

Athénaïs could not resign herself to retirement. Now and then she would let fly with a cutting remark at the King, but these tactics did not solve her problems. Her children were removed, and the Comte de Toulouse was marked out for the army (he was thirteen), while Mlle de Blois was entrusted to the Marquise de Montchevreuil.

On the Orléans side of the family, Monsieur was by now the 'paunchy, stilted little man' whom Saint-Simon knew, leading the frivolous and scandalous life to which he had been conditioned. The Chevalier de Lorraine, his old favourite, took no offence at his more recent rivals, since he remained the effective master at the Palais Royal and Saint-Cloud. Madame was completely estranged from her husband, whom she did not miss, and from the King, which reduced her to despair. She led a life of seclusion in the midst of the court, dividing her time between Monseigneur's hunting expeditions and her private apartment. A few close friends and innumerable pet animals distracted her when she was not engaged on her voluminous correspondence.

The King and the Marquise kept an apprehensive and unfriendly eye on Charlotte Elizabeth's son, the Duc de Chartres, who was too bold, too brilliant, too debauched and insufficiently devout. He had been very well educated and was proving himself in every respect the superior of his cousins of the senior branch, thus making himself automatically suspect.

This was the clan that Louis xiv terrorized without always succeeding in taming it. It also included Mademoiselle, the eccentric old cousin rebuffed by Lauzun, the 'impossible' husband from whom she was now separated, and already despoiled of part of her property, while covetous hands waited to grab the rest.

1691 began eventfully. The King decided that the Duc de Chartres and the Duc du Maine should serve together in the Army of Flanders. He was in fact considering marrying his son and Mlle de Blois to the daughter and son of Monsieur. It would crown the enterprise begun when he had married two of his natural daughters into the House of Condé. He intended to defy convention and break a law that was almost sacred to the society of his time in order to turn the fruits of his twofold adultery into authentic princes. Consequently they must be completely integrated into the royal family, which made it essential to get rid of the offending mother.

It was the Duc du Maine, her own son, who had the callousness to inform her that she must leave the Court and that the King needed her apartment, and the son moved into it the following day ... She asked for a last audience with the King, and, seeing that she no longer had anything to gain from self-restraint, flew into a rage and flung in his face what she had done for him, and his own ingratitude. The King put up with this fit of temper because he realized that it was the last to which she would ever subject him.[1]

Athénaïs retired to the convent of Saint Joseph, which she had founded in the Faubourg Saint-Germain in her heyday. It had taken her former servant eighteen years to put her there.

[4]

A 'Happy' Year

No sooner had William disposed of James II than he crossed the Channel again, assembled an army as large as Luxembourg's in the Low Countries, and summoned representatives of all the members of the League of Augsburg to the Hague. There was not a single absentee. He had the honour of presiding over a conference on an unprecedented scale, as leader and architect of the vast coalition of rival states and opposed religions drawn together by their common hatred of the King of France. It seemed as if this gigantic Alliance was bound to prove invincible, but while they talked the French army was on the march, a month earlier than usual. Louis XIV in person, accompanied by most of the princes, laid siege to Mons on 21 March.

He did so with Louvois' guarantee that the coalition powers would not attempt to rescue the town, for he was, as always, firmly resolved not to risk his prestige and fortunes on a set battle. Mons surrendered on 8 April, just in time, for on the very same day William of Orange was reported to be on his way at the head of fifty thousand men. It was the first time in well over a century that a King of England had commanded an army outside his own country.

Thanks to skilful manoeuvring by Luxembourg, the battle did not take place, but Louis did not forgive his minister for putting him at risk. As his ascendancy faded, Louvois behaved more and more brutishly. His arrogance and coarseness, hardly bearable in the days of easy victories, ceased to be so when they were no longer holding off the enemy. The King's patience with him was wearing very thin, and as a last gamble Louvois made secret arrangements to have William III assassinated. The operation failed and Louis was extremely angry at having been made a party to this affair.

It was perhaps with the idea of comforting him that Racine wrote *Athalie* – too much reliance might have been placed in men, but there was every justification for relying on Heaven, for God could destroy the usurping heretic as he had destroyed the usurping idolatress. The young ladies of Saint-Cyr performed the play behind closed doors and without costumes before Louis XIV and James II. It did not achieve the hoped-for success, being considered tedious.

On 16 July 1691 Louvois was reading a letter in Mme de Maintenon's apart-

243

ment when he felt suddenly sick and had to withdraw. Half an hour later he died, and his family and many others were convinced that he had been poisoned. Charlotte Elizabeth wasted no time in accusing Mme de Maintenon, and the agent was said to be the physician Séran, whom Saint-Simon also mentions. The Duke's story is suspect, however, for he claims to have been at Versailles on 16 July when on his own showing he was not presented until 28 October.

In any event, there can be no doubt about Louis' indifference. When an officer brought him the condolences of James II and his wife, he made the often-quoted reply: 'Tell them from me that I have lost a good minister but that my affairs and their own will not fare any the worse.' This remark proves nothing: in the midst of war, the King could not afford to appear anxious, or even distressed. Much more significant and more chilling is another remark, quoted by the Abbé de Choisy:

> He was taking supper with the ladies at Marly. The Comte de Marsan was sitting on the other side of Madame and talking about the great things the King had done at the siege of Mons. 'It is true,' the King said, 'that this has been a happy year for me. I have got rid of three men whom I could no longer endure – M. de Louvois, Seignelay and La Feuillade.'

Excess of zeal was not to the taste of the impassive demigod. Others before Louvois had lost favour by departing from the role in which the royal producer had cast them. No trace of humanity moderated Louis' displeasure, which might be compared to that of a conductor with a temperamental musician. Whether a man was a marshal of France or a gardener, his sole significance to the Sun King lay in the part he played in the majestic enterprise dedicated to the greatness of France and his own *gloire*. Saint-Simon put the matter in his own way: 'He was a uniquely personal man, and took account of others, whoever they might be, strictly in relation to himself.'

History has summarily ranked Louvois among the great ministers, whereas it would be more appropriate to reckon him as a remarkable war-minister and a disastrous statesman. Whenever he tipped the scale at crucial moments, it was always to the wrong side. The gravest mistakes of the reign bear his personal hallmark. Perhaps no other man ever did so much harm to the prestige and honour of France.

The court was both relieved and dismayed. Its state of mind is well illustrated by the epitaph:

> Ci-gît sous qui tout pliait
> Et qui de tout avait connaissance parfaite,
> Louvois que personne n'aimait
> Et que tout le monde regrette.*

* 'Here lies the man beneath whom everything bowed/And who was completely informed about everything,/Louvois, whom no one loved/And everyone misses.'

The Marquis de Barbezieux, Louvois' son, was only twenty-three years old. Louis did not think of depriving him of his father's principal post, even though this was the war ministry, an essential piece of the machinery of government. The King respected birthright, and it pleased him to have seen his new servant in the cradle. Above all, he had enough confidence in his own guiding star to believe that he could 'confer the talent along with the appointment'.

Barbezieux was brilliant, a slave to his own excesses, and no less coarse and brutal than his father. The King reprimanded him often, treated him with the severity of a teacher towards a gifted but wayward pupil, and eventually kept him to the end. He decided to recall Pomponne, who joined Colbert de Croissy and Pontchartrain, now in charge of the navy as well as finance, in an administration that is singularly unimpressive compared with the exceptional team of Louis' earlier years.

The King had no illusions about them: they were competent executives, but not capable of independent initiative, or of running the kingdom. After the extraordinary flowering of genius earlier in his reign, the species was growing rare. The army had hardly any, and there were none at all on the higher levels of the government. In matters of policy, no one had as much experience and ability as the King himself.

Having arrived at this by no means presumptuous conclusion, Louis took his decision, just as he had when Mazarin died – even more bravely, perhaps, given the situation and the state of his health. He had been ruling since 1661, but from above; now, at the age of fifty-three, he assumed full responsibility for the state, the administration and the war. His clockwork schedule changed. Except for hunting expeditions, which were essential to his health, and the equally indispensable court ceremonial, he worked tirelessly, dealing in person with the most trivial affairs. He no longer soared above ordinary mortals: instead he had to know about everyday miseries and injustices, the painful secrets, drudgeries and cruelties of the state, and take responsibility for them.

He carried his burden with bewildering ease and serenity. No anxiety or bad news ever altered his mood. He was cocooned by an unflagging faith that never allowed him to doubt the justice of his cause, the support of his God, or his own infallibility. Unchanging, monolithic, and to all appearance unfeeling, he went his way at a pace that frightened many of his followers.

As Louis became increasingly absorbed in the work of government, he ceased to be the model of his compatriots, their source of inspiration and the centre of gravity of the intellectual world. Artists began to go their own way, salons opened in Paris, writers departed from the classical vein and philosophers re-examined dogmas that had been judged immutable.

Only Louix xi, of all the Capetian, Valois and Bourbon kings, had lived to the age of sixty. As he approached this milestone, Louis was faced with the rise of a hostile generation. France was suffering from her usual unsettling financial problems, and the suggested remedies were contradictory. There was a rising tide of criticism, which even went so far as to call for a revolution. One pamphleteer announced: 'When the princes enter France as liberators, the whole nation will flock to their banner.' Another accused Louis: 'The more you have gloried in extending and augmenting your lands, the more you have crushed your subjects. The patience of your people may turn to anger.'

That was the King's situation – still dominating a dazzled Europe, but already unpopular and criticized – on 28 October 1691, when Claude, Duc de Saint-Simon, one-time favourite of Louis xiii, then aged eighty-four, presented his sixteen-year-old son, Louis, at court. The slight, sickly boy had a pinched face, thin lips and inquisitive, malicious eyes. Louis xiv hesitated before yielding to the father's entreaties and accepting the boy in his musketeers. He could not know that he had just made his first appearance before an implacable judge whose verdicts would be continually consulted by posterity. If he had had the least premonition of the literary genius this 'myrmidon' would·become, he would not have been content with granting Saint-Simon only three private audiences in twenty-four years. He would have gone out of his way to win him over, and the memoirs would have left us quite a different picture.

The first significant event attended by the young man was the strange prelude to the marriage of the Duc de Chartres and Mlle de Blois. In return for a few promises about the Prince's military career and a number of payments to the Chevalier de Lorraine, the King had forced a scandalous misalliance on his humiliated brother and outraged sister-in-law. Saint-Simon was present when Chartres, bowing to his mother, received 'a smack so resounding that it was heard at a distance of several paces and which, in the presence of the Court, covered the poor prince in confusion and utterly astonished the many onlookers.'

In spite of the lamentable state of his finances, Louis gave his daughter a dowry of two million livres (equivalent to about £2,000,000 or $4,800,000 today). She had showed whose blood ran in her veins when, informed of her fiancé's chagrin, she said: 'I do not care about him loving me, I care about him marrying me.'

The ultimate outcome of this forced marriage was Philippe Egalité, the renegade prince who was to vote for the execution of Louis xvi, and Louis Philippe, whose July Monarchy was to replace that of the senior Bourbons in 1830.

[5]

The Mirage of the Sea

FRANCE still retained her maritime supremacy, and not only because of Tourville's genius. A new figure had made his entrance, tall, fair-haired, illiterate, but endowed with Herculean strength, a comprehensive grasp of naval matters and unbelievable audacity. Jean Bart had sailed under Ruyter and as a privateer. He ravaged the English coasts throughout the summer of 1691, and even made a raid on Newcastle.

With these exploits and his agents' optimistic reports in mind, James II begged Louis to attempt the great invasion. Louvois was dead, and Louis let himself be persuaded. History has censured him for doing so, yet the prospects seemed very favourable.

The events of the Revolution had created conditions in England to which no parallel exists in later times. Many of the magnates who had dethroned and expelled James still revered him in their hearts, in spite of all the Acts of Parliament they had passed, as their real, natural sovereign. Every one regarded the imperious and disagreeable Dutchman who had had to be brought in and set up for the sake of Protestantism and civil liberty as a necessary evil. They understood that he regarded England mainly as a powerful tool for his Continental schemes, conceived primarily in the interest of Holland. With anxious eyes they watched his unpopularity increasing with the growth of taxes and distress. . . .[1]

William's favourite, Bentinck, was universally detested. Many English noblemen had permanent contacts with Saint-Germain, and one of these was Admiral Russell, the man who had gone to offer William the crown in 1688. Marlborough had been alienated by the high-handed behaviour of William, who barred him from the Council and the court in January 1692.

This political chameleon was suspected of harbouring plans to overthrow William and Mary and put Princess Anne in their place. In that same month of January the Queen asked her sister to break with Lady Marlborough, her temperamental favourite, and Anne refused point-blank. She was a gentle, timid woman, destined to bear sixteen children by her alcoholic husband, but it was Sarah whom she obeyed. Sarah had a lively, trenchant wit, blazing eyes, beautiful hair and a quick-silver tongue. She was a she-devil, subject to wild rages, and a tyrant tremblingly adored by the Princess she despised.

The two friends lived in the same house, but exchanged a voluminous correspondence in which Anne humbled herself to the lowest possible degree. She wrote under the pen-name of 'Mrs Morley', while Sarah adopted the name 'Mrs Freeman', thus declaring her own strength, the policy of the Whig party and the role she played in her relations with the weak-willed Stuart. Not surprisingly, the Queen made no headway. She lost her temper, and 'the two sisters parted in the anger of what proved to be a mortal estrangement'.[2] The defection of the Churchills had been fatal to the cause of James II, and their new volte-face might be crucial. Such was the opinion at both Versailles and Saint-Germain.

A French army assembled between Cherbourg and La Hougue. It was put under the command of Marshal Bellefonds and augmented by ten thousand Irishmen – a howling blunder, in view of the English hatred of the Irish. Three hundred vessels waited at Brest to ferry the troops to England under the protection of Tourville's forty-four warships. If the landing had been attempted in March, when the Dutch and English squadrons were dispersed, it would probably have succeeded. Unfortunately Seignelay and Louvois were no longer available to terrorize the civil servants. Tourville waited six weeks for poor-quality munitions and powder, and when he complained a clerk mistook himself for Seignelay and wrote that 'if he found that the powder did not carry far enough, he had only to sail closer to the enemy.'

In the meantime the English and Dutch fleets joined forces, a hundred ships in all, but the only naval force the Coalition possessed, under the command of Russell. James swore that when the time came Russell would go over to his true King.

The English Jacobites were straining at the leash, and their hopes were high. It is unfair that some historians should have sneered at their illusions and those of the French, for James was never closer to his revenge. He was certain of it when he went to La Hougue.

The sea goes to people's head . . . James though that it was fine, noble and loyal to play the king and declare that he was not bound by the cowardly amnesties being issued in his name by the foxes and turncoats who came and went between the two sides. He told England precisely what she could expect. Aside from certain guilty parties marked down for death, large numbers of people, whole categories, were threatened . . . This declaration laid ten thousand heads on the block . . . It is easy to guess what effect this terror had.[3]

Versailles knew nothing of this. There was growing impatience with the procrastination of Tourville, who was now waiting for d'Estrées and the thirty ships of the Mediterranean fleet. The guardian angel of the house of Orange was watching, and d'Estrées was held up by unfavourable winds.

Louis XIV has been the object of so much bitter criticism over the invasion that some effort must be made to understand his motives. For twenty-five years he had been used to forestalling and surprising the enemy. It seemed to him that this tactic applied as well on sea as on land, and he would not have been wrong if the information available had been accurate and James less stupid. Unfortunately for him, he believed that Russell was a Jacobite and he did not know about the size of the allied fleet or the wind that was holding up d'Estrées. It was in these circumstances that the King sent Tourville an order in his own hand enjoining the Admiral to seek out and attack the enemy fleet, 'strong or weak, wherever it might be found'.

A few days later (on 10 May) he left Versailles with the princes and ladies, having decided to take command of the Army of Flanders. On the way, he stopped at Chantilly and announced: 'There will be a great sea battle.' On 21 May he reviewed 120,000 men at Givry, and on the 24th he made his land objective known: Namur, a reputedly impregnable fortress. The French began the siege the next day.

Pontchartrain had discovered the true state of affairs by then, but did not dare to revoke the King's order and sent a courier. Louis immediately ordered Tourville to wait for d'Estrées, but his messenger did not reach La Hougue until the 27th – too late. Tourville did not receive the countermanding order, and he gave battle on 30 May.

The engagement was glorious and grimly contested. On the first day the English lost two men-of-war, the French none. On the second Tourville exhausted his ammunition and had to signal a retreat. Now the rout began. The Admiral's flagship, the *Soleil Royal*, was shot to pieces and had to be left a burnt-out wreck. Three other ships were sunk. On the 2 and 3 June English gunboats attacked the very coastline where James II and Bellefonds were waiting for news of victory. Owing to a shortage of powder and above all of resolution, they encountered no more than a light cannonade. The French armada perished under the eyes of the man it was to have restored.

In Flanders, Luxembourg was holding William III's eighty thousand men at bay while the siege of the 'virgin town' proceeded. The virgin succumbed on 5 June. Boileau wrote an ode and Louis himself wrote an account of the event.

Thereupon the messengers arrived from La Hougue. The King remained unmoved, except to ask after Tourville, since 'as for ships, we can find more, but an officer like him is not so easily to be found.' The Great King did not make others pay for his mistakes. The following year Tourville became a Marshal of France. The courtiers casually remarked: 'We have lost fifteen ships,' and talked only of the capture of Namur, whose last strongpoint fell on 30 June. The King once again went back to Versailles like a conquering Caesar. Mme de Maintenon, worn out, took to her bed immediately.

La Hougue has often been called 'the Trafalgar of the seventeenth century' – a misnomer, since France's naval strength was not destroyed. By 1693

Tourville had as many ships under his command as before, and won the battle of Cape Saint Vincent off the coast of Portugal. Things went better still after the King accepted a plan put forward by Jean Bart and another sailor, the Chevalier de Forbin, who organized a patrol of fast frigates to cut England's trade lines.

They were astonishingly successful, and London rang with the complaints of desperate merchants on the verge of bankruptcy. Bart and Forbin sailed back and forth from Dunkirk whenever they pleased. 'Never were there men who took such delight in the terrible game of boarding a ship and the threefold peril of a fight to the death, with no retreat, between sea and fire . . . One young man, Duguay-Trouin, who was mad about women and gambling, got quite different pleasures out of boarding.'[4] There were other famous privateers, notably Cassart, from Nantes, but no one ever matched the exploits of Jean Bart, who took or burned seven hundred Dutch and English ships.

The battle of La Hougue should therefore have been a side-issue, if not for the Stuarts, then at least for France. In fact, it was the only decisive action of the war, in that England, deeply divided for over a century, now regained her unity and her will to 'rule the waves'. That country had decided upon her natural element, while France was to go on dreaming of establishing a hold on sea as well as on land for many years.

[6]

Luxembourg's Hump

Not being an Englishman, William III went on pursuing the continental victory that kept eluding him. Thanks to the discovery of a French spy in his camp, he managed to lure Luxembourg into a trap and surprised him at Steenkerke on 3 August 1692. It was an epic battle, in which both sides suffered heavy losses, and fifteen thousand men were left on the field. Victory went narrowly to Luxembourg. Since the beginning of Louis' reign, no victory had ever been greeted with so much enthusiasm. The young princes passed through delirious crowds on their way back, and fashionable young men took to wearing 'Steenkerke cravats', carelessly tied, like Conti's when he had hurried into battle half-dressed.

The strategic benefit was insignificant, and the following year everything had to be resumed from scratch. In the spring Louis was crippled by rheumatism and suffering from pains in the throat, but he set off as usual with his usual entourage. Mme de Maintenon hated campaigns, and was accused of wanting to keep the King at Versailles, but she was quite justified if this was so: the place of the man on whom the fate of a nation depended was not in a tent in the Low Countries, as La Hougue had shown, but the French could not do without the symbolism of a paladin-King.

Early in June 1693 they believed that they were on the verge of gaining a decisive victory when Louis XIV, with two massive armies, confronted the very inferior forces of William, whose position at Louvain was vulnerable. 'Only a miracle can save me,' the King of England told the Prince de Vaudemont.

The miracle happened. In spite of the entreaties of the general staff and Luxembourg, Louis announced that Monseigneur would join Marshal Lorges in Germany with one of the armies, while he himself returned to Versailles. Jacques Roujon has explained this strange decision by drawing attention to a little-known letter from the King to Monsieur. News from Germany had convinced Louis that a big push in that area would force the Emperor to sue for peace. Contrary to his reputation, he was seeking peace at that time, rather than the hazardous glories of pitched battles. 'I gave in,' he wrote to his brother, 'to the pressing remonstrances that were presented and to the workings of my own reason, and was happy to sacrifice my personal prefer-

251

ence and satisfaction and everything that could most have set me off to advantage, to the good of the state.'

He might have reached a different decision had he foreseen the consequences of his action. Saint-Simon wrote:

> The effect of this retreat, among the officers and even the people, was unbelievable.
> ... All the enemy's insults were hardly more scandalous than what was being said in the armies, the towns and even in the court itself, by courtiers usually so delighted to find themselves back at Versailles, but who made it a point of honour to act as if they were ashamed.

Luxembourg's Frondeur spirit was showing through again, and Conti had never lost it: no modern head of state would survive the kind of campaign they now mounted against Louis – the Commander-in-Chief avoiding danger and refusing victory in order to be back with his ageing mistress (the marriage was never mentioned): coward and clownish lover both. The King's self-control never faltered, but it is easy to imagine how he must have suffered from such a direct hit on his most sensitive spot, all the more so when his sacrifice came to nothing. Instead of gaining the expected victory in Germany, Monseigneur's army merely caused further havoc before being forced on to the defensive.

Excess of caution had brought Louis as little in 1693 as excess of boldness the previous year. Nevertheless, the fiery younger element at court was soon to have the blood-bath it was demanding. The most murderous battle of the century took place at Neerwinden on 29 July. So many were killed that the resulting infection put the victors to flight.

Luxembourg's dispatch to the King was brief and striking:

> Your enemies have done wonders, your troops even more. The princes of your blood have surpassed themselves. As for myself, Sire, I have no other merit than that of having carried out your orders. You instructed me to assault a town and offer battle: I have taken the former and won the latter.

The people sang:

> Toute la France repose
> Sur la bosse de Luxembourg.*

As the King went to mass at Marly on 4 August, he was presented with the fifty-five standards and twenty-five flags captured from the enemy. They were put on show in a state room, where foreign ambassadors could see them, before being sent to Notre-Dame.

On 18 August Catinat won an equally brilliant victory against the Duke of Savoy at Marsaglia. But the French, 'victorious on every side and weakened by their successes, were fighting in the Allies a perpetually reborn Hydra ... The

---

* all of France rests / on Luxembourg's hump.

severity of the season destroyed the fruits of the earth at that time, bearing famine in its wake. People were dying of starvation to the strains of the Te Deum.'[1]

Louis XIV had bouts of fever and gout, as well as 'vapours'. He suffered in both mind and body, and was further disturbed by the Frondeur undertones of the popularity enjoyed by Luxembourg, the 'decorator of Notre-Dame', and Conti. When the Prince and the Marshal came to pay their respects at Marly in November, they received a chilly reception. Shocked historians have conveniently forgotten how the two heroes had tried to dishonour the King.

Louis, for his part, never forgot anything, except the occasional promise, as the Duc de Chartres learned to his cost. In spite of his valour, he did not receive a command, whereas the Duc du Maine became Grand Master of the Artillery, the Comte de Toulouse an Admiral, and the Duc de Vendôme General of the galleys. The King was elevating bastards and the descendants of bastards to the detriment of the Princes in whom he saw an old peril recurring.

A cabal had in fact been formed. Luxembourg had visions of becoming Constable and First Minister of France. Like his young warrior friends, he led a life of debauchery and impiety that offended the *dévot* spirit of the court. The little faction hardly even bothered to conceal that it was looking ahead to the King's death.

Luxembourg had introduced one of his relatives, Clermont-Chatte, a handsome ensign in the gendarmes of the guard, into the household of the Princesse de Conti. When he pretended to be in love with her the Princess responded, and Clermont-Chatte became involved with Luxembourg and the Prince de Conti in their plan to gain ascendancy over Monseigneur. The young ensign was to ingratiate himself with La Choin, become her lover and pretend that he wanted to marry her: he played his part, and made some headway, but the young woman did not disclose what none of them suspected – her marriage. In order to get the better of her rival, she even pretended to fall in with Clermont's matrimonial plans, which enabled her to demand the correspondence exchanged between him and the Princess.

When the campaign of 1694 got under way, the lovers wrote numerous letters to one another, without taking any precautions to keep them secret – an almost unbelievable blunder. The King naturally received their letters, together with those of his daughter, enclosed by Clermont. He saw through their plan to gain control of Monseigneur whom they referred to as 'our fat friend'. Naturally, Mme de Maintenon was also informed.

Monseigneur was in Germany. The good lady decided that the King ought to know Mlle Choin's true status before making any further move, and warned him by the method already described. As for Monseigneur, he was still completely in the dark when he wrote to the Marquise on 19 July 1694: 'I was surprised that you should speak to me of my wife, and I' am quite taken aback!'

The King sent for the Princesse de Conti, and cruelly forced her to read out loud all the terrible things that had been said about herself by Clermont and La Choin. 'At that point she thought that she did not have long to live. She threw herself at the King's feet, bathed in tears ... It was nothing but sobs, forgiveness, despair, rage and pleas for justice and revenge.'[2]

Mlle Choin was banished from court and Clermont ruined and exiled. Not until then did Louis inform his son, who found himself in no position to intervene. Nevertheless, the King's secret daughter-in-law could hardly be turned out like a common subject. The Princess 'sent Mlle Choin to the Abbey of Port-Royal in one of her own carriages and *gave her a pension** and vehicles for moving her furniture.' Saint-Simon does not seem at all surprised that these unusual favours should be granted to an unimportant creature who had been compromised in a scandal and had come close to the crime of *lèse-majesté*.

This episode surely clinches the theory that Monseigneur's marriage took place in 1690 and not at the much later date usually suggested. He would never have been able to marry the girl with the 'big bosom' after the furore of 1694, and she would have received altogether different treatment at that time if she had not been practically invulnerable.

After 1694 the war took a turn not unlike the events of 1914-18 between the two battles of the Marne. The antagonists exhausted their energies in vain attempts to fight a decisive battle, breeding death and devastation and bringing Europe to the brink of ruin.

Yielding to the remonstrances of Mme de Maintenon, Louis decided no longer to attend campaigns in person. In any case he was unwell, bound by gout to his invalid-carriage, and greatly changed. Charlotte Elizabeth, who still had some affection for him in spite of everything, wrote: 'The King is letting himself go, declining, looking fat and old. It is as if his Majesty had shrunk; the face is changed; it is hardly recognizable; it becomes daily more lined.'

The sufferings that came in the wake of famine prevented any decisive moves in the Low Countries and Italy. Noailles won a battle in Spain, but shortage of supplies prevented him from exploiting his advantage. Once again, the sea became the main theatre of operations. Dieppe, Le Havre, Dunkirk and Calais were bombarded as Genoa and Algiers had been. The English attempted a landing at Brest, but the French were expecting them and they had to make a hasty withdrawal, leaving the Bay of Camaret crammed with dead men.

* Which the Dauphin supplemented, as he would never had dared to do if he had only been her lover.

The conflict was spreading to the most distant regions. There was fighting in San Domingo, Newfoundland and Jamaica. Voltaire comments:

It is one of the results of the ingenuity and fury of men that the ravages of our wars are not confined to Europe. We drain ourselves of manpower and money so as to go to the far reaches of Africa and America for our own destruction. The Indians whom we have compelled to accept our settlements, and the Americans whose continent we have devastated and stained with blood look upon us as enemies of mankind, flocking from the end of the earth to slit their throats and then to destroy ourselves.

[7]

Fénelon's First Downfall

IN the space of a single week, both William III and Louis XIV suffered grave bereavements. Queen Mary died on 28 December 1694, and Luxembourg on 4 January 1695, These were cruel blows. William III recovered from his own, and succeeded in remaining King of England, at the cost of maintaining better relations with Princess Anne, who was now his heir. Louis, on the other hand, was never able to fill the gap left by the brilliant, dangerous little hunchback. The absurd Clermont-Choin affair now had dramatic consequences. A replacement had to be found for one of the greatest strategists of the century. Still under the influence of the pitiful conspiracies hatched in the entourage of the old Frondeur, the King wanted a general whose loyalty was above suspicion.

Childhood memories grow precious with age. Marshal Villeroy, the son of Louis' tutor, was upright, faithful and affable. 'He was a man made for presiding over a ball, judging a tournament, or, if he had had a voice, singing the part of a king or a hero at the Opera, well suited also for setting fashions, and beyond that, for nothing.' For once, Saint-Simon seems not to have tampered with the portrait.

Louis gave this trusted friend the command of Luxembourg's army, and friendship cost him Namur and the Low Countries in a single campaign. The bombardment of Brussels in reprisal for that of the French coastal towns brought down fresh curses on the King's head. His shame was completed by the conduct of the Duc du Maine, who at the moment when victory was near had hesitated, stammered, and asked for his confessor.

The King saw his plans in tatters. He had always mistrusted his family's ambitions, and had believed that he was strengthening the throne by elevating the adopted son of Mme de Maintenon. Failing Monsieur's daughter, he had given him a Bourbon-Condé in marriage. His intention had been to ease the Duc du Maine into the supreme command without causing too hostile a reaction from a public enthralled by the exploits of Chartres and Conti. Now it turned out that the appointed champion of the Crown was a coward, the laughing-stock of soldiers and pamphleteers.

Mme de Maintenon was equally distraught. The misfortune came just as a storm was threatening her spiritual oasis.

256

In spite of Bossuet, it is accepted that the relationship between Fénelon and Mme Guyon remained chaste, so it is all the more confusing to encounter the names they assumed in their correspondence: 'Bibi' for the preceptor of the grandchildren of France, 'Mother Breast' for the prophetess of quietism. In five years the odd couple had come a long way. Mme Guyon and her doctrine reigned supreme at Saint-Cyr, while Fénelon, the master of the future King's intellectual development, controlled his 'little flock' and thus infiltrated into politics. He insinuated himself between the King and Mme de Maintenon, lavishing advice on the latter: 'Behave towards him with simplicity, liberty, joy and willingness, without precaution or reflection, like a child. In the long run, he cannot but come to love and enjoy that freedom of God's children that scandalizes him at present.' When these methods failed to bring the King under the influence of the suave Abbé, it was he who became scandalized.

He wrote and handed to Mme de Maintenon a letter to the King, or rather a relentless, scorching indictment. The wildest republican of later days could not have done better. This ferocious document has generally been attributed to the year 1691, but 1694 seems more likely in the light of recent research.

You have been raised to the heavens . . . for having impoverished all France in order to introduce monstrous, incurable luxury into the court . . . They [the ministers] have accustomed you to receiving continual and exaggerated praises which amount to idolatry and which your own honour ought to have made you spurn with indignation. Your name has become odious and the entire French nation unendurable to our neighbours. . . . Meanwhile your people are dying of hunger . . . All France is nothing more than a great desolate hospital without supplies . . . The very people who loved you so much are beginning to lose their friendship, trust, even their respect. Little by little, sedition is kindling on every side. You do not love God, your religion consists of nothing but superstitition and superficial observances . . . You relate everything to yourself, as if you were the God of the earth.

Not even Mme de Maintenon and Beauvillier, Fénelon's protectors, were spared:

Your Council has neither strength nor vigour for good. Mme de M. and M. le d. B. ought at least to make use of your trust in them to disabuse you, but their weakness and timidity dishonour them and scandalize all the world. France is in desperate straits: what are they waiting for before speaking out? For all to be lost?

Mme de Maintenon read all this, apparently without ill-feeling for its rash author, but it is inconceivable that a woman of such prudence, hypocrisy and subtlety would have taken the colossal risk of showing a document of that nature to Louis XIV, or that her confessors would have let her do it. The letter remained within the circle of devout duchesses, where it must have been regarded as a kind of literary exercise. The legitimized princesses also amused

257

themselves occasionally by drawing up indictments of their father, but frivolous ones, with epigrams and songs.

It is not impossible that the Bishop of Chartres, Godet des Marais, one of Mme de Maintenon's principal spiritual advisers knew about the diatribe written by the Abbé he feared and whose influence he envied. This may explain why he decided to 'purge' Saint-Cyr.

A secret, unavowed but merciless struggle had been raging for years between Fénelon and the man whom he considered a pedantic yokel, 'by reason of his long, unwashed, emaciated, Sulpician face, his air of raw simplicity and vacuous expression . . . in a word, he took him for a man without poise or talent, of small wit and little learning.'[1]

It was a tremendous error. Godet des Marais was no publicity-seeker, and has not left the striking impression of a Bossuet or a Fénelon, but his influence on events was at least as great as theirs. Deviously at first, and then openly, M. de Chartres observed the propagation and harmful effects of 'pure love' at Saint-Cyr. Finally he bluntly informed the bewildered Mme de Maintenon that her pupils were on the brink of heresy. He thundered from the pulpit, and Mme Guyon's little works were shown to the King, who knitted his brow before her mystical visions. His Majesty had no truck with visions, and was totally ignorant of mysticism.

Together with two other prelates, Bossuet summoned Mme Guyon to a hearing and investigated her doctrines. The interview lasted for eight hours. Fénelon was not called, although he had provided his friend with theological ammunition. Bossuet was closely involved in the fight against free-thinking at the time. Now he discovered a still more imminent danger. Armed with her angelic purity, Mme Guyon was tending towards the dissolution of Christianity.

Quietism was condemned. Mme Guyon displayed utter docility and submissiveness, accepted the verdict and retired to a convent at Meaux, in Bossuet's diocese. As for Fénelon, while he did not abandon his friend in his heart, he signed her condemnation and emerged from the adventure apparently unscathed.

At this juncture, the Archbishops of Cambrai and Paris died. Harlay de Champvallon had spent his last years in semi-disgrace, in spite of his accommodating ways, supposedly because of his opposition to the 'declaration' of the secret marriage. The courtiers believed that Mme de Maintenon longed to wear as of right the ermine mantle in which the King had authorized Mignard to clothe her when he painted her as 'Sainte-Françoise'. In fact, she had gradually whittled away the power of Harlay because she wished, like the Archbishop himself, to play the part of a minister of ecclesiastical affairs, an office which she did in effect exercise, together with Father La Chaise, custodian of the roster of benefices. This time, under the influence of Godet des Marais, she made up her mind to disengage herself from the Jesuits and from the excessive demands of Fénelon.

The little flock expected to see its shepherd become Archbishop of Paris, and was thrown into despair and confusion at the news that he had been appointed instead to the Archbishopric of Cambrai. Cambrai was not only a considerable diocese but also a ducal principality and an enormous benefice of 200,000 livres a year. It amounted nevertheless to an unusually comfortable exile and a diminution in prestige. The See of Paris fell, against his will, to Noailles, the austere bishop of Châlons and steadfast opponent of the Jesuits.

The new Archbishop of Cambrai received his consecration at the hands of Bossuet. It was agreed that he was to reside for nine months in his diocese and for three at court. Louis asked the Duc de Bourgogne whether he was pleased at his preceptor's elevation or vexed at his removal. 'Both,' the young Prince answered.

Fénelon had certainly inspired lasting affection and admiration in the Duc de Bourgogne. As to whether he transformed the Prince, as has been claimed so often, we can consult Saint-Simon himself:

Fired by every variety of pleasure and of woman, and – a rare occurrence – with a simultaneous and equally powerful leaning in another direction, he was no less fond of wine, good cheer, reckless hunting, the near-rapture of music, and still more of gambling, at which he could not bear to be beaten and was extremely dangerous. In short, he was a prey to all the passions and transported by all the pleasures.

It is hard to believe that these passions and these transports erupted and then subsided before the Prince was thirteen years old, for he was thirteen when his mentor was appointed to Cambrai, fifteen when he stopped seeing him. The contrast between the Duc de Bourgogne and his teacher and the Sun King, declining but still awesome, is touching – virtue, charity, tenderness and impulses from the heart as against the cruelty of raison d'état – but deceptive. When the child and the prelate parted, the one retained his Neronian instincts, the other continued, in spite of his disappointment, to nurse boundless ambitions and a grudge against Louis xiv that may have been even more formidable in the long run than the hatred of William iii.

[8]

Farewell to Glory

THE following winter saw the failure of the last attempt to end the war by means of a victory. Louis XIV made fresh preparations for a landing in England, but stipulated that there should first be a rising in favour of James II. The Jacobites plotted to assassinate William III, and came close to success. Beacons were to be lit at Dover to inform the French fleet mustered at Calais that the usurper had been killed, but two of the conspirators informed on their colleagues at the eleventh hour, the French remained in port and from then on Louis' one consideration was how to bring about peace.

The King had at last given up the interests of his personal greatness in favour of those of his realm. Four factors contributed to this secret revolution: first, his ruinous financial position; then the question of the Spanish succession, which, after being half-forgotten when Charles II of Spain seemed likely to survive and procreate, was about to flare up again. The King did not want to find himself facing a coalition when the eventuality threatened the balance of Europe once again.

Further, even if he had not been informed of the precise terms of Fénelon's indictment, he could not fail to be aware of the undercurrents created at Versailles. It might have been just another court cabal, coming after so many, but notions akin to those of the 'Swan of Cambrai' were emerging at the various levels of society where the English revolution had made an impression.

Lastly, the King was approaching his sixtieth year, an advanced age in the seventeenth century. As a result of an anthrax, he had to undergo an operation almost as painful as the one on his fistula, and the Burgundy treatment was making his gout almost a permanent affliction.

These were the factors that led Louis XIV to modify his priorities of the previous thirty-five years. The most powerful motive was probably also the most hidden – his desire to be in harmony with his people, as he had once been.

He therefore set out to disarm his enemies one by one. Already he had toned down his hostility towards the Holy See, and an entente had been established in 1693. The King evacuated the county of Avignon and ordered that the Four Articles of 1682 were not to be written into the law of the land.* In exchange, the bishops appointed since that date finally received their canonical consecration, while the right of the *régale* was extended to the entire kingdom. It was the kind of peace treaty liable to lead to another war, for it resulted in an alliance between Gallicanism and Jansenism. No one realized this at the time, however, and the King's conscience was lightened and his position made more tenable when the Pope stopped encouraging his adversaries.

Next, Louis turned to the Duke of Savoy. 'His country was to be restored to him, he received money, and a marriage was proposed between his daughter [Marie Adélaïde] and the Duc de Bourgogne. Agreement was soon reached.'[1] Victor Amadeus of Savoy was generalissimo of the Imperial armies. When the Emperor refused to allow Italy to remain neutral, the Savoyard troops changed sides and the Duke became generalissimo of the French Armies!

The liberation of the army which had been fighting in the south and was now switched to the north gave Louis a powerful bargaining position. The exhausted, demoralized Coalition was falling apart, and the King could easily have made overtures to the struggling Spanish or the nonplussed Emperor, but this time he wanted a genuine peace, not a truce, and a genuine peace depended on the only belligerent who seemed victorious because he was still intact – William of England.

The Sun King was not compelled to humble himself before William. Four powerful armies mounted guard on his still unviolated frontiers, his fleet was strong, his subjects still completely obedient. Louis XIV is to be admired for demonstrating that the Cornelian ideals of his youth and even his pride yielded to raison d'état.

Late in 1698 the King sent secret agents to Holland to disclose his intentions to William: he was ready to restore all the territories occupied since the Treaty of Nimwegen, with the exception of Strasbourg. Heaven seemed to give him credit for so doing: 'Long live the Princess of Peace!' the crowd cried as young Marie Adélaïde of Savoy, then aged eleven, passed by on her way to marry the Duc de Bourgogne.

Peace brought the ageing King the most marvellous and unexpected of gifts, in the person of the little girl who was already endowed with the grace of her grandmother, Henrietta of England.† Louis went to meet her at Montargis, and wrote to Mme de Maintenon:

> She has grace and the finest figure I have ever seen; dressed like a picture, and her hair likewise; lively and most handsome eyes with adorable dark lids; her complexion very smooth, as white and red as one could wish; the most beautiful black hair that could possibly be seen, and thick. She is thin, as befits her age; scarlet mouth, large

* Several parlements refused to obey.

† Her mother, Anne Marie of Orléans, was the daughter of Monsieur by his first marriage.

lips, long, white, very uneven teeth . . . There is something Italian about her face, but she pleases, and I have seen it in everyone's eyes . . . I find her perfectly to my liking and would be vexed if she were more beautiful . . . I am entirely satisfied . . . She has not fallen short in anything, and *conducted herself as you yourself might do.*

The supreme compliment! The King was not usually given to such enthusiasm, and Mme de Maintenon might have been antagonized if the well-schooled child had not won her over with her first remark: 'Mother has charged me to give you a thousand friendly regards on her behalf, and to ask for yours for myself. I beg you to teach me thoroughly everything that must be done to please the King.'

She called the Marquise 'aunt', which was her true status. The court had not yet recovered from its surprise when it was taken aback to hear the Princess addressing Louis as 'Papa' and speaking to Monseigneur with the familiar *tu*. Everybody was delighted except Madame, who complained bitterly: 'I feel sorry for this child. Halfway through dinner she bursts out singing, she dances on her chair, pretends to curtsey to everybody, pulls the most frightful faces, tears chickens and partridges apart on the plate with her hands and puts her fingers in the sauces.'

The King, who would not have forgiven anybody else for the least of these liberties, smiled and said: 'What grace she has! How pretty she is!' And the pedantic *dévote* smiled with him. They had discovered tenderness.

[9]

Other Men's Ideals

WEARY of Bossuet's homilies, Mme Guyon left Meaux surreptitiously, went into hiding near Paris and began to spread the good word again. Louis was furious, and had her re-arrested. This time the author of *The Short Method of Praying* was imprisoned, first at Vincennes, then in the Bastille. Already beside himself with indignation, Fénelon rushed into battle when Bossuet sent him the manuscript of his *Pastoral Instruction on the States of Prayer*. Far from endorsing this text, which contained attacks on quietism, Fénelon responded by dashing off an *Explanation of the Maxims of the Saints on the Inward Life*, and thanks to the Duc de Chevreuse he managed to have his book published before Bossuet's. The latter retaliated by begging the King to forgive him: he had been concealing a dreadful secret, 'the heresy of M. de Cambrai'. It was a declaration of war.

A quarrel between generations . . . a clash of temperaments between the arrogant, touvcy, southern grand seigneur, lively and also simple, and the son of the Burgundian bourgeois, firmly rooted in reality, little given to dreams, and perhaps solid rather than subtle . . . All things considered, it was for doctrinal reasons that these two exceptional men were about to confront one another, each of them believing himself to be the upholder of the rights of God and the spirit.[1]

It was also for political reasons, with one man championing the absolutism that the other detested.

In the field of ideas, it was a magnificent two-year tournament . . . But the facts were sordid. Palace and police intrigues, violation of correspondence, insults and public calumnies, underhand defamation – nothing was omitted.

Louis XIV abominated theological quarrels to which he had nothing to contribute, and this particular quarrel seemed to him improper. When Fénelon threw down the gauntlet by submitting the case to Rome, he decided that he had enough. He wanted to live on good terms with the Holy See now, but had no intention of letting the Pope interfere in French affairs or act as umpire between his son's former preceptor and his grandson's. Fénelon received instructions to return to his diocese for good. The King had recognized an enemy in that 'fanciful spirit'. Mme de Maintenon was heart-broken. She spent whole nights sobbing and fell ill of a fever which left Louis unperturbed. Later she admitted: 'I have never been closer to disgrace.'

The Bishop of Chartres now began to tremble for his own schemes. What would happen if the King dismissed his pious adviser and found himself exposed to temptation once more? Godet des Marais was bold enough to write to Louis, exhorting him:

> Give back your trust to that excellent companion, full of the spirit of God, of tenderness and loyalty to your person. I know the depths of her heart, and I warrant that you could not be loved more tenderly or respectfully than she loves you. She will never deceive you, *if she is not herself deceived.*

The last remark was aimed at Fénelon.

Louis allowed himself to be persuaded. One day he smiled at his thin, dishevelled companion and asked: 'Well, Madame, are we to see you die of this business?' Mme de Maintenon recovered and the aged pair were reunited at last.

But the 'business' was not settled. The battle shifted to Rome, where Fénelon was unable to present his defence, although the papal authorities and the Jesuits were favourably disposed toward him. Father La Chaise wrote to say that the King wanted to smooth things over, and the Pope appointed a commission to bury this 'unfortunate and deplorable' controversy. Louis had other ideas. He hauled his confessor over the coals and gave Rome to understand that he required the condemnation of the Archbishop. For him, the solution of a religious problem must always be political. It was not until 31 March 1699 that he obtained satisfaction. 'The doctrine of M. de Cambrai has been condemned,' the King announced to his grandson. 'What he taught me will never be condemned,' was the impetuous reply of the Duc de Bourgogne. Not in forty years had a Prince behaved so boldly.

Fénelon made a proud exhibition of his submission and humility, but he struck back at the autocrat by publishing his *Télémaque*, a treatise on morality in action which strongly influenced the young Louis XVI. This spark kindled the first flames of the fire that consumed the Ancien Régime less than a century later.

Colbert de Croissy had died on 28 July 1696, and Louis had assured his succession in a manner that can only be understood in the light of the principle of hereditary appointments and the importance of family clans:

> The King, who had grown attached to M. de Pomponne ... had envisaged the marriage of his daughter to Torcy (the son of Colbert de Croissy) in order to unite the two families and to provide a good master for this young reversioner of the ministry of foreign affairs ... He explained his plans to Pomponne and Torcy, in a manner which brooked no objection, and ruled that the marriage was to take place without delay,

that Torcy would retain his father's post, would not yet be a minister but would see to all the despatches under the inspection and supervision of Pomponne ... The marriage took place on the following 13 August at the residence of M. de Pomponne and they all lived in a great and worthy union.[2]

French diplomacy thus had a two-headed leadership while negotiations were paving the rocky way to peace at the Castle of Ryswick, in Holland. The outcome was delayed by unbelievable scruples over procedure and protocol. France took Barcelona and burned Cartagena, the main Spanish base and storehouse. With the English Parliament determined to rid itself of this ruinous war, William finally gave way. He appointed his favourite, Bentinck, the Earl of Portland, to inform Marshal Boufflers, knowing that this was the best way to approach Louis, who replied to these overtures with great alacrity. He wrote to Boufflers:

> The Prince of Orange may be assured that I cannot see him at the head of a League as powerful as the one which has been formed against myself without having that esteem for him which seems to be required by the deference of the principal powers of Europe towards his opinion; and that his perseverance, even in alliances contrary to my interest, gives me grounds for believing that those which the welfare of Europe bids me contract with him will be equally lasting.[3]

While England was extending the olive-branch, a strange phenomenon was occurring at Versailles. Despite defeat and exile, Fénelon's policy seemed to be gaining the upper hand. It was as if the man who was trampling nations in chains in the Place des Victoires had suddenly adopted the doctrine of *Télémaque*.

France restored his estates to the Duke of Lorraine, who was married to the younger daughter of Monsieur. She restored to Spain her conquests beyond the Pyrenees (Barcelona) and the places occupied in the Low Countries since the Treaty of Nimwegen; to the Emperor, Freiburg, Breisach, Kehl and Philippsburg; to William himself, his Principality of Orange. The forts built along the Rhine were razed. Fénelon had written: 'We are never in need of other men's possessions.' These enormous concessions were still pointless as long as the English dynastic question remained unsettled. Louis resigned himself to the most cruel sacrifice of all. 'It is for you,' the Swan of Cambrai had also said, 'to seek your security through good alliances, through your own moderation.'

The representative of God permitted the downfall of one of his peers to the advantage of a sovereign chosen by the nation. Divine right gave way to the right of the people. Louis XIV did not expressly abandon James II, but he agreed to give no aid 'to the enemies of England, without exception,' which included the little Prince of Wales. He wanted the Jacobites to be allowed to return to England, but William refused to carry appeasement quite so far. On the other hand, he agreed not to press for the expulsion of his unfortunate father-in-law from Saint-Germain, and even granted a pension of £50,000 to Mary of Modena. As for the French Protestants, they had served and saved the conquering hero in vain. Not a word was said on their behalf.

History has generally interpreted the Treaty of Ryswick as a mere suspension of hostilities. Although it may appear so at a distance, in that month of October 1697 Europe fully believed in the peace which it had desired so intensely, and the monarchs wanted to eliminate latent antagonisms by embarking on further negotiations.

Louis had trampled on his own pride, ambition and principles for the sake of conforming to other men's ideals. He had every right to expect acclamation and recognition from all sides – from Mme de Maintenon, who had condemned the war so roundly, as much as from Vauban, who was so moved by the misery of the people; from the 'party of the saints' (as Fénelon's disciples were already known) as much as from the younger generation that had grown weary of conquering absolutism.

In the event, and not for the first time or the last, the French were perverse enough to resent being taken at their word, and proved to be fiercely attached to the *gloire* whose price they had grumbled at paying. The signatories of the peace did not dare to show their faces at court or in Paris, and were showered with criticism and abuse. Mme de Maintenon herself said that it was 'a kind of disgrace to restore what had cost so much effort and bloodshed.'

The King had good cause for bitterness as Paris sang:

> Les trois ministres habiles
>   En un seul jour
> Ont rendu trente-deux villes
>   et Luxembourg
> A peine ont-ils sauvé Paris
>   Charivari.*

* 'The three clever ministers / In a single day / Have given up thirty-two towns / And Luxembourg / They barely saved Paris / Charivari.'

⌈10⌉

Varieties of Love

ON 7 December 1697 and during the following weeks, large-scale celebrations accompanied the marriage of the Duc de Bourgogne. The King had ordained that the fêtes were to be confined to two balls, an opera and a fireworks display, but some families made serious inroads into their fortunes and others plunged into debt so as to deck themselves in sufficient splendour.

After the wedding, the twelve-year-old Duchesse de Bourgogne went ceremonially to bed, and her fifteen-year-old husband joined her, in the presence of the Royal Family and the ladies.

The King had the ambassador of Savoy shown in and told him that he might send word that he had seen the couple in bed together. Then the King and their Britannic Majesties withdrew, but Monseigneur remained in the bed-chamber. A moment afterward the Duc de Bourgogne got up, went out and dressed, and returned to sleep in his own apartment.[1]

The following day the court circle formed round the young Princess. There was a collation and a concert. The glowing velvets, cloth of gold and silver, cardinals' robes, Cordons Bleus, the rustle of lace, the flash of the gems sparkling on men and women alike, the innumerable candles whose reflections danced in the mirrors and on the gold of the panelling constituted a spectacle worthy of Louis' ambitions.

Crowding and confusion marred the first ball, but the second 'was admirable, and all in costumes that had never been seen before.' Mme de Maintenon made only a brief half-hour appearance.

Meanwhile, continence was not agreeing with the young Duke. With the help of a chambermaid he:

... found the secret of hiding in his wife's bedchamber and getting into her bed when he thought that Mme de Lude (the lady-in-waiting) was asleep, but this lady, who slept in the same room, woke up at just the wrong moment and made the prince go back to his own bed. The following day she was off to complain to the King in the morning, and the King told the Duc de Bourgogne very drily: 'I have learned, Monsieur, that things have been occurring which might harm your health, and I beg you to see that they do not occur again'. The Prince replied in all haste: 'Sire, I am in very good health,' and the matter was not mentioned again.[2]

Another marriage was beginning to cause a stir at court, that of Mlle d'Aubigné, the niece of Mme de Maintenon. Following their lovers' quarrel on theological issues, Louis xiv proved more affectionate than ever toward his wife, and seems to have tried to erase the memory of her anxious moments. The good lady's apartment was enlarged, and Charlotte Elizabeth was stupefied to see her one day sitting like the Queen in an armchair:

> Someone was kind enough to bring me a stool but I insisted that I was not tired. I bit my tongue so as not to laugh. How far we had come from the time when the King came and asked me to let Mme Scarron eat with me just so that she could cut up the Duc du Maine's food!

Françoise had disowned Fénelon and now held aloof from the Colbert clan. She even tried to discredit the Duc de Beauvillier. She was relying on the Archbishop of Paris to help her run ecclesiastical affairs, and decided to marry her niece to the Comte d'Ayen, heir to the Duc de Noailles. But first of all she had to dispose of her brother Charles, who was making 'frightful scenes' because he had not been made a marshal of France, was too willing to talk about his sister's former flirtations, and called his Majesty 'brother-in-law'. When she went to work, the *dévote* had a heavy hand. The d'Aubigné household was brutally split, Charles being compelled to shut himself away in a house of retreat for 'gentlemen or *soi-disant*', his wife to join a religious community.

The marriage arrangements could now proceed, and they were sumptuous. The King granted Mme de Maintenon's niece the dowry of a princess. It could well have been thought that this was the finest hour of 'old slops' (another of Madame's nicknames for Françoise), but there was more to come in September. Louis had decided to hold large-scale manoeuvres with the idea of demonstrating that his military resources were still intact. Sixty thousand men mustered at Compiègne in a 'camp'. The ladies came in crowds, but the ambassadors, knowing that the King intended to overawe them, raised insoluble problems of protocol and stayed away, much to his Majesty's annoyance.

A vast display unfolded in beautifully-decorated houses and tents worthy of the Thousand and One Nights, while the troops proceeded to the Siege of Compiègne. In spite of their recriminations, the French were still riveted by splendour and by war-games. Mme de Maintenon affected to be unimpressed and over-pitched her sanctimonious tone when she wrote to the Archbishop of Paris:

> It seems to me that a charitable gathering would better befit me than going to the camp with a twelve-year-old princess, but he wants everything to be in relation to himself, and it pains me to see that appreciation of good is not forthcoming, either for that which might be done or for that which others ought to be allowed to do.

Louis XIV may not have appreciated good, but he continued to appreciate his companion and did not hesitate to show it. On 13 September, during the assault on Compiègne, Saint-Simon witnessed a sight that horrified that bitter critic, but which now appears quite touching, and highly significant:

Mme de Maintenon was facing the plain and the troops, in her sedan-chair, behind her three windows and with her bearers at a distance. The Duchesse de Bourgogne was sitting on the left-hand carrying-pole, to the front . . . By the window to the right of the chair, the King, standing slightly to the rear . . . The King had his hat off nearly all the time, and was continually bending down to the window to speak to Mme de Maintenon and explain what she was seeing and why it was being done. On each occasion she was kind enough to open her window by four or five fingers' breadth, never half-way . . . The King frequently put his hat on top of the chair so as to speak inside, and this continual exercise must have put a heavy strain on his back.

Nevertheless, the miracle of her return to favour brought no pleasure to Françoise, whose chilly, sober old age had to suffer the still passionate attentions of her vigorous husband.

It was about this time that the King announced 'that he would not suffer anybody to scandalize his fellows.' A woman called Thaumur, who had consoled a Swiss for the loss of his wife, was locked up in the Magdalen. The bishops received instructions to look out for couples living in sin, and they were hunted out like heretics.

In the meantime, the King signed the marriage-contract of his brother's last favourite, a Poitevin called La Carte, whom he created Marquis de La Ferté. His daughter, Madame la Duchesse, made no attempt to conceal her tender feelings for Mme de Caylus, Mme de Maintenon's own niece, although this attachment did not prevent her from being the mistress of her brother-in-law, Conti,* who himself had 'Italian tastes'. As for the Duc de Vendôme, a thoroughgoing libertine, he took solemn leave of the court in order to be cured of his venereal diseases. 'The King told him . . . that he hoped it would pass off successfully enough to enable him to be embraced with safety on his return.'

A bishop was banished for having lived with a woman disguised as a man, and many more such examples could be cited among the nobility. The austerity and propriety of the King's own life was the decisive factor for the other levels of society. Little as public opinion loved them, the oddly-assorted couple at Versailles were preventing a moral collapse.

Court and town were particularly lively in 1698, and social life especially brilliant because of the throngs of foreigners who were arriving in the wake of the new ambassadors. William III had sent 'his most cherished favourite', as Saint-Simon called him, to Paris: Bentinck made a dazzling entry, and

---

* Conti had married the sister of her husband, the Duc de Bourbon.

succeeded in charming the French, but narrowly avoided losing everything when William was smitten in his absence with Keppel, later the Earl of Albemarle. This led to terrible scenes between the two friends, followed by partial reconciliation.

At the same time, an apparently trivial incident occurred in the household of the heiress to the throne of England. Sarah Marlborough had made her cousin, the morose and secretive Abigail Hill, lady of the bedchamber to Princess Anne. She comforted Anne when the tyrannical Sarah had rebuffed her too severely. At that time Anne was writing as many as five letters a day to 'Mrs Freeman', who did not bother to conceal her impatience or even her contempt. A ludicrous incident about a pair of gloves, accompanied by hurtful words that the Princess overheard made the first breach in her adoration of Sarah and brought her much closer to Abigail. So began the rise of the woman of whom Churchill wrote that she saved France as surely, if not as gloriously, as Joan of Arc.

[11]

The Ark of Versailles

THE return of peace meant that there was time to take stock of the great changes that had occurred during the past twenty years. There were now two oppositions at court, the 'saints', controlled by the Oracle of Cambrai, and the near-atheist free-thinkers whose leader was still the Grand Conti. At one time the King expected to be able to dispose of his detested cousin by having him elected King of Poland, but the plan fell through and Conti continued to be the darling and the scandal of Versailles.

The Duc de Chartres rivalled him in debauchery, irreligion and disaffection. A victim of the adulation that had surrounded him since his brave exploits in the war, this young man of twenty-four saw himself condemned to the same fatal quiescence as his father, although he was more gifted than any other member of the royal family. He avenged himself by deceiving his wife, laughing at things sacred and admiring England.

The silent reproaches of Fénelon's disciples and the epigrams of the disgruntled princes mingled with admonitions on behalf of the common people. A Norman magistrate, the sieur de Boisguilbert, demanded an end to the oppressive regimentation of Colbert's system, denounced the three hundred men who were feathering their nests by ruining fifteen million others, and dared to declare that the tax burden ought to be distributed equally.

The clergy and nobility were completely decadent. The Jesuit preacher Bourdaloue wrote: 'How many self-centred priests do we see, how many ambitious priests, vain and presumptuous priests, lazy and pleasure-loving priests, worldly priests?' Ecclesiastical benefices, regarded as sources of income, made 'men live by the altar who had never served at the altar,' as Father La Roche wrote. The Bishop of Troyes was nicknamed 'the ladies' darling'. The Bishop of Clermont 'had abasements that made him almost contemptible'. Balls were held at his residence which, according to Bishop Fléchier, instead of being 'a house of prayer and penitence was a house of merry-making and feasting.' A priest of his diocese 'used to have his clerk carry a gun when he was taking the Blessed Sacrament to farms a long way from his presbytery, and if he found any game in the countryside he would

271

leave the Blessed Sacrament.' Many convents were extremely lax in applying their rules, and did not discourage the 'spirit of the age' in their houses. Of course there were distinguished prelates, famous preachers and dutiful monks, but long before Voltaire the behaviour and disunity of the clergy themselves discouraged obedience and produced the first waverings in the faith to which the people had been loyal for so many hundreds of years.

The nobility did not guard their own status any better. Bourdaloue warned them bluntly that they were 'amassing a store of anger for the fearful day of divine retribution.' Enclosed within the court and the army, the great lords did not have the smallest part to play in the functioning of the state. Strangers to economic as well as to political life, they were gradually turning into parasites. There was grumbling about their arrogance, insolence and un-scrupulousness, which had been tolerated in previous times.

The *ducs et pairs,* like the lesser noblemen, had the perpetual problem of defraying the costs of their luxurious way of living. All of them were burdened by debts that they paid as seldom as possible, and many of them did not jib at cheating at the gaming-table. One of the court wits, the Marquis de Dangeau, had turned gambling into a profession, and worked hard at it from three o'clock until six.

Most noblemen were absentee landlords, absorbed in the task of showering praises on the King and capitalizing on his favour. Those who still lived on their own lands usually had dubious reputations, and some of them behaved like common robbers. Their crying need for cash threw the noblemen into the arms of low-born nouveaux riches who had profited from the country's problems and financial confusion to build fantastic fortunes and could afford to buy their daughters' way into the aristocracy with fabulous dowries. Mme de Sévigné's daughter, the Comtesse de Grignan, graciously wrote of her son's marriage: 'It is sometimes necessary to spread manure on the land.'

In spite of her condescending tone, these times did not really belong to the privileged nobility. It was the first golden age of the middle classes, whose prestige was still further enhanced by the intellectual situation. While La Rochefoucauld, Bussy-Rabutin, Mme de La Fayette and Mme de Sévigné were of noble birth (the writings of Saint-Simon were unknown until the eighteenth century), nearly all the geniuses who made the century of Louis XIV came from the bourgeoisie. That same ambitious, dynamic class was now producing the men who believed that their country was in decline.

The classical order reached its peak during the first twenty-five years of Louis XIV's direct rule. The subjects of the Sun King on whom the élite of Europe modelled themselves admired discipline and the authority that enforced it, unquestionable dogmas – in brief, restraint. After the upheavals of the Renaissance and Reformation, they considered the great problems settled, and would have nothing to do with dangerous curiosity, adventurism or vagabondage. Pascal stated that people's misfortunes arose from not being able to stay peacefully in their rooms. 'The classical spirit . . . would have liked to be stability itself . . . Politics, religion, society and art had been placed outside the scope of unending discussion and unsatisfied criticism . . . People feared space, which contained surprises, and they would have halted time if it had been possible.'[1]

During and after the 1680s the apparently indestructible framework began to betray its fragility, and ever bolder and more virulent ideas began to appear. If there had been any one notion that was sacrosanct, it had surely been that of the greatness of antiquity and the respect due to the ancients. From the King himself, portrayed in stone in the garb of a Roman emperor, to the meanest scribbler, everybody claimed some kind of kinship with them. Now this creed was suddenly under attack, a group of men proclaimed themselves 'modern', and using this word like a magical incantation disparaged everything belonging to the past. The quarrel of the Ancients and Moderns erupted, and innovation gathered momentum and authority.

Descartes had taught the science of reason. Reason now broke its bonds, penetrated hitherto forbidden regions and destroyed taboos. Pierre Bayle, one of the new critical breed, even wrote: 'It is purely and simply an illusion to claim that a sentiment that has come to us down the centuries and from generation to generation cannot be entirely false.' Assumptions about history, nature, astrology – in fact, about nearly everything – were seen to be in need of re-examination. Holy Scripture itself did not escape the critical spirit. Nothing was simple any longer.

Bossuet thundered against these aberrations:

Their rational faculties, which they take as guides, offer only conjecture and perplexity to their minds; the absurdities into which they fall by denying religion become more than the truths whose loftiness bewilders them, and through not wanting to believe in incomprehensible mysteries, one after the other they pursue incomprehensible errors.

The twentieth-century academician Paul Hazard describes the famous prelate as 'not the peaceful builder of a magnificent cathedral . . . but rather the busy, hard-pressed workman scurrying to repair holes that grow daily more menacing.'

The concept of the individual was undergoing a transformation. The *honnête homme* who had succeeded the worldly-wise courtier of the Spanish moralist Baltasar Gracian still represented an ideal. He abhorred excess and was exquisitely polite, seeking a balance 'between the wisdom of the Ancients and the Christian virtues, the exigencies of thought and of life, the everyday and the sublime.' Now it was his turn to fall victim to the general turmoil. Slowly he had to yield to a quite different persona, facing the future instead of the past, more concerned with earthly happiness than heavenly salvation, impatient to compare, travel, discover, an admirer of science and a believer in progress.

Louis wanted no truck with this latter figure. Full of suspicion for youth, its critical spirit and its discoveries, he was determined to remain unalterably faithful to himself and to the half-human, half-stellar character that was his own creation. Yet in spite of his devoutness he wanted to have his happiness on earth. By the very fact of the inordinate image that he presented to the world, his essential allegiance was to order. The romanticism of the nineteenth century and the anguish of the twentieth would have meant nothing to him. This does not mean that Louis was the incarnation of the *honnête homme*; he might have had some claim if he had been more open and humane, but he seems to have hardened as he grew older:

> M. d'Orléans, his brother, undertook to make representations to him about the misery of the people. He received the following reply, worthier of a tiger, if they could talk, than of a Christian king: 'If four or five thousand of that *canaille* died, who are not of much use on this earth, would France be any the less France? I pray you not to meddle in what does not concern you.'[2]

This is not far removed from Napoleon – 'What the hell do a million dead men mean to me?'

The occupational hazard of autocracy is contempt for humanity. In this case, Louis' verbal brutality can be explained by his desire to crush his brother for trespassing on politics. His real feeling about the condition of the poor was more akin to that of Marshal Joffre, who used to refuse to see battlefields lest they influence his judgement, and to that of the apostles of revolution, ready to sacrifice thousands for the cause. With this difference, that in 1698 it was a matter not of achievement but of preservation.

Much as he loved to surprise, Louis had always hated to be surprised. At sixty, his horror of the unexpected and taste for regularity and punctuality verged on obsession. To remain serene at all times was a principle of government and a rule of personal hygiene, and he more or less deliberately looked away from many things so as not to be moved. The same process gave him excessive confidence in his luck and his 'star', so that it was a very grave matter when no one dared to stand up to him, let alone remind him of unpleasant truths, as Colbert had once done.

Louis had become appallingly quick to take offence, and could not stand the slightest hint of contradiction or criticism. A good dozen subjects were now taboo in conversation, and the boredom that assailed the court did not spare its master. Like an ark that kept the past above water, Versailles resisted the rising tide of demands and ideas. It was a realm of illusions, and the man who suspected everything succumbed to their influence. Without being cut off from the outside world, Louis saw it in an unreal light. He was trapped by the temple in which he was the idol and by the gardens that created a world of fantasy around him. It must have been hard to imagine suffering amid the splendour of the trees drawn up as if on parade, the statues, groves, lakes, fountains, flowers, marble nymphs and cupids, the gilded gondolas on the canal and the gods of Olympus caught in their immortal youth.

The King himself wrote a masterly guide, the 'Way to visit the Gardens of Versailles', to introduce visitors to his earthly paradise. Walking there in his lace, his brown coat set off by gold thread and his hat with the white feather, he breathed in the uncanny, perilous satisfaction of a wizard in the grip of his own enchantments.

Louis XIV (Hyacinthe Rigaud – Louvre)

Louis XIV signing the
Revocation of the Edict of
Nantes in 1685

Louis XIV in the trenches
before Mons in 1691
(engraving)

Part Five

The Fires of Evening
[1698-1715]

[1]

Pandora's Tomb

WHEN Marie Louise of Orléans became the wife of Charles II of Spain, she left behind the pleasures of the Sun King's court and found in their stead the gloom of the Escorial, tomb of so many young queens. While she undoubtedly inspired violent passion in the unfortunate Spanish king, she was his prisoner nevertheless, and the victim of the grandees in whose eyes a Frenchwoman was the devil incarnate and who had all the fearsome apparatus of etiquette available for use against her. The Queen's French servants were eventually accused of plotting the death of Charles II, and her nurse suffered torture.

Charles II blamed his wife for not giving him an heir. As a final resort, he agreed to submit to exorcisms that had more in common with magic than religion, but to no avail. Marie Louise died at the age of twenty-eight, probably poisoned at the instigation of the pro-Austrian party (March 1689). Suspicion alighted on the Comtesse de Soissons, whom she had imprudently admitted into her circle. There was no proof, but it was tempting to imagine such a revenge, well worthy of Olympe, who would thus have been inflicting a terrible defeat on Louis XIV, winning the gratitude of the Emperor and thus forwarding the advancement of her son, Prince Eugène.

Anne of Bavaria-Neuburg, who was to be the heroine of Victor Hugo's *Ruy Blas,** succeeded Marie Louise. Beautiful, scheming, devoted to the Austrian cause, but lacking a mind of her own, she put herself completely into the hands of her Protestant favourite, Gertrude Wolf von Guteberg, Baroness von Berlepsch, nicknamed 'The Partridge' – a voracious one, who 'took with both hands and sold the highest positions.' According to the French envoy Louville, she embezzled practically all the assets of the kingdoms of Naples and Spain, as well as the funds of the military treasury.

This travesty of a reign was characterized by a regression towards the worst features of the Middle Ages and by an extraordinary shortage of money. In the time of Molière and Newton the King of Spain lived among visionary

* The poet probably derived the idea of the footman-first minister from the servant-mistress who is about to make her entrance.

279

monks, exorcists, dwarfs, nurses, duennas, clowns and black-clad gentlemen, in the aroma of incense burned to supernatural powers.

In 1696 it became obvious that neither prayers nor magic were going to provide the King of Spain with an heir. Having had to endure so much from his cousin, uncle and brother-in-law, Louis XIV, Charles II seemed bound to bequeath the Spanish possessions to the Emperor's second son, the Archduke Charles. But the Queen Mother was still alive, belonged to the House of Austria and detested her family. She persuaded the invalid Charles to make a will in favour of Joseph Ferdinand, the young son of the Elector of Bavaria and a great-grandson of Philip IV. When his mother died Charles II fell under the sway of his second wife. A Bavarian, she hated the House of Bavaria as deeply as her Austrian mother-in-law had hated her own. The will was torn up and the Emperor thought that the game was his.

This was the prevailing situation until the treaty of Ryswick. Everybody except the Emperor realized that the tomb of Charles II would be a Pandora's box that would release a general war. Torcy was probably the first man to try to avert it by making arrangements to share out the twenty-three crowns of the last Spanish Habsburg.

Louis XIV, who was so hostile to the slightest domestic innovation, was evolving remarkably in matters of foreign policy. Having already tacitly accepted the 'Law of Nature', he now recognized the concept of the European balance of power. As early as 1666 he had signed a secret treaty with the Emperor about the question of the Spanish monarchy. He attempted to do the same again, but times had changed and Leopold, conqueror of the Sultan himself at the Battle of Senta (1697), sent back a scornful refusal.

Leopold was overestimating his powers. If there had been a new star shining in the skies of Europe since 1666, it was not his, but the King of England's. European statesmen who wanted to know which way the wind was blowing kept one eye on Versailles and the other on London.

Louis and William could become the arbiters of Europe if they came to an agreement. Both of them realized this, and shelved their old grudges. In the utmost secrecy, and unknown to the major interested parties, they signed a Treaty of Partition at Loo, in Holland, giving Spain and her colonies to Joseph Ferdinand, 'the man with the strongest claim and the weakest power,' Naples and Sicily to the Dauphin and Milan to Archduke Charles. The maritime powers were to gain great commercial advantages.

This arrangement showed a great deal of wisdom. France gave up the Low Countries so as not to oppose England, and received a free hand in the Mediterranean in exchange. The Treaty of Loo was signed on 24 September 1698. On 14 November the indignant Charles II named Joseph Ferdinand his residuary legatee. The unfortunate child died less than three months later (6

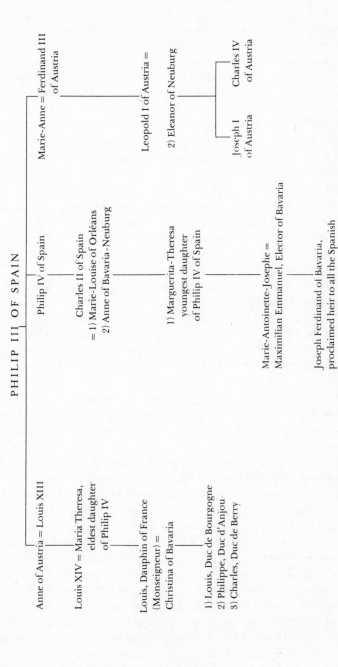

The Spanish Habsburgs: The descendants of Philip III

February 1699). No one was prepared to believe that his death was from natural causes.

At that point, the chessboard was in a state of some confusion. All the Imperial forces had been released by the signing of the Peace of Karlowitz between the Emperor and the Sultan, but this threat to France was largely nullified by the decision taken by the House of Commons, much against the will of William III, to disband the English army and declare itself resolutely 'isolationist'.

Louis XIV was consequently in a good position to resume negotiations, but he still displayed admirable moderation. By the terms of the second Treaty of Partition (11 June), Archduke Charles was to inherit Spain, the Low Countries and the colonies; the province of Guipúzcoa, Naples and Sicily would go the Dauphin; and the Duke of Lorraine would receive Milan, while his own states reverted to France. 'When this new affront became known at the court of Madrid, the King came close to dying of chagrin, and the Queen, his wife, flew into such a towering rage that she smashed the furniture in her apartment, giving special attention to the mirrors and other ornaments that were of French origin: passion makes no distinctions of rank!'[1]

Although Spain saw France as her hereditary enemy, the Spanish nation was also cursing the pro-Austrian party, since it was in power and things were going badly. Count von Harrach, the Imperial ambassador in Madrid, behaved as if he were in a conquered land, and flouted even the Queen herself. Castilian pride revolted against German arrogance. Meanwhile Louis XIV's representative, Marshal Harcourt, 'was winning every heart by his plentiful generosity, tact and great capacity for pleasing ... He accustomed the court of Spain to having friendly relations with the House of France, its ministers to being no longer alarmed by the renunciations of Maria Theresa and Anne of Austria, and Charles II himself to hovering between his own House and that of Bourbon.'[2]

Churchill and many other British historians have accused Louis XIV of double-dealing, but this was certainly not the case. The King wanted to abide by the Treaty of Partition, which was ratified on 13 March 1700 in the teeth of the Emperor's opposition: at the same time he was determined not to allow Leopold to get his hands on Spain and take France from the rear. It was for this reason that, hearing that Charles II was now proposing to leave his kingdom to the Archduke, he sent an army to the Pyrenees.

The despairing Charles went down to the vaults of the Escorial, had the tombs of his father, his mother and his first wife opened, kissed their remains and begged them for inspiration. This 'Martyr', as his subjects called him, sick in both mind and body, was more Spanish than any of his forbears. He did not know the whereabouts of his far-flung possessions, but his bemused mind retained imperial memories and a horror of dismemberment.

Realizing this, the Archbishop of Toledo, Cardinal Portocarrero, together with five grandees who were members of the Council, staged a palace revolution. When they accused the Queen's favourite, the greedy 'Partridge', before the Council, she fled to Germany, taking her treasures with her. Anne of Bavaria-Neuburg was neutralized, and Portocarrero and his allies in the Council were able to disband the German regiment in Madrid and to replace the King's pro-Austrian confessor by a priest of their own persuasion. They gave this confessor 'time to anchor himself a little', then went into the royal bedchamber and forbade the Queen to enter.

Holding Charles II at their mercy, they demonstrated to him that only Louis XIV was powerful enough to prevent the partition of the monarchy, and adjured him to leave his crowns to Philip of Anjou, second son of the Dauphin. The King consulted theologians and found that they were of the same opinion. He therefore mustered his failing strength and wrote to the Pope begging him to make the decision.

Innocent XII had just celebrated the jubilee of peace, and he himself was nearing his end. He detested the Emperor and thought that he would be rendering Italy a signal service by ousting the Habsburgs from the peninsula. On 16 July 1700 he wrote to the King that 'the laws of Spain and the welfare of Christendom required him to give preference to the House of France . . .'

While Charles II was still hesitating, the Pope died on 25 September. Fearing a change of policy in the Holy See, the French party pressed their demands. A third will was drawn up, making Philippe d'Anjou the sole heir, failing him the Archduke Charles, and failing the Archduke the Duke of Savoy. They made the King sign this document in the absence of the Queen, who was still not allowed to enter the apartment. It was 2 October 1700.

On the 23rd, hearing that Charles II was sinking fast, Louis XIV ordered Marshal Harcourt to muster an army at Bayonne and hold himself in readiness to occupy Fontarabia and other frontier strongholds. Since these places were part of Guipúzcoa, which the partition treaty assigned to France, only the Emperor could object, and his troops were a long way off.

While the fate of several million men was being played out, the court was evincing some of its former gaiety, as balls and masquerades alternated with outings to Marly and Meudon and visits to the Opéra in Paris. The King wanted to amuse the Duchesse de Burgogne, who had been authorized to live with her husband. He also treated his family generously. He paid the debts of Madame la Duchesse, and the expenses of the improvements to the Château of Meudon, the residence of Monseigneur. In return, he left the courtiers the burden of paying for the renovation of their own lodgings.

The death of Pomponne and the old Chancellor Boucherat brought changes in the Council. Torcy became a Minister, Pontchartrain succeeded

Boucherat, and the crushing responsibility of Comptroller General of Finance fell to Chamillart.

This Chamillart, originally a councillor of the Parlement, had become an intimate of the King thanks to his skill at billiards. He was an honest man, whose tact and good qualities had won over Mme de Maintenon and the party of the saints, and he had not one known enemy. Chamillart was to display 'unprecedented gentleness, patience and affability' in his task, winning himself many friends, and Louis XIV never broke with him. He seems not to have realized that he had entrusted the French economy to a worthy man who lacked the makings of a financier, let alone a statesman.

Chamillart himself mitigated the gravity of this mistake by taking on as his private adviser Samuel Bernard, the most prominent banker in Europe and a man whose international credit was greater than Louis' own. Hénault, later the President of the Paris Parlement, wrote in his memoirs:

> There never was a madman of his magnitude. He had an extravagant pride that, in a sense, ennobled him ... The most absurd adulation paled before his pretensions. I must add that he was generous, what ever the motive may have been, and that he rendered great services.

He had already proved extremely useful by securing imports of corn at the time of the recent famines and by putting secret funds at the disposal of the King's agents. It was thanks to Bernard that the terrible ordeals of the last years of the reign were made endurable.

⌈2⌉

Precarious Good Fortune

LOUIS was at Fontainebleau on 8 November 1700 when the news came of the death of the King of Spain and the contents of his will. 'After two hundred years of wars and negotiations for various frontiers of the Spanish states, France had obtained the entire monarchy by one stroke of the pen, without treaties or intrigues, and without even having had hopes of this succession.'[1]

It is a remarkable experience for a man of sixty-two suddenly to see his dearest ambitions fulfilled at a time when he has given them up. A precarious and bitter good fortune, when it comes too late and in impossible circumstances. By 1700 Louis had lost his appetite for *gloire* and conquests. His age and condition of his kingdom obliged him to desire the peace that he had just bought so dearly, and now Charles II's poisoned gift was destroying it.

The infernal machine had been constructed in 1649, by the Treaty of the Pyrenees. It should have functioned to the advantage of the Bourbons if the war of 1672, then the English revolution, had not thwarted Mazarin's plans. Louis was now in a terrible dilemma. To accept it would be to recreate the Coalition of Augsburg, minus Spain. To refuse it would make the Emperor's son King of Spain by the terms of the will – an unthinkable prospect, necessitating war with the Empire and Spain without benefit of the previous Turkish diversion.

The maritime powers had signed the Treaty of Partition, but there was no guarantee that they would side with France. In fact, the House of Commons had been so indignant about the treaty that they had just arraigned its signatory, Portland. As for William III, he had made his position clear in August: 'Having made a treaty to avoid war, I do not intend to make war to execute a treaty.'

The Council held three meetings in Mme de Maintenon's apartment. Contrary to the account by Saint-Simon, Torcy said that France should stand by the Treaty of Partition, as did Beauvillier; Pontchartrain and Barbezieux thought otherwise. To the amazement of all those present, Monseigneur flared up, and took an uncompromising stand: 'The monarchy of Spain was the possession of the Queen, his mother, therefore his own, and, for the tranquillity of Europe, that of his second son, to whom he yielded it with all his heart, but would not surrender a single inch of land to any other man.'

There was a further shock when, after listening to his son, the King consulted Mme de Maintenon. It was the first time the pious lady had found herself involved in high policy. She excused herself, was pressed to speak, then praised Monseigneur and concurred with his views.

The King made up his mind on 11 November. According to his detractors, he put his dynasty before France, but it is an unjust and oversimplified verdict. The English Parliament and the Dutch States-General were still passionately anxious for peace. Louis thought that they might possibly remain neutral in spite of William, since the two crowns were not to be united. He considered the Spanish colonies, reflected that good commercial treaties with his grandson would restore his finances, and told himself that anything was preferable to an Austrian King of Spain and the re-establishment of the Habsburg vice in which France had narrowly avoided being crushed.

Having thus appeased his reason, the old lion was bound to give way to his grand aspirations and deep conviction of fulfilling the will of Heaven. As the son and husband of Infantas, surely he was predestined to reconcile the land of Anne of Austria with that of the Bourbons?

Many historians have been indulgent toward the Dutch war because it took place during the great years of the reign, and intransigent in the matter of the Spanish succession, which, with hindsight, can be regarded as a prelude to the final tragedy. In fact, while clearly culpable in regard to the invasion of the Low Countries, Louis xiv had extremely valid reasons for accepting the will that emerged from Pandora's tomb.

16 November 1700 was perhaps Louis xiv's finest hour. On that day, as arbiter of nations, he presented a leader to a great empire and gave an unparalleled performance before his contemporaries and to history. Addressing the Spanish ambassador, the Marquis Castel dos Rios, Louis said: 'Sir, here is the King whom Spain has requested.' The ambassador fell to his knees and kissed the hand of his new master, incautiously remarking: 'Sire, how fortunate that we now have only one [king]!'

The double doors of the cabinet opened, and the court surged in. Again Louis spoke: 'Gentlemen, behold the King of Spain. His birth called him to that crown, and so too did the late King, through his will. The whole nation desired it and demanded it of myself. *It was the command of Heaven, and I have granted it with pleasure.*' Then, turning to his grandson Philip: 'Be a good Spaniard, it is now your first duty, but remember that you were born French so as to keep unity between the two nations.'

The Marquis de Sourches, author of memoirs on the French court at the end of Louis xiv's reign, noted: 'All France overflowed into Versailles, and from every side one could hear the sound of blessings upon Heaven for such a glorious event.'

With a slight smile, Louis treated the Duc d'Anjou, now Philip v of Spain, as an equal, and called him 'Majesty'. The handsome, silent boy was nonetheless causing him concern. He had been brought up in ignorance and in fear of Hell, to ensure the submission of the younger brother of a future King. It was impossible in the space of a fortnight to cram him with everything he would need in order to carry out such a superhuman task. Just as he himself had been instructed by Mazarin, so the Sun King now lavished his 'instructions in the art of ruling' upon Philip v, but time was short and the pupil was not gifted.

On 4 December, after a magnificent fête held at the Duc du Maine's residence at Sceaux, the King of Spain set out for his new country. When the time came to say farewell, Philip v asked for one last piece of advice, and the King gave him the revealing maxim: 'Never form an attachment for anybody.'

On 15 December Louis xiv wrote to Harcourt, who had just been rewarded for his services with a ducal title:

I think it needful to inform you that the King of Spain has good intentions. He loves good, and will do it if he is aware of it, but he lacks that awareness in many respects. He has had little schooling, even less than is fitting for his age. He will be easily swayed if you do not take care at the beginning to forestall the impressions that may be given him. At present, you cannot render me a greater service than to attend to this. He will trust you and will follow your advice. I have no doubt that it will be good. Finally, bear in mind that I rely upon you completely.[2]

Upon reaching the Pyrenees, Philip v was taken aback by Harcourt's advice never to breathe flowers and perfumes and never to open his letters personally – elementary precautions against poison. But he was enchanted with the enthusiasm of the Spaniards. 'There was such a throng when he arrived in Madrid that it was estimated that sixty people were suffocated . . .'[3]

The rejoicings soon came to an end, however, and the young man felt the insurmountable walls of etiquette close round him. He became prey to intolerable boredom, and in order to distract him as quickly as possible he was married in April 1701 to Marie-Louise of Savoy, sister of the Duchesse de Bourgogne, a passionate girl with all the grace of the Princesses of Savoy and in addition a fire, tenacity and courage beyond her years. Her undeveloped body aroused passions in Philip v that frightened him into feeling that the devil must surely be lying in wait for him. To satisfy his sensual longings without falling into the snare of the Evil One, he never left his wife for an instant, and became her slave.

A thirteen-year-old queen equipped with such fearful power needed a guardian angel. Louis xiv and Mme de Maintenon gave her Princess Orsini,

287

who was so French that she had changed her name to that of Princesse des Ursins. She was a member of the French family of La Trémoille, the daughter of a Frondeur, the widow first of an exiled rebel and then of a Roman nobleman. Thirty years at the papal court had taught her diplomacy, intrigue and the art of charming and influencing great men. As *camerera mayor*, she won the heart of Marie-Louise, dictated to the court, made hidalgos bend the knee and annihilated ministers. The King ruled in name, the Queen ruled the King, and the Princesse des Ursins ruled the Queen.

Mme de Maintenon was now called upon to play an important part in this family matter which was also of international importance. A secret pact was concluded between the Marquise and the Princess. Scorning ministers and ambassadors, Mme des Ursins informed her friend directly about all affairs, both public and private, describing strategic plans, risings in the provinces, disputes over precedence, the Queen's clothes and the nights of the young sovereigns. The Marquise reported to Louis XIV and then transmitted his advice and instructions.

Louis was finding himself compelled, willy-nilly, to take a hand in the affairs of the Spanish monarchy. For some time there had been no member of the Council of Madrid capable of reversing the disastrous decline of the monarchy, and in spite of his grandfather's hurried lessons the young sovereign had neither the character nor the intelligence of a statesman. To allow Spain to be consumed by famine and anarchy would be opening the door to ruin.

Already bowed under the weight of his labours, the King therefore undertook the revival of a half-paralysed nation. He strove to teach something of the order and unity to which he attached so much importance. The kingdom was centralized, the provinces lost their privileges, the government was reorganized on the French pattern and the economy revived, while the great currents of modern art and thought finally penetrated the bastion that had shut them out for so long.

The obverse side of this coin was that Europe regarded the changes in Spain as a deliberate provocation.

$\lceil 3 \rceil$

The Brink of War

By December, England and Holland were resigned to recognizing Philip v. With the exception of the Empire, the other powers soon followed them. William complained bitterly of the pacifism of the House of Commons, which was not unconnected with the influence of French gold. He wrote to his disciple Heinsius, the Grand Pensionary: 'The only game I have to play with this nation is to commit it to war by slow degrees.'

At this juncture, Louis xiv has often been blamed for having provoked the English into steering a different course through his accumulated miscalculations. The King was in the wrong when he reserved the rights of Philip v to the crown of France, but not when he ordered his troops to occupy the famous barrier of Spanish fortresses held by Dutch garrisons. It was a precaution to discourage his neighbours from attacking him, and the operation was no act of aggression since it was carried out in agreement with the King of Spain, and on Spanish territory. It was perfectly in keeping with the spirit of the will and with Charles ii's (or his ministers') design to bring his country under the tutelage of France. That Louis should have become the Regent of his grandson's states was a fatality from which circumstances allowed him no escape.

The real contest was now beginning. William managed to touch off the explosion thanks to an ignominious treaty by which Spain conceded to the French Guinea Company the monopoly on imports of negroes to the Antilles. The slave trade was a profitable source of income for democratic Holland and Puritan England, and the merchants of London and Amsterdam trembled at the prospect of France getting a grip on the East Indies trade. William was able to dissolve the Commons, which had a Tory majority, and the Whigs struck a belligerent attitude. 'Lampoons, speeches, petitions, banquets, sermons, newspaper articles, false reports, forged documents, electoral corruption and parliamentary pressure – no stone was left unturned.'[1]

The outcome of a tacit bargain between William and Parliament was that he was authorized to find allies in return for being obliged to accept the Act of Settlement that regulated his succession in a manner insulting to himself. Almost every article was an implied criticism. The future sovereign was to be the antithesis of the Dutch King. He must be an Anglican, not a Protestant, still less a Catholic. He must never leave England without the permission of Parliament, nor must he have a personal adviser. Only the Privy Council, itself responsible to the elected body, would be empowered to advise him. The descendants of James II were excluded from the throne, and so too were those of Henrietta of England, whose daughter, the Duchess of Savoy, had several children. Instead, Parliament put its faith in the descendants of the aged Electress Sophia of Hanover, James I's great-grand-daughter. Upon the death of Anne Stuart, who had just lost her only viable son, the crown would revert to the Princes of Hanover.

These arrangements annoyed so many people that the death of James II would probably have enabled his son to claim his inheritance, perhaps even with the support of William, but James remained injudicious to the last, and lived six months too long.

Having made his concessions, William now had a free hand, but he was fifty-one years old and seriously ill. For this reason, he patched up his quarrel with Marlborough and appointed him Commander of the English forces on the continent and his ambassador to the United Provinces. His real mission was to resurrect the coalition against France.

The Emperor had not waited. He had no fears about naval dangers, and was equally confident about the German states: the Elector of Hanover was in his pocket, the Elector of Saxony owed him the crown of Poland, and the Elector of Brandenburg had become King of Prussia in return for a solid alliance. With the coming of spring, the Emperor dispatched an army to Italy with instructions to occupy Milan. At the head of these troops was the conqueror of the Turks, Prince Eugène of Savoy, who might have been France's greatest champion if his mother had not dabbled in witchcraft.

Barbezieux died during this crisis, and the King, who was losing his powers of self-criticism as he grew older, put Chamillart in charge of the War Ministry. He pointed out that he would now have to carry the load of both Colbert and Louvois at the same time, but in vain. Saint-Simon, a great friend of the Minister, wrote: 'The mainspring of the King's tender affection for him was his very incapacity. He admitted it to the King at every step, and the King delighted in directing and instructing him, so much so that he was as jealous of his success as of his own, and forgave him everything.'

With the Peace of Ryswick only three years old, commanders were already having to be chosen. Not only was the Duc de Chartres not numbered among them, he was not even permitted to serve.

Monsieur was so indignant that he stood up against Louis for the first time, and their relations now deteriorated rapidly. On 8 June 1701 Louis complained bitterly about the loose life of the Duc de Chartres, and Monsieur lost his temper. The stealthy, hypocritical war that had been waged between the two brothers throughout their lives finally erupted into a furious confrontation between the Sun King in all his crushing majesty and his purple-faced victim, who had finally come to the end of his tether.

The wretched Prince, persecuted, deceived and debased in the name of raison d'état, flung forty years of suppressed home-truths and injustices in his brother's face. That same evening he had an apoplectic fit at Saint-Cloud, and he died the following day.

As usual, Louis wept. His conscience cannot have been completely clear, for he gave the Duc de Chartres a fatherly reception and let him keep Monsieur's entire estate. While not going so far as to open any sphere of activity to the new Duc d'Orléans, he refused him nothing that would make his forced inactivity more pleasant.

Having offered this sacrifice to the memory of the dead man, Louis did not want to be reminded of him again. Twenty-six hours after Philippe's death, when the evening was flagging at Marly, the Duc de Bourgogne asked the Duc de Montfort if he would play a game of cards. 'Cards!' Montfort exclaimed. 'How can you think of it? Monsieur is not yet cold.' 'I know that very well,' the Prince answered, 'but the King does not want us to be bored.'

The practice of opening hostilities without declaring war was becoming traditional. In Italy, the French army that was now the shield of the Spanish possessions faced Prince Eugène, who inflicted a severe defeat on Catinat. The furious King replaced the loser with Marshal Villeroy, whose ineptitude made him easy game for the Savoyard.

Things were not going any better on the diplomatic plane. France rallied Bavaria, Portugal and the Italian princes to her cause and fomented further risings in Hungary, but could not prevent William, Heinsius and Marlborough from achieving their aim. The Grand Alliance was signed at The Hague on 7 September 1701.

James II died on the 16th, and Louis acknowledged his son as heir to the throne of England, contrary to the provisions of the Treaty of Ryswick. Few of Louis' actions have brought such general censure on his head, and yet he had every justification. The Coalition had been sealed nine days previously and Great Britain was definitely committed. There was no point in continuing to disown divine right or incurring the blame of his supporters by withholding a gallant gesture. Recognizing the Pretender could hardly make the hostility of the Whigs any worse, and gave hope to the Jacobites.

The year that had begun so gloriously was coming to an ominous close. Louis did not have to contend merely with the Coalition, war and new prospects of economic collapse. Father Quesnel, the oracle of the Jansenists, decided to reissue a book that had appeared thirty years before, the *Abrégé de la Morale de l'Évangile*, reviving at a stroke the quarrel that had lain dormant for a third of a century and that ended only with the extinction of the monarchy.

As master of the Spanish empire, it might have seemed that Louis XIV was stronger than when he had signed the Peace of Ryswick, but a sick ally is always a hindrance to a great power. This 'dead body which does not defend itself,' as Fénelon called Spain, was no compensation for the loss of those two invaluable counterweights, Turkey, now paralysed, and Sweden, whose young King Charles XII saw himself as another Alexander the Great and was wasting his energies on conquering Poland, after having beaten the Russians.

All William's preliminaries had been completed without a hitch, and he could count on an eventual victory. He did not live to see it. To his last breath, the dark little man busied himself in affairs and laid the foundation of his revenge. He had never loved England, 'this villainous country' where he had not been allowed to rule in his own way. Before he died he gave his liquid assets to his favourite Keppel, Earl of Albemarle, and ordered him to burn his papers. Death came on 19 March 1702.

Louis banned celebrations, but did not allow anybody to wear mourning, although many princes and noblemen were related to the House of Orange.

[4]

The Instruments of Fate

ON the death of William III the throne of England passed to a Princess who was suffering in body, heart and conscience. Just before his death James II had sent his pardon to his second daughter and begged her to renounce the throne in favour of the Prince of Wales. Anne was an honest, gentle, loyal woman, of mean intelligence and without ambition. She was overwhelmed by her father's request, and would probably have acceded to it had she been free to do so. As it was, she had to serve willy-nilly as the emblem of the revolution whose success she ensured by sacrificing her filial duty to her love for Sarah Marlborough.

Two women stood at the peak of English society: the unhappy Stuart, mother of many children who had died in the cradle, riddled with gout and dropsy and tortured by remorse, and her demonic favourite, the tyrannical Sarah, who was to be the effective sovereign. Curiously allied, at least politically, with George of Denmark, the Queen's sottish husband, she was the soul of the Whig party. Anne's sentiments linked her with the Tories, to whom the government was initially entrusted. In fact, the power belonged to the favourite, her husband and one of their henchmen, Godolphin, who became Lord High Treasurer.

Sarah, Mistress of the Robes, treated her august captive harshly and did not baulk at quarrelling in public. She terrorized the court and put pressure on Parliament, while her husband was in control of both war and diplomacy. The Churchill household already had a ducal title. It was now to become immensely rich, thanks to the Duchess's ability to exploit her influence, loot from occupied countries and financial speculation. Their rise was largely based on Anne's limitless affection for Sarah, or rather Mrs Morley's for Mrs Freeman. Still using these pseudonyms, the friends went on exchanging the incredible correspondence in which the daughter of the Stuarts expressed confused feelings and her humility.

The reality by no means corresponded with the appearance. Swift confirms that by the time she came to the throne Anne had already wearied of her favourite's cruel contempt. In the utmost secrecy, she turned to the affection of Sarah's cousin, the lady-in-waiting Abigail Hill. It had taken Mme de

Maintenon ten years to supplant Mme de Montespan. Abigail took just as long to supplant the Duchess of Marlborough.

In Madrid also, a Queen ruled under the sway of a favourite. Marie-Louise of Savoy, although only fourteen, had turned her husband into a puppet. Her sixty-year-old favourite, Mme des Ursins, let nothing elude her authority. She gave their Majesties their chamber-pots and controlled their policy. In spite of her sworn obedience to Louis xiv, she often made them act in accordance with her personal views, and the French King sometimes had difficulty in bringing her to heel.

Her correspondent at Versailles, Mme de Maintenon, worked furiously away in her room while affecting to know nothing about affairs. She complained that she was a ghost, dragged from bed to bed, from niche to niche. Yet this ghost was haunting most of the rulers of Europe. A number of far-fetched stories circulated about her – that she deceived her husband, delayed a courier, even kept certain news from the King – but Louis' vast network of spies would soon have unearthed such activities. Françoise would never have risked incurring the King's displeasure, which would have been extreme in a case of that nature. Her own policy was to avoid risks by anticipating Louis' wishes and even his unspoken intentions. Philip v was perceptive enough to remind one of his agents: 'You will get no change out of Mme de Maintenon because she stands chained to the will and inclination of his Most Christian Majesty.'

She was a perpetually anxious adviser, always wondering what she was expected to say, yet her role ought not to be minimized, because she nudged the King imperceptibly in the direction he really wanted to take. She behaved similarly towards the child who mattered more to Louis than herself. At fifteen, the Duchesse de Bourgogne was the King's greatest delight, his only defence against the crushing monotony of his machine-like existence. The young favourites of earlier times never reached so exalted a position, because there was always the possibility of a rival. No one in the world could replace Marie-Adélaïde.

The Duc de Bourgogne had eventually become a disciple of Fénelon, and becoming a 'saint' meant that he changed from the raging sensualist of his younger days into a docile if cumbersome husband. Marie-Adélaïde both used and abused the situation. Her 'good aunt' secretly feared her, even while she was filling her mind with pious lessons. Charlotte Elizabeth claims that she was the secret accomplice of Marie-Adélaïde, and took steps to prevent the King from becoming aware of her foolish escapades, strange amusements with servants and flirtations, but it is difficult to believe that Mme de Maintenon could have got away with the deception. Here too the King's eyes and ears were everywhere: he may have kept them shut on purpose in order to preserve his happiness.

Louis put up with all kinds of misbehaviour from Marie-Adélaïde, on the one condition that she must always do what he asked her. When she had a miscarriage as a result of accompanying him to Marly against her doctors' advice, Louis replied to the silent reproaches of his courtiers with the appalling remark: 'Thank God that she is hurt, since He willed it so, and I shall never again be vexed on my travels and in anything I want to do by doctors and matrons . . . I shall be left in peace!'

Perhaps Louis' affection really was sheer egoism, but it did not prevent the Princess from making sallies into politics on behalf of her father, the Duke of Savoy. It was Marie-Adélaïde who precipitated the disgrace of Catinat and subsequently of Vendôme. Thanks to her, the Savoyard avoided being punished for his double-dealing until he had extracted the maximum advantage from it.

These were the women who were the instruments of fate. As for the men, the Coalition had three principal actors, with little in common beyond ambition and above all hatred of Louis xiv.

The implacable resentment of Heinsius was another legacy of Louvois, who in 1681 had threatened him with the Bastille for coming to request the restoration of the principality of Orange. William had breathed his own spirit into the Grand Pensionary, who was to be the binding element in the Coalition, its prime mover and its passion. Dressed in black, after the example of his master, Heinsius was the incarnation of Protestant republicanism.

Prince Eugène was an ailing man, like so many other great leaders, with an odd, egg-shaped face. His francophobe fanaticism was all the more powerful because it stemmed from frustrated love. Unable to serve the demigod who had been his mother's lover, he wanted to destroy his cult. Exiled from the French army, he laid the foundations of the Austrian empire.*

The Duke of Marlborough had neither the ideological passion of Heinsius nor the quasi patricidal fury of Eugène. Greed and ambition stood in their stead. Three women were his stepping-stones towards becoming the true successor of William iii: his sister, Arabella Churchill, mistress of James ii when he was still Duke of York; his mistress, Barbara, Duchess of Cleveland, Charles ii's favourite; and his wife Sarah, the friend (and later the enemy) of Queen Anne. It is a kind of miracle that his military genius and political skill should have been on so different a plane from his character and moral sense. They went with the bulldog tenacity that showed in his face just as it showed in the face of his famous descendant.

These three were comparable to the great ministers amd captains of the Sun King in his heyday. Meanwhile, on the French side, the affable Chamillart had replaced the relentless Colbert and the cruel Louvois. Agreeable men had

---

* Which was to be quite different from the empire of the House of Austria.

succeeded the plunderer Luxembourg and the marshals who had burned the Palatinate, men like the aging dandy Villeroy, the courtier-generals Tallard and Marsin and the second-in-command La Feuillade, Chamillart's son-in-law.

There was not one statesman on the Council. In the wings, the King had a financier without equal, Samuel Bernard, who was the secret banker of the expatriated Protestants. Bernard's unlimited credit enabled him to arrange numerous foreign loans, even, and particularly, from his colleagues in the maritime nations. If Louis did not succumb to the fearful expenses of the war, he would owe it to his worst enemies.

Five soldiers were potentially capable of perpetuating the tradition of Condé and Turenne, and oddly enough four of them belonged to the Royal Family. For that very reason, two of them, Chartres and Conti, were deliberately kept in the background: the poison of the Fronde was still active.

The Duc de Vendôme, who was descended from one of Henry IV's bastards and a Mancini girl, eluded this ostracism. In addition, because his princely status, due to Henry IV, constituted a precedent in favour of the Duc du Maine, the King and Mme de Maintenon forgave him everything that should have repelled them. Vendôme was an outcast in his own age, continuing the tradition of the great roaring lords of the sixteenth century and prefiguring the roués of the eighteenth. He had all the scatological wit, daring and gambling fever of his famous ancestor, as well as an enormous appetite for food and sleep. His great ability and talents were balanced by his forgetfulness and laziness, however, and his Mancini blood explains the 'Italian' morals which he took no pains to conceal. The soldiers admired him just as he was: they followed his white plume as their ancestors had followed Henry IV.

The Duke of Berwick, born of the liaison between James II and Arabella Churchill, was also a great-grandson of Henry IV. Just as the Mancini blood made Vendôme the cousin of Prince Eugène, so the Churchill blood made Berwick the nephew of Marlborough. Sheer chance had determined the camp of some of the protagonists in this family affair. Berwick had the military skill of the Bourbons and the Churchills. Fate gave his services to France.

Marshal Villars was of humble birth, whatever his claims to the contrary. Saint-Simon called him 'the most completely and most constantly fortunate man of all the millions born under the long reign of Louis XIV.' Louis had noticed him as early as 1673, at the siege of Maestricht. He was handsome, foppish and a braggart, 'a torrent of boasting, a charlatan's tongue, an over-talkative, slightly crazy figure'.[1] He loved the theatre, and turned his life into an enthralling performance. Villars' good fortune was not undeserved, and constituted one of his country's greatest assets.

Finally, there was Louis XIV himself, sixty-four years old, whose character emerges equally from the stately image produced by Rigaud's studio and the famous profile of the bitter old lion, disillusioned but still defiant, imperious and uncompromising. Far from giving way to the afflictions of age, doubt, fatigue and physical pain, the King had every intention of being supreme commander in the coming struggle. From Mme de Maintenon's apartment he would control his armies and fleets, conduct incessant secret negotiations, combat heresy, supervise the completion of the Invalides and the chapel of Versailles and choose the gentlemen of the King of Spain's bedchamber.

It was the hour of his greatest unpopularity and yet of his most total dominion. Nobody dreamed of exceeding his orders or of acting without them. By a cruel irony, the King who as a child had witnessed disasters due to the divisions of the French people, and who had laboured for forty years to make his individualist, revolutionary country the symbol of cohesion and unity, was to see the finest fruits of his success snatched from his grasp. In spite of the émigrés, Fénelon, the economist Boisguilbert, the Jansenists and the pamphleteers, France followed him as she had never followed any previous leader, but whereas the French people had paid dear for their rebellions because Louis was too young, now, when he was too old, they paid the price for their obedience.

[5]

From the Cévennes to the Danube

IMPERVIOUS to outside events, the machinery of Versailles continued to function smoothly. The Duchesse de Bourgogne played in comedy and even tragedy (*Athalie*), decked out in the Crown jewels. In February news arrived that Prince Eugène had attacked Cremona, where Villeroy had got himself captured by a scouting party. Once rid of their general, the French had proceeded to recapture the stronghold. The court gloated over his discomfiture, much to the irritation of the King, who took their delight as a disguised reproach to himself.

Philip V went to Italy to show himself to his subjects and to block the underhand stratagems of his father-in-law. Vendôme replaced Villeroy, and he and his cousin Eugène conducted a war of guile and surprise, of ineffectual but always murderous little clashes and battles in which both sides claimed victory. Paris and Vienna sang the Te Deum in unison after the Battle of Luzzara.

In spite of his commendable exertions, Philip V was fretting for his wife. An English raid on Andalusia gave him an excuse to return home and rejoin her.

In the autumn a welter of rumours filtered through from Germany. Landau was lost. Catinat did not dare to attack Prince Louis of Baden, whose troops were somewhere in the depths of the Black Forest, for fear of a defeat that might pave the way for an invasion of France. Villars was authorized by the King to take the chance and defeated the Imperial forces at Friedlingen (on 14 October 1702). His delighted men proclaimed him Marshal on the battlefield. The King confirmed it, and the Gascon thanked him by taking Kehl.

In the heat of success, the court paid scant attention to the troubles in the Cévennes. Since the Treaty of Ryswick and the cruel blow it dealt to Protestant hopes, prophets and preachers of the proscribed religion had been roaming the mountains and holding assemblies there. The Abbé du Chayla, Inspector of Missions to the Bishop of Mende, inflicted reprisals so enthusiastically that he was assassinated. It was the signal for an uprising.

Gédéon Laporte, leader of the Camisards (Cévenol Calvinists, so called because they fought in shirt-sleeves), died soon afterwards and was succeeded by his nephew Pierre Laporte, known as Roland, whose second-in-command was a fair-haired, blue-eyed youth of twenty-two, Jean Cavalier, a shepherd turned baker. The partisan warfare that now broke out brought terrible atrocities.

The religious frenzy of the insurgents was no less destructive than the rage of their enemies. At the beginning of 1703 Louis XIV had to accept that after half a century he must once again face civil war, the nightmare of his infancy. He chose a savage leader, Marshal Montrevel, to stamp it out.

Underneath his imperturbable exterior, the King was soon enduring further shocks. The Duke of Savoy, father-in-law of his two grandsons, went over to the enemy, and the King of Portugal followed suit. Fortunately he still had Vendôme, who disarmed the Savoyard forces, and Villars.

Bavaria was in jeopardy, and Villars received instructions to go through the Black Forest to help the Elector, Max Emmanuel. He wrote in his memoirs that the expedition 'was only possible because it was believed impossible.' When the French and Bavarian armies joined forces at Willingen, the Imperial army was taken off balance and the way to Vienna lay open. At the same time there was an uprising in Hungary.

Villars, however, was 'better fitted to serve the state by following his own genius than by acting in concert with a prince'.[1] The Elector wanted to protect his domains and capture the Tyrol, but Villars dragged him practically by force over the Danube and decided to give battle to prevent the Imperial army under Count von Styrum from joining the army of Prince Louis of Baden. The Bavarian opposed the idea, but Villars overrode him, and he was infuriated to have to fight against his will. Victory came at Höchstadt, a narrow one, since at one point both armies panicked simultaneously and it was Villars who rallied his men first. The Elector entered Augsburg on 20 September 1703.

Tallard and Vauban, under the nominal command of the Duc de Bourgogne, captured Breisach and Landau and defeated the Imperial army at Spires. The bayonet decided the outcome of the day, and the battle was probably the swan-song of side-arms as the decisive factor in battle.

Louis XIV thought that he had mastered fortune. The Emperor was contemplating fleeing from Vienna, the Hungarian revolt was gaining ground under the leadership of Prince Rakoczy, the Habsburg monarchy seemed on the point of collapse, while Marlborough was paralysed by the dissensions between the Dutch and the English in the Low Countries. The Sun of the Bourbons was rising towards its zenith again.

Yet there were discordant notes in the harmony of the Te Deums. The war was spreading in Languedoc, where Marshal Montrevel had instituted a reign of terror. On one occasion he burned three hundred Huguenots who had taken refuge in a windmill. The executioners were never idle. A hermit preached a new Albigensian crusade, there were massacres, and many people were broken on the wheel. None of this daunted the elusive Camisards, who also inflicted terrible tortures on their prisoners. They received unsolicited aid from Geneva, Turin, Holland and eventually England.* A fully-fledged army, complete with artillery, was mobilized against them, and failed.

In September 1703 the King accepted a proposal to raze five hundred highland villages. It was winter, and the rebellion was bound to succumb to cold and starvation. Women, children and old people were evicted from their homes by the soldiery. Able-bodied men went to swell the ranks of the combatants, then, driven by hunger, descended and marauded around the towns, fighting savagely when cornered.

The Camisards all belonged to 'the dregs of the people', in Saint-Simon's parlance, and the gentlemen of their own religion looked on them with a very jaundiced eye. One of the Protestant lords, the Baron d'Aigalliers, went to Versailles and told Chamillart 'that persecution alone was keeping the rebellion alive, and that if matters were left to the newly converted and they were given arms, they would either persuade the Camisards or fight them.'

The King was pondering the suggestion when further echoes reached him of the quarrel between the Elector and Villars. Max Emmanuel had set his heart on the Tyrol, and went to fight there. His relations with the Marshal became so strained that he asked for the insufferable champion to be recalled. Here too historians have unanimously condemned Louis, but the Elector was France's only ally, as well as her candidate to succeed Leopold, and it would have been utter folly to throw him into the arms of the enemy. In any case, the matter of the Cévennes was becoming urgent, and Villars had precisely the qualities required to implement the policy of appeasement that had just been adopted. The King therefore had good reason to recall the Marshal and send him to Languedoc.

Upon taking up his new post, Villars subordinated his usual impetuosity to unscrupulous deceit. He promised liberty of conscience (with no chance of its being granted), the release of prisoners and cessation of torture. Aigalliers helped him to win over the young Cavalier, who was nicknamed David. He succumbed to the lure of a colonelcy, a pension of twelve hundred livres, the command of a regiment, but above all the hope of seeing the King. This fanatic sacrificed his terrible God to his admiration for the living demigod. Villars paraded him through Nîmes in triumph.

Roland tried to stem the tide, but failed. Villars dismantled the gibbets and spoke of tolerance, and the country was eager for peace. The following summer Roland was killed and the rebellion fizzled out, to be replaced by the fires of the stake. While Villars went back to Versailles covered in glory,

---

* Queen Anne could not abide Puritans or the common herd. She had to be persuaded of the existence of a 'Count of the Cévennes'.

judicial repression was organized locally, backed by the forces now under Berwick's command. There is no way to calculate the number of victims involved. The figure of twelve thousand has been suggested, and may not be an exaggeration.

Cavalier too went to Versailles, as he had hoped, and was stationed on a staircase that the King was to descend. Louis XIV went by, curious about the heroic 'David' with whom he had had to negotiate. He saw only a little man with fair hair, and shrugged his shoulders. Cavalier's pride was hurt, and he left France and entered the service of the English. He too directed all the resentment of a slighted lover towards fighting his King. No Head of State ever provoked so many impassioned responses as Louis XIV.

[6]

The End of a Dream

THE year 1704 began auspiciously. The Duchesse de Bourgogne was pregnant, and Louis was in the happy position of being a prospective great-grandfather, 'at a time when he still enjoyed full strength and health'. Now that his dynasty was assured, the ageing King might reasonably envisage his descendants as masters of the western world. For the fourth time the vision of universal dominion* was passing through his mind. Already it had dissolved three times in contact with reality: in 1668, when the maritime powers 'halted the sun'; in 1672, when the Dutch flooded their country; and in 1683, when Sobieski routed the Turks.

Circumstances looked far more favourable in 1704. The Spanish empire had passed from the House of Austria to the Bourbons. Leopold's was falling apart. One successful campaign would suffice to replace the Habsburg by the loyal Wittelsbach, and Vienna by Munich as the capital of central Europe. It would deal a hard enough blow to shake the new and fragile political system of England to its foundations, and Anne would be only too happy to see the throne restored to her brother. The whole of Europe would bask under the Sun King's rays.

With the approach of spring, Louis, Chamillart and the generals laid their plans. They decided that Villeroy, who had been appointed Commander of the Army of Flanders, was to remain on the defensive, while Germany would be invaded by three armies, one Bavarian and two French, the latter under the command of Marshals Tallard and Marsin. In Italy, Vendôme was to mount an all-out offensive against the Duke of Savoy.

The snag was that although he was not yet aware of it, Louis XIV no longer had at his disposal the great machine built by the brutal genius of Louvois.

Military appointments and rewards were squandered under the ministry of Chamillart. Too many young men were authorized to buy regiments when they were barely out of their childhood, whereas among enemy nations a regiment was the reward of twenty years' service. The Cross of the Order of Saint Louis, an award instituted by the King in 1693 and which had been an object of competition among the officers, was put

---

* This is to be understood in the sense of an authoritarian suzerainty, not as a Napoleonic dictatorship or a Hitlerian oppression.

up for sale from the onset of Chamillart's ministry. It could be bought for fifty crowns at the war office. Military discipline deteriorated into a fatal laxity: companies were without their full complement of men, and regiments lacked officers . . . Stores were no longer large enough, nor quickly enough available, and the quality of munitions was no longer reliable.[1]

Louis XIV was no military genius. He had had very little to do with strategy in the days when his troops had been commanded by the best generals in the world, but considered himself more experienced than their successors, whose incompetence – Villeroy apart – has been exaggerated. Unfortunately these men, brought up at court, had courtiers' weaknesses. Knowing the King's leanings, they encouraged them, inducing him in effect to play the part of generalissimo and to run the war from Versailles.

Hostilities were resumed in May in a reassuring fashion for the French. The combined armies of Marsin and the Elector were heavily reinforced in spite of the efforts of the Imperial forces, and made ready to march on Vienna. Then they hung fire because Marlborough had left the Low Countries and was heading no one knew where. They were waiting for him on the Moselle and in Alsace when they heard that he had crossed the Main into Suabia and that Prince Eugène had left Italy and was marching to join him.

The Elector and Marsin called for help. Villeroy forfeited a number of excellent opportunities for action, but finally joined forces with Tallard, whereupon they both turned to their master. Louis received not one plan but four, and sent a long despatch explaining his view of the situation but giving no definite order. Villeroy, who had no intention of risking the King's displeasure, replied: 'Your Majesty understands war better than those who have the honour to serve you.'

This was on 18 June. On the 22nd Lieutenant-General Legalle explained the terrible danger to the King: Bavaria could be conquered, the Elector destroyed and his and Marsin's troops annihilated. Prodded into a decision, Louis instructed Villeroy to take up his position at Offenburg and Tallard to cross the mountains and reinforce the Elector and Marsin with forty battalions of foot and fifty squadrons of cavalry. Unhappily for France, Tallard had none of Villars' initiative and was demoralized before he set out. He wrote a deplorable despatch: 'Your Majesty cannot arrive at a single decision that is not hedged round with tremendous difficulties . . . I shall find myself completely dependent on the enemy's decisions.'

The enemy's own preparations were assisted by possession of the French plan, thanks to a spy in Chamillart's office. Marlborough and Eugène joined forces, and on 2 July, at Donauworth, the Allies defeated Count Arco, the Elector's General, in a bloody battle, and took the fortress of Schellenberg. Marlborough laid waste Bavaria, extending the olive branch to its sovereign at the same time, and in spite of Marsin's threats Max Emmanuel was on the verge of changing sides when he was informed of Tallard's imminent arrival.

When the King discovered that Eugene's threat to Alsace had been a ruse to keep Villeroy occupied, he ordered the Marshal to go to the assistance of Tallard. This time he was not obeyed. Villeroy was intimidated by the formidable lines of Stollhofen, manned by only a handful of troops. He made no move, and stayed out of the reckoning. Tallard reached Augsburg on 4 August. Once their forces were joined, he, the Elector and Marsin plucked up their courage, and Louis received a reassuring letter from Tallard:

We shall observe the enemy's action from the heights of Biberbach, and adjust our own movements accordingly, until the thirteen battalions and sixteen squadrons with which the Elector has undertaken to reinforce his army enable us to surround the enemy even more thoroughly. After that, we shall not let him come off lightly.

The Marquis de Feuquières, a trenchant military critic, was to count twelve major blunders made by the Elector and the two Marshals before and during the battle. The worst of these undoubtedly lay in separating the two armies and tying the infantry to a static position at the village of Blenheim. The action was fought on 13 August around Höchstädt, where Villars had beaten the Imperial army the year before. In the morning the military supremacy of France was overpowering. By evening it no longer existed, and Louis xiv's high hopes joined those of his ancestor Charles v in the land of lost illusions.

The Duc de Bretagne, son of the Duc de Bourgogne, had been born on 25 June, and there had been continual celebrations ever since. Villeroy's courier arrived amid a scene of general rejoicing on 21 August (eight days after the battle) bearing letters from a number of captured officers who had received permission to inform their families. Villeroy confined his own news to saying that Tallard's army had been destroyed. The anguished King opened the prisoners' letters, but did not find what he was looking for, and remained for six days:

. . . in the terrible situation of knowing that all was lost in Bavaria without knowing how; the few people whose letters did arrive had merely written personal news . . . nobody was in a hurry to describe the disaster; they feared for their letters and dared not give any account of either events or people . . . The cruel surrender [of the infantry at Blenheim] was nevertheless the first thing to emerge . . . Neither the King nor anybody else could understand how an entire army entrenched in and around a village had been made prisoners by means of a signed capitulation. It was bewildering.[2]

Bewilderment was what Louis wanted least of all. He displayed imperturbable coolness and resolution, and cancelled none of the prearranged festivities in honour of the new-born prince. On 22 August Monseigneur held a fireworks display at Meudon. On the 28th the city ordered a still more magnificent display. From the windows of the Louvre, the princes and the court saw in the sky the Seine triumphing over the Thames and the other rivers of Europe.

The following day Louis discovered at last how the battle had been lost, Marlborough having allowed one of his prisoners, the Marquis de Silly, to go to Versailles to explain. The disaster was on a frightful scale. Of the sixty thousand Frenchmen involved, barely twenty thousand had escaped. Nine generals had been killed, Tallard captured, and 100 cannon, 24 mortars and 171 standards had fallen into enemy hands.

There was worse news yet. Villeroy had gone to the assistance of the defeated armies and had had the opportunity to halt the rout and hold at least part of Bavaria. Instead, the ragged remnants of Marsin's forces had thrown his own into a panic. Marshals and privates alike had but a single thought – to go home. A hundred leagues of territory had been abandoned in three weeks.

Marlborough did not let matters rest there. He followed hard on Villeroy's heels, hoping to force another battle on the lines of the rivers Queich and Lauter. Villeroy preferred to abandon these positions, knowing that his men's morale was too low, and Landau fell into enemy hands again. Chamillart wrote to Marsin: 'I would never have believed that the consequences of the Höchstadt encounter could be so disastrous.' Germany was lost, the Habsburgs saved and triumphant.

Louis XIV showed his true greatness by assuming total responsibility for the defeat. Although he saw his plans in ruins, the ruthless King did not address a word of reproach to his ally or his generals, and even wrote to tell the Elector, who had taken refuge in Brussels, that he was more touched by his misfortune than by the French defeat. He reassured Marsin and commended his conduct. Of the luckless Tallard he only said: 'I sympathize with the marshal and am deeply touched by his grief at the loss of his son.' Finally, he wrote to his friend Villeroy:

> Put yourself above public gossip . . . You acted in the manner which, to your own mind, best served my interests. Ignoring a misplaced pride that would have been groundless, you cared more for my army and my state than for your personal reputation. Nothing could more convince me of your devotion to my person.

August 1704 is one of the most glorious months in the entire history of England. Nine days before Blenheim Admiral Rooke had captured Gibraltar, the impregnable but undefended fortress. The English broke in while the fifty men of the garrison were at mass. A French squadron that went to the rescue under the Comte de Toulouse was repulsed, and a subsequent expedition was destroyed by a storm, the faithful ally of the British at crucial moments. 'Since that day, no great French fleets have appeared in either the Atlantic or the Mediterranean. The navy relapsed almost into the state from which Louis XIV had retrieved it, like so many other splendid things that had their rise and fall under his reign.'[3]

That the political axis of the world had altered became clear when the son of the Caesars, the young Archduke Charles, went to London and made a humble appeal to the usurper Queen. The fleet, troops and money he received from her enabled him to land at Lisbon and conquer the kingdoms of Valencia and Murcia. The Earl of Peterborough, an individualist who was financing his own contribution to the war, gave him Catalonia and Barcelona. Marshal Tessé was repulsed with heavy losses when he tried to retake the town. It was an open question whether it had once cost France more to conquer Spain than it was now costing to support her.

The Emperor owed everything to England, and had become her client. Even so, Leopold still flatly refused to address Queen Anne by the title of 'Majesty', and would only thank 'Her Serenity.'*

---

* The head of the Holy Roman Empire considered that he himself was the only 'Majesty'.

[7]

The Olympian Mask

ANY number of contemporary witnesses and later historians have asserted that after the bombshell of Blenheim Louis XIV soon regained his optimism, illusions and hopes. His Olympian mask undoubtedly created such an impression, but research into state secrets reveals quite another picture. Louis immediately realized the implications of his defeat and saw that he must extricate himself from the war as quickly as possible. In Holland, a minority was strongly opposed to the tutelage of the English, and he approached them to suggest a return to the Treaties of Partition. A number of possibilities were discussed, and peoples and provinces distributed and bartered like so much real estate, but Heinsius prevailed, and in April the negotiations were broken off. All the same, seeds of dissension had been sown between the Dutch and the English, especially among the generals.

Both sides made colossal preparations for the campaign of 1705. The Allies raised 250,000 men, France and Spain about 200,000, an astonishing feat in view of the state of their finances. In Colbert's day France had had an annual revenue of 112 million livres and had spent 116 million. The deficit had now reached 160 million, with a revenue of 50 million, and expenditure of 220 million, and a national debt of $1\frac{1}{2}$ thousand million. *Billets de monnaie,* the ancestors of banknotes, were proliferating.

Samuel Bernard miraculously provided the army with 36 million livres in 1704 and 1705, and 42 million in 1706.[1] It never entered Louis' head to reduce his scale of living or call a halt to the round of fêtes that enabled him to keep an eye on anybody who might be nursing factional ambitions. Unfortunately, the system was rebounding on its creator: having broken the spirit of rebellion, it was paralysing initiative and talent.

The death of the young Duc de Bretagne at the hands of his doctors hit Louis at the very moment when the issue of his country's future was coming to a head once again. Marlborough meant to force a decision within the year, and the fiery Villars, recalled to his former command, confronted his increasingly formidable adversary near Trier. It was the Englishman whose nerve failed. His personal enemy, Prince Louis of Baden, did not bring up the expected reinforcements, and Marlborough fell back. He took the extraordinary step of sending apologies to Villars: 'Do me the justice of believing that my retreat is the fault of the Prince of Baden, and that I esteem you even more than I am angry with him.'

Two months later in Flanders, not far from Waterloo, Marlborough thought that revenge was in his grasp. The armies he proposed to attack belonged to Villeroy and Max Emmanuel, now Governor of the Spanish Netherlands. The Dutch generals liked him no better than did the Germans, however, and when they prevented him from moving Villeroy had the unexpected distinction of saving Flanders.

Italy too was saved, this time by Vendôme, who defeated Eugène at Cassano (on 16 August 1705). The King now decided to lay siege to Turin and, much to the distress of Marie-Adélaïde, to annihilate the Duke of Savoy. In Spain, where Berwick had been appointed commander of the French forces, a near-miracle was taking place. The burning affection of Marie-Louise of Savoy for her new country had turned her husband into a true Spaniard, and the people adored them both. On the French side, it seemed that the only conceivable purpose of the war was to leave the former hereditary enemy a dynasty of its own choice.

The Emperor Leopold had been ailing for some time, and never saw the outcome of the conflict. Saint-Simon summed up his character and his reign:

Ignoble ugliness, a base mien and a simplicity far removed from the pomp of empire did not prevent him from spreading its authority much further than had any of his predecessors, Charles v excepted; and his outward life, more monkish than princely, did not prevent him using every kind of means to achieve his ends ... He always waged [war] through his generals, in whom he was singularly fortunate. Nor was he less so in his ministers, whom he chose so wisely that his Council was always the best in Europe ... In a word, he was able and proud, always steadfast in his plans and conduct, fortunate in everything, and in his family.

His eldest son succeeded him under the title of Joseph i. Louis xiv wore violet mourning, but, whatever his feelings at the death of his brother-in-law, he did not betray the least sign of any weakness or discouragement that might have laid France open to wholesale confusion.

So the balls and masquerades continued at Versailles and Marly.

The Grand Dauphin, son of
Louis XIV (after J. Parrocel)

Louis XV (the Duc d'Anjou,
great grandson of Louis XIV –
Rigaud)

The Duc de Saint-Simon
(lithograph by Delpech)

Voltaire aged 24 (engraving
by N. de Largillière)

[8]

'There is no Good Fortune'

As long as he felt that luck was on his side, Louis had hidden a wealth of guile and caution behind his flamboyant pose. His fear of great battles made him sacrifice pride itself to caution, notably at Heurtebise and Gembloux. All at once, like a gambler uncertain of his luck, he became hasty and rash. He wanted to offer peace, not receive it. He ordered Chamillart's swaggering son-in-law, Marshal La Feuillade, to besiege Turin, because Vauban was showing signs of apprehension – as well he might, since it was he who had fortified the town when the Duke of Savoy looked like a staunch ally.

In the Low Countries, the King expressly instructed Villeroy to give battle – so expressly that Villeroy was nettled and forgot another and equally impera-tive order, which was to wait for Marsin's forces to arrive before attacking. The result was the catastrophe of Ramillies, which cost eight thousand lives and put paid to the hope of regaining lost ground (on 23 May 1706). In rapid succession, Marlborough took Brussels, Antwerp, Malines, Louvain, Ostend and Menin. Less than a month later the Archduke was proclaimed King of Spain in Madrid.

Hoping to retrieve his fortunes, the King gave Vendôme command of Villeroy's army, but Vendôme had the mentality of a feudal lord. He had defeated Eugène again at Calcinato (on 19 April 1706), and was holding him at bay across the Adige river while La Feuillade besieged Turin. As soon as his orders transferred him to another fief, he let Eugène cross the river. The crisis in the high command was then at its height. When Villeroy refused to tender his resignation the King had to overrule him.

Shaken by these setbacks, Chamillart wanted to prepare for the future and revive the morale of the army by putting a prince of the blood at their head. Not without difficulty, he persuaded first Mme de Maintenon, then the King. Louis could not overcome his bias against the Prince de Conti, but on 22 June, to the astonishment of the political pundits, he summoned the Duc d'Orléans and gave him command of the army of Italy.

Early in July the Duc d'Orléans arrived at Turin, where La Feuillade showed him the siegeworks with all the arrogance of an unassailable favourite.

Although Philippe was determined to maintain friendly relations with the son-in-law of the man to whom he owed his appointment, he was stunned by La Feuillade's inanity and complacency. He pointed out the most glaring of his positional errors, but his warnings were ignored.

The prince then went on to Vendôme's headquarters on the bank of the Mincio, only to receive a further shock. The Duke had made no attempt to prepare for his successor. He got up at four in the afternoon and stuffed himself to the point of indigestion, paying no attention whatsoever to the military situation, despite the proximity of Prince Eugène's Imperial army. Philippe wanted to prevent the enemy from crossing the river, but Vendôme shrugged and told him that it could not be done. A few days later Eugène did cross, and the eccentric general set out for Flanders, leaving his young colleague in the lurch. Thereupon an adviser arrived from the King – none other than Marsin, the man who had been defeated at Blenheim.

Marsin, an intimate of Mme de Maintenon, brought with him the secrets of the inner sanctums where the Marquise ruled and the Duchesse de Bourgogne playfully opened state despatches. With great respect and frequent genuflections, he conveyed to Philippe that from now on he was under supervision.

They were an ill-matched pair. Philippe wanted to trap Prince Eugène on the Tanaro. Marsin vetoed the suggestion. It therefore became necessary to fall back on Turin and join forces with La Feuillade. Fortified by vanity and the power of his father-in-law, the latter easily swayed the compliant Marshal, and got all his own way.

To begin with, he insisted on the two armies camping inside the over-extended lines that he had drawn around the town. Seeing the danger of such a position, the Prince wanted to attack. When Marsin obstructed him again, he lost his temper and demanded a council of war. Although he spoke with impressive authority, the staff officers, anxious about their promotion, kept their eyes on the two nominees of Versailles, Marsin and La Feuillade. They voted almost unanimously against Philippe.

Beside himself with anger, he declared that since he had no control over anything it was unjust that he should take the blame for the impending defeat, and called for his post-chaise, intending to leave the army on the spot. They hung on his coat-tails begging him to remain, and Philippe yielded, although he announced that he would relinquish his command. He wrote the King an explanatory letter, which he nobly gave into the keeping of Marsin, and then withdrew to his tent.

During the night of 6–7 September a breathless officer woke the Duc d'Orléans and informed him that the Imperial troops were advancing on the camp. Forgetting his resolutions, the Prince hurried to Marsin's tent, shook him awake and showed him how the army could win a certain victory by leaving the lines and taking the initiative. The dauntless Marshal advised his

Highness to relax, and went back to sleep. In two minds between indignation and despair, Philippe swore once again to take no further part in the proceedings.

The enemy advance guard appeared at sunrise, amid the consternation and recriminations of men suddenly faced with the consequences of their errors. Philippe decided to save Marsin and La Feuillade in spite of themselves, and might have succeeded had not each of his orders received an immediate countermand. He felt so betrayed that he slashed with his sword at an officer of the Anjou regiment who was obstinately ignoring his orders.

Eugène attacked and was quick to seize his advantage. Philippe 'performed wonders, always in the thick of the firing, with a sang-froid that saw everything, took everything into the reckoning and brought him wherever his example would do the most good . . . Wounded first of all in the thigh, fairly lightly, and then near the wrist, dangerously and very painfully, he was unshakeable'.[1] However, he could not repair so many mistakes so wantonly accumulated.

The French troops wavered and broke. Marsin, grievously wounded, fell into the hands of the enemy. In the blockhouse where he was taken, he begged somebody to restore to Philippe the letter that he had not forwarded to Versailles, called for a confessor, and died, taking with him the secret of his fatal lethargy. At the time he was accused of having sacrificed success to the desire to ingratiate himself with La Feuillade by reserving for him the honour of a victory. Later there was speculation that he might have been obeying mysterious instructions from the Duchesse de Bourgogne.

Seeing that the battle was lost, the Prince prepared to retreat. The two routes open led to France or Lombardy. If it took the former, the army would be leaving Italy in the hands of the Imperial army: he therefore boldly chose the latter, with the idea of rallying a Spanish corps that had won a recent battle at Castiglione and blockading Prince Eugène before Turin in his turn.

When Philippe announced his plan, La Feuillade and most of his staff, who had pillaged the countryside and whose one thought was to get their loot to safety, cried out in horror. The exasperated Prince ordered them to be quiet and gave instructions to set out, but once again his hands were tied by treachery. While the soldiers were making for Milan, the supply convoys were going in the opposite direction and Philippe had to call a halt. Hordes of scouts now appeared with tales of ambushes that the enemy was supposed to be laying. Exhausted and in considerable pain from his injury, the luckless hero flung himself into his carriage and told his officers to go where they pleased.

The ensuing retreat over the Alps would have turned into a rout if the prince had not been everywhere at once, risking his life in the process, but the army passed through at last and the Duc d'Orléans re-entered Versailles in

311

triumph. Louis' affectionate reception communicated itself to the courtiers at once.

Outstanding though it was as a moral victory for Philippe, the Turin disaster set France back fifty years. Although the King of Spain returned to Madrid in September to a frenzied reception, Germany, Belgium and Italy were lost for good,* and the Archduke remained in control of Catalonia, Aragon and Granada.

'The King bears it all like a great man,' Mme de Maintenon wrote to the Princesse des Ursins, 'but he is suffering.' He was also suffering from old age, and had identified himself with France to such a point that she was sinking with him. He must have had this in mind when he told Villeroy, with something approaching resignation: 'Marshal, at our age there is no good fortune.'

---

* The Spanish possessions in Italy now fell into Austrian hands, annexed by the Emperor to the detriment of his brother's interests.

[9]

The Death of Vauban and the
Birth of Parties

ON 1 January 1707 Louis XIV told the foreign ambassadors: 'Gentlemen, my affairs are going well.' Vauban did not agree. He was in favour of leaving Spain to her own devices and sending Philip V to rule in America, nor would there have been any lack of support if Marie-Louise of Savoy had not rallied public feeling on her husband's behalf. But Vauban was not only concerned with the disasters of war. He had been pondering on the deficiencies of the system and on ways to rebuild the economy.

His conclusions had produced a book, *Project for A Royal Tithe*, which added yet another voice to the chorus of evocations of the wretched condition of the common people:

The sickness is going from bad to worse, and if no cure is found this same people will be plunged into a distress from which they will never recover ... The common people have never been paid sufficient heed in any age. They are ruined, they are despised, and yet it is they who are most worthy of attention, both because of their numbers and because of their real services.

Vauban proposed a revolutionary cure, the abolition of all taxes and their replacement by a levy, a 'tithe' calculated on the basis of individual income and from which nobody was to be exempt, not even the King himself. The Marshal was two hundred years before his time.

He kept his powder dry until the moment when the troubles of 1706 decided him to touch it off, whereupon he quietly handed his book to a Rouen printer and collected and distributed it himself. The reaction of the privileged classes and the tax-farmers needs no imagining. The ministers told the King that his authority was being flouted, but although Louis undoubtedly responded, his action must be judged without reference to the malice of Saint-Simon or to modern fiscal concepts.

However pure Vauban's intentions may have been, and however impartial his concept, his book, appearing as it did in the thick of war and after so many defeats, could only aggravate the confusion of public opinion. As for his financial revolution, it would not have been possible to embark on it in the middle of a crisis, even if Louis XIV had been prepared to consider the

L *

technical aspects of the question. His genuine friendship for a man to whom he owed the capture of so many towns did not prevent the book being banned on 14 February 1707. There was talk of an inquiry, even of a *lettre de cachet*,* but Vauban was ill with bronchitis and died on 30 March.

His fall from grace had undoubtedly shattered him. Many voices were raised to assert that he was the victim of Louis' displeasure, but it is surely difficult to believe that a broken heart could kill so automatically and so quickly. The materials out of which this legend was constructed are exemplified by Saint-Simon's false claim that 'the King was so unmoved that he did not seem even to have noticed that he had lost so useful and illustrious a servant'. The fact is that Louis sent his personal physician to the marshal, and when he was informed of Vauban's death exclaimed: 'I have lost a man who loved my person and my state.' He spoke of Vauban subsequently 'with much esteem and affection'.[1]

The upshot of the Vauban affair was only to increase the general confusion. In 1701 the King's power had exceeded Charlemagne's; now, a mere six years later, a band of enemy raiders kidnapped his first equerry, Beringhen, on the road from Versailles to Paris, mistaking him for the Dauphin. In the margin of the pathetic reports of Chamillart, who was angling for retirement, Louis noted: 'We are all to be pitied and in a shattered state, but we must not lose heart and must do our best.' When Chamillart said that he would die if he was not allowed to retire, Louis merely answered: 'Well, we shall die together.'

In circumstances like these, there was no possibility of stifling the development of different schools of thought. At court, two opposing parties speculated on the future and made stealthy attempts to influence the present. The group around the Dauphin and La Choin drew its inspiration from Madame la Duchesse and Vendôme. Monseigneur, reacting against his teacher Bossuet, cultivated ignorance and boasted of not having read a book for thirty years. He did not understand his eldest son, and invested all his affection in the King of Spain. Consequently he advocated out-and-out war. His coterie was aggressive, perfidious, free-thinking and clogged with feminine rivalries and promiscuity.

The côterie of the Duc dê Bourgogne, the old 'party of the saints', was devious, evangelical and puritanical. The exiled Fénelon, eaten up with ambition and resentment, directed the conscience of his beloved 'Télémaque' and of the 'little flock' that preached a pacifism verging on treason, rejecting the ill-gotten gains of Lille, Strasbourg, Besançon, Arras and Valenciennes, and asking the King to accept defeat as the judgement of God. They condemned the un-Christian resistance of Philip v, and the Duc de Bour-

---

* Document issued by order of the King for the incarceration, internment or exile of individuals – Tr.

gogne was secretly advising his brother to safeguard the peace of the world by abdicating.

Philippe d'Orléans was now a piece on the chessboard. His dissolute morals and fighting spirit ought to have inclined him towards Meudon, but his way was blocked by his sister-in-law, Madame la Duchesse, who hated him with all the force of a slighted woman. On the other hand, his favourite niece, the Duchesse de Bourgogne, his friendship with Saint-Simon and his admiration for Fénelon ranked him paradoxically among the 'saints'. Their furtive condemnation of Philip v must also have played its part, since the Prince had not forgotten that he too had claims to the Spanish crown. He was delighted, therefore, when he was put in command of the forces dispatched to his nephew's assistance.*

Tensions were beginning to arise between the plaintive Marquise de Maintenon, who was secretly in favour of Philip v's abdication, and the indomitable Princess des Ursins. Françoise had advised her friend to ask the nuns of the Incarnation to pray, and received a stinging reply: 'Instead of turning to [the nuns] for help, we have recourse to good troops who give no quarter to anybody and cut off the arms, head and legs of those whom they cannot take prisoner.'

The Princess's tone modulated into one of barely-veiled contempt, and Mme de Maintenon replied: 'The King and Queen of Spain have good reason to love you, Madame, when your passion for them makes you quite forget that you are French. We must forgive you, and pray God that it may please him to change your attitude.' The riposte arrived by return: 'I only ventured my letter, Madame, to persuade you that in pressing for war I am perhaps a better Frenchwoman than any other.'

Events confirmed the Princess's view. Before Philippe d'Orléans had reached his headquarters, Berwick defeated the English and Imperial forces commanded by the Earl of Galway at the Battle of Almanza (on 25 April 1707). The British title was a cover for a French Protestant, the Comte de Ruvigny, whose army contained a refugee regiment led by Cavalier in person. They were burning for revenge, and fell upon their fellow-countrymen at the point of the bayonet. Few of the combatants survived this fratricidal engagement.

Orléans had no intention of playing second fiddle to Berwick. He retook the province of Valencia, pushed the Allies back in Aragon, and captured Saragossa and, after a superb siege, Lérida, which had once repulsed the Grand Condé himself. This brought him great popularity in Spain, and he asked Mme des Ursins to appoint his mistress, Mme d'Argenton, lady-in-waiting to the Queen of Spain, by way of a reward. Mme de Maintenon was consulted and sent back a scandalized veto. By setting the prince at logger-

---

* Through her mother, the Queen of Spain was the granddaughter of Monsieur.

heads with these two powerful women, this incident was to have far-reaching consequences.

In the Rhineland too, the French were having some success under Villars, but the Duke of Savoy and Prince Eugène crossed the Col di Tenda in the first incursion onto French soil for half a century. The Allies believed that they had Provence and Dauphiné at their mercy. They laid siege to Toulon, which was rescued in the nick of time by forces detached from Villars' army. An epidemic completed the defeat of the enemy, who retreated across the Alps leaving a trail of devastation in their wake.

In the press of events, the death of Mme de Montespan went almost unnoticed. The King's ready tears did not fall, but Mme de Maintenon was overcome by tears of unexpected grief which 'for want of a better refuge, she went and shed on her night-stool.'[2]

[10]

The Rout of Oudenarde

F O R a time the decisive force in Europe was neither at Versailles, London nor Vienna, but was sweeping through northern and eastern Europe driving Danes, Russians and Saxons before it and conferring on Poland a sovereign of her own choice. Charles XII of Sweden, a bald giant who hardly ever took his boots off, had visions of re-living the epic of Alexander the Great. Louis XIV sent emissaries to him, and England deputed Marlborough himself. Charles XII was in a position to sway the outcome of the war and the Spanish succession, and to remodel the continent to suit his fancy, but he was not interested in high diplomacy, and was motivated only by his love of battle and hatred for Peter the Great of Russia. His ambitions and passions were focused exclusively on the Tsar, and western Europe had nothing to fear or to hope from him, to the disappointment of Louis and the relief of Marlborough. There was nothing to do but prepare for the operations of 1708.

In spite of everything, the King was determined to make a powerful effort. Many Scotsmen were showing signs of dissatisfaction with the Act of Union of 1707, which welded their country to England. A fleet gathered at Dunkirk to carry the son of James II to the cradle of his dynasty, and a large army was mustered in Flanders.

The problem was to find enough money in the midst of galloping inflation and with Louis' credit at rock-bottom. Chamillart's health had collapsed under the weight of his responsibilities, so the King had to relieve him of Finance, but left him the War Ministry. Desmarets, a nephew of Colbert, was recalled out of a long exile to take over the Ministry of Finance.

The new Minister was reduced to financial expedients that took no account of the future. One of his measures was to double the amount of inland excises, thus dealing the final blow to his uncle's industrial achievement. When this was still not enough, he had to turn to the inevitable Samuel Bernard, who was impatient and unhelpful. So it was that at Marly, on 6 May 1708, Desmarets presented the financier to the King, who showed him over the gardens. Bernard still produced only 900,000 livres, which was much less than in the preceding years. The costs of the campaign were finally met thanks to a

317

number of Saint Malo merchants, who brought thirty million livres over from Peru and lent half to the state.

The Jacobite enterprise was destroyed by unfavourable weather, still on the side of the English. As for the prospects of settling accounts with the Low Countries, the 'Saints' made a grave mistake: they managed to have the Duc de Bourgogne appointed Commander of the Army of Flanders, not realizing that the virtues of this modest, devout and sensitive Prince would work against him when he came face to face with the enemy. As a guide, he received none other than the leader of the rival côterie, the outrageous, cynical rake, Vendôme.

Few campaigns have ever been more fatal. The French army of eighty thousand men outnumbered the Allies. It took Ghent, Bruges and Ypres before being paralysed by the division between its leaders. Prince Eugène was able to effect his junction with Marlborough undisturbed.

An almost accidental battle was fought at Oudenarde on 11 July. In place of Louvois' magnificently arrayed army, there was a tangle of infantry and cavalry, each acting on the spur of the moment. Most of the regiments merely watched the action develop. When the time came to withdraw, the retreat became a rout. Regiments received no orders, and milled about aimlessly. Four thousand men were captured, while the quarrel between the generals festered.

The Duc de Vendôme was immensely popular with the masses, and for the first time since the Fronde court rivalries produced grave political repercussions:

The cabal broke out by degrees ... Its emissaries paraphrased letters from the front among the gossip-mongers in cafés, public places, gaming rooms and private houses. Even Les Halles was full of them, and their satires, verses and atrocious songs about the heir to the throne that built up Vendôme as a hero were rife in Paris and throughout the realm.[1]

Vendôme may have had the people on his side, but the Duc de Bourgogne had his wife, who did not love him but 'was nonetheless affected by his reputation, on which all her consequence depended for many years'. From being a charming girl totally involved in pleasure she now became a harsh, arrogant Princess. After praying at great length beside Mme de Maintenon, she complained to the King and threw tantrums that exasperated her grandfather.

Meanwhile the Allies had entered France and were boldly laying siege to Lille, Louis' personal conquest and one of the most dazzling emblems of his *gloire*. Berwick, who was commanding an army near Douai, was instructed to join Vendôme. He was a Marshal of France, as much the great-grandson of Henry IV as Vendôme himself, and refused to take his cousin's orders. The result of their disagreements was that an army of 120,000 men merely looked on while Boufflers put up a heroic defence of Lille against Prince Eugène. Mme de Maintenon wrote to Mme des Ursins: 'I see only wailing and weeping, and those about me are even more anxious than I. Only the King is steadfast in his determination to give battle for the relief of Lille and the honour of the nation.'

The nation's pride was at a low ebb, and there was no battle. Lille fell on 23 October, then Ghent and Bruges. The King opened his arms wide to his grandson when he returned to Versailles and did not address a word of reproach to him. He said nothing to Vendôme either, but Marie-Adélaïde won her point and the Duke was out of favour again.

In Spain the Duc d'Orléans had to restrict himself to capturing Tortosa, having found 'general want and even greater negligence', which he blamed on Mme des Ursins and, indirectly, on Mme de Maintenon. On one drunken evening he made coarse remarks about them that turned their ill will into outright hostility.

In the Peninsula too, there was disaffection. Although the people adored Philip v, many grandees could not stand being ruled by a woman, and no longer had any confidence in Louis xiv. They led the Duc d'Orléans to understand that there were bright prospects for a descendant of Philip iii* who was not bound to the King of France and was capable of governing efficiently and winning battles.

Certain Englishmen, ill-satisfied with Archduke Charles and finding little to choose between him and his rival Philip v, had arrived at the same conclusion. Among them was Stanhope, the Commander of the English army and one of the Whig leaders, who had once been received and fêted at the Palais Royal. On a fateful October day in 1708 M. Flotte, his Highness' secretary, appeared at the English camp to negotiate an exchange of prisoners. Stanhope received him like an ambassador, told him what he had in mind and handed him a letter meant for the Dutch and English plenipotentiaries who were discussing peace conditions at The Hague. The Prince rejected the poisoned gift, but when winter brought him back to France he left behind him an audacious, foolish intriguer, Deslandes de Rignault, who began to recruit support for his master.

Anarchy was spreading like gangrene. The great empire of the Sun King seemed like a dismantled fortress, his sceptre a rotten branch. Fénelon wrote: 'The old machine will fall completely to pieces at the first jolt.' Yet an odd event in London might have warned a perceptive observer that this was not the end. Sarah Marlborough had at last discovered the relationship between Queen Anne and Abigail Hill, and learned that her cousin had secretly

---

* Philippe d'Orléans was a grandson of Anne of Austria and great-grandson of Philipp iii of Spain.

married a page named Samuel Masham, with the Queen as a witness. The Duchess had been seething with rage ever since. She kept the Queen short of money, sent her insulting letters and picked quarrels even in the bedchamber where the unhappy sovereign was watching over her dying husband. She even tried to have the House of Commons table a motion requesting the Queen to dismiss Abigail, but the House refused to make itself a laughing-stock.

Anne put up with all this, not because of any lingering affection, but out of fear. The terrible Sarah was openly casting slurs on her morals and threatening to publish her pitiful letters. The Queen trembled all the more at the prospect of such a scandal because she had become very popular. The oligarchy was delighted by her physical and moral shortcomings, thanks to which she presented the perfect example of a constitutional monarch. Although she could not even spell, the intellectuals, who had had a thin time under William, were grateful to her for encouraging the magnificent renaissance in the arts and sciences (she knighted Newton). The middle classes saw their own language, tastes and prejudices reflected in their Queen. Finally, the people worshipped her for her good works, and above all for the very English reason that she did not conceal that one of her ancestors had been a washerwoman.* If the letters were ever published, 'Good Queen Anne' would become the object of shame and derision. Nevertheless, Abigail's astute scheming was gradually strengthening Anne's will to resist her former favourite.

In February 1708 the Queen tried to loosen the Marlborough grip by replacing Godolphin with Robert Harley, former Speaker of the House of Commons and Abigail's cousin. The response was savage. In the course of a violent scene in the Privy Council, the Duke of Somerset dropped all pretence of speaking respectfully to the Queen. Harley was dismissed, and his secretary arrested, then hanged. The Marlboroughs remained all-powerful, and the Duke's prestige reached its zenith with Oudenarde.

In August of that year Queen Anne went in solemn procession to Saint Paul's to give thanks for the victory. The procession had already set out when Sarah saw that, contrary to her instructions, the Queen was not wearing jewels. She at once began to argue with her mistress, and a quarrel broke out between the two 'friends'. When they had taken their places in the cathedral, Sarah was heard silencing the Queen.

A day or two after the ceremony she renewed her complaints in a letter, and for the first time, Anne replied with dignity: 'After the commands you gave me in the church . . . of not answering you, I should not have troubled you with these lines, but to return the Duke of Marlborough's letter† safe into your hands, and for the same reason do not say anything to that, nor to yours

---

* On the side of her mother, Anne Hyde.
† Which Sarah had sent in her own support.

which enclosed it.' This unwonted tone made Sarah more cautious. A further letter from her, in a far more subdued tone, finished with: 'I shall never forget that I am your subject, nor cease to be a faithful one.'

Things were beginning to change in England, and Marlborough must have sensed it immediately. Five days after the incident in the cathedral he wrote to his nephew Berwick:

I would also assure you that no one in the world wishes for peace with more sincerity than I . . . Circumstanced as I am, I am inclined to think that the best way to set on foot a treaty of peace would be for the proposal to be first made in Holland, whence it will be communicated to me, and I shall be in a better position to help, of which you may assure the King of France.[2]

Secret talks had already started between France and Holland. Realizing that his footing was less solid in London, Marlborough wanted to counteract them so as to claim the credit for the negotiations and above all to profit from them. The day after the fall of Lille he advised, still through the medium of Berwick, that France should openly request an armistice and peace. He wrote on 30 October: 'You may be assured that I shall be wholeheartedly for peace, not doubting that I shall find the kindness [amitié] that was promised to me two years ago by the Marquis d'Alègre.'

Louis xiv had in fact offered him the enormous sum of two million livres in 1706.[3] Chamillart wrote to Torcy: 'If he is sincere, his friendship could be used.' But the King could not bring himself to buy the man whom he regarded as an adventurer and who had destroyed his power. He preferred to deal with genuine traders, his old enemies the Dutch.

The illustrious victor of Blenheim, Ramillies and Oudenarde was deeply offended that no one would condescend to subvert him.

[11]
Article IV

EXCESS of adulation at home and execration abroad had finally created an inhuman, artificial image of Louis XIV. He was generally regarded as a graven idol with a pedestal of forty years' success, which would crumble under the blows of ill fortune. Events proved otherwise. The Great King had been truly great when he incarnated a France worthy of being an example to the world. He surpassed himself now that, identifying himself more than ever with the nation, he bore his setbacks with incomparable steadfastness and nobility. 'I am as much a Frenchman as a King. Anything that tarnishes the *gloire* of the nation concerns me more than any other interest.'

His strength lay in his majesty and his calm. He was rightly compared to an oak feeling the strength of its century-old roots while the storm raged all around. Saint-Simon wrote:

> What stung the King was the torrent of exceedingly bold and immoderate lampoons against his person, his conduct and his rule that were to be found for some time posted at the gates of Paris, in churches, in public places and especially on statues of him, which were defaced by night ... There was also a multitude of verses and songs in which nothing was spared.

A threatening underground pamphlet was passed from hand to hand, which recited the notorious litany: 'Our unhallowed father which art in Versailles...'

The King found no support in his private life. Instead, he had to stave off the pious cowardice of Mme de Maintenon, openly committed to peace at any price. Nature provided her with a terrible argument. Since the beginning of December 1708 the temperature had been daily below freezing, and on 6 January 1709 the cold in Europe became so intense that even the Rhône, the canals of Venice and the mouth of the Tagus froze over. Livestock, and even rabbits in their warrens, died. There was a brief thaw, and then from 6 February to 6 March the cold grew still worse. By 4 February the next season's wheat was frozen in the ground: it was a disaster comparable to an earthquake or a tidal wave.

Mme de Maintenon wrote to the Princesse des Ursins:

How can you say, Madame, that God is not declaring himself against us, when he sends us a winter unexampled for a hundred and five or six years ... which not only spares not a single fruit for the present, but freezes all the trees? The olive trees in Provence and in Languedoc, the chestnuts in Limousin and the walnut trees all over France are ruined for years to come. We see the poor dying of hunger, but cannot succour them because our lands no longer yield!

The women of Les Halles marched on Versailles, bands of desperate vagabonds fled from the countryside, brigandage developed on a frightening scale, convents and châteaux were attacked and the mortality rate doubled. In Paris the poor were dying and the rich were becoming poor. In response to the unversal cry for 'bread and peace', Louis sent Rouillé de Marbeuf, an officer of the Parlement, to The Hague. He was received with an arrogance and rudeness worthy of Louvois himself.

Louis had renounced Spain on behalf of his grandson, and hoped to obtain the Two Sicilies for him in return, but the Allies had other ideas. To begin with, Marlborough was no longer anxious to end the war. During the winter Abigail had been working like a beaver. Queen Anne was slipping further and further out of Sarah's clutches, and the victor of Blenheim now feared that peace would also bring disgrace for them both. Since the Dutch were expecting England to leave them with seventeen Flemish towns at the expense of the Archduke and of France (Barrier Treaty, October 1709), he experienced no difficulty in having the luckless Rouillé shown out.

The King wept when he informed the Council of this rebuff. This time his tears came from the heart, and the ministers were thoroughly shaken. Torcy offered to go to The Hague in person to deliver the surrender of France, for Mme de Maintenon and the 'saints' had the upper hand. The old lion was ready to submit to the enemy's terms, but Torcy had to suffer great humiliations before finding out what they were. The Allies kept increasing their demands for spoils, and the Minister wrote that 'each sovereign prince would have felt dishonoured had he not demanded something to the detriment of the Crown.' He took advantage of a private conversation to offer Marlborough four million livres, but to no avail. Queen Anne was too dubious a factor.

The Allies meant to keep their conquests, compel France to relinquish much of Alsace and numerous towns (Lille and Strasbourg among them), and to dispossess Philip v co npletely. Torcy accepted, but now the young Queen and the near-septuagenarian Mme des Ursins confused the issue and proved so intransigent that the abdication of Philip v could not be guaranteed. The 'Duc d'Anjou' might refuse to go, and if he did agree, his people might not let him.

A long debate ensued, and became particularly heated after the Spanish had defeated an Anglo-Portuguese army without the support of France. This led to the drafting of the ambiguous Article IV: 'If the said term [two months] ends without the Duc d'Anjou consenting to the execution of the present convention, his Most Christian Majesty and the signatory princes and States will take the appropriate concerted measures to ensure its entire effect.'

Most historians have regarded this clause as an exorbitant, vindictive demand. The reality was not so straightforward. It is not over-fanciful to interpret Torcy's and Marlborough's behaviour as tacit complicity in breaking an agreement that neither of them welcomed, the former because it would destroy France, the latter because war safeguarded the power of the Marlboroughs and the Whigs. At all events, in spite of Rouillé and his free hand, Torcy refused to sign the forty-four articles of the 'Preliminaries', already ratified by the Allies, and succeeded in representing them as an ultimatum.

The unsuspecting Allies gave Louis XIV a week's moratorium, starting from 28 May. If he had signed at that date, hostilities would have been suspended during the two months that were supposed to see the downfall of Philip V: otherwise they were to be resumed at once. When Torcy sent the Preliminaries to Versailles, he wrote: 'Your Majesty is thus entirely at liberty to reject these conditions altogether, *if, as I believe, the state of his affairs permits*; or to accept them if he should deem it his unhappy duty to terminate the war at all cost.'

Torcy arrived at Versailles on the evening of 1 June, and the Council met the next morning. An anxious, excited crowd thronged the anterooms. Everybody wanted to know what was happening, and no one succeeded, nor would posterity be any better informed if the Hungarian Prince Rakoczy had not had a secret agent, Vetes, at Versailles, and above all if the war office had not been harbouring a spy in the pay of the English, very much better informed than Dangeau or Saint-Simon.

Vetes' report, dispatched on 3 June, was published together with his memoirs in 1855. Those of Marlborough's anonymous agent are in the Sunderland archives.[1] They reveal that the Grand Dauphin, Bossuet's unworthy pupil, rediscovered the instincts of his race on that day of 2 June, and tipped the scale of fate.

The Duc de Beauvillier, spokesman of the party of the Saints, delivered an eloquent speech in favour of surrender. Opinion was swinging towards him when Monseigneur, finding that his favourite son was in danger of being deposed and dispossessed, discarded years of caution and spoke out to his father so vehemently that their audience was dumbfounded. Then he turned on the startled ministers and reminded them that he would be their master some day, and that if they held out for peace now, they would have to answer to himself later. Having said this, he stamped out of the room.

Rouillé was on his way back to The Hague that same evening to announce the breakdown of the negotiations. 'What!' cried Marlborough, seemingly taken aback, 'Is there then no counter-proposal?' There was not. While Prince Eugène and Heinsius bitterly regretted the lost opportunity, Marlborough wrote to his wife: 'If I were in the place of the King of France, I should venture the loss of my country much sooner than be obliged to join my troops for the forcing of my grandson.'

He thought that the Queen would no longer be able to refuse him the coveted title of Lord High Constable, but domestic warfare had broken out between Sarah and Abigail, and the Queen had no wish to humour the husband of her persecutor.

Beaten on that ground, Marlborough was also beaten in the battle of wits by Louis xiv. The King knew the power of propaganda. Flourishing Article iv, which he interpreted as brutal coercion, he did what would once have been unthinkable and made the French the judges of his conduct by means of an open letter to the Governor of Paris:

Although my affection for my people is no less keen than that which I bear towards my own children, although I share all the hardships that the war is inflicting on such loyal subjects and have demonstrated to all Europe that I sincerely long for them to enjoy peace, I am convinced that they would of their own accord refuse to accept it on conditions contrary to both the justice and the honour of the French name.

This immensely effective appeal enabled extreme measures to be passed: the creation of a general ten per cent tax, ancestor of present-day income tax, and the conscription of forty thousand recruits on conditions that anticipated compulsory military service.

The King sent his gold tableware to the Mint, and no courtier dared eat off silver any longer. A spate of dishes, tureens and pieces of plate went to be melted down, although many people followed the example of Saint-Simon, an unwilling patriot: 'I confess that I brought up the rear ... I sent a thousand pistoles' worth to the Mint and locked the rest away.'

What the inquisitive little Duke seems not to have scented was that the nature of the war had been altered by Louis' actions. The failure to make peace was much regretted in Holland and England, where the tax-burden was becoming equally intolerable and ruin threatened. To ordinary Englishmen, the only purpose of keeping up such efforts when the Alliance had achieved its aim and France was on her knees was to go on lining the pockets of the London bankers and especially the Marlborough family. The lampoons against Louis xiv were matched by the pamphlets against the Duke, who had made the error of not getting the world of letters on his side.

The French reaction was exactly the reverse. It was no longer a matter of defending an empire on behalf of the Bourbons, or of being the chief power on the Danube, the Ebro, the Adige and the Scheldt, but of defending native soil. Louis said as much to his grandson, and suggested that he leave Spain.

Philip v answered through the medium of his wife that he would rather die than abdicate, whereupon the French troops (with the exception of twenty-six battalions obtained by the Dauphin), the French advisers and the French ambassador himself abandoned the peninsula.

The masses were stirred by a war that had become a national struggle for survival. Not since the time of Charles vii had there been such a sense of unity in France, and not until the Revolution did it reappear. The fact that the demigod obsessed with his own greatness was able to lead this movement proves that he really was what Goethe was to call him, the *man-king*. Louis xiv had in a sense taken to himself the *gloire* due to the victories and masterpieces of his reign. When the time came he assumed the misfortunes also, and incarnated the will of a nation determined to triumph over them.

[12]

Family Matters

A NATIONAL recovery demands its sacrificial victims and its popular heroes. The kind-hearted Chamillart had managed to league against himself Meudon and the Saints, the princes and the marshals, Mme de Maintenon and La Choin. 'There arose a kind of dull murmur at Court . . . that either the State or Chamillart must perish.'[1] The King's attachment to his honest, loyal, if mediocre minister was practically a unique phenomenon, a crack in his granite exterior. However, he reluctantly bowed to the inevitable and Chamillart fell, to be succeeded by Voysin, a Councillor of State whose wife had gained Mme de Maintenon's friendship by finding her a dressing-gown during the siege of Namur. According to Saint-Simon, Voysin was:

. . . barely visible and hating to be seen, sullen and dismissive, abrupt, replying drily and in a few words, then turning his back on the rejoinder or closing his mouth to people out of some sort of dry, decisive, imperious quality; and his letters, devoid of all politeness, were nothing but laconic, authoritative answers or a master's brief announcement of his requirements.

Such a man was unlikely to arouse enthusiasm in the French, so Louis turned to Boufflers, the hero of Lille, and especially to Villars. Stifling his own objections, he had also made up his mind to recall Conti, another popular idol, but an exclusive diet of milk that his doctors had been foisting on him for some time cost the prince his life at the age of forty-five.

The summer months did not undo the damage caused by the winter. Famine was still rife and there were riots in Dijon, Rouen and even Paris. A further crisis arose when Samuel Bernard went bankrupt in Lyons, but Desmarets was able to limit the failure to that town, and Bernard retained his credit abroad. He remained the providential banker of the war.

Then, in July, yet another blow fell in the shape of a prodigious scandal within the royal family. With Mme des Ursins determined never to lay eyes on him again, the Duc d'Orléans had not returned to Spain.[2] Louis allowed him to send Flotte, his secretary, on the pretext of bringing back his baggage. Flotte stayed too long, saw too many people and talked too much. When he was about to leave for Paris, he was apprehended by the King of Spain's dragoons and thrown in jail. The seizure of his papers revealed Stanhope's letter, *still sealed*, and a memorandum by whose terms 'the principals of the high nobility' resolved that if France abandoned them they would 'put the Duc d'Orléans at their head and sacrifice their possessions and their lives in his support.' The arrest of two Lieutenants General, friends of his Highness, followed at once.

The news created an uproar at Versailles. Having provoked this scandal against the will of Louis XIV, Mme des Ursins could congratulate herself on her achievement. All those who hated or envied Philippe d'Orléans – jealous women, bastards, *dévots*, princes of the blood of lesser precedence and incompetent generals – scrambled for the kill. Madame la Duchesse even claimed that her brother-in-law had poisoned his wife, who was feeling very ill following the birth of her fourth daughter, Mlle de Montpensier. The monster was planning to marry the Queen of Spain, Charles II's widow, whose wealth would enable him to topple Philip V with more despatch. As soon as he was crowned he would inflict a similar fate on his second wife and place the diadem on the head of Mme d'Argenton.

Spurred on by the furies of Meudon, and always ready to enter the lists on behalf of his favourite son, the credulous Dauphin demanded his cousin's head without more ado. This exalted example, and the obvious hostility of Mme de Maintenon, drew the mass of opportunist courtiers into the fray. There is no telling what might have happened if Philippe's wife had not fortunately recovered.

Orléans attempted to vindicate himself, saying that he might have committed an imprudence, even a culpable one, but that he had never conspired against his nephew. His transactions had provided only for the contingency whereby events might force Philip V to relinquish his throne. Was it not preferable, if this happened, that the inheritance should remain in French hands?

These explanations could not gloss over so obvious an offence. A member of the Royal Family, and above all a military leader, was failing in his duty when he assumed the failure of a cause which it was his mission to defend. At the same time there was no proof of actual treason, otherwise there would not have been so much guile and dishonesty invested in bringing to light a non-existent crime.

Louis reserved judgement on his son-in-law's pleas. Although his ever-present suspicions of the aspirations of younger sons had been aroused, he would rather have hushed up such a chaotic affair. The party of the Saints, grateful to the Duc d'Orléans for his loyalty to Fénelon, came timidly to his defence. The Duc de Bourgogne even tried to placate his brother, but nothing could prevail against the shrill slanders of Mme des Ursins and Madame la Duchesse, and the more insidious voice of Mme de Maintenon. The King of

Spain, Monseigneur, the Duc du Maine (despite a show of helping his brother-in-law), everybody except the fair-minded Comte de Toulouse and the scrupulous friends of the Duc de Bourgogne wanted to dispose of the one Prince capable of acting like a statesman.

Louis consulted his ministers, none of whom dared to offend the heir to the throne, still less the unspoken wishes of Mme de Maintenon. The Chancellor received instructions to prepare the Duke's impeachment. Just when Philippe's hopes had been rising, he now found them savagely destroyed. His pleasures were depicted as base orgies and what had seemed venial in the Grand Condé or Gaston d'Orléans was condemned in himself as unforgivable wantonness. The triumphant cabal was already arguing over the appropriate ceremonial for the execution of a prince of the blood.

Fortunately, despite the harassments of the royal family and Mme de Maintenon's mute obsession, the King's sense of dignity and infallible equilibrium soon showed him the proper course of action. His eyes were opened to the dangers inherent in the gratuitous besmirching of his family and the crown itself, and a few casual remarks gave the court to understand that his Majesty considered the affair to be of no consequence and was astonished by all this commotion. The rumours died down at once, and the Chancellor shelved his files.

Nevertheless, the affair was not at an end. The King's suspicions and Monseigneur's resentment cast threatening shadows on Philippe, and the court avoided him as if in fear of catching the germ of his disgrace. After three years of hope, he relapsed into solitude and idleness. Discouragement and worry did their work, and the luckless hero became less rebellious and more vulnerable. It was at this moment that he acquired or gave vent to a timidity, indecision and frivolous indifference that were the legacy of his father.

It was the fate of this easy-going Prince to arouse violent hatred in others. Philip v's bitter resentment of his uncle never abated, to the great misfortune of Spain and France alike. Mme de Maintenon and Mme des Ursins must have been given pause a few years later when they saw the antagonism fostered by their own malice shatter the Franco-Spanish unity that had cost so much in bloodshed.

[13]

A Nation Aroused

ON 10 June Marlborough's spy sent the following report:

The King has written that peace is at an end. Mons. de Villars was delighted at this letter. He read it to the whole army, and asked the soldiers and officers if they did not wish to avenge the honour of the King which his enemies were insulting. So saying, he called for cheers from them all, and when they threw their hats in the air he threw his up too. It is felt here that this General, although light and vain in his talk, inspires audacity in the soldiers and leads them well *and as the French like to be led*, and that he is a lucky risker. Thus all hope he will do well.[1]

Villars had the soul of a hero and the tongue of a braggart. Both proved invaluable. Although he declared himself ready to fight a decisive battle in the open, he took defensive measures and threw up a solid line of fortifications against the Allied armies of 120,000 men, an utter Babel of tongue and uniforms.

The French army, by contrast, displayed complete cohesion. Many peasants had been driven into enlisting because they could find no food elsewhere. They were desperate enough to prefer a glorious death under an indomitable leader to slow starvation. The general mood had also infected the court, where the ageing Boufflers asked to be appointed second-in-command.

The French defensive line could be outflanked if the enemy took Ypres at one end or Tournai at the other. Marlborough wanted to lay siege to the former, while Prince Eugène opted for the latter. The previous year, the Englishman's strategy would certainly have prevailed. Now, palace intrigues had weakened his position so much that he fell in with the prince's opinion without a murmur.

The Coalition was exasperated by the vigorous defence put up by the garrison of Tournai. In May the spoils of France had been theirs for the taking: now they were stubbing their toes on a molehill. When Tournai eventually fell and the Allies invested Mons, Louis authorized Villars to stake everything on a single throw. The result was Malplaquet (11 September 1709), the most terrible battle the West had seen, or would see again until the last campaigns of Napoleon.

The Allies were disconcerted to find themselves opposed not by the demoralized Frenchmen of Ramillies and Oudenarde but by the 'insolent nation' of Neerwinden. The outcome hung in the balance for a long time and the Allies suffered enormous losses. They won narrowly thanks to Marlborough and to the fact that Villars was wounded in the leg and knee. Boufflers ordered a withdrawal, but prevented the confusion that had proved fatal after Blenheim and Oudenarde and halted the army in good order between Quesnoy and Valenciennes. The Allies lost 24,000 dead, the French 12,000. At Versailles 'the honour of having fought for so long and lost only the possession of the field was accounted a victory.'[2]

Eighteenth-century Europe, less blasé than that of today, was horror-struck by the news that after peace had been so close, thirty-six thousand men had fallen in a single day. The Allies could not admit that all this carnage had barely enabled them to capture Mons. On the other hand the French, who had grown accustomed to defeat, were elated at having stemmed the tide. Villars was created a duke on his sickbed and became a national hero at the very time when Marlborough ceased to be one.

The Whigs voted him an address of thanks, but one of his lieutenants, the Duke of Argyll, blamed him in the House of Lords for wasting human lives. The Queen refused him the title of Constable once again.* She was a gentle woman who never signed a death warrant without trembling, and was horrified by the butchery which Abigail kept describing as so many burnt offerings to Marlborough's greatness.

The termagant Duchess made matters even worse:

Sarah's judgement was warped by her hatred of Abigail, and she was tormented out of all prudence or proper self-respect by jealousy of her triumphant rival. She obtruded herself upon the Queen; she protested her party views; she asked for petty favours, and attributed the refusals to the influence of Abigail. Abigail Masham had become an obsession to her, and she acted as if it were possible to tear the Queen away from her by force.[3]

This being his ancestor, Churchill dutifully leaves the main point unspoken: if the Duchess paid no heed to her husband's entreaties and refused to restrain herself, it was because she counted on the scandalous potential of 'Mrs Morley's' letters, and was openly threatening to publish them. Her recriminations finally succeeded in rousing the spirit of Mary Stuart in the timid invalid, and gave her the courage to prepare one of the greatest coups d'état in history.

Every evening Abigail Hill conducted Harley, the secret Tory leader, to Anne by way of a secret passage. This strange conspiracy spelled trouble for

* By a curious coincidence, Boufflers asked for the same reward. In Saint-Simon's version, the King was displeased, and the marshal relapsed into semi-disgrace of which he died two years later.

the Whigs, who were pilloried by a fire-eating clergyman, Doctor Sacheverell, during a sermon on the text 'In perils among false brethren'. The Whigs made the mistake of impeaching Sacheverell, and the trial gave the people the chance to demonstrate their violent hostility to the government, for while the oligarchy had been growing tremendously wealthy the masses had been suffering almost as much as the French. The price of bread was rising steadily and the debtors' prisons were crammed.

The Doctor received a fairly light sentence, but the popularity of the Whigs had crumbled. Sarah now requested an audience in order to acquit herself of the accusations made against her, for the court was still reverberating with the scandalous stories retailed by the Queen's former favourite. 'What I have to say in my own vindication will have no consequence in obliging Her Majesty to answer,' the Duchess wrote, in a letter that, after many hesitations, decided the Queen to face the ordeal. The Queen listened to an hour-long spate of complaints, reproaches, protestations and tears. When Sarah paused, Anne told her calmly: 'You desired no answer and you shall have none.' The two women never saw one another again. It was the end of a reign and, for Europe, the beginning of a new era.

The world was changing rapidly. While France was escaping dismemberment, her old ally Sweden was succumbing to Peter the Great at Poltava, and Russia made her unexpected entry onto the international scene.

[14]

The Sacrifice of Port Royal

In a deplorable perversion of the spirit of religion, devout monarchs had a tendency to expiate their sins and ingratiate themselves with Heaven by means of persecution. It was no accident that the year 1709 found Louis xiv's greatest difficulties coinciding with an example of his deepest intolerance.

The trials of humanity had not diverted the theologians from their debates. A formulary devised by the bishops to condemn the five 'propositions' of Jansenius half a century previously was still a matter of contention. 'Should the sacraments be administered to a man who had signed the formulary while believing in his heart that the Pope and even the Church can be mistaken in the facts?' This problem had flared up again in 1701. In 1703 the Jesuits persuaded Philip v to order the arrest of Father Quesnel, the Jansenist theologican, who had taken refuge at Malines. Two years later Pope Clement xi issued the bull *Vineam Domini Sabaoth*, which the nuns of Port-Royal refused to accept. In spite of his Jansenist leanings, Cardinal Noailles deprived them of the sacraments by an ordinance that the Archbishop of Lyons, Primate of the Gauls, broke on 8 April 1708.

Louis xiv was exasperated by these quarrels. They meant nothing to him and he took any manifestation of non-conformity as an affront.

Father La Chaise had wanted to retire for some time, but the King was becoming more and more averse to seeing new faces around him, and would not hear of it. Saint-Simon describes the situation in which Father La Chaise now found himself: 'The infirmities and decrepitude which soon overtook him could not release him. Splayed legs, dim memory, shaky judgement and blurred understanding – strange inconveniences in a confessor – nothing discouraged the King, and to the very end he sent for this corpse and dispatched the usual business with it.'

When Father La Chaise died the King, much to Mme de Maintenon's annoyance, instructed Beauvillier and Chevreuse to find him a new Jesuit confessor. How was it that these virtuous and gentle dukes picked on a wild man, a stranger to the court, who was the scourge of his order? Obviously they did not assume such a responsibility without consulting their oracle. Fénelon was obsessed by hatred of Jansenism, as well as by his grievances against Cardinal Noailles, who had been one of his judges at the time of the Quietist controversy. The Jesuits, who by an unwritten law provided the royal confessors, happened to have available a man who was a bitter enemy of both Jansenism and Noailles. Indifferent to anything that did not contribute to the greatness of his order, Father Tellier was wedded to his old grudge against the author of the *Provinciales* and against those whose ideas Pascal had shared. He also nursed a personal grudge against Noailles, who had been responsible for the condemnation in Rome of Tellier's book about Chinese rites.

One final consideration swayed Fénelon and Colbert's brothers-in-law during the disaster of the winter of 1709, to which their decision added another: all three were convinced that the wrath of God must be appeased, and that this involved making the King redouble his intransigence where orthodoxy was at issue.

Of all the portraits in Saint-Simon's frightening gallery, Father Tellier's is the most sinister:

> ... violent enough to terrify the most respectable Jesuits ... insolent, impudent, impetuous, knowing neither manners, moderation, degree nor regard for others ... to whom all means were good if they achieved his ends, and whose blind, gloomy, terrible features ... encountered in some dark woodland corner, would have inspired fear.

This is a harsh verdict, and it is tempting to disregard it, seeing that the shrill little Duke holds it against Father Tellier 'that he never proposed anything for himself'; 'that he belonged to the dregs of the people and made no attempt to hide it'*; and that he had a mind 'ceaselessly diligent, devoid of any other interest, hostile to all dissipation, society and amusement'. But the evidence is overwhelming: it was Tellier who gave the proportions of a tragedy to an old dispute that had been dormant for a century.

He found little difficulty in egging on the King. Louis xiv had been brought up to detest Jansenism, which ran counter to the teaching that legitimized his own power, and to fear Port-Royal, the powerhouse of a seditious philosophy. When he was exhorted to propitiate the God of Armies by sacrificing a handful of disobedient nuns, no great reflection was required. For Louis, humane emotions never outweighed raison d'état.

It was therefore decided to remove and disperse the nuns and to destroy Port-Royal. 'They proceeded to raze house, church and all the buildings, as is done with the houses of regicides, so that not a single stone was left standing.'[1] The dead themselves were hauled out of the desecrated cemetery and dumped elsewhere, 'as offensively as can be imagined'.

The Jesuits were not yet satisfied, for Cardinal Noailles remained. Father

---

* When the King asked him whether he was related to the Le Telliers, the Jesuit shocked the court by replying: 'I am a poor peasant from Lower Normandy, where my father was a farmer.'

Tellier said 'that either he must lose his own position, or the Cardinal his.' A new kind of war of religion broke out. Mme de Maintenon, who was linked so closely with Noailles, merely groaned. She wrote to him: 'It is not for me to judge and condemn, I can only be silent and pray for the Church, the King and yourself.' The Cardinal suspended all Jesuits from preaching or hearing confession. Voltaire wrote: 'Those who persist in all these disputes would do well to cast an eye over the general history of the world, for observation of so many nations, customs and different religions shows how small a figure is cut by a Molinist or a Jansenist on this earth.' That kind of talk would have been beyond the understanding of a son of Anne of Austria.

[15]

The Posthumous Return
of Mme de Montespan

THE Grand Conti had died on 22 February 1709. M. le Prince, his father-in-law, followed him to the grave on 31 March, and M. le Duc, his brother-in-law, on 3 March 1710. To compensate for these losses, on 15 February the Duchesse de Bourgogne gave birth to a sturdy little boy who received the title of Duc d'Anjou. It was the future Louis xv,

Mourning and rejoicing did not prevent the court from indulging in intrigues as devious if not as gay as during the palmy days of the 1660s. At their centre was a new figure, a fourteen-year-old child, a half-siren, half-demon, whose autopsy was later to reveal an abnormal, 'cracked' brain.

Elizabeth of Orléans, Mademoiselle, daughter of the Duc d'Orléans and grand-daughter of the King, bore a striking resemblance to her grandmother, Mme de Montespan. She had her beauty, wit, seductiveness, temper, perversity, monstrous pride and taste for strong drink and affairs. The absence of education, the neglect of a mother she had been taught to hate, and the weakness of an indulgent father had left a clear field to her errant passions. Already she was mistress of the Palais Royal. The King himself showed real affection for the ravishing and somewhat disquieting creature who restored to him Athénaïs in her dawn, just as the Duchesse de Bourgogne had given him back Henrietta of England.

A marriage was being arranged between Mademoiselle and the Duc de Berry, third son of the Dauphin, when the events in Spain placed the Orléans family beyond the pale. During this ordeal the young girl was the mainstay of her father, and became his confidante, friend and inseparable companion. In the meantime, Madame la Duchesse was taking advantage of the situation to net the Duc de Berry and marry him to the eldest of her six daughters, Mlle de Bourbon. The party of the Saints was thrown into an uproar at the prospect of the second son of France enlisting among the enemy, that is, into the Meudon faction.

The Duc de Saint-Simon acted as their emissary. He persuaded the Duc d'Orléans to restore himself to grace by relinquishing Mme d'Argenton and then leading an edifying life at last. The tactic worked. A league was formed between Mme de Maintenon, the Duchesse de Bourgogne, the Duchesse d'Orléans and the Saints, all of them determined to prevent the Bourbon-Berry match. Madame la Duchesse was furious, and chose this moment to circulate the tale of the incestuous relationship between Mademoiselle and her father, a slander that the Duc d'Orléans never lived down. The King, who knew his formidable daughter, disregarded the story, and Elizabeth was married to the Duc de Berry on 10 July 1710 in the chapel at Versailles, whose recent completion had put the finishing touch to the palace.

Hardly a week after the wedding the Duchesse de Berry began to display her folly and malice. Jealous of the Duchesse de Bourgogne, who had worked so effectively on her behalf, and annoyed at owing her new station to the party of austerity, she separated two loving brothers and dragged her husband into the Meudon camp.

At twenty-four, the Duc de Berry was a good-natured young man, plump, fair, and a great eater, hunter and lover of horses and violent exercise. 'He would not be such a simpleton,' wrote Charlotte Elizabeth, 'if he had not been brought up so ignorant, but he knows absolutely nothing.' He thought of himself as 'a dolt and an ass, incapable of anything', and was infatuated with his young wife, who had him at her beck and call.

Elizabeth took such unfair advantage of him that the Duchesse de Bourgogne complained to Louis, and he had to pause from his strenuous labours to scold her. The Princess flared up at first, then burst into tears. Another reminder of the Montespan era.

[16]

Miracle in London and Madrid

ALTHOUGH the French had recovered their spirit, their situation was still critical. Louis XIV, once so contemptuous of public opinion, realized that he could not ask for enormous sacrifices without being prepared to do as much himself. He reopened negotiations with the Allies and offered to abandon Philip V; leave Strasbourg and Breisach to the Empire and Lille and Maubeuge to Holland; give up his sovereignty over Alsace and retain only the 'prefecture'; block up the port of Dunkirk; raze all his fortresses from Basle to Philippsburg; and finally to contribute subsidies to help the Archduke to dethrone his grandson.

This was a gamble. Louis XIV could not conceivably have resigned himself to so many losses and humiliations at the precise moment when the wind was changing in London, but it was necessary for the King to have done his utmost for the peace of his subjects, and for his enemies to have given him the attributes of a martyr. Only then would it be possible to continue the struggle. It is impossible not to admire the iron nerve of the old man worn out by moral and physical trials, who could still risk such an outrageous gamble.

The allies fell into the trap. At Gertrudenberg, in Holland, they heaped insults on the French ambassadors Huxelles and Polignac before communicating their demands: the King must 'with his forces alone compel his grandson to cede Spain and the Indies within a term of two months . . . It was a case of take it or leave it.'

As he broke off the negotiations, Louis was able to speak the words that would rally his people around him: 'Since it is necessary to fight, I would rather fight my enemies than my children!' At the same time Huxelles and Polignac were writing to the indignant Dutch: 'We are convinced that we shall soon see the English generalissimo relieved of his post and disgraced, or treated in such a fashion that he could not continue to serve with honour, and then the fall of the present ministry and the dissolution of Parliament.'[1]

Fénelon had other ideas. He wrote a new impassioned letter – whether inspired by love of the public good or hatred of Louis is open to question – to the Duc de Chevreuse, meant for the King:

You will tell me that God will uphold France, but I ask where is the promise. Do you deserve miracles at a time when your imminent and total ruin cannot make you change your ways, when you are still hard, haughty, ostentatious, unapproachable, insensitive and ever ready to vaunt yourself? Will God be placated when he sees you humbled without humility, confounded by your own faults without wanting to confess them, and prepared to begin anew if you could have two years' breathing-space?

It is most improbable that Louis ever saw this high-flown appeal for surrender. Marlborough took Douai, but the Queen succeeded in dismissing the Secretary of State, his brother-in-law Sunderland. The negotiations had ended on 20 July. On 2 August the Duke wrote to his wife: 'The French king is so reassured by our most recent events in England that all the letters from Paris make a point of the zeal being displayed in prosecuting the war.'[2] On his side, the Imperial ambassador informed Prince Eugène: 'My fears are stronger than my hopes.'[3]

His fears were justified: on 8 August Queen Anne dismissed Marlborough's ally Godolphin, who had been acting as Prime Minister. Harley became Chancellor of the Exchequer, and not long afterwards Henry St John (subsequently Viscount Bolingbroke) was promoted secretary of state. Sarah, quite beside herself, went from one house to another disseminating her sorry secrets, quoting 'Mrs Morley's' letters, exaggerating, blackening and besmirching everything.

At the end of September the Queen announced the dissolution of Parliament. Electoral feeling rose higher than many could remember. The Whigs were overwhelmed, losing 270 seats and composing barely a third of the new Parliament. This event was as vital to the destiny of France as the entry of the United States into the two world wars of the twentieth century.

As soon as he saw his hopes realized, Louis summoned Mesnager, a Rouen businessman and a convenient go-between with his Dutch and English colleagues. Mesnager was to attest: 'It is impossible for me to describe the King's transports of joy.'* Louis had intended to send him to London at once, but had to contain his impatience. Although the Tory government had resolved to make peace, it did not dare to publish its intentions. Feeling was still running high against France, and party strife too bitter. Ministers were afraid that they might be accused of treason if their opponents should get the upper hand again. Consequently they announced their decision to pursue the war, and confirmed Marlborough in his command until the right moment came. Europe had to remain at war.

In the archives of the French foreign ministry there is a curious fragment: the minute of the dispatch in which Louis XIV informed Blécourt, his chargé d'affaires in Madrid, of the impending breakdown of the Gertrudenberg

---

* Minutes of Mesnager's negotiations with the English court.

talks. It contains four lines in Torcy's handwriting, lightly scored out in pencil by Louis, which read: 'At the same time, the King of Spain must make the most of these circumstances favourable to himself, since affairs could otherwise come to such an extreme pass that it would no longer be possible for me to refuse what I have rejected hitherto [the dethronement of Philip v].'

Philip's grandfather disapproved of this tone. He intended to heal the wounds he had inflicted by abandoning his grandson in the thick of the fray, and to restore family harmony with the help of Mme des Ursins. Following Louis' 'advice', Philip v made his way to the army, but asked for Vendôme to be sent to him. Louis agreed, at the instance of the Duc de Bourgogne, nobly practising the forgiveness of trespasses. However, before Vendôme arrived on the scene the Allies defeated Philip v at Saragossa and captured Madrid. A miracle of loyalty now occurred. From grandees in their carriages down to the last beggar trudging through the dust, the population of the capital accompanied the Queen and her son in their flight from the invader. The Archduke who had been dubbed 'the horror of the people' did not even dare to enter Madrid, although it is true that he placed little reliance on the English.

Vendôme finally made his appearance. He sent a report to Versailles, and the King replied: 'I have reached a decision about the situation you describe in Spain, and you are to use my troops for a minimum of six months to facilitate the success of the enterprises of his Catholic Majesty to keep him on the throne.' 'A lot can be done in six months,' Vendôme commented. He forced the Allies to evacuate Madrid, pursued them and cut them to pieces at Villaviciosa. Stanhope surrendered. Louis' gamble was paying off.

These events in Spain decided Harley. An unsuccessful attempt on his life had made him very popular, and he was bubbling with ideas. One of them enabled the Tories to increase their financial strength to rival that of the Whigs. Since banking was the mainstay of his opponents, his mind turned to commerce and to its most profitable branch, the slave trade. As part of the campaign against Philip v, the British navy had been blockading the shipment of Africans to South America. There could be no better basis for an agreement with France and Spain than the restoration of this traffic, especially if England could make substantial profits from it. The problem was how to conduct negotiations without the knowledge of the people, Parliament and the government itself, in which Shrewsbury was the only minister who shared the secret of the Queen, Abigail and Harley.

One of Louis' minor spies in London was the Abbé Gautier, deliberately forgotten by Tallard when he had left his embassy in 1702. Gautier had become chaplain to the Imperial embassy, where a great Jacobite noblewoman, Lady Jersey, attended mass. She mentioned Gautier to Harley. One day in February 1711 Torcy was flabbergasted to see his own agent, in the guise of a travel-stained priest, transformed into a diplomatic envoy of England. Without more ado Gautier asked: 'Do you want peace? I bring you the means of negotiating it independently of the Dutch, who are beneath the King's attention.' Torcy noted in his memoirs: 'It was like asking a man who had been dangerously ill for a long time whether he wanted to be cured.'

Peace is difficult to restore after the horrors of a relentless war. It was pursued for months with infinite pains and precautions, facilitated by the death through smallpox of Joseph I at the age of thirty-three, and the accession of Archduke Charles to his throne, but hindered by the efforts of Marie-Louise of Savoy. With death now hovering over herself, the fiery Queen would not let her husband be plundered now that he was finally victorious.

Marlborough resumed the campaign and captured Bouchain, while Duguay-Trouin took Rio de Janeiro and returned laden with wealth. Nevertheless, peace drew slowly nearer.

The lowly Abbé was succeeded by the poet Matthew Prior, who went to Paris with plenipotentiary powers from the Queen, no minister having dared to receive or delegate them. The first demand transmitted to Torcy by Prior concerned an English monopoly on the importation of slaves to America. Naturally it was followed by a host of others, in particular the cession of Gibraltar, the demolition of Dunkirk and the expulsion of the Pretender. Torcy argued, and Mesnager crossed the Channel in his turn. He stayed at the house of a midwife and only went out at night. The Preliminaries to a general peace, together with a Franco-British Treaty, were signed on 8 October.

There was uproar in Vienna and Holland and among the Whigs and the household of the Elector of Hanover, heir to the throne, when the public learned what were given out as the French proposals (the Treaty remained a secret). The Tories retaliated, and Swift published *The Conduct of the Allies*, a merciless indictment of the innumerable failures of the Habsburg Empire and the United Provinces to stand by their commitments. The Coalition was in pieces.

The government was defeated in the House of Lords at Marlborough's instigation, but had an overwhelming majority in the Commons. The victor of Ramillies was charged with misappropriating public funds, and the Queen at last had a lever to prise him out of his appointments. A general conference opened at Utrecht on 29 January 1712. Only the Emperor refused to be represented.

Torcy wrote in his memoirs:

Who would have thought at the time that the prosperity of that formidable league of the enemies of France and Spain had reached its furthest limit . . . that the supreme Being . . . would so abruptly put an end to the spate of so many victories . . . that in spite of the efforts of the League and the advantages it had won, the descendant of

Saint Louis, chosen by Providence to rule Spain, would remain firmly on his throne, recognized ... by an enemy army that returned home with nothing ... but the crushing burden of the debts contracted to sustain their vast designs?

Yet neither Louis xiv nor Philip v had seen the last of their ordeals.

[17]

Genesis of a Golden Age

On 16 April 1711 Monseigneur died of smallpox at Meudon, where the King had taken up residence together with those rare individuals who had survived the disease and were immune.

Versailles, jolted awake in the middle of the night by this bombshell, looked like an overturned ants' nest. A rumbling like the sound of an army on the march heralded from one storey to another the arrival of messengers, the confusion of people pulled out of bed and the scurry of dazed servants. Never in the fifty years of his drab existence had the Dauphin caused so much feeling and commotion. Mob-capped ladies and half-dressed gentlemen crowded into the apartments of the Duchesse de Bourgogne, casting sidelong glances at one another and trying to anticipate the consequences of the upheaval. With a single pin-prick, hopes, plans and ambitions had been exploded. In place of the timid heir whose survival would have seen the triumph of Vendôme's cynical clique, the greed of Madame la Duchesse and the unfettered whims of the Duchesse de Berry, the pallid Télémaque with his entourage of peers and confessors now came to the fore. War was giving way to peace, debauch to asceticism, laxity to austerity.

Sitting on a settee between his wife and his brother, the new Dauphin was quietly weeping – 'in good faith', as Saint-Simon admiringly noted – for a father who had detested him. The Duc de Berry was sobbing aloud, as was the duchess, who was seeing all her calculations reduced to nothing. Marie-Adélaïde was painfully squeezing out a few tears and dabbing them over her face. Mme d'Orléans, the intimate enemy of Monseigneur and Madame la Duchesse, had to delay her entrance to mask her jubilation. Everyone's feelings seemed to be dictated by self-interest. The fat, kindly Charlotte Elizabeth arrived in tears, and caused considerable surprise because no valid reason could be found for her grief.

At Meudon, Louis was visibly distressed, but by an odd quirk that may have been the final manifestation of his unconscious jealousy of his heir, 'after giving a general order to do what was needful, he left all the arrangements to the officers of ceremonies.' Fearing infection, they fled the château with the other servants as soon as the King had departed. Six Capuchin monks from a nearby monastery had to assume the task, with the result that the body of the King's son received the treatment of a beggar. It did not even occur to anybody to have it embalmed. 'The workman who made the coffin made it too narrow, and only got the body into it by dint of bouncing on the Dauphin's stomach with his knees.'[1]

This was the sad epilogue to the sad life of a prince born to reign over half the world. Saint-Simon, a fanatical supporter of the Duc de Bourgogne, states that he would have made a 'pernicious' king, but this is by no means certain. Monseigneur had become extremely popular with the common people, in particular with those denizens of Les Halles who played no small part when times were troubled. At the moment of the death of Charles II of Spain and above all at the decisive Council of 2 June 1709, he had proved that he would lack neither resolution nor authority once he escaped the clutches of his father. Free of the appalling complex that Louis XIV induced in him from the cradle onwards, his character, in spite of his lack of schooling, might have revealed itself in a surprising light.

Jacques Roujon has written:

The son of the Sun King would undoubtedly have proved less dazzling on the throne than his father. Might he not have resumed the tradition of the father-figure kings in close contact with their subjects? ... Nature seems to have created him to serve as a transition between a magnificent but outworn system and the sweeping reforms that would become feasible when time had healed the scars of a long and terrible war.[2]

After this warning from Heaven, Louis XIV won a great victory over himself. For the first time he ceased to regard himself as the be-all and end-all of the interests of France. He relinquished part of his power to the Duc de Bourgogne, the new Dauphin and treated him as the personification of the future. He ordered the ministers to work with the Prince, and even opened his almost inaccessible heart to the grandson who was so unlike himself at the same age.

The Dauphin, deeply moved, responded with all imaginable respect and submission. He soon acquired the ease and authority he had hitherto lacked, without losing any of his scruples and application. Almost immediately he attracted to himself genuine admiration, respect and love, and came to incarnate everybody's hopes. As for the Sun King, he was transformed to the point of appearing modest, altruistic and patriarchal. He told the Assembly of the Clergy: 'Here is a prince who will soon succeed me and who, by his virtue and piety, will make the Church flourish still more and the realm more fortunate.'

But Louis XIV's good deeds were almost always destined to have painful consequences. Behind the touching façade, the machine that was to destroy the Bourbons was being constructed. At Cambrai, Fénelon had no doubt that his dreams were about to become reality: the exile would soon be a Cardinal and First Minister. Lacking the patience to wait, he was preparing for the future reign.

He corresponded regularly with his former pupil, using Beauvillier and Chevreuse as his permanent representatives. Throughout the summer they whispered, scribbled and held secret conclaves. Saint-Simon took great pains to explain the prominent part he played with the Dauphin in this situation. He claims to have sent him innumerable memoranda of which not a trace remains because the King is supposed to have burned them, without having the curiosity to examine them, immediately after the Prince's death. This biased evidence is unfortunately all we have. No contemporary seems to have suspected the intimacy between the heir to the throne and the little duke who was generally regarded as a pest. The obvious inference is that thirty years later Saint-Simon described things as his pride and imagination created them in retrospect. It would not have been the first time.

With or without his assistance, Fénelon drafted the blue-print of a state founded not on human opportunism but on the divine laws and an inflexible morality. First of all, the Archbishop dealt with the main objects of his aversion. The tender cleric nursed a ferocious hatred of Calvinists and above all of Jansenists. The first step he proposed was their annihilation. The way would then be clear for a reform that was to suppress luxury, licence, ostentatious buildings, carriages that were too comfortable and those modern houses where some people were so far gone in sybaritism that they no longer wanted to crowd their family into a single bed!

Each individual would assume the position for which his birth marked him out. A caste-system would petrify the realm. State functions and service, military rank and judicial power would be the exclusive preserve of the nobility. Its privileges – even the occasionally extravagant relics in which some professed to see the real causes of evil – would be confirmed and reinforced.

The administration that Louis XIV had packed with commoners was to disappear. The sovereign, reduced to a benevolent authority-figure, would be assisted, not by ministers, but by councils and assemblies of varying degrees of influence (provincial, diocesan). At the summit of the hierarchy, the Estates General would assemble compulsorily every three years and be free to sit for as long as they pleased. Procrastination, chicanery and the dangers of anarchy were thus instituted on every level. M. de Cambrai was entrusting absolute power to a tiny minority, but organizing it in such a manner as to expose it to the worst failings of democracies. In addition, he assumed that this minority would spring up fully-fledged with the requisite skills, and made no proposals for preparing it for its task. *

All these fantasies were to be handed down devoutly from generation to generation to the future Louis xvi, who at the age of twelve was collecting the *Moral and Political Maxims* garnered from *Télémaque*.

In effect, the reign that could be predicted for the grandson of Louis xiv already prefigured that of the guillotined king, for while the Dauphin drew his inspiration from *Télémaque* in the same way as his unfortunate descendant, and was, like him, virtuous and good-natured, he too had his Marie-Antoinette, in the person of Marie-Adélaïde, whom he idolized. She was shallow, imprudent and fickle (she was in love at the time with the handsome Abbé de Polignac), but strong-willed when it came to conducting an intrigue, paying off a score or simply satisfying a whim, and had every intention of ruling in his name. After all, her sister Marie-Louise was doing likewise in Spain.

For the time being, however, the young Princess was another welcome adjunct to the happy prospects of the French people, who after so many disasters watched the war drawing to a close and the monarchy flowering anew.

---

* The substance of Fénelon's ideas is to be found notably in the *Essay on Civil Government* edited by Ramsay, based on conversations between Fénelon and the Chevalier de Saint-Georges (the pretender James Stuart); the Letter of 4 August 1710 addressed to Beauvillier and Chevreuse; and the *Examination of the Conscience of a King* written by the Duc de Bourgogne and published in 1734, then censured and forgotten until the accession of Louis xvi.

[18]

The Harvest of Death

ON 7 February 1712 the Dauphine, who had been ill with a fever for two days, was unable to get out of bed. Her head throbbed painfully and her body was covered with ominous blotches. Her Highness's chief physician, Boudin, vainly went through the gamut of blood-lettings, emetics, opium and even chewing-tobacco.

Married since childhood and worn out by nine pregnancies including six successive miscarriages and by the reckless sacrifice of her health to pleasure or etiquette, Marie-Adélaïde had no reserves of energy to combat the illness (probably measles or scarlet fever) that mystified her entourage. She died on 12 February, in her twenty-seventh year. Overcome with grief, the King and Mme de Maintenon took refuge at Marly. 'There will never be a moment of my life when I shall not miss her,' wrote Louis, to whom the young woman's charms had brought the one ray of brightness in his declining years. The Dauphin was inconsolable, but he had contracted the fever at his wife's bedside, and had to take to his bed upon his arrival at Marly.

In accordance with custom, the post-mortem was conducted in the presence of the Dauphine's ladies-in-waiting. There were two conflicting diagnoses: the first was that some noxious substance had 'burned' the patient's blood, the second that the Princess had been poisoned. The ensuing arguments were long, bitter and unenlightening.

Faced with two theories, the King wisely ordered silence, but it was already too late. The news was spreading among the sensation-loving courtiers and had already reached the drawing-rooms, shops and taverns of Paris. The ambassadors were sharpening their quills: like her grandmother, Henrietta of England, the Dauphine had been murdered.

There was further hissing from the vipers of the Meudon coterie and the little court of the bastards. How unfortunate for the reputation of M. d'Orléans that he concocted so many mysterious potions in the laboratory of the chemist Humbert! What a regrettable reminder of his former friendship with the Marquis de Feuquières, a man once implicated in the Poisons Affair! As for his motive for such a revolting crime, perhaps the solution might lie with the Duchesse de Berry, who had been so violently jealous of her sister-in-law and was taking few pains to disguise her joy at being henceforward the first lady of the kingdom.

Meanwhile, one by one, the Dauphin was traversing the same painful stages that his wife had already completed. He breathed his last on 18 February, and the whole nation mourned him. There followed another autopsy, and further contradictory diagnoses by the physicians. This time the sinister rumours became a fanfare. The Saints could not admit that their idol had died of natural causes. They were the first to cry murder, closely followed, for differing reasons, by all the other Versailles factions. Charlotte Elizabeth wrote of her son: 'They are already afraid that he will have a part in the government. It is for that reason that they strive to make him hated in Paris and at Court.'

The Dauphin left two young children, the Duc de Bretagne and the Duc d'Anjou, of whom the elder took his father's title at the age of five. The designated guardian of the young Prince, who would certainly be inheriting the throne in the not far distant future, was the Duc de Berry, but everybody knew what a cypher he was and how firmly he was under the thumb of his wife. On Louis' death the only member of the royal family in any position to exercise power would therefore be the Duc d'Orléans. Too many people were dead set against such a prospect: immediate steps must be taken to eliminate the free-thinker, the spoil-sport, the revolutionary.

Out of the smouldering ruins of the party of Monseigneur and the party of the Saints, the party of the bastards had risen. Since his military discomfiture, the Duc du Maine had been quietly forging ahead. Limping on his club foot and alertly deferential, he heaped smiles, politeness and promises on the most humble gentlemen, flattered officials and danced attendance on members of the Parlement. With constant modesty, discretion and timidity, he had extracted one disproportionate favour after another from the King – the Cordon Bleu, a peerage, command of the Swiss and Grisons guards, the artillery, the five brigades of carabineers (with reversion), spoils from La Grande Mademoiselle, the wealthiest heiress in the realm, the governorship of Languedoc, and honours identical to those of the princes of the blood. He dogged the footsteps of his father and former governess, diverting and wheedling them.

Forgetting his former disappointments, Louis xiv admired the young man's looks, subtlety and zeal. Mme de Maintenon could never recall without emotion the struggle she had put up to preserve the life of the condemned child, the dramatic nights when she thought that she had lost him, and the cruel visits to bone-setters and quacks. Such devotion gives powerful claims to the recipient.

In the charming palace of Sceaux, the tiny, turbulent Duchesse du Maine – Bénédicte de Condé – had become the focus of a group of artists, writers, scholars and men of pleasure, which was gradually extended to include financiers, magistrates, soldiers and a host of flatterers and intriguers. Here the infamous slanders that were only whispered at Marly were sounded aloud – the Duc d'Orléans wanted to give the crown to his daughter (his mistress!); he wanted to become King himself; it was well known that he summoned up the devil; the chemist Humbert was the heir to La Voisin's secrets!

With meteoric speed, these rumours 'filled the Court, Paris, the provinces, the darkest corners, the depths of the most distant monasteries, the most useless and desolate wildernesses, and eventually foreign lands and all the nations of Europe.'[1] Mme de Maintenon was already prejudiced against Monsieur's son and shocked by his scepticism and his morals. She believed, possibly in good faith, that an unbeliever like Philippe was capable of anything. For his own part, the King was in the grip of the direst uncertainty.

As early as 22 February Philippe was insulted by the mob while on his way to take holy water to the unfortunate Dauphin. The following day he had to lead the gloomy procession that took the two bodies from Versailles to Saint-Denis. Having left the palace at six o'clock in the evening, the cortège did not pass the walls of Paris until two in the morning. Sixty grey and sixty black musketeers and two companies of gendarmes and light cavalry preceded the six mourning carriages, each drawn by eight horses. Innumerable torches raised dull gleams from swords, armour, capes and helmets. The King's pages went three abreast. The Dauphin's and Dauphine's crowns and the insignia of the Saint-Esprit were carried by three noblemen. Four mounted chaplains were the pall-bearers.

The rapt, silent crowd at the gate suddenly flared up at the sight of the carriage emblazoned with the Orléans arms. Fists were shaken, whistles blended with shouts, insults and curses. Near the Palais Royal, the angry mob tried to break through the cordon of guards and tear the murderous uncle in pieces. Horses reared and women screamed. Without the wise precautions taken the previous day, the Prince would not have come out alive.

Philippe had to accept that the French regarded him as a poisoner. It came as a terrible blow to a man whose close friends reproached him with being over-sensitive. The Duke loved his nephews and had great expectations of their accession. If he had really harboured criminal intentions, he would have protected his interests better by getting rid of a sovereign who was for ever hostile to him. Raging with despair and indignation, Philippe sought out the King, demanded justice and offered to commit himself to the Bastille forthwith, in order for a public trial to broadcast his innocence. Louis refused.

A few days later, it was the turn of the Dauphin's two sons to go down with the 'purple', the mystery disease that was ravaging Paris and Versailles. The doctors took charge of the little Duc de Bretagne, bled him and made him vomit until he died (7 March). The Duc d'Anjou would have suffered a similar fate had not his governess, the Duchesse de Ventadour, torn him from the clutches of science by administering a counter-agent that was luckily incompatible with any other remedy. The child recovered, but remained extremely weak, and there was a widespread conviction that he would soon go the way of his brother and parents.

The outcry from the cabal redoubled: Philippe d'Orléans was going to exterminate the royal family so as to carve out his passage to the throne! From Madrid, Mme des Ursins added fuel to the flames. She had a Franciscan friar arrested in Poitou on a charge of plotting the murder of the King of Spain, and Philippe had to take the blame for this new outrage also.

Bombarded from every side, the luckless Duke tried in vain to redeem himself. The storm of recriminations was gradually replaced by an even more unbearable calm as a silent ostracism reduced him to the condition of a pariah. If he appeared in company, conversation died at once. If he mingled with a group, it moved off and re-formed at a distance. The hero of Turin, Lérida and Tortosa could no longer find a walking-companion, a partner for lansquenet, or even someone to talk with.

Everything fades in France and is quickly forgotten – especially scandal – but the Duc du Maine had staked his future on his brother-in-law's downfall and proved diabolically skilful at keeping the abominable rumour alive in Paris, at Versailles, in the provinces and even abroad. In the public eye, Philippe d'Orléans was an incestuous poisoner, another Cesare Borgia, a Richard III.

Behind his waxen mask, the aged King was riddled with anxiety at the sight of his dynasty reduced, apart from the King of Spain, to a great-grandson who seemed to have one foot in the grave, an utterly incapable grandson and a dishonoured nephew.

[19]

The Blazing Sunset

THE deaths in the House of France had caused consternation at Utrecht, where the negotiators watched their fragile edifice collapsing. There was only one point on which everybody was agreed, namely that the two-year-old Dauphin did not have long to live. Once he was dead, Louis xiv's crown would revert to Philip v, whose rights had been solemnly enshrined in 1700, but neither Holland nor England would ever accept the union of France and Spain under a single sceptre.

As early as March, St John demanded that Philip v renounce his claim to the French throne on behalf of himself and of his heirs, withdrawing in favour of the Duc de Berry and then the other members of the Bourbon family. Speaking for his master, Torcy invoked the organic law of the realm, based on the rights of primogeniture, and wrote:

> This law is regarded as the work of Him who has established all monarchies, and we in France are convinced that God alone can repeal it. Consequently, no renunciation can set it aside, and if the King of Spain gave his own ... it would be a mistake to receive it as an expedient capable of preventing the trouble that it is intended to avoid.

St John's quick riposte was: 'You will allow us in Great Britain to be convinced that a prince may relinquish his rights by a voluntary cession.'

It took Louis xiv only five days to subordinate his dynastic scruples to raison d'état, but when he tried to persuade his grandson he came up against a brick wall.

Philip v's resentment after being left in the lurch by France in 1709, followed by the rapture of a victory that he attributed to divine intervention, seemed to have eradicated the last of the young man's Capetian leanings. Sequestered between a wife of twenty-five, not far from death, and a septuagenarian power behind the throne, and worn out by carnal and mystical excesses, he inhabited, like Charles ii himself, a universe peopled with visions and fantasies. The time was past when the sun of Versailles shining into the palace of Madrid had reminded him of a forgotten life. Muttering his paternosters with dull eye and pendent lip, His Catholic Majesty was a worthy successor to the series of Velasquez' models.

351

Already, Louis xiv only maintained his influence by courtesy of Mme des Ursins, yet he was obliged at every turn to threaten to withdraw his troops and subsidies. Philip v had allowed his grandfather to extract – painfully – the plenary powers that authorized him to negotiate on his behalf, and was indignant, in spite of so many reverses, that his states were destined to be reduced to Spain and the Indies. In exchange for the lost provinces, he demanded the French Mediterranean province of Roussillon.

To him, the idea of renouncing the heritage of his ancestors was sacrilege. Divine law required him to reign in Madrid and Paris, or at least, if the Dauphin survived, to be King of Spain and Regent of France. Nothing could make him violate this sacred principle. The immediate consequence was that the English govern nent was unable to defer sending an expeditionary force under the Duke of Ormonde to support Prince Eugène in a new campaign, the Allies having appointed him supreme commander in Marlborough's place.

The Tories were not prepared to reverse their policy, however, and St John wrote to Ormonde:

Her Majesty, my Lord, has reason to believe that we shall come to an agreement upon the great article of the union of the two monarchies, as soon as a courier, sent from Versailles to Madrid, can return; it is therefore the Queen's positive command to your Grace that you avoid engaging in any siege, or hazarding a battle, till you have further orders from her Majesty.

The postscript was no less significant:

I had almost forgot to tell your Grace that communication is given of this order to the Court of France; so that if the Mareschal de Villars takes, in any private way, notice of it to you, your Grace will answer accordingly. If this order is changed on either side, we shall, in honour, be obliged to give notice of it to the other.[1]

There exists another and even more sensational document that appreciably alters the account given by most historians of the events of 1712. It is a report from the Abbé Gautier to Torcy, dated 21 M. St John what Marshal Villars should do if Prince Eugène and the Dutch took the offensive. *He answered that there would be nothing to be done but fall on him and cut him to pieces, him and his army.*'

While Prince Eugène, wary of Ormonde, was hesitating over his objectives, a last effort was being made in Madrid. The English ministers had devised a transaction by which – since the Dauphin was going to die – they invited Philip v to cede Spain to the Duke of Savoy and become ruler of the Duke's estates, Savoy, Piedmont and Montferrat, with Sicily thrown in. When the time came, Philip would don the French crown and keep the three North Italian provinces, while Sicily would go to Austria.

Louis XIV was delighted with the plan. It reassured Europe, spared France a formidable dynastic struggle and provided an unexpected reward for all her hardships. True, the Bourbons would lose the empire of Charles II, but experience had proved the fragility of the union between the two courts, and the Great King, learning from past misfortune, set the nation's interests above the *gloire* of his House.

Louis wrote an urgent letter to his grandson, combining political reasoning with appeals to sentiment: Philip V would be able to make frequent visits to Versailles and re-create the family circle so tragically broken. Marie-Louise, so like her sister, would take the place of poor Adélaïde. . . .

Mme des Ursins' morose pupil, who managed to combine rabid obstinacy with non-existent will-power, resorted to his usual weapons, silence and inertia. Weeks passed. Prince Eugène went into action and laid siege to Le Quesnoy in northern France. Louis XIV then sent an ultimatum: his grandson must choose between the British proposal and the succession of Charles II, bearing in mind that in opting for Spain he would be renouncing the country of his birth for ever. In default of a prompt reply, France would conclude a separate peace and leave her ally to confront eight angry nations single-handed.

This firm attitude enabled a truce to be negotiated with the English ministers. The King did not baulk at suggesting that they should occupy Dunkirk, 'as a guarantee of good faith'. He did so because of the pressing danger from the Empire. Between 10 and 14 June a force of two thousand horsemen ravaged Champagne with impunity and almost succeeded in carrying off the Archbishop of Rheims.

Le Quesnoy fell on 1 July, but a few days later Ormonde parted company with the Allies and withdrew to Ghent, followed by his twelve thousand British troops. Most of the foreign mercenaries in the pay of the British refused to go with him.

With 130,000 men, Eugène still easily outnumbered Villars. He resolved to force the hand of fate by marching on Paris, and laid siege to Landrecies on 17 July. Versailles was in the grip of panic, but Louis refused point-blank to move when courtiers begged him to withdraw to Chambord. According to Voltaire, who obtained a great deal of information from the Duchesse du Maine, he now told Marshal Harcourt 'that in the event of a further setback he would summon all the nobility of the realm, lead them against the enemy, in spite of his age, and perish at their head.'

Eugène was in a hurry to settle the issue, and had adopted a 'strategy of exasperation' that led him to make mistakes. His lines were dangerously stretched, with his stores at Marchiennes, a long way from his headquarters on the far side of Le Quesnoy. Between these two points one of his lieutenants, General Albemarle, had been stationed to secure his lines of communication, and was dug in at Denain with seventeen battalions. The question of who first realized the vulnerability of his position and who deserves the credit for the resulting manoeuvre has been argued for two and a half centuries, and will never be settled. Once again it is Voltaire who provides one of the best accounts:

A curé and a Douai councillor named Le Fèvre d'Orval were the first to envisage how easy it would be to attack Denain and Marchiennes while taking a walk together in that direction ... Le Fèvre passed on his opinion to the intendant of the province, the intendant to Marshal Montesquiou, who commanded under Marshal Villars: the general approved and executed it. This action was indeed the saving of France, more so than the peace with England.

Marshal Villars sent Prince Eugène off on a false scent: a corps of dragoons advanced within view of the enemy camp, as if preparing to attack it, and while these dragoons then withdrew towards Guise the marshal marched on Denain with his army in five columns (24 July 1712). He stormed General Albemarle's entrenchments, killing or capturing every defender. The general surrendered together with two princes of Nassau, a prince of Holstein, a prince of Anhalt and all the officers. Prince Eugène came up in haste, but at the end of the action, with what troops he could muster. He attempted to attack a bridge that led to Denain and was in French hands, but lost men and returned to his camp, after having witnessed this defeat.

One after another, the positions along the River Scarpe towards Marchiennes were rapidly carried. The French pushed on to Marchiennes, defended by four thousand men, where the siege was pressed home so keenly that in the space of three days they were taken prisoner and all the military and food supplies accumulated for the campaign by the enemy were captured (30 July 1712). All the superiority was then on the side of Marshal Villars: the disorganized enemy raised the siege of Landrecies and saw Douai, Le Quesnoy and Bouchain retaken. The frontiers were secure. Prince Eugène's army withdrew, reduced by close on fifty battalions, of which forty were captured between the battle of Denain and the end of the campaign. The most signal victory would not have yielded greater advantages.

Although Louis was sick at heart, the news brought him a moment of indescribable joy. After coming close to foundering in one of the worst disasters in the history of France, the Sun King had finally preserved his realm and his gloire. His unshakeable courage in the face of misfortune had redeemed his mistakes. He shone once more in a blazing sunset.

[20]

Balance Sheet of a
Policy of Grandeur

MME DES URSINS intervened 'as suppliant and mother', but failed to bring Philip V round to his grandfather's point of view. Having prayed, communicated and consulted his confessor, he received a mystical illumination and made his decision known: he had become a Spaniard, and a Spaniard he would remain. As for France, he announced unexpectedly that her crown seemed to him to be 'too dazzling', and he made a gift of it to the Duc de Berry.

At Versailles, the aged King heaved a sigh of relief, while in London and Utrecht anxiety alternated with delight. The killjoy of Europe might be surrendering, but how was his renunciation to be made effective? Partisans of divine right in every capital declared that no such disclaimer could be valid: a prince could not discard his legitimacy.

As a pledge of good faith, Philip V consented to commission the Spanish Junta to formulate the renunciations itself, in the most binding terms. This text was then submitted to the scholars of Oxford University, as were the declarations by which the Dukes of Berry and Orléans relinquished their rights in Spain. The Queen and the Tories showed their satisfaction. Both Houses passed votes of thanks to the Duke of Ormonde, and Harley and St John were created respectively Earl of Oxford and Viscount Bolingbroke. This inequality of titles caused considerable friction between the two Ministers.

The new Viscount went to France, and was made welcome by the King and the court, who were at Fontainebleau. Louis presented him with the diamond that the Duc de Bourgogne had worn in his hat. Paris showed its enthusiasm in the course of a celebration at the Opera. Torcy extended lavish hospitality to Bolingbroke, and introduced him to a beauty who was also an expert at ferreting out state secrets, Mme de Tencin. The resultant affair was not unhelpful to French diplomacy.

Bolingbroke negotiated a renewal of the truce, then, in the privacy of Mme de Maintenon's apartments, a problem of a different nature was raised. Since the Sacheverell trial in 1710, Queen Anne had as good as recognized the legitimacy of her brother, the Prince of Wales, whom she called the Pretender.

She had been having references to her own divine right struck out of official acts.

True, she sometimes managed to disconcert her entourage by demanding measures against the son of James II, to whom she had no intention of deferring, but she was willing for the crown to pass to him rather than to her disagreeable cousin, the Elector of Hanover. Bolingbroke himself was in two minds on the question, and popular feeling remained violently opposed to the Papist prince, but Louis XIV still got the impression that on the Queen's death James Stuart would be able to return to London. He therefore agreed to recognize the Act of Succession of 1701, since it was destined to become a dead letter, to sacrifice the Dunkirk fortifications, the bugbear of the English, and even to banish the Pretender from France, in expectation of a triumphant return.

Now that these hindrances were removed, the final negotiations proceeded in an atmosphere of hope, almost of gaiety. Now and then, Philip V would stir up old fears in the diplomats and make them doubt his sincerity. In his subsequent proclamation to the Spanish people, he told them: 'I did not hesitate for an instant about the decision that I had to make, and in any case I was not given the least respite in which to take counsel and to deliberate.'

A report from Bonnac, the French ambassador, indicated one specific threat: 'The King of Spain will cede France to his brother, the Duc de Berry, but if the Duc de Berry were to die childless, he would not wish to have made a cession that benefited the Duc d'Orléans.' The antagonism between uncle and nephew had not abated in the slightest since 1709.

But there was no point in borrowing trouble. The future seemed clear and reassuring. The French were resigned to losing the Dauphin, and the sceptre would go the Duc de Berry, then to the little Duc d'Alençon, to whom Elizabeth had just given birth. Mme des Ursins' influence on the Queen of Spain would keep that country a satellite of France, while England would also gravitate towards her with the accession of a Catholic Stuart. It would be a resounding victory, so few years after the humiliations of The Hague.

In spite of dangerous advice from various quarters, Philippe d'Orléans made no attempt to dispute the new order in which he would have no part to play. After the King of Spain had solemnly pledged 'his faith and his royal word that he would procure the observance and accomplishment' of the renunciation in the Cortes, Berry and Orléans went in solemn procession to the Parlement to register the act that enshrined the surrender of their rights to the Habsburg inheritance.

That same evening the jubilant Spanish ambassador wrote to his master that French opinion set no store by these formalities and expected to see the Spanish monarch cross the Pyrenees as soon as the Dauphin had breathed his last. This foolhardy dispatch fortunately remained unknown to the chancellories of Europe.

On 11 April 1713 the Treaty of Utrecht was signed by France, Great Britain, Holland, Prussia, Portugal and Savoy. The Emperor refused to subscribe to it, and Philip v would certainly have followed suit without his grandfather's pressure. The Treaty restored Lille, Aire, Béthune and Saint-Venant to France, leaving her, apart from a few strongholds, with her frontiers of 1679. Holland got possession of the famous barrier of fortresses, but the war had ruined the Dutch, and they never regained their great power status. An irony of fate thus enabled Louis xiv to see the belated success of the enterprise launched by himself and Colbert, and which had cost him so dear. But instead of accruing to the mortal enemy of the Low Countries, the advantage went to their associate, England. In the same way, after their common victory in 1945 the United States caused the disintegration of the British Empire and made Great Britain its satellite.

That empire had just been born at Utrecht. England received Gibraltar, Minorca, Hudson's Bay, Nova Scotia and Newfoundland. She acquired the right to send a ship annually for thirty years to trade with South America, in addition to the slave treaty. Colbert's dream was dead, and France had lost her chance of maritime hegemony.

If the Emperor had agreed to negotiate, Louis xiv would have ceded Landau, Strasbourg, Huningen and Breisach to him. When he refused France demonstrated how strong she still remained in spite of her fatigue. Assured of the benevolent neutrality of England, she crushed the Imperial armies in a single campaign, in spite of the genius of Prince Eugène.

Villars carried Spires, Worms and Landau, broke through the enemy lines and besieged and captured Freiburg. Threatened even in his hereditary states, the Emperor gave way. The two Commanders-in-Chief, both of them objects of general admiration and courtiers' malice were appointed to negotiate the peace.

The Treaty signed at Rastadt was ratified by the German princes. Not only did Louis xiv make none of the concessions he had originally offered, but he also obtained the reinstatement of his allies the Electors of Bavaria and Cologne. The Emperor finally relinquished Alsace and Franche-Comté, although he also received vast compensations at the expense of Philip v – the Spanish Netherlands, Milan and Naples. The Duke of Savoy recovered Nice and became king of Sicily, and the Elector of Brandenburg was recognized as king 'in' Prussia. This time it was Philip v who did not want to sign.

According to the textbooks, the English hegemony of 1713 succeeded the French hegemony of 1659. This is a misconception. In spite of her fleets and her wealth, England was in no position to impose her will on whomsoever she pleased, as Louis xiv had been when Mazarin died. The same was true of the other victor, the Emperor Charles VI. France remained holding the scales between them, always provided that there was no revival of the old Alliance.

This was the Europe produced by the immense diplomatic and military effort of Louis XIV, neither what he had envisaged at the height of his powers, nor what he had been resigned to at his lowest ebb.

It is impossible to evaluate the King's policy fairly without examining its twin aspects. Two centuries previously Francis I and Charles V had inaugurated the battle of giants that concluded with the treaties of 1713–14. As heir of the one and descendant of the other, Louis XIV combined the ambitions of a Capetian and a Caesar. As a Capetian, he wanted to enlarge his 'duelling field' and make it invulnerable, and he succeeded: in 1713 France numbered more towns and provinces than in 1661, towns and provinces permanently integrated into the nation. It was no longer necessary to stand guard over the Pyrenees, and the kingdom no longer had a single dangerous enemy at its gates. It was to remain secure from invasion until the end of the Ancien Régime.

Louis XIV was unable to lay hands on the whole of the Spanish Netherlands, and has been criticized for letting the opportunity slip, but the truth is that it never arose. Either England or Holland was always strong enough to deny France access to Antwerp. The dynasty had begun the patient extension of its boundaries in the eleventh century, when Philip I had seized the castle of Montlhéry only a few leagues from Paris. Louis XIV pushed them back to Lille, Besançon, Strasbourg and Landau.

He would probably have enlarged his realm still further had not the Habsburg blood and the teachings of Mazarin, steeped in the Roman tradition, aroused a dream of empire. The man cast by the Treaty of the Pyrenees as the arbiter of nations had hopes on a number of occasions of dominating them all, confiscating the crown of the Germanic Caesars, absorbing the Spanish monarchy and bringing the West under the Capetian sceptre from the Danube to Canada and from Brabant to Peru. In this he failed, like many others before and after him, but Louis XIV took a revenge that none of his peers achieved.

The intellectual flowering of France replaced the triumph of her arms. Europe, or at least its élite, became French by speaking the language, drawing inspiration from the creations and copying the customs of the land where the Great King reigned. Even among his bitterest enemies, there was not one prince whose descendants were not obsessed by his example. Because he succeeded in becoming both the sovereign and the patron of the great men of his age, Louis XIV left an indelible imprint on civilization. His was a more difficult and more glorious masterpiece than a great many conquests.

[21]

Expiatory Schism

WITH the loss of his grandchildren, Louis XIV rediscovered human suffering. He had forgotten it since the departure of Marie Mancini half a century earlier. Yet neither his work nor his timetable changed, and he remained as impassive as ever: 'Our reason should conceal these vulgar emotions when they detract from the public welfare, for which alone we are made.'

The court was nonetheless sunk in despondency, and Mme de Maintenon wrote: 'Everything is dead here, life has been taken away.' There were no more fêtes or receptions, and even the games of faro flagged among those in whom Louis had encouraged a gaming mentality so as to keep them under his control. The Duchesse de Berry, dazzled by her new status, cavorted like an unbridled mare, laughed, shouted and made no secret of her affair with M. de La Haye, but all her excitement only caused a few bubbles to break on the surface of a stagnant lake.

Peace came, and with it the animal assertion of life that follows disasters. Curbed at Versailles, youth ran unfettered in Paris, which after a long eclipse became the centre of cultural life and the capital of pleasure once again.

Mme de Maintenon was mortified by the wreck of all her plans for the future, which had counted on her influence over the Dauphine. Worn out and desperate, she trembled at the prospect of amusing an 'unamusable' man by herself. She was seventy-eight, and the King nearly seventy-five – extreme senility in that era. Torn between grief, memories and fear of tomorrow, they no longer had a word to say to one another. Now and then Louis' eyes would fill with tears. The Marquise was paying the price of her extraordinary rise to fortune. She would have preferred to retire to Saint-Cyr, but could not abandon the aged tyrant, still all too youthful in spite of his dismal moods, or the sun-temple that had become a necropolis.

She summoned Louis' childhood friend Villeroy to her assistance and gave him free access to the private rooms. Villeroy managed to bring smiles to the King's tragic countenance by recalling the days of their youth and telling stories of the events of 1660. They were often joined by the Duc du Maine. Affectionate, sober, devout, intelligent, adroit and in touch with events, he went out of his way to appear not so much the King's son as his respectful disciple. His calculations were correct. As he looked distastefully about him, Louis mused that only the Duke would be capable of following the path that he himself had marked out.

His health does not seem to have been undermined by his ordeals. He still rode and hunted, and drove his little barouche through his beloved gardens, which he never stopped improving. Little by little he regained his taste for amusements, and especially for music.

Private parties became more and more frequent in the apartments of Mme de Maintenon. Dinners, concerts, scenes from plays and acts from operas, lotteries where all the tickets were black [i.e. winners], even dinners at Marly, or sometimes the Trianon, and always the same small numbers and the same ladies, always Marshal Villeroy at the concerts and performances.[1]

Extracts from *Le Bourgeois gentilhomme*, *L'Avare* and *Georges Dandin* were performed. France might have been spared any number of misfortunes if Molière's wit had protected the King against the fanatics who surrounded him.

This society, already ruffled by the first breath of the revolution and preparing itself for the monstrous orgy of the Regency, was drunk with theological disputes. As might have been foreseen, the tragedy of Port-Royal had given a new lease of life to Jansenism. Father Tellier, Cardinal Bissy and Cardinal Rohan (who may well have been Louis' own son since his mother, the Princesse de Soubise, had been the King's mistress at the time of his birth) had persuaded him that before he died he must rid the Church of this cancer in payment for the remittance of his sins.

The old monarch fell into the trap. He repudiated Gallicanism and adopted the Ultramontane doctrine of his worst enemy, Fénelon. Father Tellier and his friends 'employed the royal authority to kindle the sparks that could have been extinguished. Instead of copying Rome, which had imposed silence on both parties on several occasions; instead of curbing a monk [Tellier] and controlling the cardinal [Noailles]; instead of banning these combats in the same way as duels and reducing all the priests, like all the lords, to being useful without being dangerous ... Louis xiv asked Rome for a declaration of war.'[2] Clement xi yielded. He issued the bull *Unigenitus,* which condemned the work published by Father Quesnel forty-two years previously and promulgated a kind of charter of Ultra-montanism. The papal nuncio delivered this bombshell to Versailles on 2 October 1713.

Intending to prevent a schism, Louis had provoked one. An immense uproar ensued, and Noailles and seven other bishops rejected the bull. They had the backing of the majority of the Sorbonne and the Parlement. Gallicans and Jansenists rose in revolt against the Holy See. There had never been a graver breach in the theological foundations on which the Church's strength and the monarch's authority rested.

The moral prisoner of a small group of fanatical priests, the King once again made the fatal blunder of using violence against ideas. Noailles was banished from Versailles, the 'recusant' bishops were exiled to their dioceses and the Jansenists suffered more concrete persecution, two thousand being thrown into jail. Such severity naturally inflamed passions ever further. The Parlement, tamed and docile ever since 1652, refused to register the bull. Paris was also aroused, turned the affair into a laughing-stock and jeered at Rome, Jesuits, clergy and dogma.

The struggle went on until the Revolution. It spelled total failure for the policy of Louis xiv, whose desire to establish unity of faith discredited the Church, provoked a schism and dangerously undermined the foundations of the régime. Nothing contributed more to the rise of free-thinking than his aspirations towards regimenting people's consciences.

[22]

Death Plays Tricks

DEATH continued to cast its shadow over royal families, sowing confusion, shaking the fragile foundations of the peace and falsifying the calculations of men. Scorning the little Dauphin, whom the entire world had written off, it removed first the son of the Duc de Berry, then the valiant Queen of Spain. Since Christmas 1713 it had been hovering above Queen Anne, to the detriment of any rapprochement between France and England.

Another shattering blow came on 26 April 1714, when the Duc de Berry had a riding accident that ruptured a vein in his stomach. He mentioned it to no one, did not curb his spectacular appetite and was dead on 4 May. Some weeks later his widow gave birth to a daughter who lived for barely twelve hours. There was further talk of poison.*

Berry's death caused as much consternation in Europe as that of his elder brother. By the terms of the Treaty of Utrecht, the heir of the Dauphin was now Philippe d'Orléans, and to break this commitment would be putting a match to the powder-keg, but the idea of adhering to it revolted Philip v, horrified Mme de Maintenon, shocked the partisans of divine right and profoundly disquieted Louis xiv.

The King did not believe in his nephew's guilt, but severely condemned his conduct. Without sharing the extreme feelings of his immediate entourage, Louis could not entirely shake off the doubts that were fostered so sedulously by Mme de Maintenon.

To avert a terrible dilemma, he clung to the unlikely hope of the Dauphin's miraculous survival. The letter, if not the spirit, of the Utrecht treaties did not provide for the eventuality of a regency. No legal obstacle therefore debarred Louis xiv from entrusting the guardianship of the future king to Philip v, his nearest relative. It was out of the question to put the child in the hands of a man suspected of the wholesale murder of his family, but this argument might not allay the fears of the English.

---

* Since the affair between the Duchesse de Berry and M. de La Haye, the Berry ménage had been going from bad to worse. The Duke wanted to be rid of his wife. Elizabeth was unbalanced, and was the only person who had it in her character to commit a crime against those who got in her way. She has been accused, but there is no evidence.

The Duc d'Orléans found himself in a demoralizing situation. In spite of his new status as guardian of the balance of power in Europe and defender of the dynasty's national traditions, he was still a suspect and a pariah. The intrigues of chancelleries and the dispatches of ambassadors were full of him, yet he knew no more than the rawest Versailles kitchen-lad.

Philip v was trembling with anxiety and hope. He sent an ambassador extraordinary, Cardinal Giudice, who pestered Louis so continuously that he had him recalled.

Louis did not want to jeopardize the treaties, but neither was he resigned to seeing his nephew mount the steps to the throne, and the members of his entourage were aware of it. They took advantage of an attitude implanted in him seventy-three years previously when, as a small child, he had had to act out an appalling performance for Louis XIII on pain of being parted from his mother. His subsequent execration of his father had to some extent alienated the Sun King from him and from his forebears; the almost immemorial tenure of the Crown had induced him to think of it as his personal property. His pride was another factor that enabled him to consider his own blood a more valid title to the succession than that of his predecessors. Furthermore, it was surely the duty of the head of a dynasty in peril to graft a new shoot onto the withered old branch.

Mme de Maintenon succeeded in making insidious use of these suppressed motivations, and the King came to an unprecedented decision. On 29 July 1714 he solemnly announced that his natural children had been elevated to the rank of genuine princes of the blood, entitled to inherit the crown if the legitimate lines became extinct. By taking this extraordinary step, he was tacitly entrusting his favourite son, the Duc du Maine, with the destinies of the kingdom.

The higher nobility was beside itself with envy, and although it registered the Edict, the Jansenist Parlement seized this fresh pretext for demonstrating its opposition, but in spite of the mutterings of Saint-Simon there was no real upheaval in France.

Grave news arrived from London at this point. Bolingbroke, who had become Oxford's mortal enemy, had assumed the single-handed direction of the government with the avowed intention of repealing the Act of Succession. He claimed that six weeks would suffice to disbar the Hanoverian and restore a Stuart to the throne. He did not get his six weeks. The Queen died, and the Whigs, who had laid secret plans for such a contingency, had the Elector proclaimed King George I. Bolingbroke had to escape to the continent, where he became chief adviser to the Pretender.

Nothing now survived of the hopes that had been nursed at Versailles for the past two years. England had fallen into the hands of intransigent francophobes, ready to resume friendly relations with the Emperor and perhaps to embark on a new war.

It was in this atmosphere of rising crisis that the King resolved, against his better judgement, to make a will. It is possible that Mme de Maintenon, always so careful not to oppose him, plucked up the courage to exert pressure, but the decisive factor must once more have been the influence of the confessor and the cardinals. On 27 August he summoned the First President and the Procureur Général and handed them a large packet closed with seven seals, saying: 'Gentlemen, this is my will. Only I know what it contains.' Smiling sourly, he added: 'The example of the kings, my predecessors, and that of the will of the King, my father, do not let me be unaware of what could happen to this one. But they wanted it, they tormented me, they gave me no peace whatever I might say. Very well then, I have bought my peace. There it is – take it away. Whatever may come of it, at least I shall receive forbearance and not hear it mentioned again.'

Mme de Maintenon would have preferred Philip v to be Regent and the Duc du Maine to be Lieutenant Général and consequently in control. Fearing a revival of the war, Louis named the Duc d'Orléans President of a Regency Council, but one that would be packed with his enemies, reaching its decisions by a majority vote that was bound to go against him. The real power would be in the hands of the Duc du Maine, who was also appointed guardian of the young sovereign.

This will was unquestionably Louis xiv's most feeble action. Harassed by prayers and exhortations, the old man thought that he was paying a low price for the calm of his last days when he gave instructions that could not be enforced. In fact, the will was to have the effect of a time-bomb set to destroy the monarchy. Philippe d'Orléans had no choice but to nullify Louis' seed of dissension a year later, but had to restore its old prerogatives to the Parlement at the same time. Once re-established, the magistrates proved to be die-hards, jealous of their privileges and hostile to the most trivial reforms. Until 1788 they prevented the Crown from taking the measures that would have averted the Revolution. Louis xiv had bought his peace at the expense of his dynasty.

The document was concealed inside one of the pillars at Versailles, and its contents remained secret. Nevertheless, it still caused immediate trouble. At home, where Orléanists and supporters of Philip v confronted each other in violent disputes, it revived the party politics that had been unknown for sixty years. Abroad, England considered forming a new Coalition on the pretext of the general anxiety.

The exhaustion of Europe disposed of that danger, but another appeared before the year was out. Confined in the Medina-Coeli palace, with Mme des Ursins his sole companion, Philip v mourned his wife and waited impatiently for her replacement. The uneasy Princess pored over genealogies to find a queen poor enough to become a docile tool in her hands.

The former secretary of the Duc de Vendôme – dead of indigestion not long after his triumph – a devious Italian named Giulio Alberoni, son of a gardener in the employ of the Duke of Parma, suggested his master's niece, Elizabeth Farnese. Although the princess belonged in some measure to the Austrian clan, being also the niece of the dowager empress and of Charles II's widow, her poverty and smallpox-ravaged beauty singled her out for the role of grateful pupil. Mme des Ursins rose to the bait.

Elizabeth Farnese, married symbolically in Italy, prolonged her journey for several months, received numerous messages and much advice and caused great apprehension to the agents of the King of France. She met Mme des Ursins on 23 December 1714, in the little town of Jadraque. The two women had withdrawn for a brief tête-a-tête when the crowd was stunned by the sound of exclamations, an order, and the clatter of arms. Already the gilded coach with its escort of guards was carrying Mme des Ursins, still in full court dress, towards the Pyrenees, disgrace and exile.

A revolution had occurred. Philip V came under the control of an impulsive, violent woman whose will was guided by the wily Alberoni. In thirty years the besotted husband never left his wife's side: she was to exhaust his senses until he lapsed into complete dementia. Even their night-stools were placed side by side in a single alcove.

Louis XIV realized that from now on the Franco-Spanish unity that was the key-stone of his achievement would be at the mercy of a whim, a caress, a pair of adventurers. He tried to prevent the disaster, addressed not one word of censure, wrote graciously to the Queen and paid Alberoni a pension with six years' back-pay!

The Duc d'Orléans reacted violently to the arrival of the Princesse des Ursins, whom he considered as his worst enemy, and swore that he would not show his face at Versailles if she received an apartment there. The King, strangely eager not to alienate his son-in-law, relegated the Princess to Paris and kept her waiting for several months before granting a single audience. Her former friendship with Mme de Maintenon had cooled considerably, and she plunged from the most dazzling light to the most ignominious darkness.

It needed just such an astounding reversal of fortune to bring home to Louis that it was time to reconcile the King of Spain and the Duc d'Orléans. The opportunity to shift the entire responsibility for their mutual antipathy onto Mme des Ursins was too good to miss.

Philip V pretended to yield to his grandfather, but did not relinquish any of his ambitions. He fed on fantasies. 'It is likely,' he wrote, 'that the King has named me guardian in his will and that he has appointed the man who will deputize for me. There is no ground for believing that he has replaced me with a prince, *my adversary*, who would disunite the two Crowns.'

In November 1714 death played tricks that might well have caused total confusion. While the King continued to enjoy miraculous good health, the

Duc d'Orléans caught a fever and nearly died. Death then fell back on Fénelon. Worn out, feverish and in despair at the loss of his pupil, the archbishop had still gone on laying the foundations of his revenge. Whether the victor was Philip v, so close to his brother, or the Duc d'Orléans, a fervent admirer of the Swan of Cambrai, the latter was assured of imminent victory. Then all at once the interminable waiting broke down his health, and he died in January 1715.

[23]

The Twentieth Century's
Lost Opportunity

'HE was beginning to be so sick at heart because of his family's misfortunes
that he hardly took part in anything except where he was committed.'
Saint-Simon, who wrote these words, never suspected that the King, who was
so close to the grave, was thinking of the future and searching for the means to
secure true peace for Europe. During the last weeks of 1714 Louis realized that
the English Whigs were irremediably hostile, and conceived a bold new
diplomatic depature that might have changed the course of history. He saw
that the old nations, France, Austria and Spain, must unite against the
ambitions of the newcomers, England, Prussia and Russia, and took the
unwonted step of appointing to Vienna an ambassador* whose task would be
to promote this policy. He chose his representative, the Comte du Luc, from
Switzerland.

The instructions drawn up for Luc by Torcy in accordance with the
directives of the King, who signed them on 3 January 1715, constitute a 'grand
design' so breathtakingly radical as to induce speculation on how many
subsequent disasters mankind might have averted had it been pursued.

First of all, Louis averred:

... the happy dispositions that exist on either side towards the formation of a union
between the Houses of France and Austria as advantageous to their interests as it will
be essential to the maintenance of the general repose of Europe ... Their divisions, the
source of so many wars, have acted hitherto as a counterbalance to their mutual
greatness, and it will be by means of a perfect understanding that they will henceforward uphold the superiority that belongs to them.

The Bourbon-Habsburg rivalry was indeed an anachronism, and the
misfortunes of modern times arose out of its artificial survival for half a
century and subsequent perpetuation in the form of a stubborn prejudice.†
Only Louis XIV had enough authority to eliminate this prejudice from the
thinking of the Emperor, Philip V, and the statesmen of Europe. He continued:

---

* Since the start of his reign, Louis XIV had appointed only minsters to Vienna.
† Until 1917, when Austria offered a separate peace.

Never has there been a situation in which the designs of the King and the interests of the Emperor have been as mutually compatible as they are at present . . . Although that prince [Charles vi] may still have difficulty in divorcing himself from his views on Spain, yet it appears that he understands how useful it would be henceforward for him to maintain a good understanding with the King . . . He is beginning to realize that his views on Spain are becoming fanciful . . . and that it is not even in the interests of Europe to support them.

With extraordinary lucidity, Louis discerned the threat of an alliance that unleashed the Seven Years War forty years later, and paved the way for so many of the tragedies of modern times:

The King of Prussia,* the son-in-law of the King of Britain, has nearly sixty-thousand men in readiness, and the unity between these two princes seems all the more solid in that it is based on a common interest and on the hope they both have of enlarging their States . . . If it should happen, therefore, that the troubles in the North [the war between Russia and Sweden] came to an end . . . the Protestant party will find itself formed, and in a position to provoke wars far more unfortunate than those we have taken such pains to snuff out.

The King indicated the bases on which peace could eventually be signed between Philip v and Charles vi:

Since the King of Spain is willing to negotiate, there will be no time to lose in agreeing as soon as possible on the means of opening negotiations and the place where the conference will be held. When these have been started, it is the King's intention to do his utmost to surmount the difficulties liable to retard their success.

A Triple Alliance between France, Spain and Austria would have prevented the absurd war of the Austrian Succession in 1740, and thus the rise of Prussia and Russia, the former to the ranks of the great powers, the latter to becoming arbiter of Europe.† The twentieth century therefore had an opportunity to avoid the cataclysms it has suffered. Unfortunately the Comte du Luc, busy rebuilding the alliance between France and the Swiss Cantons, could not reach Vienna until July. Six weeks later Louis xiv was dead, and the opportunity with him. When Louis xv finally revived his grandfather's plan in 1756, it was already too late to halt the process that led inexorably towards two world wars.

Doubts have been thrown on the King's peaceful intentions, for while he was groping towards a rapprochement with the Emperor he was also taking measures against England. Major construction work had begun at the port of

---

* Frederick-William, father of Frederick ii, had been on the throne since 1713. He had married the daughter of George i of England.

† The arrival of Russian troops on the Rhine in 1748 determined Louis xv to sign the bootless peace of Aix-la-Chapelle, in spite of three years of victories. In 1762 Russia's volte-face saved Frederick ii.

Mardyk (although these had to be halted), and Louis was resuming relations with the Pretender, who had taken refuge at Commercy.

While the bankers, the Puritans and the army supported George I, the landowners put their hopes in James II's son. A Scottish uprising was being prepared, and the Pretender requested four hundred thousand livres and a ship to enable him to rejoin and revitalize his supporters. The King's treasury was empty, and he asked Philip V to advance the money. Louis was not seeking war, but knowing the hostility of the Whigs he expected aggression and tried to forestall it.

At this point the new English ambassador, the Earl of Stair, arrived on the scene. He ingratiated himself with Parisian society, the Parlement, the Jansenists and especially the Duc d'Orléans, a near relation of his own king,* and had secret talks with the Abbé Dubois, the Prince's former preceptor and adviser. At Versailles he gave such an exhibition of arrogance and rudeness that one day he went too far, and Louis XIV told him: 'I have always been master in my own house, and sometimes in others'. Do not remind me of it.' Stair remained silent, and later admitted that he had been overawed.

---

* George I's mother, the Electress Sophia, was the aunt of Charlotte Elizabeth.

[24]

Final Splendour, Final Anger

LOUIS XIV had a passion for order. He used his waning energies to restore it among the nations and above all in the Church of France, whose internal dissensions were causing him great distress. Father Tellier and the *dévots* of his entourage took advantage of his concern. Far from treating the aged monarch gently, they badgered him incessantly about the bull and the indomitable Cardinal Noailles, and threatened him with the anger of God. Louis tried to 'buy his peace' again by acceding to extremist measures: the convocation of a Council to depose Noailles, who had become the idol of Paris, and a Declaration by which any bishop not declaring his complete allegiance to the bull would be prosecuted.

The Parlement resisted and Louis found himself cónfronting one of the nightmares of his childhood, the men in red robes standing their ground against the monarchy and obstructing its aims. After trying in vain to persuade them individually, the furious King announced his intention of holding a *lit de justice*.

Towards Whitsun, these annoyances gave him a slight fever. The surgeon mareschal mentioned it to Fagon, the King's chief physician, and Mme de Maintenon, but they ignored him and the pious lady even showed signs of anger. However, the King was visibly wasting and sinking. People in England were laying bets about when he would die. Louis found out, and joked about it at supper, but was shaken nonetheless.

On 12 June he went to Marly, where he received the new Spanish ambassador, the Prince of Cellamare, whom Philip V had instructed to form a faction, corrupt ministers and generals and suborn the Jesuits – which meant that if Louis' will did not grant the Spanish king custody of the Dauphin, the ambassador was to secure it by a coup d'état. The friends of the Duc d'Orléans were making their own arrangements. As for Mme de Maintenon and the Duc du Maine, they wanted the King to institute a Regency Council and set it to work at once, so as to tie the Duke's hands, but the old man flew into a rage at the idea that they considered him no longer able to rule.

He went stag-hunting on 9 April, and attended a concert in the evening. The following day, after a last walk in the gardens of Marly, he returned to

Versailles yellow, ravaged, stumbling and unrecognizable. He was suffering from senile gangrene in one leg, although the physicians remained optimistic.

Too feeble to hold a *lit de justice*, the King sent for d'Aguesseau, the Procureur Général, on 11 August and ordered him to give instructions for the registration of the Declaration relative to refractory bishops.

The King tried every possible approach, and made no headway. Whilst displaying the utmost respect and devotion, d'Aguesseau eluded, declined and continually escaped. His smooth eloquence and long-winded circumlocutions, the stock-in-trade of the Palais, moulded and re-moulded all the forms of obedience so as to avoid obeying. The King was exasperated, as anybody will be when he finds resistance in what he took to be submissive.[1]

He lost his legendary calm, dignity and courtesy in a fit of temper that was all the more tragic for being his last, threatened to sack d'Aguesseau, stamped his foot and broke his cane over a marble table, but to no avail.

Everybody wanted to give the King the consolation of appearing once again in all his glory. The governor of a Persian province had sent an agent to France to discuss trade. When the man pretended to be the ambassador of Persia, the court fell in with the deception to amuse the King, and on 13 August the Easterner received the honour of a grand farewell audience in the Galerie des Glaces. Louis xiv, clad in black and gold and decked out in diamonds worth thirteen million livres, stood in front of the throne in spite of his painful leg and received the impostor's homage with all his customary majesty. The little Dauphin stood at his right, the Duc d'Orléans and the princes at his left. Drums rolled. The enchanted splendours of Versailles glittered as they had in his prime. It was the final splendour of the Sun King.

A Great Artist's Farewell

ALL the great figures of Louis' age possessed the art of dying magnificently and calmly. At the moment of leaving the stage, the most illustrious of royal performers achieved a masterpiece. Jean and François Anthoine, *valets intérieurs*, have passed on every detail of Louis XIV's last days, and the genius of Saint-Simon has added a sombre, stately poetry.

Only one regret tormented Louis as death approached, that of leaving the Church in the throes of anarchy. The persecution of the Protestants appeared to him as the guarantee of his salvation. For the rest, his Most Christian Majesty did not doubt that his slate was clean.

The Great King was not able to prepare himself as he would have wished. The further he declined, the more his entourage feared Philippe d'Orléans, strove to aggravate the old man's prejudices against his nephew and redoubled their pleas for restraining measures. Torn between these entreaties and the fear of committing an injustice fatal to his dynasty, the King experienced the final bitterness of his once 'delightful' *métier*.

He still would not hear of changing the rhythm of his life, and worked his usual hours in spite of the cruel ministrations of his physicians. One of their methods was to cause him to sweat profusely and then swallow forty figs and three glasses of water immediately afterwards. Fagon betrayed no anxiety. He had great faith in baths of aromatic wine, cinchona and ass's milk.

There was a significant pointer to future events on 22 August, when the King was in no state to review his troops, had the Dauphin take his place and gave him the Duc du Maine for a guide. The Duc d'Orléans, at the head of his companies, saluted the Dauphin in the capacity of a simple captain. There was such a striking contrast between the humility of the true prince and the airs of the bastard, the hero of Turin and the pathetic soldier who had been a universal laughing-stock, that M. du Maine realized it and lost countenance. When the troops went back to their quarters the officers flocked round the Duc d'Orléans and left the legitimized prince to stew in his disappointment. It was now that the physicians finally had to acknowledge that the King's leg had turned black with gangrene.

On 25 August, after a painful night, His Majesty ordered the feast of Saint

Louis to be celebrated in the customary fashion, dined in the presence of the court, received respects and listened to the drums and oboes echoing beneath his windows.

After the ceremony he sent for the Chancellor and wrote a last codicil to his will, in the presence of Mme de Maintenon. He was yielding, out of sheer fatigue, to his wife and confessor, probably with the reservation that this extraordinary action would be set aside after his death, like the will itself. Otherwise he would have been deliberately condemning his kingdom to perpetual strife, for the codicil appointed the Duc du Maine commander of the civil and military Household, with Villeroy as his second-in-command. 'By this arrangement they became the sole masters of the person and residence of the King; of Paris . . . and all the internal and external guard; of the entire service . . . so much so that the Regent did not have even the shadow of the slightest authority and found himself at their mercy.'

On the evening of 25 August the King fainted, and when he recovered consciousness he received the sacraments. Later he had an audience with his son-in-law, whom he had not seen in private since the tragic day when the prince had demanded to enter the Bastille. He spoke affectionately to Philippe:

You will find nothing in my will that should displease you. I commend the Dauphin to you, serve him as loyally as you have served me. Do your utmost to preserve his realm. If he were to die, you would be the master. I know your good heart, your wisdom, your courage and breadth of spirit. I am confident that you will take care to bring up the Dauphin well, and that you will leave nothing undone for the relief of the people of my realm . . . I have made what I believed to be the wisest and fairest arrangements for the well-being of the realm, but, since one cannot anticipate everything, if there is something to change or to reform, you will do whatever you see fit . . .

He finished with a surprisingly romantic remark: 'You are about to see one king in the grave and another in the cradle. Always bear in mind the memory of the one and the interests of the other.'

In spite of all the pressures from those who were closest to him, the dying man was therefore sanctioning the prerogatives of the Duc d'Orléans. His statement that Philippe should find nothing objectionable in his will caused Saint-Simon to accuse him of appalling double-dealing, even 'with Jesus Christ on his lips', but this is hardly believable, for at a moment when his son-in-law could well have thought himself disinherited in favour of Philip v, the old King was at least promising that he had not rescinded the renunciations of Utrecht, nor repudiated the rights created by that treaty.

On 26 August Louis mentally discarded the crown that he had worn for seventy-two years. He referred to the Dauphin as 'the young King', and talked

373

of the time 'when I was King'. In answer to protestations, he said: 'Why? It does me no hurt.'

The hurt still lay in the matter of the papal bull. His words to Cardinals Rohan and Bissy explain, without excusing, his attitude to religious problems: 'I have merely followed your advice. If I have done ill, it is on your own consciences and you will answer before God!' He added that he bore no ill will towards Cardinal Noailles. Fagon and Mareschal at once suggested that he should receive the Archbishop of Paris, but Father Tellier and Mme de Maintenon overruled them.

After the Cardinals' visit, the farewell ceremonials began. The King conducted them with the majesty, self-mastery and sureness of utterance that had never failed him in fifty-four years. He spoke first to the dignitaries and servants who had invaded his bed-chamber:

Gentlemen, I ask forgiveness for the bad example I have set you. You have served me loyally and with a desire to please me. It vexes me not to have rewarded you better. Bad times are the cause. I ask on my grandson's behalf for the same application and the same loyalty that you have shown to me. He is a child who may have many setbacks . . . Follow the orders that my nephew will give to you, *he is to rule the realm.* I hope that he will do it well. I also hope that you will all contribute towards unity, and that if anybody strays you will rescue him. I sense that I am becoming emotional and that I am making you emotional also. I ask your pardon. Farewell, gentlemen, I rely on you to remember me sometimes.

Emotion does not last long among courtiers. These were hardly out of the room before they were repeating the key words – the Duc d'Orléans was to rule. Until then the issue had been in doubt. Everybody crowded into the apartments of the future master. Philippe now made his first gesture of authority when he ordered d'Argenson, the reliable lieutenant of police, to detain the couriers until the moment of death. It was a wise move, and may have saved France from civil war, for the King of Spain received the news a week too late to do anything but accept the fait accompli of Orléans' Regency and abandon his designs.

At the King's bedside, princes and princesses took the place of noblemen. The dying man gave them some final words of advice. Madame, who had loved him, wrote later: 'He bade me farewell in such tender words that I am astonished that I did not fall down in a swoon.' The little Dauphin was the last to be shown in, and his great-grandfather told him:

My dear child, you are about to become the greatest king in the world. Never forget your obligations to God. Do not imitate my taste for war. Try to relieve your people as much as you can, something that it has been my misfortune to be unable to do, because of the necessities of the state. Always think of accounting to God for your actions. I give you Father Tellier as a confessor: follow his advice and always remember your obligations to Mme de Ventadour.

He embraced the future Louis xv and blessed him twice. In the evening he recalled the Duc d'Orléans and suggested that he take the little King to Vincennes, where the air was very healthy, while Versailles was put in order. He called for a casket containing a plan of the old château, which had not been used since the death of Mazarin.

Louis had been too fond of parades not to make arrangements for his own funeral procession. With breathtaking thoroughness, he even went so far as to fix the length of the mourning coats and order the gentlemen to 'prepare their carriages and equipages and not to wait for his death before doing so, so that the workmen would have time to do their job with less fatigue'.

27 August and the morning of the 28th were devoted to his wife.* Mme de Maintenon, discreetly assisted by Mlle d'Aumale, remained alone with the dying man. They went through pockets, made inventories of the various caskets and burned sheafs of papers, among them Françoise's letters to Louis, who asked her to burn his own letters to herself. Almost nothing survives of this correspondence: if we possessed it, many of history's pages might have to be rewritten.

Louis xiv remarked: 'I have heard it said that it is difficult to bring oneself to die: for myself, now that I am on the point of this moment that men fear so much, I do not find it so hard.'

Mme de Maintenon answered in her pedantic tone: 'That depends on one's attachment to individuals, the hatred that remains in one's heart and the atonements one has to make.'

'Ah!' Louis sighed, 'as for atonements, I owe them to no particular person, *but for those I owe to the realm, I trust in the mercy of God.*'

Together with his remark about war, this was Louis' only indication of remorse. He told his companion that his sole regret was that he was leaving her. In the same calm, dry voice he enjoined her 'to think only of God.' The scene now achieved a pathos through which their strange and often melancholy union acquired its claim to nobility at the eleventh hour. The man who had been the Sun King wept as he said to the former governess: 'Madame, I ask your pardon for not having lived with you well enough. I have not made you happy, but I have always loved and esteemed you.'

A brief resurgence of decorum made him ask whether there was anybody else in the room, but he soon realized: 'In any case, if anybody saw that I was becoming emotional with you, they would not be surprised.'

Mme de Maintenon did not reply. 'What is to become of you?' the King suddenly went on. 'Madame, you have nothing.' She replied: 'I am nothing, concern yourself only with God,' and left him. Then, overcome by

---

* She took notes of the King's last words. This manuscript evidence is in the archives of the Duc de Mouchy.

a sudden fear, she retraced her steps and begged Louis to commend her to the Duc d'Orléans. It was a humiliating action for the woman who had worked so industriously to obstruct the Prince, but the King deferred to her request.

When she left him again, worn out and no longer able to act her part, she set out for Saint-Cyr in one of Villeroy's carriages, under the protection of his guards, fully resolved never to leave. It was 28 August. On the 29th a quack introduced by Orléans administered a remedy that seemed to revive the dying man. He ate two biscuits, drank a little wine and called for Mme de Maintenon. 'Sainte Françoise' had to return to her post.

During the night the last hopes faded, and the King lapsed into the penultimate coma. He recovered consciousness on the afternoon of the 30th, recognized the Marquise and croaked: 'You must have a great deal of courage and friendship, Madame, to stay so long.' Then: 'Do not sit there any longer, Madame, it is a sad spectacle. I hope that it will soon be at an end.'

Françoise consulted her confessor, Father Briderey. The monk observed the dying man, then spoke the words of release: 'He no longer needs you.'

Mme de Maintenon went to her apartment and shared out the furniture among her servants. At five o'clock in the evening she left Versailles for good, at least as a living creature. Two hundred and thirty years later her remains were brought back, and are now in the chapel royal at Versailles.

On the evening of 30 August the courtiers slipped away and left the King to the chaplains, the physicians and the *valets de chambre*. The Duc du Maine was giving a celebration supper, and the Duc d'Orléans was making the final preparations for his coup d'état.

At eleven o'clock on the evening of the 31st the prayers for the dying echoed through the deserted antechambers. When the King regained consciousness his voice rose above those of the priests. He received the sacraments again from Cardinal Rohan, the last person to whom he spoke, saying: 'These are the last favours that the Church can do me.' Then he was heard to murmur: 'Oh my God, come to my aid, make haste to succour me!'

On 1 September 1715, at a quarter to eight in the evening, death finally freed that 'happy prince, if ever there was one, unique in aspect, strong in body, uniform and firm in health, with hardly an interruption, and in a century so fertile and lavish towards him in every degree that in this sense it could be compared with the century of Augustus.'[1]

The deaths of Henry IV and Louis XIII had produced paroxysms of grief throughout France. Louis XIV atoned for the excessive adulation that had gratified him all too much by being conveyed to the basilica of Saint-Denis amid the abuse of a brawling, drunken populace, howling with barbaric joy. This unprecedented spectacle gave food for thought to the young son of the notary Arouet. He did not dream that one day public opinion would make him the heir of the fallen idol, and that men would speak of 'King Voltaire' as once they had spoken of the Sun King.*

---

* Voltaire has been quoted extensively because, twenty years old in 1715, he represents a generation that had immediate impressions of the reign of Louis xiv, and found Louis xiv a natural subject on whom to exercise his critical spirit.

[26]

Sunbeams and Shadows

LOUIS XIV was the resplendent incarnation of a monarchy that – setting aside the brief Napoleonic epic – brought France to the highest peak of her power and influence. It has often been said that he also dug his country's grave, particularly as regards his religious policy, his will and the isolation of the monarchy in Versailles.

The mistakes he made in his role as 'sergeant of God' were the outcome of a simplistic upbringing. 'Does God no longer remember what I have done for him?' the son of Anne of Austria once exclaimed. He was unable to prevent the Church from tearing itself apart, but the prime responsibility rests with the spirit of theological dissension that was the bane of the late seventeenth and early eighteenth century.

It is difficult to find any extenuating circumstances in the matter of the will by virtue of which the Parlement was able to resume a political role, but it was not Louis XIV who gave the magistrates the right of remonstrance. In any case, if Louis XV had reacted against them in 1750 instead of 1770, their opposition would have been broken in time.

As for the isolation of the monarchy, until the King became a martyr to gout in his fifties he was continually travelling and going to war. His successors were at liberty to follow this example, instead of conforming to the practice of his old age.

The adoration enjoyed by Louis XV, 'the Well-Beloved', during the first part of his reign, and above all the attachment to the Crown still reflected in the records of the Estates General in 1789, prove that Louis XIV had done nothing irrevocable. He did, however, make one cardinal error: he turned kingship into a burden too heavy for an ordinary man to carry. By concentrating the state into his own person, he laid it open to the infirmities of nature.

It should not be disregarded that from the Dutch war to the Revocation his worst mistakes were acclaimed by his contemporaries – the same contemporaries who waxed so indignant about enterprises which, like Versailles, are his greatest claims to fame in our own eyes.

The face of historical events alters with the passage of time. Today this unique reign presents a different picture. The lost hegemony, the lasting resentment of ravaged countries, financial bankruptcy, economic hardship, the persecution of Protestants and Jansenists, the chaos of the Church and the crumbling foundations of the monarchy constitute the sum total of a crushing debit. Yet the credit side is just as extensive. The despot who was worshipped in 1661 and execrated in 1715 freed his country from civil war and invasion, strengthened the frontiers, tamed a factious aristocracy and shattered for ever the vice in which the House of Austria had been trying to crush France for two centuries. From being a still rough and uncouth nation, he transformed France into the cynosure of the civilized West.

'Never did a more insensitive body guard a more imperturbable soul,' Lemontey has written. Louis xiv could identify himself with his function to such an extent that it is almost impossible to judge him as a man. His harshness and courage, his pride and his passion for order, his devoutness and his worship of beauty can only be appreciated in terms of the exigencies of government. Convinced that he personified France, the King wished her to be supreme, glorious, radiant and therefore, as a nation, happy, without paying overmuch heed to the happiness of the French. In essence, it was charity, and especially social charity, that he lacked.

Absorbing his subjects as he himself was absorbed by the state, Louis was a forerunner of the totalitarian rulers, and he might even have succumbed to the pitfalls that have swallowed up modern dictators had his divine right not caused him to despise the type of prestige that these must maintain at all costs. Yet he was also a true revolutionary, for not only did he shake his kingdom from top to bottom, but also his all-embracing spirit and overwhelming need for unity made him forget the practical realism of his ancestors, and on several occasions he departed from their tradition for the sake of inordinate dreams.

Louis xiv loved power, like Napoleon after him, as an artist does. For more than half a century he remained an unfaltering performer on the world's stage, the central figure in a proud, heroic spectacle in which horror mingled with splendour, the laughter of favourites with the groans of galley-slaves. In this too, he enforced his own example. After him, every national leader had to have the bearing, attitudes and inspiration of a man of the theatre.

Stonelike in his fearless, secret majesty, Louis xiv can have no power over the heart. He will always arouse admiration, however, because he had 'an elevation in his soul that bore him towards great things'[1] and because he deserved the final tribute of his enemy, Saint-Simon: 'That is what is meant by living and reigning.'

Appendix

References

The quotations of Louis XIV's own words are taken from his memoirs (*Mémoires de Louis XIV pour l'éducation du Dauphin*, ed. Charles Dreyss, Paris, 1869, and ed. Jean Longnon, Paris, 1923) and from the memoirs of a number of contemporaries, including those of La Porte, Brienne, Mme de Motteville, La Grande Mademoiselle, Primi Visconti, Dangeau and Saint-Simon; from the letters of la Palatine; and from ambassadors' reports, including those of Venice and Savoy (the Marquis of Saint Maurice). Voltaire (*Le Siècle de Louis XIV*), drawing on verbal communication with the Duchesse du Maine, daughter-in-law of Louis XIV, is also quoted.

Part One: THE TRAGIC DAWN (1637–61)

   3 *The Queen and* Frère Coupechou
1 Jacques Roujon, *Louis XIV*, London, 1943.
2 Voltaire, *Le Siècle de Louis XIV*, Berlin, 1751.
3 *Ibid.*

   4 *The Childhood of a Living God*
1 Mme Françoise Langlois de Motteville, *Mémoires pour servir à l'histoire d'Anne d'Autriche*, Amsterdam, 1723.

   5 *Encounter with Revolution*
1 *Ibid.*
2 Roujon.
3 Pierre-Georges Lorris, *La Fronde*, Paris, 1961.

   6 *The Lessons of Adversity*
1 *Ibid.*
2 *Ibid.*

   7 *Folly and Anarchy*
1 *Cf.* Georges Mongrédien, *Colbert*, Paris, 1963.
2 Quoted, *ibid.*
3 Michel Le Tellier (Chancelier), Mémoires, Bibliothèque Nationale, Paris.

   9 *The Cannon of the Bastille*
1 Mme de Motteville.

10 *The Lord's Anointed*

1 Jean de La Varende, *Anne d'Autriche, femme de Louis XIII*, Paris, 1947.

2 Roujon.

11 *Pangs of Youth*

1 Voltaire.

2 Maurice Schumann, *Mazarin*, Paris, 1959.

3 Henry Bordeaux, *Marie Mancini*, Paris, 1952.

15 *Armed Vigil*

1 Voltaire.

2 For the way they were composed, see the introduction and notes to the edition by Jean Longnon, Paris, 1923.

Part Two: THE RISING SUN (1661–80)

1 *Dictatorship by Divine Right*

1 *Cf.* Philippe Erlanger, *Monsieur, frère de Louis XIV*, Paris, 1953.

5 *National Self-Sufficiency*

1 Primi Visconti, *Mémoires sur la cour de Louis XIV*, ed. (with introduction) Jean Lemoine, Paris, 1908.

6 *The Science of Tears*

1 Abbé de Choisy, *Mémoires pour servir à l'histoire de Louis XIV*, Utrecht, 1727; and *Mémoires de M. le Duc Saint-Simon*, Paris, 1788.

7 *Mars and Venus*

1 Voltaire.

8 *The Sun Palace*

1 Voltaire.

2 Letter dated Chantilly, 24 April 1671.

9 *The Infernal Machine*

1 The accounts of Charlotte Elizabeth and Saint-Simon deserve no credence. The most interesting contemporary versions are those of Mme de La Fayette, Canon Feuillet and La Grande Demoiselle. Among the modern studies the following may be singled out: Littre, Lair, Brouardel, de Baillon, Loiseleur, Walckenaer, Paul Lacroix, Michelet, Sainte-Beuve, Anatole France, Legendre, Fabre, Pierre Clément, Funck-Brentano, Claude Darblay. *Cf.* also Philippe Erlanger, *Monsieur*.

2 Saint-Simon.

3 Voltaire.

References

10 *The Surprises of War*
1 Papers of M. de Chamlay, French National Archives.
2 Jacques Madaule, *Histoire de France* (chapter entitled 'Les Guerres de Louis XIV'), Paris, 3 vols, 1965–6.
3 Sir Winston S. Churchill, *Marlborough: His Life and Times*, 4 vols, London, 1933–8 (vol. 1, p. 85).
4 Voltaire.

11 *The Crusade Rebounds*
1 Churchill, vol. 1, p. 104.
2 Voltaire.

12 *The Rage to Live*
1 Saint-Simon.

13 *Fêtes, Massacres and Conspiracies*
1 Sandras de Courtilz, *Le Prince infortuné*, Amsterdam, 1713.
2 Voltaire.
3 *Ibid.*

14 *Retribution*
1 Memoirs of Jean Joseph Languet de Gergy (subsequently chaplain to the Duchesse de Bourgogne), in Théophile Lavallée, *La Famille d'Aubigné et l'enfance de Mme de Maintenan. Suivi des Mémoires inédits de Languet de Gergy*, etc., Paris, 1863.
2 According to the Comtesse de Caylus, *Souvenirs*, Amsterdam, 1770.
3 Voltaire.
4 Visconti.
5 Churchill, vol. 1, p. 125.
6 Visconti.

16 *The Onset of Middle Age*
1 Comte Roger de Bussy-Rasbutin, *La France galante, ou Histoires amoureuses de la cour de Louis XIV*, Cologne, 1740.
2 Marquis de Sourches, *Mémoires secrets et inédits de la cour de France sur la fin du règne de Louis XIV*, 13 vols, Paris, 1882–93.

17 *Pride and Distrust*
1 La Fare.

Part Three: HEAVEN AND OCEAN (1680–9)

1 *From Scandal to Hypocrisy*
1 Bussy-Rabutin.
2 Languet de Gergy.

2 La Raison du Plus Fort
1 Voltaire.
2 *Ibid*.

3 *The Triumph of Equivocation*
1 Comtesse de Caylus.
2 Mme Sainst-René Taillandier, *Mme de Maintenon,* Paris, 1923.

4 *The Ides of September*
1 Jean Racine, 'Fragments historiques', in Louis Racine, *Mémoires, sur la vie de Jean Racine*, Lausanne and Geneva, 1747.
2 *Cf.* P. W. Platzkoff, 'Louis xiv and the crisis of 1683' (in German), *Historische Zeitschrift,* 1920.

5 *The Interests of Heaven*
1 Languet de Gergy.
2 Abbé de Choisy.

6 *Stoicism and Violence*
1 Jules Michelet.
2 Official report drafted by Louvois.

7 *The Tide of History*
1 Churchill, vol. 1, p. 262.
2 Voltaire.
3 Churchill.
4 Saint-Simon.

Part Four: THE LOOMING SHADOW (1689–98)

1 *Splendid Isolation and 'Pure Love'*
1 Roland Mousnier, *14 mai 1610: L'Assassinat de Henri IV*, Paris, 1964.
2 Henri Daniel-Rops, *L'Eglise des temps classiques*, Paris, 1960.

3 *Family Affairs*
1 Anne-Marguerite Petit, Mme Du Noyer, *Lettres historiques et galantes*, Cologne, 1713.

5 *The Mirage of the Sea*
1 Churchill, vol. 1, pp. 337–8.
2 *Ibid*., p. 391.
3 Michelet, *Histoire de France et de la Revolution*, Paris, 28 vols, 1885–8.
4 Michelet.

6 *Luxembourg's Hump*
1 Voltaire.
2 Saint-Simon.

7 *Fénelon's First Downfall*
1 Saint-Simon.

8 *Farewell to Glory*
1 Voltaire.

9 *Other Men's Ideals.*
1 Daniel-Rops.
2 Saint-Simon.
3 Paul Grimblot (ed.), *Letters of William III and Louis XIV*, etc., 2 vols, London, 1848.

10 *Varieties of Love*
1 The magazine *Mercure galant*.
2 Mme Du Noyer.

11 *The Ark of Versailles*
1 Paul Hazard, *La Crise de la conscience européene*, Paris, 1935.
2 *Un Colonial au temps de Colbert. Mémoires de Robert Challes, écrivain du Roi*, Paris, 1931.

Part Five: THE FIRES OF EVENING (1698–1715)

1 *Pandora's Tomb*
1 Voltaire.
2 *Ibid.*

2 *Precarious Good Fortune*
1 Voltaire.
2 Harcourt archives.
3 Saint-Simon.

3 *The Brink of War*
1 Pierre Gaxotte, *La France de Louis XIV*, Paris, 1946.

4 *The Instruments of Fate*
1 Saint-Simon.

5 *From the Cévennes to the Danube*
1 Voltaire.

6 *The End of a Dream*
1 Voltaire.
2 Saint-Simon.
3 Voltaire.

7 *The Olympian Mask*
1 Jacques Saint Germain, *Samuel Bernard, banquier des rois*, Paris, 1960.

8 *'There is no Good Fortune'*
1 Saint-Simon.

9 *The Death of Vauban and the Birth of Parties*
1 Marquis de Dangeau, *Journal de la cour de Louis XIV depuis 1684 jusqu'à 1715*, etc., London, 1770.
2 Saint-Simon.

10 *The Rout of Oudenarde*
1 Saint-Simon.
2 Archives of the Ministry of Foreign Affairs, Paris.
3 *Cf.* Arsène Legrelle, *La Diplomatie française et la Succession d'Espagne*, 4 vols, Paris, 1888–92.

11 *Article IV*
1 Sunderland, the Duke's sonèinèlaw, was Secretary of State. The Sunderland archives are among those of Blenheim. Cf. Churchill.

12 *Family Matters*
1 Saint-Simon.
2 This episode, like most of those in which the Duke was involved, is dealt with in the author's *Le Régent*, Paris, 1938.

13 *A Nation Aroused*
1 Blenheim documents, quoted in Churchill, vol. 4, p. 98.
2 Voltaire.
3 Churchill, vol. 4, p. 197.

14 *The Sacrifice of Port-Royal*
1 Saint-Simon.

16 *Miracle in London and Madrid*
1 Onno Klopp, *Der Fall des Hauses Stuart*, etc., 14 vols, Vienna, 1875–88.
2 Coxe, *Memoirs of Marlborough*, London, 1885.
3 Klopp.

17 *Genesis of a Golden Age*
1 François Albert Duffo (ed.), *Le Baron Louis-Nicolas de Breteuil à la cour du Duc de Mantour, 1648–1728* (*Mémoire de M. le Baron de Breteuil,* etc.), Paris, 1934.
2 Jacques Roujon, *Le Duc Saint-Simon (1675–1755)*, Paris, 1958.

18 *The Harvest of Death*
1 Saint-Simon.

19 *The Blazing Sunset*
1 Letters and correspondence of Lord Bolingbroke, quoted in Churchill, vol. 4, pp. 541-2.

21 *The Expiatory Schism*
1 Saint-Simon.
2 Voltaire.

24 *Final Splendour, Final Anger*
1 Michelet.

25 *A Great Artist's Farewell*
1 Saint-Simon.

26 *Sunbeams and Shadows*
1 Voltaire.

Select Bibliography

Maurice Andrieux, *Henri IV dans ses années pacifiques*, etc., Paris, 1954. *Rome*, 2 vols, Paris and Ottawa, 1960.

Octave Aubry, *The King of Rome, Napoleon II* ..., Philadelphia and London, 1932, *The Second Empire*, Philadelphia and New York, 1940.

Auguste Bailly, *Byzance*, Paris, 1939. *St Louis*, Paris, 1949. *Louis XI*, Paris, 1936. *François I*, *restaurateur des lettres et des arts*, Paris, 1954. *The Cardinal Dictator: a Portrait of Richelieu*, London, 1936. *Mazarin*, Paris, 1035. *La sérénissime république de Venise*, Paris, 1946.

Jacques Bainville, *History of France*, New York and London, 1926. *Napoleon*, London, 1932. *The French Republic, 1870–1935*, London, 1936.

Jules Bertaut, *1848 et la Seconde République*, Paris, 1937.

Louis Bertrand, *Louis XIV*, New York and London, 1928.

Georges and Germaine Blond, *Histoire pittoresque de notre alimentation*, Paris, 1960.

Marcel Brion, *Histoire de l'Égypte*, Paris, 1954.

Joseph Calmette, *Charles V*, Paris, 1945.

Joseph Calmette and Henri David, *Saint Bernard*, Paris, 1953.

Eugène Cavaignac, *Sparte*, Paris, 1948.

Jacques Chastenet, *Elisabeth I*, Paris, 1953. *William Pitt*, Paris, 1941. *Wellington, 1769–1852*, Paris, 1945. *Le Siècle de Victoria*, Paris, 1947. *Winston Churchill et l'Angleterre du XXᵉ siècle*, Paris, 1956. *Une Époque pathétique: la France de M. Fallières*, Paris, 1949.

Henry Contamine, *L'Europe est derrière nous*, Paris, 1953.

Henri Daniel-Rops, *The Book of Books: the Story of the Old Testament*, London, 1958. *Jesus in His Time*, London, 1955. *History of the Church of Christ*, London and New York: Vol. I – *The Church of Apostles and Martyrs*, 1960; Vol. 2 – *The Church in the Dark Ages*, 1959; Vol. 3 – *Cathedral and Crusade. Studies of the Medieval Church, 1050 – 1350*, 1957; Vol. 4 – *The Protestant Reformation*, 1961; Vol. 5 – *The Catholic Reformation*, 1962; Vol. 6 – *The Church in the 17th Century*, 1963; Vol. 7 – *The Church in the 18th Century*, 1964. *The Church in an Age of Revolution, 1789–1870*, London and New York, 1965. *A Fight for God, 1870–1939*, London and New York, 1966.

Jean Descola, *The Conquistadors*, London and New York, 1957. *Les Liberatadores*, Paris and Ottawa, 1957. *A History of Spain*, New York, 1963.

Frantz Funck-Brentano, *The Renaissance*, London, 1936.

Pierre Gaxotte, *The French Revolution*, London and New York, 1932. *Frederick the Great*, London, 1941. *Louis XV and his Times*, London, 1934.

Appendix

Claud Joseph Gignoux, *Turgot*, Paris, 1945.

René Grousset, *The Rise and Splendour of the Chinese Empire*, London, 1952.

Jean Héritier, *Catherine de Medici*, London and New York, 1963.

Léon Homo, *Nouvelle histoire romaine*, Paris, 1941. *Le Siècle d'Or de l'Empire Romain*, Paris, 1947. *Alexandre le Grand*, Paris, 1951.

Paul Léon, *La Guerre pour la Paix, 1740–1940*, Paris, 1950.

Ferdinand Lot, *La Gaule, les fondaments ethniques, sociaux et politiques de la nation française*, Paris, 1947. *Naissance de la France*, Paris, 1948.

Jean Lucas-Dubreton, *L'âge d'or de la renaissance italienne*, Paris, 1957. *The Borgias*, London and New York, 1954. *Napoléon devant l'Espagne: ce qu'a vu Goya*, Paris, 1948. *Le Marechal Ney, 1769–1815*, Paris, 1941. *Louis-Philippe*, Paris, 1938. *Aspects de Monsieur Thiers*, Paris, 1948. *Charles Quint*, Paris, 1958. *Madrid*, Paris, 1962.

André Maurois, *A History of England*, London, 1937.

Pierre Miquel, *Poincaré*, Paris, 1961.

Maurice Muret. *Guillaume II*, Paris, 1940.

Jean de Pange, *L'Allemagne depuis la Révolution française, 1789–1945*, Paris, 1947.

René Ristelhueber, *Histoire des peuples balkaniques*, Paris, 1950.

Pierre Rousseau, *Histoire de la Science*, Paris, 1945. *Histoire des techniques et des inventions*, Paris, 1958. *Histoire des Transports*, Paris, 1961.

Georges Roux, *Néron,* Paris, 1962.

Firmin Roz, *Histoire des États-Unis*, Paris, 1930.

Comte de Sainte-Aulaire, *Françoise-Joseph*, Paris, 1945.

René Sédillot, *A Bird's-eye View of World History*, London and New York, 1951. *Histoire des Colonisations*, 2 vols, Paris, 1958. *Paris*, New York and Ottawa, 1962. *Histoire des marchandes et des marchés*, Paris, 1964.

Henry Vallotton, *Yvan le Terrible*, Paris, 1959. *Pierre le Grand*, Paris, 1958. *Catherine II*, Paris, 1955. *Marie-Thérèse, Impératrice*, Paris, 1963. *Bismarck*, Paris, 1961.

Pierre Varillon, *Joffre*, Paris, 1956.

Bernard de Vaulx, *History of the Missions. From the Beginning to Benedict XV – 1914*, London and New York, 1961.

Pierre Verlet, *Versailles*, Paris, 1961.

Emile Vuillermoz, *Histoire de la Musique*, Paris, 1948.

Family tree showing
Louis XIV's descendants

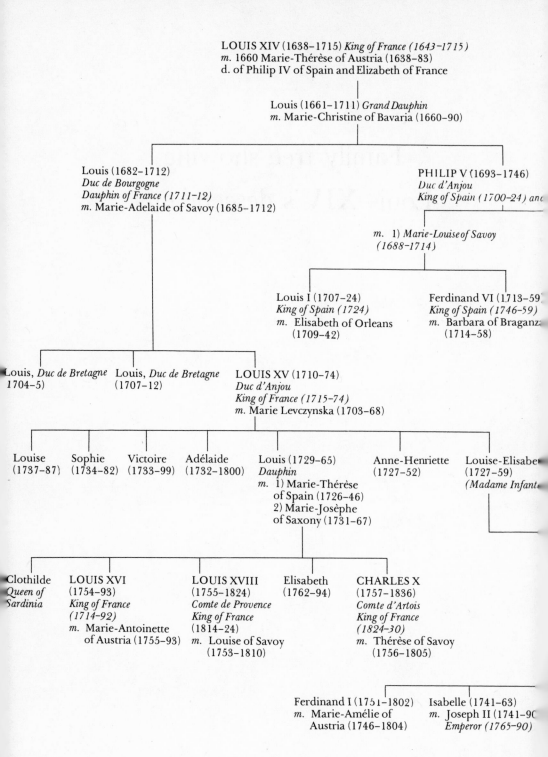

LOUIS XIV (1638–1715) *King of France (1643–1715)*
m. 1660 Marie-Thérèse of Austria (1638–83)
d. of Philip IV of Spain and Elizabeth of France

Louis (1661–1711) *Grand Dauphin*
m. Marie-Christine of Bavaria (1660–90)

Louis (1682–1712)
Duc de Bourgogne
Dauphin of France (1711–12)
m. Marie-Adelaide of Savoy (1685–1712)

PHILIP V (1693–1746)
Duc d'Anjou
King of Spain (1700–24) and

m. 1) *Marie-Louise of Savoy*
(1688–1714)

Louis I (1707–24)
King of Spain (1724)
m. Elisabeth of Orleans
(1709–42)

Ferdinand VI (1713–59)
King of Spain (1746–59)
m. Barbara of Braganza
(1714–58)

Louis, *Duc de Bretagne*
1704–5)

Louis, *Duc de Bretagne*
(1707–12)

LOUIS XV (1710–74)
Duc d'Anjou
King of France (1715–74)
m. Marie Levczynska (1703–68)

Louise
(1737–87)

Sophie
(1734–82)

Victoire
(1733–99)

Adélaide
(1732–1800)

Louis (1729–65)
Dauphin
m. 1) Marie-Thérèse
of Spain (1726–46)
2) Marie-Josèphe
of Saxony (1731–67)

Anne-Henriette
(1727–52)

Louise-Elisabeth
(1727–59)
(Madame Infante

Clothilde
Queen of
Sardinia

LOUIS XVI
(1754–93)
King of France
(1714–92)
m. Marie-Antoinette
of Austria (1755–93)

LOUIS XVIII
(1755–1824)
Comte de Provence
King of France
(1814–24)
m. Louise of Savoy
(1753–1810)

Elisabeth
(1762–94)

CHARLES X
(1757–1836)
Comte d'Artois
King of France
(1824–30)
m. Thérèse of Savoy
(1756–1805)

Ferdinand I (1751–1802)
m. Marie-Amélie of
Austria (1746–1804)

Isabelle (1741–63)
m. Joseph II (1741–90
Emperor (1765–90)

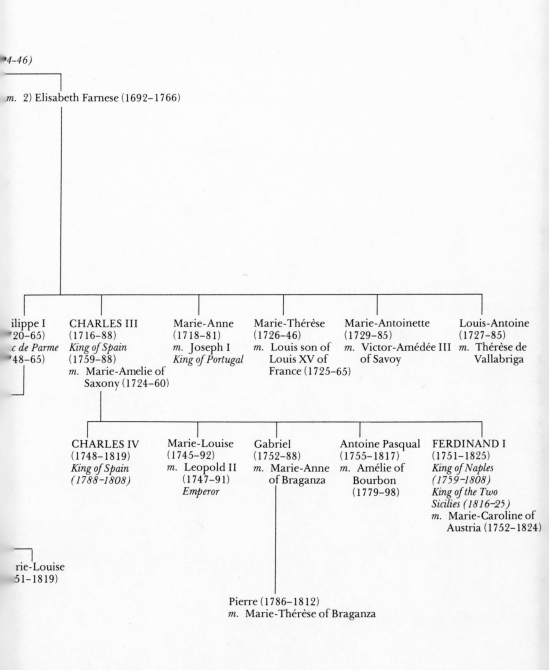

4-46)

m. 2) Elisabeth Farnese (1692–1766)

ilippe I
'20–65)
c de Parme
'48–65)

CHARLES III
(1716–88)
King of Spain
(1759–88)
m. Marie-Amelie of
Saxony (1724–60)

Marie-Anne
(1718–81)
m. Joseph I
King of Portugal

Marie-Thérèse
(1726–46)
m. Louis son of
Louis XV of
France (1725–65)

Marie-Antoinette
(1729–85)
m. Victor-Amédée III
of Savoy

Louis-Antoine
(1727–85)
m. Thérèse de
Vallabriga

CHARLES IV
(1748–1819)
King of Spain
(1788–1808)

Marie-Louise
(1745–92)
m. Leopold II
(1747–91)
Emperor

Gabriel
(1752–88)
m. Marie-Anne
of Braganza

Antoine Pasqual
(1755–1817)
m. Amélie of
Bourbon
(1779–98)

FERDINAND I
(1751–1825)
King of Naples
(1759–1808)
King of the Two
Sicilies (1816–25)
m. Marie-Caroline of
Austria (1752–1824)

rie-Louise
51–1819)

Pierre (1786–1812)
m. Marie-Thérèse of Braganza

Index